Anecdote Lives of the Later Wits and Humourists
by John Timbs

Address:
HardPress
8345 NW 66TH ST #2561
MIAMI FL 33166-2626
USA
Email: info@hardpress.net

ANECDOTE LIVES

LATER WITS AND HUMOURISTS:

CANNING, CAPTAIN MORRIS, CURRAN, COLERIDGE,
LAMB, CHARLES MATHEWS, TALLEYRAND, JERROLD, ROGERS,
ALBERT SMITH, HOOD, MAGINN, THACKERAY, DICKENS, POOLE,
LEIGH HUNT, FATHER PROUT, ETC.

By JOHN TIMBS, F.S.A.,

AUTHOR OF "A CENTURY OF ANECDOTE."

IN TWO VOLUMES.
VOL. II.

LONDON:
RICHARD BENTLEY AND SON.
1874.

CONTENTS OF VOL. II.

TALLEYRAND.

ARCHBISHOP WHATELY.

SAMUEL ROGERS.

SIR JOHN SOANE LAMPOONED.

MRS. PIOZZI.

THOMAS HOOD.

BAD SPELLING.

WORTHIES OF ISLINGTON.

WALTER SAVAGE LANDOR.

ALBERT SMITH.

LEIGH HUNT.

DOCTOR MAGINN.

WILLIAM MAKEPEACE THACKERAY.

CHARLES DICKENS.

RELIQUES OF FATHER PROUT.

APPENDIX.

ANECDOTE BIOGRAPHY.

TALLEYRAND.

CHARLES MAURICE DE TALLEYRAND PERIGORD was born February 2, 1754,[*] the eldest of three brothers. His family was ancient and distinguished; but he was neglected by his parents, and placed at nurse in one of the faubourgs of Paris. The effects of a fall when about a year old rendered him lame for life, and being, on this account, unfit for the military career, he was obliged to renounce his birthright in favour of his second brother, and enter the church. The contempt and aversion for him, which his parents did not attempt to conceal, impressed a gloomy and taciturn character on the boy. From the charge of his nurse, he was transferred to the Collége d'Harcourt, and thence successively to the seminary of St. Sulpice and to the Sorbonne. In all these institutions he maintained the character of a shy, proud, bookish lad. He showed, in after-life, a taste for literature, and such an extensive acquaintance with and appreciation of science as sits gracefully on the statesman; and the taste and knowledge must have been acquired at an early age, for his turbulent career, after he was fairly launched into busy life, left little leisure for that purpose.

By the time he had attained his twentieth year, his reputation for talent and his confirmed health, appeared to have reconciled the vanity of his parents to the necessity of acknowledging him. They introduced him to the society of his equals in rank for the first time at the festivities with which

[*] The date of M. de Talleyrand's birth is stated, on, apparently, the best authority, on the 7th of March, on the 1st of September, and on the 2nd of February. This last, Sir Henry Bulwer had reason to believe the correct date.

the coronation of Louis XVI. was celebrated (1774), under the title of the Abbé de Périgord. His opinions and tastes, and his temperament, combined to render the clerical profession an object of detestation to him, but he could not escape from it. He availed himself to the full extent of the indulgence with which his age and country regarded the irregularities of the young and noble among the priestly order ; but the pride and reserve with which twenty years of undeserved neglect had inspired his strong character—served him in part as a moral shock. He was a strict observer of the appearances excited by the conventional morality of society ; and this good taste exerted a powerful influence over his whole future career.

Talleyrand's recklessness as to the means by which he attained his ends is no evidence of insincerity, but merely want of faith in men, which the treatment he had experienced in early life, and his observation of the society he habitually mixed in, had instilled into him. It was his weakness through life to pride himself upon his power of refined mockery, regardless of the enemies he created ; he gave vent to his spirit of raillery in actions as well as in words; and thus lent a grotesque colouring to his *coup d'état*, which rendered them more startling than if they had been as prosaic as those of other men. The world, perhaps, is less startled with the atrocity of a passion in a statesman, than for a laughing air which shows its contempt for it. The most startling of his devices is his solemn inauguration of the constitutional monarchy by the religious celebration of the 14th of July. But the love of theatrical presentation, and the delusive belief that good may be effected by it, is strong in every man at some period of his life. Talleyrand, in all likelihood, looked forward at that moment to being the founder and future primate of a church which should be to France what the Anglo-Episcopal has been to England. The means to which he was driven to have recourse in order to carry through the installation of the national bishops, undeceived him, and brought back his early disgust for the profession ; and he, not long after, resigned the bishopric of Autun, and at the same time renounced his ecclesiastical character.

In 1776, Voltaire visited Paris ; M. de Talleyrand was introduced to him, and the two interviews he had with him left such a deep impression that he was accustomed to talk of them with a lively pleasure till the close of his life. Voltaire and Fontenelle were M. de Talleyrand's favourite authors :

upon whom he had formed his written, and still more his conversational, style. Conversational talent was in great demand at Paris, when he entered the world, and both his love of pleasure and his love of power prompted him to cultivate that which he possessed. This he did with eminent success. Excellence of this kind is like excellence in acting; it is impossible to convey an adequate impression of it to posterity. The reporters of flashes of wit and felicitous turns of conversation uniformly communicate to them something of their own inferiority, and vulgarize them in the telling. Again, superior excellence in conversation is an art; the artist is and ought to be judged not by his materials but by the success with which he uses them. Written *bon mots* are necessarily estimated by their originality, the quantity and quality of thought expressed in them : they are judged as we judge the writings of a poet; whereas the person who introduces them with effect in conversation ought to be judged as we judge the actor, of whom we do not think less because he merely says what the poet has put into his mouth.

Much as Talleyrand's reputation has declined of late years, and low as his political honesty stood at all times, would anything be now thought to justify such a diatribe as—

"Where at the blood-stain'd board expert he plies,
The lame artificer of fraud and lies ;
He with the mitred head and cloven heel ;—
Doom'd the coarse edge of Rewbell's jests to feel ;
To stand the playful buffet, and to hear
The frequent inkstand whizzing past his ear ;
While all the five Directors laugh to see
'The limping priest so deft at his new ministry.'"

According to a current story, Rewbell, exasperated by Talleyrand's opposition at council, flung an inkstand at his head, exclaiming : "*Vil emigré, tu n'as pas le sens plus droit que le pied.*"

In the centre of the troop who are introduced singing the praises of Lepaux, were inconsiderately placed a group of writers, who, with equal disregard of their respective peculiarities and opinions, were subsequently lumped together as the Lake School :—

"And ye five other wandering bards, that move
In sweet accord of harmony and love,
Coleridge and Southey, Lloyd, and Lamb and Co.,
Tune all your mystic harps to praise Lepaux !"

1—2

PORTRAIT OF TALLEYRAND, IN 1789.

Let us picture to ourselves a man of thirty-five, and appearing somewhat older ; his countenance of a long oval ; his eyes blue, with an expression at once deep and variable ; his lips usually impressed with a smile, which was that of mockery, but not of ill-nature ; his nose slightly turned up, but delicate, and remarkable for a constant play in the clearly-chiseled nostrils. "He dressed," says one of his many biographers, "like a coxcomb, he thought like a deist, he preached like a saint. At once active and irregular, he found time for everything : the church, the court, the opera. In bed one day, from indolence or debauch, up the whole of the following night to prepare a memoir or a speech. Gentle with the humble, haughty with the high ; not very exact in paying his debts, but very scrupulous with respect to giving and breaking promises to pay them."

A dull story is related with respect to this last peculiarity. The new bishop had ordered and received a very handsome carriage, becoming his recent ecclesiastical elevation. He had not, however, settled the coachmaker's small account. After long waiting and frequent letters, the civil but impatient tradesman determined upon presenting himself every day at the Bishop of Autun's door, at the same time as his equipage.

For several days, M. de Talleyrand saw, without recognizing, a well-dressed individual, with his hat in his hand, and bowing very low as he mounted the steps of his coach. "And who are you, my friend ?" he said at last. "I am your coachmaker, my lord." "Ah ! you are my coachmaker ; and what do you want, my coachmaker ?" "I want to be paid, my lord." "Ah ! you are my coachmaker, and you want to be paid ; you shall be paid, my coachmaker." "And when, my lord ?" "Hum !" murmured the bishop, looking at his coachmaker very attentively, and at the same time settling himself in his new carriage. "You are very inquisitive !"

Such was the Talleyrand of 1789, embodying in himself the ability and frivolity, the ideas and the habits of a large portion of his class. At once the associate of the Abbé Sièyes, who had just published a celebrated pamphlet ; a profligate fine gentleman, a deep and wary thinker ; and above all things, the delight and ornament of that gay and graceful society which, crowned with flowers, was about to be the first victim to its own philosophy. As yet, however, the sky, though troubled, gave no evidence of storm ; and never, perhaps, except on the 1st of May, did a great assembly meet with less gloomy anticipations than that which, in the pomp and gallantry of feudal show, passed through the royal city of Versailles.—*Talleyrand, the Politic Man,* by Sir H. L. Bulwer.

THE FESTIVAL OF THE FOURTEENTH OF JULY.

To celebrate the destruction of the Bastille, and to do honour to the new government which had risen on its ruins, a festival was held on the 14th of July—a day of joy.

A magnificent amphitheatre was erected on the Champ de Mars : there the hereditary sovereign of France, and the temporary president of an elected assembly—the joint symbols of two ideas and of two epochs—are seated on two equal thrones, resplendent with the arms which the nation has taken from its ancient kings ; and there is the infant prince, on whom an exulting people look kindly as the inheritor of his father's engagements, and who is to perpetuate the race of St. Louis ; and there is that queen " decorating and cheering the sphere she moves in, glittering like the morning star, full of life, of splendour, and of joy ;" and there that royal maiden, beauteous with the charms of the palace, blessed with the virtues of the cloister—a princess, a saint, destined to be a martyr ! And there is the vain but honest Lafayette leaning on his citizen sword ; and there the terrible Mirabeau, his long hair streaming to the wind. . . . And behold, in yonder balcony, the most splendid court in Europe, for such even at that time was still the court of France ; and lo ! in the open space, yon confederated bands, bearing their respective banners, display every portion of that great family which, at this moment, is enjoying the triumph it has achieved. On a sudden, the sky—the light of which mingles so well with the joy of men, but which had hitherto been dark and sullen—on a sudden the sky clears up, and the sun blends his pomp with that of this noble ceremony ! And now, robed in his pontifical garments, and standing on the altar thronged by three hundred priests, in long white robes and tricoloured girdles, the Bishop of Autun blesses the great standard, the oriflamme of France, no longer the ensign of war, but the sign and token of peace between the past and the future—between the old recollections and the new aspirations of the French people.

Who that had been present that day in Paris, could have believed that those who wept tenderly with the children of Bearne, at the foot of the statue of Henry IV., would so soon laugh horribly round the scaffold of his descendants ; that the gay multitude, wandering in the Champs Elysées, amidst garlands of light, and numberless breathing sounds of gentle happiness and affection, would so soon be the ferocious mob, massacring in the prisons, murdering in the public streets, dancing round the guillotine dripping with innocent blood ; that the monarch, the court, the deputies, every popular and princely image of this august pageant, the very forms of the religion with which it was consecrated, would, in two or three brief years, be scoffingly cast away ; and that even the high-priest of that gorgeous solemnity, no longer attached to his sacred calling, would be a miserable exile on foreign shores, banished as a traitor to the liberty for which he had sacrificed the prejudices of his caste, the predilections of his family, the honour and wealth of his profession ?—Sir H. L. Bulwer's *Historical Characters.*

TALLEYRAND'S MISSION TO ENGLAND.

In 1791, it was an object with all who denied that the French Revolution should have fair play, to preserve peace with England. The court party hated M. de Talleyrand for having taken part frankly with the Revolution ; the republicans hated him for his advocacy of a limited monarchy ; all parties distrusted him on account of his eternal sneer ; but all parties agreed that he was the only man whose talents fitted him for the delicate mission to England. And it was impossible to appoint him to it. He was despatched, however, in January, 1792, to sound the English ministry and attempt to commence negotiations. His want of an official character allowed the queen to indulge her feelings of personal dislike to the ex-bishop of Autun by turning her back upon him when he was presented at St. James's ; and this reception insured at once his exclusion from general society, and rendered him powerless. Next, the attempt to insure neutrality on the part of England was renewed. Chauvelin was sent to England as nominal, along with Talleyrand as real, ambassador. By this time, however, the French Government had become as obnoxious to the general public of England as to the court circles : the torrent was, probably, too powerful to have been stemmed by Talleyrand, even though he had been in a condition to act directly and in person. He could do nothing, forced as he was to act by the instrumentality of a man too jealous and opinionative to conform honestly to the directions of one whose authority necessarily made him feel himself a mere puppet. Talleyrand's good faith at this· period, in labouring to preserve peace between England and France, as the only means of rendering a constitutional monarchy possible in the other country, and the steadiness with which he pursued this object, undaunted by the most gross personal insults, are satisfactorily established by the narrative of Dumont.

" M. de Talleyrand, during his mission in England, not only sustained his previous reputation, but added very considerably to it. What struck the vulgar, and many, indeed, above the vulgar, who did not remember that the real crafty man disguises his craft, was the plain, open, and straightforward way in which he spoke and dealt with all public matters, without any of those mysterious devices which distinguish the simpleton in diplomacy from the statesman who is a diplomatist. In fact, having made up his mind to consider the English alliance at this time essential to his country, he was well aware that the best and only way of obtaining it was by such frank and fair dealing as would win the confidence of British statesmen."—*Sir H. L. Bulwer.*

Talleyrand was thus placed when the event of the 10th of August put an end to the monarchy ; and it required all his dexterity to enable him to obtain passports from Danton, to enable him to quit Paris. He fled to England, and having saved little of his property, he was obliged to sell his library there to procure himself the means of support. The English Government, jealous of his presence, after some time, ordered him to leave the country in twenty-four hours ; and proscribed in France, he was obliged, with a dilapidated fortune, to seek refuge in America when he had almost attained his fortieth year.

NAPOLEON AND TALLEYRAND.

Napoleon and Talleyrand may be said to have understood each other, and that in a sense not discreditable to either. The good sense of both was revolted by the bloodshed and theatrical sentiments, the blended ferocity and the coxcombry of the Revolution ; both were practical statesmen, men with a taste and talent for administration, not mere constitution-makers. Like most men of action, neither of them could discern to the full extent the advantage an executive government can derive from having the line of action to a considerable extent prescribed by a constitution : but Talleyrand saw better than Napoleon that the laws which protect subjects by limiting the arbitrary will of the ruler, in turn protect him by teaching them legitimate methods of defending their rights. In another respect they resembled each other—neither was remarkably scrupulous as to the means by which he attained his ends, though the laxity of moral sentiment was kept in check by the natural humanity of both. Their very points of difference were calculated to cement their union. The observant, self-centred mind of Talleyrand was lamed by its want of power to set others in motion : it is only through sympathy that the contagious love of action can be conveyed.

The impassioned and imaginative soul of Napoleon was made to attach others to him, and whirl them along with him ; and this power was often too strong for itself. Napoleon, though capable of reflection, was too often hurried away by his instinctive impulses. Each of these men felt that the other was a supplement to himself : Talleyrand really admired and appreciated Napoleon. If he flattered him, it was by the delicate method of confirming him in the opinions and intentions which met his approbation. He dared to tell the First Consul truths which others were afraid to utter ; and he ventured to arrest at times the impetuosity of Napoleon, by postponing the fulfilment of his orders until he had time to cool. He opposed, as long as there was any prospect of success, the divorce from Josephine ; but his virtue gave way in the business of the Duke d'Enghien ; for even though we exculpate him from participation in the execution of that prince, to gratify his master he sanctioned the violation of a neutral territory. This was, however, the only instance, in so far as Bonaparte is concerned, of his sacrificing the duty of a friend to flattery that can be brought home to him. Napoleon's frequent recurrence, in his *Conversations at St. Helena,* to the subject of Talleyrand's defection, and his attempts to solve the question at what time that minister began to betray him, show his appreciation of the services he had received from him.

TALLEYRAND A KING.

" When M. de Talleyrand created the government of Louis XVIII. he wanted to give it a backbone, consisting of a party of able, practical, and popular men of moderate opinions. But

Louis XVIII., as a principle, distrusted all men in proportion to their popularity and ability, his ministers especially, M. de Talleyrand, therefore, was, in his eyes, a person who should be constantly watched, and constantly suspected. Louis XVIII. held also in horror the idea of his cabinet being a ministry, *i.e.*, a compact body agreeing together. His notion as to driving was that horses who always kicked at each other, were the less likely to kick at the carriage ; furthermore, he considered that everything which was not as it had been thirty years back, was really wrong, though he did not mean to take the trouble of changing it, and that all this new set of persons he had to deal with were *coquins*—not a gentleman amongst them—that it was proper manners, since they existed, to treat them courteously, and proper policy, since they had a certain power in their hands, to temporize with them ; but in his heart of hearts he looked upon them as yahoos, who had got into the stalls of horses, and were to be kicked out directly the horses, strengthened by plentiful feeds of corn, were up to the enterprise. In the meantime, nothing was to be risked, so he sat himself down as comfortably as he could in his arm-chair, received all visitors with an air, which an actor, about to play Louis XIV., might have done well to study ; wrote pretty billets, said sharp and acute things, and felt that he was, every inch, a king."—*Sir. H. L. Bulwer.*

"M. de Montrond was a specialty of his epoch : a type of that French *roué* whom Faublas, and more particularly the '*liaisons dangereuses*,' had produced. He had ruled the world of fashion by his loves, his duels, and his wit, which was superior to any man's, for nearly forty years. He was one of M. de Talleyrand's pets, as M. de Talleyrand was one of his admirations. Each spoke ill of the other, for each said he loved the other for his vices. But no one could speak to M. de Talleyrand with so much intimacy as M. de. Montrond, nor obtain from him so clear an answer. For they trusted each other, though M. de Montrond would never have told any one else to trust M. de Montrond."—*Ibid.*

THE WORSHIP OF DUTY.

Shortly, previous to the last illness of M. de Talleyrand, he appeared in the Tribune of the Institute, and bade the world a sort of dignified adieu, his essay being M. Reinhard, who had long served under him, and was just dead ; and between whom and himself, even in the circumstance of their both having received an ecclesiastical education, there was some sort of resemblance.

In spite of certain difficulties, M. Reinhard always succeeded in doing, and doing well, whatever was entrusted to him. How, then, did he find the means of succeeding ? Whence did he derive his inspirations ?

" He received them " (says M. de Talleyrand) " from a deep and true feeling, which guided all his actions—*from the sense of duty.* People are not sufficiently aware of the power derived from this feeling. A life wholly devoted to duty is very easily diverted from ambition ; and that of M. Reinhard was entirely taken up by his professional avocations, while he never was influenced in the slightest degree by an interested motive, or a pretension to premature advancement.

" This worship of duty, to which M. Reinhard continued faithful to the end of his days, comprised entire acquiescence in the orders of his superiors—indefatigable vigilance, which, joined to much penetration, never suffered them to remain ignorant of anything which it was expedient for them to know. Strict truthfulness in all his reports, however un-pleasing their contents—impenetrable discretion—regular habits, which inspired esteem and confidence—a style of living suited to his position—and, finally, constant attention in giving to the acts of his government the colour and lucidity which their importance demanded.

" Although age seemed to invite M. Reinhard to seek the repose of private life, he would never have asked permission to retire from active employment, so much did he fear to be thought lukewarm in the duties of a profession which had occupied the greater part of his days."

THE WATERS OF CARLSBAD.

When, in 1814, M. de Talleyrand was more or less in disgrace with the politicians, who were already disputing about the re-distribution of the places that their mistakes had just lost, bearing this disgrace with his usual superstitious negligence, he declared that his health required the waters of Carlsbad, observing that a diplomatist's first duty after a congress was to take care of his liver.

M. de Metternich's secret negotiation with Fouché, is de-scribed as a proposition which, as long as its success was uncertain, could not but affect considerably the state of M. de Talleyrand's liver.

The same conviction was arrived at about the same time at Carlsbad, where the distinguished invalid began to think that he ought no longer to delay a personal account of the services he had rendered at Vienna.

When M. de Talleyrand's disgrace was resolved upon,—as he was rarely the last to know what concerned himself,—when he waited on Louis XVIII., the day after the battle of Waterloo, it was to request his gracious permission to continue his cure at Carlsbad ; nor was his Majesty so ill-natured as to do otherwise, by saying : " Certainly, M. de. Talleyrand ; I hear those waters are excellent !"

Nothing could equal the amiable and contented mien with which M. de Talleyrand limped from his most Christian Majesty's presence after this considerate reply, and eating an excellent dinner that evening with the Mayor of Mons, he was never known, says one of the guests, to be more gay, witty, or agreeable ; dilating to one or two of his intimate friends on the immense pleasure it was to find that he had no longer to disturb himself about the affairs of a clique which it was impossible to serve and to please.

END OF M. DE TALLEYRAND'S DIPLOMATIC CAREER.

The quadruple alliance—and alliance* of the western and constitutional government of Europe—was, in fact, a mere extension of the alliance between England and France, and a great moral exhibition of the trust placed by the parties themselves in that alliance. With this remarkable and popular compact—a compact which embodied the best principles on which an Anglo-French Alliance can be formed—the diplomatic career of M. de Talleyrand closed. He felt, as he himself said, that there " is a sort of space between death and life, which should be employed in dying decently."

On leaving England, Talleyrand quitted not only diplomacy, but public life, and passed the remainder of his days in the enjoyment of the highest position, and the most agreeable and cultivated society that this country could afford.

" His fortune and ability might now, according to the Grecian sage, be estimated ; for his career was closed ; and, as the old sought his saloon as the hearth on which their brighter recollections could be revived, so the young were glad to test their opinions ' of the politic man,' who had passed through so many vicissitudes and walked with a careless and haughty ease over the ruins of so many governments, at the fall of which he had assisted.   He himself, with that cool presence of mind for which he was so remarkable, aware that he had but a few years between the grave and himself, employed them in one of his great and constant objects, that of prepossessing the age to succeed him in his favour, and explaining to those whom he thought likely to influence the coming generation, the darker passages of his brilliant career.   To one distinguished person, M. Montalivet, who related to Sir H. L. Bulwer the fact, he once said : ‘ You have a prejudice against me, because your father was an Imperialist, and you think I deserted the Emperor.   I have never kept fealty to any one longer than he has himself been obedient to common sense. But, if you judge all my actions by this rule, you will find that I have been eminently consistent ;’ and where is there so degraded a human being, or so bad a citizen, as to submit his intelligence, or sacrifice his country, to any individual, however born, or however endowed ?”

“ This, indeed, in a few words,” says Sir H. L. Bulwer, “ was M. de Talleyrand’s theory ; a theory which has formed the school, that without strictly adhering to the principle that common sense should be the test of obedience, bows to every authority with a smile and shrug of the shoulders, and the well-known phrase of ‘ La France avant tout.’ ”

TALLEYRAND AND COUNT MONTROND.

“ To Talleyrand is generally attributed the well-known saying : ‘ La parole a été donnée à l’homme pour l’aider à cacher sa pensée :’ whereas, Captain Gronow, in his Recollections and Anecdotes, second series, asserts positively that the above saying is Montrond’s and not Talleyrand’s. Apropos of the Count, he is said to have been ‘ the most agreeable scoundrel, and the greatest reprobate in France.’ He was an inveterate gambler, and rarely lost.   When very young, at the Court of Marie Antoinette, a Monsieur de Champagne, an officer of the Guards, who was playing at cards with him, said : ‘ Monsieur, vous trichez.’   Monsieur answered with the greatest sang froid, ‘ C’est possible ; mais je ’n’aime pas qu’on me le disé,’ and threw the cards in the face of Champagne.   Montrond is said to have been one of the wittiest men of the age.   His death was a very wretched one.”—The Antiquary, vol. iv.

DEATH OF PRINCE TALLEYRAND.

The force of nature, which a long life had expanded in a variety of ways, seemed now unequal to any further struggle.

A disease which, at Prince Talleyrand's age, was almost certain to be fatal, and which had already made its appearance, assumed a more formidable character.

An operation was devised. The prince submitted to it, and bore it with a fortitude that surprised even those who most knew the stoicism which he on all occasions affected, and usually practised. Dangerous symptoms, however, soon followed, and his physician judged it an act of duty to warn him that his disorder might be fatal.

He was urged to do so by the noble patient's relations, who were especially anxious that he should die in peace with the Church; and when convinced that he could not recover, he assented to all that was asked him in this respect, as a favour that could not hurt himself, and was the wish of those about him.

The following account of his last moments is given by a person who was present at them :—

" When I entered the chamber where reposed the veteran statesman, he had fallen into a profound slumber, from which some amendment was augured by his physicians. The slumber, or rather lethargy, had continued for about an hour after my arrival, when it became curious to observe the uneasiness which was manifested, as the time drew on, even by those dearest and nearest, lest this repose, however salutary, should endure beyond the hour fixed for the King's visit, for the sovereign intended to pay M. de Talleyrand this last homage.

" With some difficulty he was at last aroused, and made to comprehend the approaching ceremony ; and hardly was he lifted from his reclining position, and placed at the edge of the bed, when Louis-Philippe, accompanied by Madame Adelaide, entered the apartment.

" ' I am sorry, prince, to see you suffering so much,' said the King, in a low, tremulous voice, rendered almost inaudible by apparent emotion.

" ' Sire, you come to witness the sufferings of a dying man ; and those who love him can have but one wish, that of seeing them shortly at an end.' This was uttered by M. de Talleyrand in that deep, strong voice so peculiar to himself, and which the approach of death had not power to weaken.

" The royal visit, like all royal visits of a disagreeable nature, was of the shortest duration possible. Indeed, the position was to all parties embarrassing and painful. Louis-Philippe rose, after an effort, and some few words of consolation, to take his leave ; and not even at this last moment did the old prince lose his wonted presence of mind, or forget a duty which the etiquette he had been bred in dictated, that of introducing those formally to the sovereign who found themselves in his presence. Slightly raising himself, then, he mentioned by name his physician, his secretary, his principal valet, and his own private doctor, and then he said slowly, 'Sire, our house has received this day an honour worthy to be inscribed in our annals, and which my successors will remember with pride and gratitude.' Shortly afterwards, the first symptoms of dissolution were observed, and a few persons were then admitted to his chamber ; but the adjoining room was crowded, and exhibited a strange scene for a room so near the bed of death.

"The flower of the society of Paris was there. On one side, old and young politicians, gray-headed statesmen, were gathered round the blazing fire, and engaged in eager conversation ; on another was to be seen a coterie of young gentlemen and ladies, whose sidelong looks, and low, pleasant whispers, formed a sad contrast to the dying groans of the neighbouring sufferer.

"Presently, the conversation stopped—the hum of voices was at an end. There was a solemn pause, and every eye turned towards the slowly opening door of the prince's chamber. A domestic entered, with downcast looks, and swollen eyes, and advancing towards Dr. C——, whispered a few words in his ear. He rose instantly, and entered the prince's chamber. The simultaneousness with which this movement was executed but too plainly revealed its cause. There was an instantaneous rush to the door of the apartment within which M. de Talleyrand was seated on the side of his bed, supported in the arms of his secretary. It was evident that death had set his seal upon that marble brow ; yet I was struck with the still existing vigour of the countenance. It seemed as if all the life which had once sufficed to furnish the whole being was now contained in the brain. From time to time, he raised up his head, throwing back, with a sudden movement, the long, gray locks which impeded his sight, and gazed around ; and then, as if satisfied with the result of his examination, a smile would pass across his features, and his head would fall again upon his bosom. He saw the approach of death without shrinking or fear, and also without any affectation of scorn or defiance.

"If there be truth in the assertion that it is a satisfaction to die amidst friends and relations, then, indeed, must his last feeling towards the world he was for ever quitting have been one of entire approbation and content ; for he expired (on the 17th of May, 1838) amidst royal pomp and reverence, and of all those whom he, perhaps, would have himself called together, none were wanting.

"The friend of his maturity, the fair young idol of his age, were gathered, on bended knees, beside the bed, and if the words of comfort whispered by the murmuring priest failed to reach his ear, it was because the sound was stifled by the wailings of those he had loved so well. Scarcely, however, had those eyes, whose every glance had been watched so long, and with such deep interest, for ever closed, when a sudden change came over the scene.

* * * * * * *

"One would have thought that a flight of crows had suddenly taken wing, so great was the precipitation with which each one hurried from the hotel, in the hope of being the first to spread the news among the particular set or coterie of which he or she happened to be the oracle. Ere nightfall, that chamber, which all day had been crowded to excess, was abandoned to the servants of the tomb; and when I entered in the evening, I found the very arm-chair, whence I had so often heard the prince launch the courtly jest, or stinging epigram, occupied by a hired priest, whispering prayers for the repose of the departed soul."

M. de Talleyrand was buried at Valençay, in the chapel of the Sisters of St. André, which he had founded, and in which he had expressed a desire that the family vault should be placed.

TALLEYRAND'S WEALTH.

In the sequel to the Will of Prince Talleyrand was found a sort of manifesto, in which the celebrated diplomatist asserted the principles which had guided him in his political life, and explained his way of looking at certain events. In that declaration, dated in 1836, the prince declares that, before all things, he had preferred the true interests of France. In his opinion, the Bourbons, in 1814, did not re-ascend the throne in virtue of a pre-existing and hereditary right.

He refutes the reproach of having betrayed Napoleon. · If he abandoned him, it was when he discovered that he could no longer blend, as he had up to that time done, France and the Emperor in the same affection. *This was not without a lively feeling of sorrow, for he owed to Napoleon nearly all his fortune. He enjoins his heirs never to forget obligations; to tell them to their children, and to instruct those, again, to tell them to their offspring; so that, if some day a man of the name of Bonaparte should be found in want of assistance, he should always find it in the family of Talleyrand.*

" Replying to those who reproached him for having served successively all governments, he observes, that he had done so without the least scruple, guided by the idea that, in whatever situation the country might be, there were always means of doing it some good, and that to do this good was the business of a statesman."

Supposing the testament thus spoken of to exist, it is curious ; and the expression of gratitude to the Bonaparte family is the more creditable from the fact that it could not have been made with any idea that it would be rewarded.

As to the defence set up for serving all dynasties and all causes, it cannot apply to any country where public men have the power, out of office, to put down a bad government, as they have, in office, the power to uphold a good one.

WIT, HUMOUR, CHARACTERISTICS, AND PERSONAL OPINIONS.

The wit of Talleyrand was the wit of intellect, not of temperament. It was often full of meaning ; always suggestive of thought ; most frequently caustic. His reserve, constitutional, but heightened by the circumstances of his early life, and cultivated upon principle, was impenetrable. In advanced life, it seemed to have affected his physical appearance. When at rest, but for his glittering eye, it would have been difficult to feel certain that it was not a statue that was placed before you. When his sonorous voice broke upon the ear, it was like a possessing spirit from a graven image. Even in comparatively early life, his power of banishing all expression from his countenance, and the soft and heavy appearance of his features, was remarked as contrasting startlingly with the manly energy indicated by his deep, powerful voice.

Mirabeau in the beginning, Napoleon at the close, of the Revolution, threw him into the shade; but he outlasted both. The secret of his power was patience and pertinacity ; and his life has the appearance of being preternaturally lengthened out, when we recollect the immense number of widely-removed characters and events of which he was the contemporary. It may be said, on the one hand, that he accomplished nothing which time did not, in a manner, bring about ; but, on the other, it may be said, with equal plausibility, that scarcely any of the leading events which occurred in

France in his day would have taken the exact shape they assumed, had not his hand interfered to give them somewhat of a bias or direction. Next to Napoleon, he certainly is the most extraordinary man the extraordinary period of France has given birth to.

Not long before the death of Talleyrand, an able English writer, speaking of his brilliant apothegms, said : "What are they all to the practical skill with which this extraordinary man has contrived to baffle all the calamities of thirty years, full of the ruin of all power, ability, courage, and fortune? Here is the survivor of the age of the Bastille, the age of the guillotine, the age of the prison-ship, the age of the sword. After baffling the Republic, the Democracy, the Despotism, and the Restoration, he figures in his eightieth year as the Ambassador to England, the Minister of France, and retires from offices only to be the chief counsellor, almost the coadjutor of the king. That where the ferocity of Robespierre fell, where the sagacity of Napoleon fell, where the experience of the Bourbons fell, this one old man, a priest in a land of daring spirits, where conspiracy first, and soldiership after, were the great means of power, should survive all, succeed in everything, and retain his rank and influence through all changes, is, unquestionably, among the most extraordinary instances of conduct exhibited in the world."

Bourrienne is not the best of authorities, but the earlier volumes of the memoirs which pass under his name, are less falsified than the later ; and an anecdote which he relates of Talleyrand's interview with the First Consul, after being re-appointed Minister of Foreign Affairs, is so characteristic, that its truth is highly probable :—

"M. de Talleyrand, appointed successor to M. Reinhard, at the same time that Cambacères and Lebrun succeeded Sièyes and Roger Ducas as consuls, was admitted to a private audience by the First Consul. The speech which he addressed to Bonaparte was so gratifying to the person to whom it was addressed, and appeared so striking to myself, that the words have remained in my memory: ' Citizen Consul, you have confided to me the department of foreign affairs, and I will justify your confidence ; but I must work under no one but yourself. This is not mere arrogance on my part. In order that France may be well governed, unity of action is required. You must be First Consul, and the First Consul must hold in his hand all the mainsprings of the political machine—the ministers of the interior, of internal police, of foreign affairs, of war, and the marine. The ministers of these departments must transact business with you alone. The ministries of finance have, without doubt, a powerful influence upon politics; but it is more indirect. The Second Consul is an able jurist; and the Third a master of finance. Leave these departments to them; it will amuse them; and you, general, having the entire management of the essential parts of government, may pursue, without interruption, your noble object, the regeneration of France.'

"These words accorded too closely with the sentiments of Bonaparte to be heard by him otherwise than with pleasure. He said to me, after M. de Talleyrand had taken his leave, ' Do you know, Bourrienne, Talleyrand's advice is sound. He is a man of sense.' He then added, smilingly, ' Talleyrand's a dexterous fellow. He has seen through me. You know, I wish to do what he advises, and he is in the right. Lebrun is an honest man, but a mere bookmaker; Cambacères is too much identified with the Revolution. My government must be something entirely new.' "

Sièyes, who, with a more profound, had a less sagacious, intellect, imagined that as he, a man of letters, had handed the state to a daring, unscrupulous man of the world, he could govern that man. But M. de Talleyrand rather despised and underrated Sièyes, whom he looked on as a tailor who was always making coats that never fitted—a skilful combiner of theories, but without any tact as to their application; and when some one *apropos* of the new constitution, which Sièyes had undertaken to frame, said, " After all, Sièyes has a very profound intellect," he replied, " Profound ! Hem ! You mean, perhaps, *hollow.*"

Bonaparte's conduct justified this witticism; for, when the first project of the constitution alluded to was presented to him, he treated it with ridicule, in the well-known phrase, " A man must have little honour or intellect who would consent to be a pig put up in a sty, to fatten on so many millions a year."

One of the causes which facilitated Napoleon's early steps towards the great object of his ambition was the general incredulity as to the possibility of his attaining it.

A gentleman in company was one day making a somewhat zealous eulogy of his mother's beauty, dwelling upon the topic at uncalled-for length—he himself having certainly in-

herited no portion of that kind under the marriage of his
parents. "It was your father, then, apparently, who may
not have been very well favoured," was Talleyrand's remark,
which at once released the circle from the subject.

When Madame de Staël published her celebrated novel of
Delphine, she was supposed to have painted herself in the
person of the heroine, and M. de Talleyrand in that of an
elderly lady, who is one of the principal characters. "They
tell me," said he, the first time he met her, "that we are
both of us in your novel, in the disguise of women."

Rulhières, the celebrated author of the work on the Polish
revolution, said, "I never did but one mischievous work in
my life." "And when will it be ended?" was Talleyrand's
reply.

"Is not Geneva dull?" asked a friend of Talleyrand.
"Especially when they amuse themselves," was the reply.

"She is insupportable," said Talleyrand, with marked
emphasis, of one well known; but, as if he had gone too
far, and to take something off what he had said, he added,
"It is her only defect."

"Ah! I feel the torments of hell," said a person, whose
life had been supposed to be somewhat of the loosest. "Already?" was the inquiry suggested to M. Talleyrand. Certainly, it came naturally to him. It is, however, not original;
the Cardinal de Retz's physician is said to have made a similar
exclamation on a like occasion.

On the murder of the Duke d'Enghien by the order of
Bonaparte being mentioned, Talleyrand is reported to have
said, "It was worse than a crime, it was a blunder." "We
believe," says Charles Butler, "that such an expression was
never uttered by an Englishman, and that it would be heard
by no Englishman without disgust."

Talleyrand was one of the few men who had the art of
doing witty things. On the death of Charles X. he drove
through Paris for a couple of days, wearing a white hat. He
carried a crape in his pocket. When he passed through the
faubourg of the Carlists, the crape was instantly twisted
round his hat; when he came into the quarter of the Tuil-
eries, the crape was instantly stripped off and put into his
pocket again.

At a public dinner Talleyrand's health was drank. Before
the noise was over, he got up, made a mumbling as if speaking, spoke nothing, made a bow, and sat down; at which the

applause redoubled, though all those immediately about him
knew he never said a word.

The only *mot* recorded of Charles X., as uttered on his
return to France in 1814, on seeing that the adversaries of
his family had disappeared, was—" There is only one Frenchman the more." This was the suggestion of M. Talleyrand.
He afterwards proposed, in like manner, to Charles's successor, that the foolish freaks of the Duchess de Berri should
be visited with this rescript to her and her faction : " Madame, no hope remains for you. You will be tried, condemned, and pardoned."

The prince was enjoying his rubber when the conversation
turned on the recent union of an elderly lady of respectable
rank. " How ever could Madame de S—— make such a
match ?—a person of her birth to marry a valet-de-chambre !"
" Ah," replied Talleyrand, " it was late in the game ; at nine
we don't reckon honours."

Talleyrand being asked if a certain authoress whom he had
long since known, but who belonged rather to the last age,
was not " a little tiresome"—" Not at all," said he ; " she
was perfectly tiresome."

From Sir Henry Bulwer's lucid and comprehensive development of the career and character of M. de Talleyrand, we
select the following passages :—

" I can hardly think, looking calmly and dispassionately at
each of the epochs, that any sensible and moderate man will
deny that the side taken by M. de Talleyrand was the one on
which, in every instance, lay good sense and moderation. It
cannot be said that in the various changes that marked his
career he ever acted disinterestedly ; but at the same time, it may
be urged that every time he accepted office he did thereby a
real service to the cause he espoused, and even to the country to
which he belonged.

" No party had to complain of treachery or ingratitude from
this statesman so frequently stigmatised as fickle.

" The rule of his conduct and the cause of his success may be
generally found in his well-known and wise maxim, that, ' The
thoughts of the greatest number of intelligent persons in any
country are sure, with a few more or less fluctuations, to become
in the end that public opinion which influences the state.'

"The particular and especial talent of M. de Talleyrand, his
tact, the art of seizing the important point in an affair, the
peculiar characteristic of an individual, the genius and tendency
of an epoch. His great merit was to have served governments

when in serving them he served the public interests. I never heard any clear justification of his great wealth, though that which, it is said, he gave to Bonaparte, 'I bought stock before the 18th Brumaire, and sold it the day afterwards,' has wit and *àpropos* to recommend it.

"There was something in his silent way of doing business which disappointed those who expected a more frequent use of the brilliant weapons which it was well known the great wit of the day had at his command. But in the social circle which he wished to charm, or with the single individual whom he wished to pain, the effect of his peculiar eloquence generally overran the expectation."

Lord Alvanley used to relate of Talleyrand, some one stated before him that Châteaubriand complained he was growing deaf. Talleyrand replied, "Il se croit sourd, parcequ'il entend plus parler de lui."

A brief was taken by M. de Talleyrand as a permission to become a layman, and even to take a wife. The lady he married, born in the West Indies, divorced from Mr. Grand, and mentioned in connection with a scandalous story in the life of Sir Philip Francis, was as remarkable for being a beauty as for not being a wit. Every one has heard the story (whether true or invented), of her asking Sir George Robinson after his man "Friday." But M. de Talleyrand vindicated his choice, saying, "A clever wife often compromises her husband; a stupid one only compromises herself."

When, in 1813, Napoleon wavered, and with a momentary doubt as to his own judgment, and a remembrance very possibly of happier times, offered the portfolio of foreign affairs to his ancient minister, but on the condition that he should lay down the rank and emoluments of vice-grand elector. The object of the emperor was thus to make M. de Talleyrand entirely dependent on his place, but M. de Talleyrand, who would have accepted the office, refused the condition, saying, "If the emperor trusts me he should not degrade me; and if he does not trust me he should not employ me; the times are too difficult for half measures."

When the Comte d'Artois wished to be present at the councils of Louis XVIII., M. de Talleyrand opposed the project. The Comte d'Artois was attended, and reproached the minister. "Un jour," said M. de Talleyrand, "votre majesté me remerciera pour ce qui déplait à votre altesse royale."

Some person saying that Fouché had a great contempt for mankind, " C'est vrai," said M. de Talleyrand, " cet homme est beaucoup étendié."

" One evening at Holland House, the company had got into groups, talking over some question of moment in the House of Commons; and thus M. de Talleyrand, left alone, got up to go away, when Lord Holland, with his usual urbanity following him to the door, asked where he was going so early. ' Je vais aux *Travellers*, pour entendre ce que vous dites ici.' " —*Sir H. L. Bulwer.*

" We could prolong almost indefinitely" (says Sir H. L. Bulwer) " this record of sayings from which M. de Talleyrand, notwithstanding his many services and great abilities, derives his popular and traditional reputation ; but, in reality, they belong as much to the conversational epoch at which he entered the world, as to himself."

Lord Palmerston told Sir Henry Bulwer that Talleyrand's manner in diplomatic conferences was remarkable for its extreme absence of pretension, without any derogation of authority. He sat, for the most part, quiet, as if approving, sometimes, however, stating his opinion, but never arguing or discussing, a habit foreign to the natural indolence which accompanied him throughout his active career, and which he also condemned on such occasions as fruitless and impolitic. " I argue before a public assembly," he used to say, " not because I hope to convince any one there, but because I wish my opinions to be known to the public. But in a room in which my voice is not to extend, the attempt to enforce my opinion against that which another is engaged to adopt, obliges him to be more formal and positive in expressing his hostility, and often leads him from a desire in the sense of his instructions to go beyond them."

Whatever M. de Talleyrand did, therefore, in the way of argument he usually did beforehand and alone, with the parties whom he was afterwards to encounter, and here he tried to avoid controversy. His manner was to bring out the principal point, in his own opinion, and present it to the best advantage in every possible position.

Napoleon complained of this, saying he could not conceive how people found M. de Talleyrand eloquent. He always turned round the same idea. But this was a system with him as with Fox, who laid it down as the great principle for an orator who wished to leave an impression.

As a general rule in business, M. de Talleyrand held that a chief should never do anything that a subaltern could do for him. " You should always," he used to say, " have time to spare, and rather put off till to-morrow what you cannot do well and easily to-day, than get into that hurry and flurry which is the necessary consequence of feeling one has too much to do."

Talleyrand had a confidential servant, excessively devoted to his interests, but withal superlatively inquisitive. Having one day entrusted him with a letter, the prince watched his faithful valet from the window of his apartment, and, with some surprise, observed him coolly reading the letter *en route*. On the next day a similar commission was confided to the servant, and to the second letter was added a postscript couched in the following terms :—" You may send a verbal answer by the bearer ; he is perfectly acquainted with the whole affair, having taken the precaution to read this previous to its delivery."

Talleyrand's cook, Marie Antoine Carême, contrasting the good and evil features of his vocation, exclaimed enthusiastically, " The charcoal kills us ; but *n'importe*, our years are few in number, but full of glory."

Talleyrand, only three months before his own death, said : " A minister for foreign affairs must possess the faculty of appearing open, at the same time that he remains impenetrable ; of being in reality reserved, although perfectly frank in his manner." The precept was his own portrait. His power of concealing his opinion, and his steady adherence to the principle of allowing attacks upon his character to dissipate by time for want of opposition, have had the effect of keeping his contemporaries ignorant of his real character.

" Towards the close of his existence the likenesses of M. de Talleyrand that are common are sufficiently resembling. His head, with a superfluity of hair, looked large, and was sunk deep into an expanded chest. His countenance was pale and grave, with a mouth, the under lip rather protruding, which formed itself instantly and almost instinctively into a smile that was sarcastic without being ill-natured. He talked little in general society, merely expressing at intervals some opinions that had the air of an epigram, and which produced its effect as much from the manner with which it was brought out as from its intrinsic merit. He was, in fact, an actor, but an actor with such ease and nonchalance, that he never seemed more natural than when he was acting."—*Sir H. L. Bulwer.*

When the Austrian alliance was formed by the Emperor Napoleon it did not meet with M. de Talleyrand's approval, although he had at one period advised it, and had been also mixed up in the question of a marriage with the imperial family of Russia. The change might have proceeded from his now seeing that such an union as he had at one time favoured, in the hope that it would calm the restless energy of Napoleon, would only stimulate his ambition; or it might have been because, having had nothing to do with the resolutions adopted at Vienna, he had gained nothing by them. At all events, what he said with apparent sincerity was, " Nothing is ever got by a policy which you merely carry out by halves." " If the emperor wants an alliance with Austria he should satisfy Austria; does he think that the house of Hapsburg considers it an honour to ally itself with the house of Bonaparte? What the emperor desires is to have his provinces restored, and his empire raised and revived; if the government of France does not do this, it disappoints him, and the worst enemies we can have are those we disappoint."

The reputation of M. de Talleyrand was now at its height, and many were disposed to consider him as great a master in the science of politics as Napoleon was in that of war. He acquired, moreover, immense wealth, as it is said, by extorted gifts from the powers with which he had been treating; and more especially from the small princes of Germany, whom, in the general division of their territory, he could either save or destroy, and also by successful speculations on the Stock Exchange, means of acquiring riches highly discreditable to his character, but thought lightly of in a country that teaches the philosophy of indulgence, and had recently seen wealth so rudely scrambled for that *Res si possis recte* had become as much a French as ever it was a Roman proverb. His health, moreover, was broken, and unequal to the constant attendance upon the emperor's person, which had become inseparable from his office; while the elevation of Berthier to the rank of vice-consul established a precedence exceedingly galling to his pride. Under these circumstances he solicited and obtained permission to retire, and already Prince de Benevento, received the title of " Vice Grand Electeur," raising him to the rank of the great dignitaries of the empire, a position which, it appears—so small are men, even the greatest—he denied.

THE PRINCESS TALLEYRAND.

This strange lady is described by Prince Talleyrand as the most eccentric person he ever met with ; " the last of a race of which it will be impossible, from the change in human ideas, ever to behold another specimen." In her youth she had been most beautiful, and still retained, saving the loss of an eye, traces of loveliness, even in advanced age. She could not be called either clever or witty, but was the cause of such interminable wit on the part of others, and of such endless good sayings on the part of the prince, that Valençay, to those who were accustomed to her society, seemed dull à *perir* when she was not there. She had the greatest fund of originality and natural vivacity that could be possessed by any human being. Her ideas could not be made by any force of reasoning or persuasion to follow the tide of improvement of the times ; and she could never be taught to believe that the revolution had wrought any change in the relative positions of the aristocracy and the people, but continued, to the latest period of her life, to treat all plebeians and *roturiers* as though they had still been serfs and vassals subject to her will and pleasure. She was an invaluable specimen of the old insolent *noblesse ;* and after a day spent in her company you might retire to rest, no longer wondering at the horrors of the revolution, nor yet at the hatred by which they had been instigated.

On one occasion she had nearly set the whole province in an uproar by an unseasonable display of what the prince was wont to call her *impertinence régente.* A large party had been invited to dinner at the *château* at Valençay, it was one of the gaudy days of the castle ; there were scions of royalty among the guests. The antique silver, and the royal gifts were all displayed. Of course, the *préfet* of the department, the *maire* of Valençay, the curé, and in short all the authorities of the place had been invited, and arrived with true provincial punctuality at the hour named in the invitation. None of the family had as yet appeared. In a short time, however, the drawing-room doors were thrown open, and in sailed the Princess T——. The troubled *provincials* moved in a body towards the fair princess, who stood for a moment and gazed as they advanced ; then turning suddenly round to the grinning domestic who remained standing at the door, " Fool !" indignantly exclaimed her Highness, " did I not bid you ascertain if anybody had arrived, before I troubled myself to come down to the *salon ?*" " Yes, princess, and I came myself to see," answered the servant, looking puzzled and embarrassed, first at his mistress, then at the guests, who stood wondering where the questioning would lead to ; " and when I found these gentlemen here I—" " Idiot !" interrupted the princess, " not to know your business better ; remember that such as these are not anybody, but *nobody.*" With these words she flounced out of the room, pointing with her fan over her shoulder at the poor duped provincials, whose rage and mortification defy description.

PRESENTIMENTS TO TALLEYRAND.

Dr. Sigmond received from the widow of Mr. Colmache, the private secretary and friend of M. de Talleyrand, the following remarkable narrative :—

" One day, in the presence of the minister, the conversation had turned upon the subject of those sudden warnings which have been looked upon as communications from the world of spirits to man ; some one observing that it would be difficult to find a man of any note who had not, in the course of his life, experienced something of the kind—

" ' I remember,' said Talleyrand, ' upon one occasion, having been gifted, for one single moment, with an unknown and nameless power. I know not to this moment whence it came ; it has never once returned, and yet upon that one occasion it saved my life. Without that sudden and mysterious inspiration I should not have been here to tell my tale. I had freighted a ship in concert with my friend Beaumetz. He was a good fellow, Beaumetz, with whom I had ever lived on the most intimate terms. I had not a single reason to doubt his friendship. On the contrary, he had given me, on several occasions, most positive proof of his devotion to my interest and well-being. We had fled from France ; we had arrived at New York together, and we had lived in perfect harmony during our stay there. So, after having resolved upon improving the little money that was left by speculation, it was still in partnership and together that we freighted a small vessel for India, trusting to all the goodly chances which had befriended us in our escape from danger and from death, to venture once more conjointly to brave the storms and perils of a longer and yet more adventurous voyage. Everything

was embarked for our departure ; bills were all paid, and fare-
wells all taken, and we were waiting for a fair wind with most
eager expectation, being prepared to embark at any hour of
the day or night, in obedience to the warning of the captain.
This state of uncertainty seemed to irritate the temper of poor
Beaumetz : he grew remarkably restless : one day he entered
our lodging, evidently labouring under great excitement,
although commanding himself to appear calm. I was engaged
at that moment in writing letters to Europe ; and looking over
my shoulder he said, with forced gaiety, " What need to waste
time in penning those letters ? they will never reach their
destination. Come with me, and let us take a turn on the
Battery ; perhaps the wind may be chopping round ; we may
be nearer our departure than we imagine." The day was very
fine, and though the wind was blowing hard, 1 suffered myself to be persuaded. Beaumetz, I remembered afterwards,
displayed an unusual officiousness in aiding me to close my
desk, and put away my papers, handing me with hurried
eagerness my hat and cane, and doing other services to
quicken my departure, which, at the time, I attributed to his
restless desire for change. We walked through the crowded
streets to the Battery. He had seized my arm, and hurried
me along. When we had arrived at the broad esplanade—
the glory of New York—Beaumetz quickened his step still
more, until we reached close to the water's edge. He talked
loud and quickly, admiring in energetic terms the beauty of
the scenery, the Brooklyn heights, the shady groves of the
island, the ships riding at anchor, and the busy scene on the
peopled wharf, when suddenly he paused in his mad, incoherent discourse—for I had freed my arm from his grasp, and
stood immovable before him. Staying his wild and rapid
steps, I fixed my eye upon his face. He turned aside, cowed
and dismayed. " Beaumetz," I shouted, " you mean to murder
me : you intend to throw me from the height into the sea
below. Deny it, monster, if you can." The maniac stared at
me for a moment ; but I took especial care not to avert my
gaze from his countenance, and he quailed beneath it. He
stammered a few incoherent words, and strove to pass me, but
I barred his passage with extended arms. He looked vacantly
right and left, and then flung himself upon my neck, and
burst into tears. " 'Tis true—'tis true, my friend ! The
thought has haunted me day and night, like a flash from the
lurid fire of hell. It was for this I brought you here. Look !

you stand within a foot of the edge of the parapet : in another instant the work would have been done." The demon had left him ; his eye was unsettled, and the white foam stood in bubbles on his parched lips ; but he was no longer tossed by the same mad excitement under which he had been labouring, for he suffered me to lead him home without a single word. A few days' repose, bleeding, abstinence, completely restored him to his former self, and what is most extraordinary, the circumstance was never mentioned between us. My Fate was at work.'

" It was whilst watching by the bedside of his friend that Talleyrand received letters which enabled him to return to France ; he did so, and left Beaumetz to prosecute the speculation alone. The Prince Talleyrand could never speak of the preceding event without shuddering, and to the latest hour of his existence believed that ' he was for an instant gifted with an extraordinary light, and during a quick and vivid flash the possible and the true were revealed to a strong and powerful mind,' and that upon this the whole of his destiny hinged. This species of momentary exaltation," says Dr. Sigmond, "which is not again repeated, but is remembered with the most vivid impression, is what is more immediately known by the name of fantasia ; in France and England it is named *presentiment*."—Dr. Forbes Winslow's *Psychological Journal*.

M. de Talleyrand was, up to the last hour of his life, almost indifferent to praise, but singularly enough (considering his long and varied career) exquisitely sensitive to censure.

" The art of putting the right men in the right place, (the phrase is not of to-day's invention)," M. de Talleyrand observes profoundly, "is, perhaps, the first in the science of government ; but," he adds, " the art of finding a satisfactory position for the discontented is the most difficult. To present such to their thoughts and desires, is," he says, " I think, one of the solutions of this social problem."

ARCHBISHOP WHATELY.

THIS eminent theologian and writer on logic and political economy was descended from a distinguished family, who have contributed notably on their part to Church and state. Among them we find Charles Whately, remembered for a tract impugning the orthodoxy of Bishop Hoadley. Then there was William Whately, the powerful Puritan preacher of Banbury, who (says Wood) " laid such a foundation of faction in Stratford-on-Avon as could never be removed." This divine occupied a prominent niche in the late archbishop's ancestry, is traditionally recognised as the " Roaring Boy of Banbury," and was a popular person, whose epitaph is quaint :—

> " It's William Whately that here lies,
> Who swam to's tomb in's people's eyes."

The Whately family had their doctors of physic as well as divinity. The Rev. Joseph Whately having accepted, under Bishop Bagot, a prebend of Bristol, he removed to that city. The prebendary and his wife sometimes came to London during the season, and in Cavendish Square, on February 1, 1786, Richard, afterwards Archbishop of Dublin, was born. He was the youngest of eight children, most of whom died " unsung," though neither " unwept nor unhonoured." He received a comprehensive course of general instruction at Bristol. At the age of eighteen he was placed in Oriel College, Oxford, the then great school of speculative philosophy, where his originality at once attracted attention. But he did not rise like a rocket. John Keble, famed in late years as author of the *Christian Year*, was in the same class with Whately, who won a double-first at the age of eighteen. He is well remembered in Oxford as the " Boy Bachelor." From the hour he entered Oxford he was remarkable for a certain amount of originality both of thought and action, which sometimes amounted to rank eccentricity ; his ways were often unequal, and he had great points of character. In 1808 he graduated, and in 1810 he produced a valuable English essay, "What are the arts in the cultivation of which the ancients were less successful than the moderns?" which won the twenty-guinea prize. The college of Oriel is famous for having some of the greatest thinkers of which English churchmen of the present generation may boast, such as Dr. Arnold, Dr. Copleston, Dr. J. H. Newman, and the subject of this sketch. Whately was appointed to read the Bampton Lectures in 1822, in which year he accepted the rectory of Halesworth, in Suffolk, value £450. In the contest which took place in the University, when Sir Robert Peel appealed to his learned constituents upon the Roman Catholic question, Whately voted for the right honourable baronet. In 1830 he was appointed president of St. Alban's Hall, and professor of political economy, and in 1831 he was consecrated Archbishop of Dublin and Bishop of Glendalough; the diocese of Kildare was subsequently added to his charge.

"Whately's master at Oriel was Edward Copleston, the subsequently famous Bishop of Llandaff. The vigour, clearness, and thought, which was a specialty with Dr. Copleston, he at last succeeded in engrafting on Richard Whately, who, in dedicating to him his great work on logic, many years after, proudly records the advantages which 'he derived from Dr. Copleston's instruction both in regular lectures and in private conversation.' Of this invaluable intercourse the future archbishop seems to have made ample notes; and he repeatedly declared, both in print and in private, that this memorable "Logic," on which his fame mainly rests, contains quite as much of Copleston as of Whately."

The work below-mentioned,* which extends to 700 pages, not only presents a vivid picture of Dr. Whately's public life, but "illustrations of the inexhaustible fund of wit and humour which was constantly flowing from the late archbishop," and it originated in a suggestion from Oxford for a biography of this class. While it glances at the Archbishop's contemporaries and times, it details the leading events of his active life with the relief of the *characteristics* of well-stored minds; and, in accordance with the object and plan of our "Anecdote Biography," we have

* *Memoirs of Richard Whately, Archbishop of Dublin; with a Glance at his Contemporaries and Times.* By John Fitzpatrick, J.P. 2 vols. (Richard Bentley, 1864.)

noted the following passages selected from the Doctor's memoirs.

M. Guizot describes Dr. Whately as "startling and ingenious, strangely absent, familiar, confused, eccentric, amiable, and engaging, no matter what unpoliteness he might commit, or what propriety he might forget." In short, a mind with a little of the Sydney Smith's leaven, whose brilliancy lay in precisely these odd analogies. It was his recreation to take up some intellectual hobby, and make a toy of it, just as, years ago, he was said to have taken up that strange instrument the boomerang, and was to be seen on the sands casting it from him, and watching it return. It was said, too, that at the dull intervals of a visitation, when ecclesiastical business languished, he would cut out little miniature boomerangs of card, and amuse himself by illustrating the principle of the larger toy by shooting them from his finger.

Homœopathy was a medical paradox, and was therefore welcome. Yet in this he travelled out of the realms of mere fanciful speculation, and clung to it with a stern and consistent earnestness, faithfully adhered to through his last illness. Mesmerism, too, he delighted to play with. He had, in fact, innumerable *dadas*, as the French call them, or hobby-horses, upon which he was continually astride.

Dr. Whately, after he had received the mitre, still continued the same jovial, free-and-easy man in manners that he had been as a Fellow and College Master at Oxford. With an abundant fund of anecdote, enlivened with humour and brilliant flashes of wit, he was quite at home in convivial meetings of an intellectual kind in Dublin. All sorts of stories are current about his love of fun ; how he got rid of a pompous professor of grammar, by challenging him to decline the word " cat," and when the professor came to the vocative case, " O cat," laughing at him, and asking him who ever called to a cat " O cat," and not " Puss." How, on another occasion, an English clergyman on a visit to Dublin, on being chaffed by the Archbishop more than he thought proper, stopped him by saying, " You forget, your grace, that I am not in your diocese." In 1831, when he was appointed to the archbishopric, Dr. Arnold could write of him thus : " In point of essential holiness, there does not live a truer Christian than Whately. It grieves me that he is spoken of as dangerous and latitudinarian, because his intellectual nature

in the intensity of the effort to solve it, the Archbishop said, "Sir, you resemble an ignorant pedagogue, who keeps his pupil in darkness."

WHAT IS A MIRACLE?

Dr. Whately often amused a chosen few by telling this odd story :—An Irish parson of the old school, in whom a perception of the ludicrous was developed with a Rabelain breadth of appreciation, was asked by a clodhopper to explain the meaning of a miracle. "Walk on a few paces before me," said his reverence, which having done, the peasant was sur-prised to feel in the rear a kick, administered with telling energy. "What did you do that for?" exclaimed the young man, angrily. "Simply to illustrate my meaning," replied the cleric, blandly. "If you had not felt me, it would have been a miracle."

There were some eccentric parsons in Ireland in those days. One having been interrupted by two dogs, which began to fight in church, he descended the pulpit and endeavoured to separate them. On returning to his place, the clergyman, who was rather an absent man, asked the clerk, "Where was I a while ago?" "Wasn't your rivirence appaising the dogs?" responded the other.

QUID PRO QUO.

A puffy parson from Donegal, with more hat than head, one day swaggered into the model school, and in loud and pompous accents requested that a teacher of unexceptionable acquirements should be trotted out before him. "In addition to his duties," he added, "he should act as parish-clerk, assist the sexton, take care of the registries, and be capable of leading the chorus in my church." An inspector inquired, "What amount of salary the rev. gentleman would consider equitable for these varied services?" "Five pounds a year," he replied, "in addition, of course, to his pay from the Board." "Here is the Archbishop himself," proceeded the inspector, "and you had better tell him the exact sort of person you require." Dr. Whately heard the litany of accomplishments recited, with the remuneration proposed. "You can get beer at any price, sir," said his Grace, "small price, small beer; but I tell you, sir, you disgrace the cloth you wear and the diocese from which you come."

SACRAMENTAL WINE.

Dr. Whately (observes a monthly reviewer) was jesting with Dr. Pusey in reference to his alleged practice of mingling water with wine at early communion. "The people," replied Pusey, "complain of the wine getting into their heads." "Oh, come now, Pusey," rejoined Dr. Whately—"a thimble-full of wine to get into people's heads!" Dr. Pusey's only answer, according to the Archbishop, was a laugh and a nod of the head, expressive of sympathy, and indicative of utter disbelief in all such frippery. Now, a smile, we believe, did play across the features of Dr. Pusey; but it was one which, if not over hastily scrutinised, might possibly be found indicative of compassion for what he believed to be undeniable infidelity.

The writer of the *Anecdotal Memoirs* has not much belief in the above story. When he began early communion at Oxford, one or more communicants applied to him to the effect that, as the wine was strong, and on account of its strength was unpleasant to them the first thing in the morning, for that reason he mixed the water with it. It must be recollected that the so-called wine used for the Anglican communion used to be a strange composition called Tent, and made up, whether of brandy, or of treacle, raspberry vinegar, or what else, he did not know; but it used to be a very strong compound. In mass, not only is the wine light and unbrandied, but after the first ablution the strength of the wine is counteracted. The sacramental wine at —— was complained of, not so much as getting into men's heads, as leaving an unpleasant taste in the mouth.

PALACE FESTIVITIES.

No strait-laced whine ever penetrated Dr. Whately's festive meetings. The fullest unreserve and the heartiest enjoyment reigned around. Fun, almost juvenile in its exuberance, was often the order of the evening, as logical puzzles or metaphysical speculations, and trying who should make the worst pun, quite as frequently occurred as higher tests and tournaments of wit. At a farewell dinner to Dr ——, Bishop-elect of Cork, a bottle of rich old Waterloo port, instead of making a rapid circuit, rested before him. "Come," cried the Archbishop from the head of the table, "though you are John Cork, you must not *stop* the bottle here."

The reply attributed to the Archbishop was quite in the Whateleian vein. "I see your Grace is disposed to *draw me out*. But, though charged with *cork*, I am not going to be *screwed*." "We are all most anxious to see you *elevated*," exclaimed the host. "I leave to your Grace, as a disciple of Peel, the privilege of *opening the port*," was the reply.

DR. WHATELY'S LOVE OF GARDENING.

The Archbishop was in the habit of making two daily circuits in the demesne, attended by a ponderous stock, with a steel blade at the end, whereby he served both his own health and that of the trees by lopping off decayed branches. He was also especially fond of grafting ; and his domain at Redesdale contained 1000 standing specimens of the art, straight from his grace's hands. When cutting down trees, or grafting, Dr. Whately wore an apron, a veritable bishop's apron— which had been worn out in episcopal service, or at least, had become too shabby to wear in ordinary.

Dr. Whately had also, while residing at Stillorgan, a complete set of garden utensils, with which he used to work constantly, and often stripping himself to his shirt-sleeves. He was specially fond of horticulture. And here ends all illustration of his system of self-culture, which discouraged gaudy flowers, then so fashionable in Ireland, under the leadership of Mr. Shiel, the Brummel of modern Irish oratory. Whately's brain was a nursery of young oaks, albeit they often grew up gnarled and knotty.

When the Archbishop was one day engaged in his gardening operations, a companion referred, among other matters, to the great revolution in the medical treatment of lunatics introduced by Pinel, who, instead of the strait waistcoat and other maddening goads, awarded to each patient healthful and agreeable occupation, including agriculture and gardening. "I think gardening would be a dangerous indulgence for lunatics," observed Dr. Whately. "How so ?" said his friend, surprised. "Because they might *grow madder*," was the witty rejoinder.

THE TICKET-OF-LEAVE SYSTEM

Found little favour in Dr. Whately's sight : he lost no opportunity to make a cut at it, and if he could contrive to make the sarcasm cut two ways, the joke was all the pleasanter. The Rev. W. M'Naught and others, having forsaken the Anglican Church, joined the Sectaries, and finally came back to the Anglican Church again, Dr. Whately quietly remarking : " I hope they are not going to send us ticket-of-leave clergymen."

The Archbishop would seem to have been averse to all capital punishments, which he regarded as anything but a capital cure for crime. " Every instance," he said, " of a man's suffering the penalty of the law is an instance of the failure of that penalty in effecting its purpose, which is, to deter."

In a social circle he continued to be the idol of the few rather than of the many. He " delighted in the oddities of thought, in queer, quaint distinctions," observed a gentleman who knew him well ; " and if an object had by any possibility some strange distorted side or corner, or even point, which was undermost, he would gladly stoop down his mind to get that precise view of it ; nay, would draw it in that odd light for the amusement of the company."

THE OPERATION OF HANGING.

" Why does the operation of hanging kill a man ?" asked Dr. Whately. A physiologist replied : " Because inspiration is checked, circulation is stopped, and blood suffuses, and congests the brain." " Bosh !" replied his Grace ; " it is because the rope is not long enough to let his feet touch the ground."

ECCENTRICITIES.

" Pray, sir," he said to a loquacious prebendary, who had made himself active in talking at the Archbishop's expense when his back was turned ; "pray, sir, why are you like the bell of our own church-steeple ?" " Because," replied the other, " I am always ready to sound the alarm when the church is in danger !" " By no means," replied the Archbishop ; " it is because you have an empty head and a long tongue."

By some he was voted a bore ; by others, a bear ; and with formidable co-operation, they baited him as cruel people sometimes bait a bear or a *boar*.

When Lord Gough returned to Ireland wreathed with laurels by the subjugation of Runjeet Singh, and the Sikhs,

Dr. Whately asked him what had been the proportion of the belligerent parties. Lord Gough was proceeding into a numerical statement, when the Archbishop cut it short by saying : "They were Sikhs (six), and we won (one)."

A man directed the Archbishop's attention to a valuable draught horse, as sagacious as he was powerful. "There is nothing," said the horse-dealer, "which he cannot draw." "Can he draw an inference?" inquired Dr. Whately.

A friend who had been to visit Madame Tussaud's, and expressed great pleasure at beholding the many heroes and heroines made of wax. "What was Joan of Arc made of?" inquired a lady. "She wasn't there," replied the sight-seer ; "but I have seen her generally in plaster-of-Paris." "Joan of Arc was made (maid) of Orleans," sang out the Archbishop, with a hearty laugh.

Turning to a junior clergyman, Dr. Whately asked : "What is the difference between a form and a ceremony? The meaning seems nearly the same, yet there is a very nice distinction." Various answers were given. "Well," he said, "it lies in this : you sit upon a form, but you stand upon a ceremony."

A remarkable conundrum of his was : "Why can a man never starve in the Great Desert?—Because he can eat the *sand which* is (sandwiches) there. But what brought the sandwiches there?—Noah sent Ham, and his descendants mustered and bred (mustard and bread)."

The answer to the following—one of the latest charades given forth by him—he withheld :—

> "When from the Ark's capacious round
>   The earth came forth in pairs,
> Who was the first to hear the sound
>   Of boots upon the stairs?"

He once asked a room-full of divines why white sheep eat so very much more than black sheep. One person advanced the opinion that black being a warmer colour than white, and one which never fails forcibly to attract the sun, black sheep could do with less nutriment than their white contemporaries. At these profound speculations, Dr. Whately shook his head gravely, and then proceeded to explain : "White sheep eat more because there are more of them."

Much of the extravagant humour peculiar to the Archbishop, was a stimulant deliberately applied to elicit laughter, which he considered a wholesome exercise tending to renovate the nerves relaxed in the progress of his often jaded life. There can be no doubt that laughter promotes a free respiration, quickens the circulation, and consumes, to some extent, the splenetic humours. Old medical writers attribute laughter to the fifth pair of nerves, which, sending branches to the ear, eye, lips, tongue, palate, and muscles of the cheek, mouth, and præcordia, a pleasant sympathy is awakened between all other parts. "Cultivate, not only the cornfields of the mind, but the pleasure-grounds also," was a motto of Dr. Whately's.

This cultivation was often a labour rather than a luxury. His hilarity was not always the result of happiness. "Gay spirits," he once said, "are always spoken of as a sign of happiness, though every one knows to the contrary. A cockchafer is never so lively as when a pin is stuck through his tail, and a hot floor makes Bruin dance."

Often, when the old Archbishop seemed most exuberant with drollery, stab after stab was making sad havoc in his heart.

CONCEALED AUTHORSHIP.

"Concealment," says Dr. Whately, "is the great spur to curiosity, which gives an interest to investigation. . The celebrated *Letters of Junius* would, probably, have long since been forgotten, if the author could have been clearly pointed out at the time."

In *Moore's Diary*, vol. vii., p. 60, we find : "Rogers, in speaking of Brougham, and remarking how well he often puts some points in his speeches, gave as an instance what he had said in a late speech on the subject of very young men at college signing the Thirty-nine Articles, viz., that they swallowed them first and digested them afterwards. On hearing this I could not help putting in a claim for my own property, which the thought in question decidedly was ; as, not more than a week before Brougham made this speech, my verses on Philpotts's famous explanation of the signing had appeared in the *Times*, and that Brougham must have read those verses ; his immediate interest in the subject was a sufficient guarantee. In that squib were the following lines :—

"'Both in dining and signing we take the same plan,
First swallow all down, then digest as we can.'

When I mentioned this, Rogers seemed a little ashamed of

himself.   It is too hard, when a great gun like the Chancellor
condescends to discharge one of my pellets from his muzzle,
that the original *popgun* should be thus forgotten.   But, as it
is, station makes all the difference, even in a joke, and Shakspeare was for once wrong, when he said, ' A jest's posterity lies
not in the tongue of him who makes it ; for it does sometimes
lie wholly there.' "—Fitzpatrick's *Memoirs of Dr. Whately*, vol.
ii. p. 129, note.

" HISTORIC DOUBTS."

In 1819 appeared Dr. Whately's *Historic Doubts relative to
Napoleon Bonaparte.*   Some persons with a superficial knowledge of this and other apparently trifling performances of
the Doctor, have taken them up as a piece of light reading.
But to quote his own felicitous illustration, such persons, in
stooping to pick up a stone, find that they have caught the
point of a rock.   The object of the Napoleon pamphlet was
to show the fallacy of scepticism or criticism in general, and
of the German neology in particular.   Dr. Whately used to
say, at the time he published this pamphlet, the heresy of the
German rationalists had formidably penetrated Oxford ; and
it has been asserted by one of his chaplains that even Dr.
Pusey was tinged by its progress.

It is easier to tear down than to build up ; and it has been
said that so ingeniously are the arguments devised and stated,
that the reader rises from the perusal half inclined to doubt
whether Napoleon the Great ever existed, or the battle of
Waterloo was ever fought.   " Dr. Whately," remarks Mr.
Blacker, " attained his object, which was to show that it is
possible to give a philosophic denial to the most notable facts
of history, as well as the doctrines of the Christian religion,
and the statements of Revelations."   But it would seem that
Dr. Whately himself caught the contagion which he aimed
to subdue.

The *Historic Doubts*, which ran through thirteen editions,
Dr. Whately long intended to supplement by a tract upon the
evidence of the Old Testament, from which he would have
essayed to show that no fiction, however carefully constructed,
could stand the test of critical examination.   He intended to
take De Foe's great work as an illustration, demonstrating by
internal evidence that Robinson Crusoe could not be true.

Some of the Oxford divines, whose scepticism Dr. Whately

had sharply ridiculed, were, ere long, gratified by detecting in his discourses some profoundly original views, and which proved that Whately's doubts were not confined to Napoleon Bonaparte, and that it was possible for even an extinguisher to take fire.

"Gibbon," writes Dr. Whately, "affords the most remarkable instances of that kind of style, in which the assumption of the point in question is never stated distinctly, but some other proposition inserted which implies it. He keeps it out of sight (as a dexterous thief does stolen goods), at the very moment he is taking it for granted. His way of writing reminds one of those persons who never dare look you full in the face."

WHATELEIAN PROVERBS AND PRECEPTS.

Among the energetic services of Dr. Whately to the Board of National Education in Ireland, is the completion of a set of proverbs and moral precepts for use as regular copy-books in all the schools. These copy-lines are designated " rough stones," and are thoroughly *Whateleian*. Here are a few specimens :—

" ' A man will never change his mind if he has no mind to change.'

" ' The brighter the moon shines the more the dogs bark.' Some say, ' The moon does not regard the barking of dogs.' It is a curious propensity in most dogs to howl at the moon, especially when shining brightest. In the same manner, it may be observed, that any eminent person who is striving to enlighten the world, is sure to be assailed by the furious clamour and abuse of the bigoted and envious. This is a thing disgusting in itself (as the howling of dogs is an unpleasant sound), but it is a sign and accompaniment of a man's success in doing service to the public. And, if he is a truly wise man, he will take no more notice of it than the moon does of the howling of the dogs. His only answer to them is, ' to shine on.'

" ' A proverb is the wisdom of many and the wit of one.'

" ' If you will not take pains, pains will take you.'

" ' Be old when young that you may be young when old—or, old young and old long.'

" ' Better to wear out shoes than sheets.' That is, to go about your business actively than to lie a-bed. Some say, ' Better wear out than rust out.' A knife, or other iron tool, will wear out by constant use, but if laid by useless the rust will consume it.

" ' Lose an hour in the morning and you will be all day hunting it.'

" ' The tree roots more fast,
That has stood a tough blast.' ·

" This is literally true, for it is always found that winds which do not blow a tree down make it root the better.

" ' As the fool thinketh so the bell clinketh.' When a weak man is strongly biassed in favour of any opinion, scheme, &c., everything seems to confirm it, the very bells seem to say the words that his head is full of.

" ' A man is one knave, but a fool is many.' A weak man in a place of authority will often do more mischief than a bad man, for an intelligent, but dishonest, man will only do as much hurt as will serve his own purpose ; but a weak man is likely to be made the tool of several dishonest men. A lion only kills as many as will supply him with food ; but a horse, if ridden by several warlike horsemen, may prove the death of more than ten lions would kill." ·

THE BEST MEDICINE.

Dr. Whately avowed a scepticism as regards drugs, and was very much of opinion with Dryden, that—

" Better to seek the fields for health unbought,
Than fee the doctor for a nauseous draught."

The physic from the fields and draughts " of vital air," of which the Archbishop partook copiously, carried in his own face an advertisement of their potency, quite as effective, and perhaps more truthful, than the ubiquitous credentials of the Methuselah pills.

CRANIOLOGY.

Dr. Whately was a devout believer in Craniology. Provost Sadlier's head was peculiarly flat on the top. " Did you hear of the new phrenological test, gentlemen?" inquired the Archbishop, glancing significantly at the provost. " Take a handful of peas, drop them on the head of the patient, the amount of the man's dishonesty will depend on the number which remain there. If a large number remain tell the butler to lock up the plate."

Shortly after the publication of Moore's *Travels of an Irish Gentleman in search of a Religion*, a reply appeared containing some acrimonious remarks of a polemical character, which

Dr. Whately—at least just then—would have been very unlikely to write, and yet Moore found from Lady Elizabeth that the Archbishop of Dublin was at first supposed to have been the author of the answer. "After all," adds Moore, "it is, probably, no bishop at all, but merely somebody who wants to be a bishop." The author was, we believe, the Rev. Mortimer O'Sullivan ; but we have also seen the work attributed to Blanco White.—*J. W. Fitzpatrick, J.P.*

There are several anecdotes related of Dr. Whately's attempts to eradicate the seed of disunion sown in the vineyard of Dublin by industrious predecessors, and of his desire to lop off such offshoots of illiberal feeling as occasionally flung themselves forth before him. The caustic way in which he snubbed a young aide-de-camp, who at one of the Castle levées asked, *apropos* of Dr. Murray, who wore a cross, what was the difference between a Roman bishop and a jackass, was very characteristic. "One wears a cross upon his back and the other upon his breast," explained the A.D.C. "Do *you* know the difference between an aide-de-camp and a donkey?" asked Dr. Whately. "No?" said the other, interrogatively. "Nor I, either," was the reply.

"DRESSING THE STATUE."

When Dr. Whately first came to Ireland, he found traces of the old and silly fashion of dressing the statue of William III. on College Place, a ceremony often attended with midnight discord and outrage. Dr. Whately strongly denounced these odious practices ; and, in reference to the fashion of painting the statue and its pedestal in the vulgar brilliancy of orange and blue, he adds, "Even the Pagans would never paint a trophy."

NAPOLEON.—O'CONNELL.

The actual history of Napoleon Bonaparte consisted, according to Dr. Whately, of a great number of incidents, not only very improbable of themselves, but attended by evidence to which suspicion must attach.

At the period of the memorable De Grey proclamation, in 1843, Dr. Whately, although opposed to the prosecution of O'Connell, was equally opposed to a surrender of the great measure for which O'Connell struggled. "To expect," he said, "to tranquillize and benefit a country by gratifying its agitators, would be like the practice of the superstitions of old, with their sympathetic powders and ointments, who, instead of applying medicaments to the wound, contented themselves with *salving the wound* which it had inflicted."

POPULAR PREACHERS.

Dr. Whately was a little jealous of some of the popular preachers. "Many a meandering discourse one hears," he said, "in which the preacher aims at nothing, and hits it." "A preacher," he exclaimed, "should ask himself, ' Am I about to preach because I want to say something, or because I have something to say?' "

"Almost every one," says Dr. Whately, "is aware of the infectious nature of any emotion excited in a large assembly. The power of this reflects sympathy in increasing any feeling, whether pity, indignation, contempt, bashfulness, the sense of the ludicrous, &c., and may be compared to the increase of sound by a number of echoes, or of a light by a number of mirrors, or to the blaze of a heap of firebrands, each of which would speedily have gone out if kindled separately, but which, thrown together, help to kindle each other."

Dr. Whately's preaching was too sober for a people accustomed to strong appeals, and fervour and favour more equally far from him. He belonged to a different genius from the cleric who, whenever he struck the old pulpit cushion, raised such a cloud of dust as to lose sight of his congregation for several minutes.

In conversation with his chaplains, Archbishop Whately referred to the charge of Socinianism, Arianism, and even the Sabellian heresy, which had been brought against him by persons who imparted passages from his work apart from their context. "Why the same might be said of the Bible itself," said Dr. Whately, "else we should not have heard of these sects, which appeal to it in support of their views."

"Weak arguments are often thrust before my path, but although they are most unsubstantial, it is not easy to destroy them. There is not a more difficult feat known than to cut through a cushion with a sword."

A young chaplain had preached a sermon of great length. "Sir," said Lord Mulgrave, bowing to him, "there were some things in your sermon I never heard before." "Oh, my lord," said the flattered chaplain, "it is a common text, and I could not have hoped to say anything new on the subject." "I never heard the clock strike twice," said Lord Mulgrave.

PRACTICAL SERMONS.

Dr. Whately's flock liked practical sermons, but he declared war to the knife against all such sermons. "Any Christian minister," he said, "who should confine himself to what are sometimes (erroneously) called 'practical sermons,' *i.e.*, mere moral essays, without any mention of the peculiar doctrines of Christianity, is in the same condition with the heathen philosopher, with this difference—that what was their *misfortune* is his *fault*."

DR. WHATELY'S PREACHING.

His style of charging and preaching exposed him to not a few hits, including a paraphrase on an old epigram, by Rogers :—

"Whately has got no heart, 'tis said, but we deny it ;
He *has* a heart, and gets his sermons by it."

The Doctor rarely let an opportunity pass of perpetrating a pun, and in reference to the Rev. Maurice Day, he said that " The ladies of Dublin ran *to-day* for a sermon, and *to-morrow* for a novel." " Morrow," we may add, is the Mudie of Dublin. And on a false report of Mr. Day's death, he is said to have exclaimed, in the words of the Roman emperor, " Alas ! my friends, I've lost a day !"

TAKING THE MEASURE.

Dr. Whately was often constrained to assume a repellent sternness of manner, in order to keep at a distance the host of hungry applicants for preferment, who daily taxed his patience. Excuses and pretexts dropped inexhaustibly from their glib tongues. Of these gentlemen, the Archbishop, as he said, " took the measure," and he was soon able to recognise even the knocks and rings which heralded their approach.

THE RASHLY CAUTIOUS.

There is many a *rashly cautious* man. A moth rushes into a flame, and a horse obstinately stands still in a stable on fire, and both are burnt. Some men are prone to moth rashness, and some to horse rashness, and some to both.

SOLITARY THOUGHT.

Newman was fond of the luxury of solitary thought. In one of his walks round Christ Church meadow, he met Dr. Copleston, who, bowing as he passed, said, "*Nunquam minus* solus quàm cum solus."

Upon occasions when all redeeming gifts on Whately's part failed to popularise him, wags paid him in his own coin, and said, if he proved himself an *augur*, it only confirmed their original opinion of him as a *bore*.

SELF-INTEREST AND SELF-DENIAL.

Quoting La Rochefoucauld, Dr. Whately once said that self-interest speaks all sorts of languages, and personates all kinds of parts, even that of self-disinterestedness. "There is none which greedy petitioners for places personate so often. The transparent and disgusting hypocrisy of desiring preferment purely for the good of the country and from a sense of public duty, is stated by Lord Brougham to be incessant. Once, on his remarking to Lord Melbourne that nobody could tell till he came into office how base men were, the latter humorously replied, "On the contrary, I never before had such an opinion of human virtue, for I now find that self-denial is the sole motive in seeking advancement, and personal gain the only thing that is never dreamt of.'"

ERROR AND TRUTH.

The fame of clever but puzzle-headed advocates of vulgar errors will be like a mushroom, which springs up in a night and rots in a day ; whilst that of the clear-headed lover of truth will be a tree, "*seris factura nepotibus umbram*." He must take his chance for the result. If he is wrong in the doctrines he maintains, or the measures he proposes, at least it is not for the sake of immediate popular favour. If he is right it will be found out in time, though perhaps not in his time. The preparers of the *mummies* were (Herodotus says) *driven out of the house* by the family who had engaged their services, with execrations and stones ; but their *work* remains sound after three thousand years."

"TWO OF A TRADE NEVER AGREE."

Sydney Smith, who was himself a marvellous talker, once said, in reply to a remark, that Dr. Whately appeared to great advantage in conversation, " Yes, there were some splendid flashes of silence."

"THE MAGIC-LANTERN SCHOOL."

" Copleston said of writings of this school, that ' children like it, but grown people tire of it.' Much of what is now admired as originality and profound wisdom, would appear, if translated into common language, to be mere commonplace matter. Many a work of this description may remind one of the supposed ancient shield which had been found by the antiquary, Martinus Scriblerus, and which he highly prized, incrusted as it was with venerable rust. He mused on the splendid appearance it must have had in its bright newness ; till one day an over-sedulous housemaid having scoured off the rust, it turned out to be merely an old pot-lid."

A LEGAL KNOT.

Charles Phillips relates that he never saw Lord Redesdale more puzzled than at one of Plunket's best *jeux d'esprit.* A cause was argued in Chancery, wherein the plaintiff prayed that the defendant should be restrained from suing him on certain bills of exchange, as they were nothing but " kites." " Kites !" exclaimed Lord Redesdale ; " Kites, Mr. Plunket? Kites never could amount to the value of those securities ! I don't understand the statement at all, Mr. Plunket." " It is not to be expected that you should, my lord," answered Plunket. "In England and in Ireland, kites are quite different things. In England, the wind raises the ' kites,' and in Ireland the ' kites ' raise the wind."

THE OVERTASKED MIND.

" Physiologists are of opinion that the brain expends its energies and itself during the hours of wakefulness, and that they are recuperated during sleep ; if the recuperation does not equal the expenditure, the brain withers—this is insanity. Thus it is that, in early English history, persons who were condemned to death by being prevented from sleeping, always died raving lunatics. Thus it is, also, that those who are starved to death become insane ; the brain is not nourished, and they cannot sleep. The practical inferences are these :— 1. Those who think most, who do most brain-work, require most sleep ; 2. That time saved from necessary sleep is infallibly destructive to mind, body, and estate."—*Rev. D. Wills.*

One of Dr. Whately's last retorts conveyed a telling stroke of delicate irony. " They will begin to pelt me now," said a freshly-fledged bishop, who sought consolation under the weight of a mitre laden with some suspicion of a temporizing compliance on the Education Question.

"They have nearly given over that practice upon me," observed the Archbishop.

" Well, no one can say that I ever threw a stone at you," retorted the other.

" Certainly not," was the reply ; " you only kept the clothes of those who did."

The following charade, said to be one of the latest by Dr. Whately, has puzzled many wise heads :

"Man cannot live without my *first*,
    By day and night it's used ;
My *second* is by all accursed,
    By day and night abused.

" My *whole* is never seen by day,
    And never used by night ;
Is dear to friends when far away,
    But hated when in sight."

A Correspondent of *Notes and Queries* suggests the following solution :—

"*Ignis*, or fire, all men will own,
    Essential to the life of man ;
Fatuus, a fool, has been, 'tis known,
    Cursed and abused since time began.
Some *Ignis Fatuus*, Will-o'-wisp,
    Not seen by day, nor used by night,
Men love, and for their phantom list,
    When 'tis unseen, but hate its sight."

ELEGY ON A GEOLOGIST.

Archbishop Whately, one day, with genial humour, wrote

a supposed " Elegy on Dr. Buckland," of which the follow
ing is a portion :—

" Where shall we our great professor inter,
  That in peace may rest his bones ?
If we hew him a rocky sepulchre
  He'll rise and break the stones,
And examine each stratum that lies around,
For he's quite in his element underground.

" If with mattock and spade his body we lay,
  In the common alluvial soil,
He'll start up and snatch these tools away
  Of his own geological toil ;
In a stratum so young the professor disdains
That embedded should lie his organic remains.

" Then exposed to the drip of some case-hardening spring
  His carcass let stalactite cover,
And to Oxford the petrified sage let us bring
  When he was encrusted all over ;
There, 'mid mammoths and crocodiles, high on a shelf,
  Let him stand as a monument raised to himself."

EPIGRAM BY DR. WHATELY.

Dr. Whately is said to have made but one attempt at versification — an epigram, stinging as well as ringing. The
following parody on a nursery jingle, and written in " satirical
allusion to Dr. Wordsworth's well-known volume, *Who wrote
Icon Basilike ?*' has been attributed to Dr. Whately :—

" ' Who wrote, who wrote Icon Basilike ?'
  ' I,' said the Master of Trinity,
  ' I, with my little divinity,
    I wrote Icon Basilike.' "

Other versions make the third line read, " I, with my small
ability," and as some think, for the better.

" The last straw breaks the horse's back."

" When a man is loaded with as much work, or as much
injury as he can bear, a very trifling addition (in itself trifling) will be just as much beyond what he can bear."

LAST DAYS.

Until disabled, the Archbishop was to be daily seen on St.
Stephen's Green, drinking fresh air and seeking strength.

Sometimes he would work his arms round and round like a windmill; at other times he threw pebbles at birds, or romped with his exuberant dogs. During the closing years of his life the prelate's mind would often seek repose; but, like the pendulum of a clock, it only needed the slightest touch to set the machinery in active motion.

Whately's mind frequently bounded, and even wounded by its strokes; but after a storm comes a calm, and a reaction often exceeded these bounds. Othello's occupation, however, was not wholly gone : touch him with a genial allusion, or a pleasant poke, and RICHARD was himself again.

Leaning on the arm of his chaplain, the Archbishop was sometimes met by an old friend, with, "I hope your Grace is very much better to-day."—"Oh, I am very well indeed, if I could only persuade some strong fellow like you to lend me a pair of legs," was the reply. "I shall be only too happy to lend you *my* legs, if your Grace has no objection to give me *your* head in exchange." The Archbishop brightened up at the touch of wit, and delicately conveyed compliment, and exclaimed, "What, Mr. ——, you don't mean to say that you are willing to exchange two *understandings* for one?"

One retort led to another. Touching the word "either," he was asked whether *E-ther* or *I-ther* was the correct pronunciation. "*Ni-ther*," replied his Grace.

Dr. Whately has been styled the "Sydney Smith" of the Irish capital. The style of their wit, however, is not identical. When the witty canon of St. Paul's spoke of a cannibal inviting an omnivorous friend to partake of roast rector and corned curate, it was rich humour; when Whately said to a clerical valetudinarian who consulted him on the propriety of going to New Zealand for his health, "By all means go— you are so lean, no Maori could eat you without loathing," it was a telling stab.

On some few occasions the Archbishop got a "Roland for an Oliver." It was, we believe, the Hon. D. Le Poer Trench, last [Anglican] Archbishop of Tuam, who in casual conversation, slightly misquoted a classical passage. Dr. Whately having indicated the error, rather with the rough whirl of a teacher's birch than with the gentle touch of an episcopal crosier, was interrupted with, "My lord, I cannot lay claim to much scholarship or erudition, but I must congratulate myself on not being of the number of those whom learning has made mad!" To give the Archbishop his due, he took retorts of this sort in good part.—*Fitzpatrick.*

" The censure of frequent and long parentheses " (said Dr. Whately), " has led writers into the preposterous expedient of leaving out the marks by which they are indicated. It is no cure to a lame man to take away his crutches."

The Archbishop's death was slow and excruciating ; but a troop of faithful friends surrounded him, and it was not their fault if they failed to smoothe the dying prelate's pillow. He would have no nurse but them.

The bulletins issued during the last two days of Dr. Whately's life were to the effect that " his Grace was sinking rapidly." On Wednesday, October 7th, he lost the power of speech ; but the mind struggled to the last against its threatened dethronement. A few minutes before noon on the following day, all was over. Dr. Whately having died in the country, his remains were removed to the Palace, where they lay in state for some days. The funeral was a public one. It included, among other attending bodies, the clergy of Dublin and Kildare ; the provost, professors, and scholars of Trinity College, Dublin, with its representatives in Parliament ; the Senate of the Queen's University, and the Royal Irish Academy, with its mace. His Excellency the Lord Lieutenant, the Lord Chancellor of Ireland, the Lord Mayor, the Dean of St. Patrick's, and F. M. Lord Gough were also present.

It may be said that Dr. Whately, having attained his seventy-sixth year, outstripped the average age. The Whately family are proverbial for longevity. His sister, Lady Barry, aged eighty-four, was living in 1863 ; and the same remark applies to Thomas Whately, then entering on his ninetieth year.

SAMUEL ROGERS.

THE poetry of Mr. Rogers, author of the *Pleasures of Memory*, is that of a school of refinement which has very high merit. "We have," says a well-qualified critic, "everywhere in his works a classic and graceful beauty ; no slovenly or obscure lines ; fine cabinet pictures of soft and mellow lustre ; and occasionally trains of thought and association that awaken or recall tender and heroic feelings." His diction is clear and polished—finished with great care and scrupulous nicety. On the other hand, it must be admitted that he has no forcible or original invention, no deep pathos. that thrills the soul, and no kindling energy that fires the imagination. In his shadowy poem of *Columbus*, he seems often to verge on the sublime, but does not attain it. His late works are his best. Parts of *Human Life* possess deeper feeling than are to be found in the *Pleasures of Memory ;* and in the easy half conversational sketches of his *Italy*, there are delightful glimpses of Italian life, and scenery, and old traditions.

The life of Mr. Rogers was as calm and felicitous as his poetry ; he, for more than half a century, maintained his place in our national literature. He was born at Newington Green, in 1762, in an ancient porch-house. His father was a banker by profession ; and the poet, after a careful private education, was introduced in the banking establishment, of which he subsequently became a partner. He was fixed in his determination of becoming a poet by the perusal of Beattie's *Minstrel*, when he was only nine years of age. His boyish enthusiasm led Rogers to sigh for an interview with Dr. Johnson ; and to obtain this he twice presented himself at the door of Johnson's well-known house in Bolt Court, Fleet Street. On the first occasion the great moralist was not at home ; and the second time, after he had rung the bell, the heart of the young aspirant misgave him, and he retreated without waiting for the servant ; Rogers was then in his fourteenth year : he appeared as an author in 1786, the same year in which Burns was born. The first production of Rogers was a thin quarto of a few pages, an *Ode to Superstition*, and other poems. In 1792 he produced the *Pleasures of Memory;* in 1812 the *Voyage of Columbus* (a fragment); and in 1814 *Jacqueline*, a tale, published in conjunction with Byron's *Lara*—

"Like morning brought by night."

In 1819 appeared *Human Life*, and in 1822 *Italy*, a descriptive poem in blank verse.

"When a young man," says Rogers, " I went to Edinburgh, carrying letters of introduction (from Dr. Kippis, Dr. Price, &c.) to Adam Smith, Robertson, and others. When I first saw Smith, he was at breakfast, eating strawberries, and he descanted on the superior flavour of those grown in Scotland. I found him very kind and communicative. He was (what Robertson was not) a man who had seen a great deal of the world. Once, in the course of conversation, I happened to remark of some writer, ' that he was rather superficial—*a* Voltaire.' ' Sir,' cried Smith, striking the table with his hand, ' there has been but *one* Voltaire !' Robertson, too, was very kind to me. He one morning spread out the map of Scotland on the floor, and got upon his knees, to describe the route I ought to follow in making a tour on horseback through the Highlands. The most memorable day perhaps which I ever passed was at Edinburgh—a Sunday, when, after breakfasting with Robertson, I heard him preach in the forenoon, and Blair in the afternoon, then took coffee with the Piozzis, and supped with Adam Smith. Robertson's sermon was excellent both for matter and manner of delivery. Blair's was good, but less impressive, and his broad Scotch accent offended my ears greatly."

Of the manners and amusements of the period he presents us with some curious pictures. " Before his going abroad, Garrick's attraction had much decreased. Sir William Weller Pepys said that the pit was often almost empty. But, on his return to England, people were mad about seeing him ; and Sir George Beaumont and several others used frequently to get admission into the pit before the doors were open to the public, by means of bribing the attendants, who bade them ' be sure, as soon as the crowd rushed in, to pretend to be in a great heat, and to wipe their faces, as if they had just been struggling for entrance.' At the sale of Dr. Johnson's books,

I met General Oglethorpe, then very, very old, the flesh of his face looking like parchment. He amused us youngsters by talking of the alterations that had been made in London, and of the great additions it received within his recollection. He said that he had shot snipes in Conduit Street. By-the-bye, General Fitzpatrick remembered the time when St. James's Street used to be crowded with the carriages of the ladies and gentlemen who were walking in the Mall—the ladies with their heads in full dress, and the gentlemen carrying their hats under their arms. The proprietors of Rane-lagh and Vauxhall used to send decoy-ducks among them, that is, persons attired in the height of fashion, who every now and then would exclaim in a very audible tone, 'What charming weather for Ranelagh' or 'for Vauxhall!' I recollect when it was still the fashion for gentlemen to wear swords. I have seen Haydn play at a concert in a tie-wig, with a sword at his side. I have gone to Ranelagh in a coach with a lady who was obliged to sit upon a stool placed at the bottom of the coach, the height of her head-dress not allowing her to occupy the regular seat."

Rogers' conversation was rich and various, abounding in wit, eloquence, shrewd observation, and interesting personal anecdote. He had been familiar with almost every distinguished author, orator, and artist. It is gratifying to mention, that his benevolence was equal to his taste : his bounty soothed and relieved the deathbed of Sheridan, and was exerted to a large extent, annually, in behalf of suffering or unfriended talent.

> " Nature denied him much,
> But gave him at his birth what most he values :
> A passionate love for music, sculpture, painting,
> For poetry, the language of the gods,
> For all things here, or grand or beautiful,
> A setting sun, a lake among the mountains,
> The light of an ingenuous countenance,
> And, what transcends them all, a noble action."
>
> *Italy.*

Lord Byron dedicated his poem of the *Giaour* to " melodious Rogers ;" but Byron maintains that one of its beautiful ideas was borrowed from the *Pleasures of Memory,* a " poem so well known as to render a reference almost superfluous, but to whose pages all will be delighted to recur."

An interesting memorial of Rogers is preserved at Holland

House, where in the north-garden wall is an arbour, with this distich, by Vassall Lord Holland :—

" Here ROGERS sat, and here for ever dwell,
  With me those 'Pleasures,' which he sang so well.—V^{ll} H^{».}"

At No. 22, St. James's Place, built by James Wyatt, R.A., Rogers lived from 1808, until his death in 1854. In this house, during three generations, Rogers gathered round him the most celebrated statesmen, poets, painters, sculptors, and those who in science or in other ways were honourably distinguished. Going into the house, from Park Place (No. 22), we find in the hall some choice Greek and other sculptures, busts and vases of large size ; and we enter the dining-room which overlooks the Green Park. This room, wherein so many noted persons have met together, is lighted by a bow window which occupies the whole of one end ; near the window on one side of the room was a fine head by Rembrandt ; on the other side, the famous head of Christ crowned with thorns, by Guido. Other portions of the walls were covered with choice examples of the works of Rubens, painters of the Italian and Spanish schools, and some of the best of Sir Joshua Reynolds's pictures ; for instance, the Strawberry Girl, and Puck—that wonderful personification of frolic and mischief. The library is a square-looking apartment. On the top of the book-cases was a variety of Etruscan vases. The working patterns of the ceiling were supplied by Flaxman, who also designed and executed the sculpture on the mantelpiece. Leaving the library we passed through a vestibule, containing works of art, to the drawing-room, in which there was a glorious display of fine pictures of different schools. The mantelpiece in this room is of white marble, and, like that in the library, by Flaxman. The paintings were lighted by lamps with reflectors. Among the sculpture were : Cupid pouting and Psyche couching, and Michael Angelo and Raphael, statuettes by Flaxman. Here also were seven pictures by Stothard (including a copy of the Canterbury Pilgrims), and a cabinet with his designs. Among the autographs was the original assignment of Dryden's *Virgil* to Tonson, witnessed by Congreve. Milton's agreement with Symons for *Paradise Lost*, long possessed by Mr. Rogers, was presented by him to the British Museum in 1852.

Many smart sayings were assigned to Mr. Rogers, with

which he had nothing whatever to do. The Rev. Mr. Dyce selected the genuine of the many good things attributed to the banker-poet; they are printed in two volumes of "Table Talk," and Mr. Peter Cunningham contributed to the number; from these sources we have selected the following:—

Of Lord Holland, whose face was full of sunshine, Rogers observed most happily: "Lord Holland always comes to breakfast like a man upon whom some sudden good fortune has just fallen." On another occasion, he exclaimed (alluding to the same nobleman),

"His was the smile that spoke the mind at ease"—

a line of Rogers's own composing, though not in his printed works.

He could, however, be severe upon his own friends. Of the same nobleman he observed: "Painting gives him no pleasure, and music absolute pain."

"In Italy," he said, "the memory sees more than the eye."

Rogers envied no man of his time any saying, so much as he envied Lord John Russell that admirable definition of a proverb—"The wisdom of many and the wit of one."

"What a lucky fellow you are," said Rogers to Moore: "surely you must have been born with a rose in your lips, and a nightingale singing on the top of your bed."

Rogers said: "When Croker wrote his review in the *Quarterly* of Macaulay's *History*, he intended murder, but committed suicide."

Of Sydney Smith, Rogers observed: "Whenever the conversation is getting dull, he throws in some touch which makes it rebound, and rise again as light as ever. There is this difference between Luttrell and Smith: after Luttrell you remembered what good things he said—after Smith you merely remembered how much you laughed."

An old gentleman asleep before the fire was awakened by the clatter of the fire-irons at his feet. "What! going to bed without one kiss?" he exclaimed. He mistook one noise for another.

When Dean Milman observed, in Rogers's hearing, that he should read no more prose translations from poets—"What," exclaimed Rogers, "not the Psalms of David to your congregation?"

That was a happy reply of Sydney Smith. "When I began to light my dinner-table from the reflection of the pictures about me, I was not very successful. The light was thrown above the table, and not on it. I asked Sydney what he thought of the attempt. We were at dinner at the time. 'I do not like it at all,' was the reply; 'all is light above, and all below is darkness and gnashing of teeth.'"

"I was pleased with what I saw you about this morning," Rogers observed once at Broadstairs to an artist, who naturally expected, from such a commencement, some reference to the labours of his pencil: "I was greatly pleased: I saw you brushing your own coat. A gentleman who can brush his own coat is very independent."

Sheridan told Rogers that he was aware he ought to have made a love-scene between Charles and Maria, in the *School for Scandal,* and would have done it, but that the actors who played the parts were not able to do justice to such a scene.

J. T. Smith told Rogers that the little landscape by Claude, for which the poet gave at West's sale two hundred guineas, was bought by West at an old iron-shop for ten shillings and sixpence.

Mr. West said that Beckford called upon him before he went to Spain to borrow two small pictures, to take in his carriage with him wherever he went, and that the two pictures he selected were the little octagon Claude, and the Domenichino (afterwards in Mr. Rogers's collection).

There is a couplet in Cowper which Rogers admired exceedingly :—

> "Knowledge is proud that he has learned so much,
> Wisdom is humble that he knows no more."

Rogers adds : "When I am at Fine Arts Commissions, where good paper and pens abound, I copy out these lines for the people who trouble me for my autograph. 'How much he improves,' was the remark of one who mistook them for mine. These lines (and they are very good)—

> "Oh ! if the selfish knew how much they lost,
> What would they not endeavour, not endure,
> To imitate, as far as in them lay,
> Him who his wisdom and his power employs,
> In making others happy !"

I transcribe in the same manner.

Rogers was observing one day to Sydney Smith, that he should not sit again for his portrait unless he was taken in an attitude of prayer. "Yes," said Sydney, "yes, with *your face in your hat*."

"Here is Hallam, who has spent a whole life in contradicting everybody, is now obliged to publish a volume to contradict himself." (Mr. Rogers referred to the supplemental volume to the *Middle Ages*.)

Lord Byron wrote the following verses on Mr. Rogers, in Question and Answer:—

"QUESTION.

" Nose and chin would shame a knocker,
Wrinkles that would puzzle Cocker;
Mouth which marks the envious scorner,
With a scorpion in each corner,
Turning its quick tail to sting you,
In the place that most may wring you;
Eyes of lead-like hue, and gummy:
Carcass pick'd out from some mummy;
Bowels (but they were forgotten,
Save the liver, and that's rotten);
Skin all sallow, flesh all sodden—
From the Devil would frighten God in.
Is't a corpse stuck up for show,
Galvanised at times to go?
With the Scripture in connection,
New proof of the resurrection?
Vampyre, ghost, or ghoul, what is it?
I would walk ten miles to miss it.

ANSWER.

Many passengers arrest one,
To demand the same free question.
Shorter's my reply, and franker—
That's the Bard, the Beau, the Banker.
Yet if you could bring about,
Just to turn him inside out,
Satan's elf would seem less sooty,
And his present aspect—Beauty.
Mark that (as he marks the bilious
Air so softly supercilious)
Chastened bow, and mock humility,
Almost sickened to servility:
Hear his tone (which is to talking
That which creeping is to walking;

Now on all-fours, now on tiptoe ;)
Hear the tales he lends his lips to ;
Little hints of heavy scandals ;
Every friend in turn he handles ;
All which women, or which men do,
Glides forth in an innuendo,
Clothed in odds and ends of humour—
Herald of each paltry rumour,
From divorces, down to dresses,
Women's frailties, men's excesses,
All which life presents of evil
Makes for him a constant revel.
You're his foe, for that he fears you,
And in absence blasts and sears you ;
You're his friend, for that he hates you ;
First caresses, and then baits you ;
Darting on the opportunity
When to do it with impunity.
You are neither—then he'll flatter
Till he finds some trait for satire ;
Hunts your weak point out, then shows it
Where it injures to disclose it,
In the mode that's most invidious,
Adding every trait that's hideous,
From the bile whose black'ning river,
Rushes through his Stygian river.

Then he thinks himself a lover—
Why, I really can't discover,
In his mind, eye, face, or figure ;
Viper-broth might give him vigour ;
Let him keep the caldron steady,
He the venom has already.
For his faults—he has but *one*—
'Tis but envy, when all's done.
He but pays the pain he suffers,
Clipping, like a pair of snuffers,
Lights which ought to burn the brighter
For this temporary blighter.
He's the cancer of his species,
And will eat himself to pieces,
Plague personified, and famine—
Devil, whose sole delight is damning !

For his merits, would you know 'em ?
Once he wrote a pretty poem."

Rogers was silent about these verses, while he would turn
with satisfaction to the following entry in the Diary of Sir

Walter Scott :—" At parting (they were at Holland House together), Rogers gave me a gold-mounted pair of glasses, which I will not part with in a hurry. I really like S. R., and have always found him most friendly.".

Boddington had a wretchedly bad memory, and in order to improve it he attended Feinagle's lectures on the Art of Memory. Soon after, somebody asked Boddington the name of the lecturer, and for his life he could not recollect it. When Rogers was asked if he had attended the said lectures on the Art of Memory, he replied, " No ; I wished to learn the Art of Forgetting."

Witticisms are often attributed to the wrong people. It was Lord Chesterfield, not Sheridan, who said, on occasion of a certain marriage, that " Nobody's son had married Everybody's daughter." Lord Chesterfield remarked of two persons dancing a minuet, that " they looked as if they were hired to do it, and were doubtful of being paid." Rogers once observed to a Scotch lady, " how desirable it was in any danger to have presence of mind." " I had rather," she rejoined, " have absence of body."

We first hear of Rogers as an author in print in the year 1786, when he published with Cadell, in the Strand, his *Ode to Superstition*, leaving his poem at the shop of the publisher, with a bank-note to pay for any loss by the publication.

Lord Byron wrote the following complimentary lines on a blank leaf of a copy of the *Pleasures of Memory*, presented to him by the author :

> " Absent or present, still to thee,
>   My friend, what magic spells belong ?
> As all can tell, who share, like me,
>   In turn thy converse and thy song.
>
> " But when the dreaded hour shall come,
>   By friendship ever deemed too nigh,
> And ' Memory ' o'er her Druid's tomb
>   Shall weep that aught of thee can die,
>
> " How fondly will she then repay
>   Thy homage offered at her shrine,
> And blend, while ages roll away,
>   *Her* name immortally with thine."

Mr. Rogers relates that Fox used to read Homer through once every year. On R. asking him, " Which poem had you rather have written, the 'Iliad' or the 'Odyssey?'" he answered, "I know which I had rather read" (meaning the "Odyssey").

He was a constant reader of Virgil, and had been so from a very early period. There is at Holland House a copy of Virgil covered with Fox's manuscript notes, written when he was a boy, and expressing the most enthusiastic admiration of that poet.

One of Rogers's poems, *Jacqueline*, glided into public notice anonymously. In August, 1814, appeared from the shop of Mr. Murray a thin duodecimo volume, entitled *Lara, a Tale; Jacqueline, a Tale*, to which was prefixed a brief advertisement, written anonymously by Lord Byron, in which he hints at his own authorship of *Lara*, and states that *Jacqueline* is the production of a different author, "added at the request of the writer of the former tale, whose wish and entreaty it was that it should occupy the first pages of the volume." The union was not thought happy. Murray, the publisher, solicited a divorce. "*Jacqueline*," Jeffrey wrote to Moore, "is not advantageously placed with *Lara* as a companion." Byron himself was fond of making fun of this joint production—"Larry and Jacky," as he delighted to nickname them. An acquaintance of Byron, who was reading the book in the Brighton coach, was asked by a passenger the name of the author, and on replying that there were two, "Ay, ay," rejoined the querist, "a joint concern, I suppose —*summat* like Sternhold and Hopkins."

In Rogers's third publication, his *Epistle to a Friend*, the poet had admitted the description of an ice-house, of very inferior description to other parts of the poem, and somewhat out of place. That no lines of so careful a writer may be lost, Mr. Peter Cunningham transcribed them from the quarto copy of the first edition :—

" But hence away ! yon rocky cave forbear !
A sullen captive broods in silence there.
There though the dog-star flame, condemn'd to dwell
In the dark centre of its inmost cell,
Wild winter ministers his dread control,
To cool and crystallize the nectar'd bowl !
His faded form an awful grace retains—
Stern though subdued, majestic yet in chains !"

Few will recognise in this description a cartload of ice from an adjoining pond, packed for summer use in a solitary ice-house, half concealed at the end of an overgrown shrubbery.

When the absurdity of tight lacing was in-fashion, Lady Crewe told Rogers that, on returning home from Ranelagh, she had rushed up to her bedroom, and desired her maid to cut her laces without a moment's delay, for fear she should faint.

Further, he could remember how, during his youth, umbrellas were far from common. At that time every gentleman's family had *one umbrella*—a huge thing made of coarse cotton—which used to be taken out with the carriage; and which, if there was rain, the footman held over the ladies' heads as they entered, or alighted from, the carriage.

He also recollected how, at Paris, a bottle of English porter was placed on the table by a French nobleman as a great rarity, the dark " Entire " being sipped from tiny glasses as if it were Tokay.

The poet's recollections of Sheridan are very characteristic. Mr. Rogers was present on the second day of Hastings' trial in Westminster Hall, when Sheridan was listened to with such attention that you might have heard a pin drop. Sheridan was in the habit of putting by, not only all papers written by himself, but all others that came into his hands. Ogle said that, after his death, he found in his desk sundry unopened letters written by his (Ogle's) mother; who had sent them to Sheridan to be franked. Sheridan, Sir Walter (then Mr.) Scott, and Moore were one day dining with Rogers, and Sheridan was talking in his very best style, when, to Rogers's great vexation, Moore (who had that sort of restlessness which never allowed him to be happy where he was) suddenly interrupted Sheridan by exclaiming, " Isn't it time to go to Lydia White's?" Sheridan had very fine eyes, and he was not a little vain of them ; he said to Rogers on his death-bed, "Tell Lady Besborough that my eyes will look up to the coffin-lid as brightly as ever."

" I was taking a drive with Lady Jersey in her carriage, when I expressed (with great sincerity) my regret at being unmarried, saying that ' if I had a wife I should have some-body *to care about me*.' 'Pray, Mr. Rogers,' said Lady J., 'how could you be sure that your wife would not *care more about somebody else than about you ?* "

Mrs. Richard Trench tells the following characteristic dialogue story of Rogers, and a gentleman whom he did not estimate very highly : " So, Mr. Wilmot, you are going to the

Duchess of ——'s? Mr. Wilmot.—Yes, immediately. R.— How *fat* you'll grow! Mr. W.—*Fat!* how so? R.—You will sleep so much. They go to bed so early. Mr. W.—No, I never go to bed early. R.—You will, indeed. Mr. W.— I always read in my own room. R.—You will not. *Measure your candle.* (*Exit* Mr. Wilmot.) Rogers (to the remaining circle).—That Mr. Wilmot is a sensible man. I don't say so from my own knowledge; not the least. He wrote a book, too. That, you'll say, was *nothing.* And printed it. I don't say that from my own knowledge either, for I never read it— never met anybody that had."

It is curious how fashion changes pronunciation. In Rogers's youth everybody said "Lonnon," not "London:" Fox said "Lonnon" to the last; and so did Crowe.

As Mr. Rogers advanced in life, the colour retreated altogether from his face, and his looks afforded a fine field for sarcastic comment. Theodore Hook recommended his friends to induce him to abstain from attending Lord Byron's funeral. He stood in danger, he said, of being recognised by the undertaker as a corpse he had screwed down some six weeks before.

A critic annoyed Mr. Rogers in the *Quarterly Review* by asserting that his author was a hasty writer: yet his literary life extended over sixty years, and the produce of his life only fills a pocket volume: his were hard-bound brains, and not a line he ever wrote was produced at a single sitting. This was well exemplified in a favourite saying of Sydney Smith: "When Rogers produces a couplet, he goes to bed, and the knocker is tied up, and straw is laid down, and the caudle is made, and the answer to inquiries is, that Mr. Rogers is as well as can be expected."

Captain Gronow relates that, at an evening party, at Lady Jersey's, every one was praising the Duke of B—, who had just come in, and who had lately attained his majority. There was a perfect chorus of admiration to this effect:— "Everything is in his favour; he has good looks, considerable abilities, and a hundred thousand a year." Rogers listened to these encomiums for some time in silence, and at last remarked, with an air of great exultation, and in his most venomous manner, "Thank God, he has got bad teeth!" His well-known epigram on Mr. Ward, afterwards Lord Dudley,

"They say that Ward's no heart, but I deny it,
He has a heart, and gets his speeches by it,"—

was provoked by a remark made at table by Mr. Ward. On Rogers observing that his carriage had broken down, and that he had been obliged to come in a hackney-coach, Mr. Ward grumbled out in a very audible whisper, "In a hearse, I should think," alluding to the poet's corpse-like appearance. This remark Rogers never forgave; and he is said to have pored for days over the retaliatory epigram.

Comparatively few men have attained very great age, and enjoyed it to the end, like Mr. Rogers. Even so late as 1843, four years before his death, Rogers continued his yearly epicurean visits to Paris, to enjoy the Italian opera, and other refined sources of pleasure. The hand of age had then begun to bow him down, but his intellect was clear as ever, and his talents and taste for society were in full vigour. He had refined upon the art of telling a story, until he brought it to the most perfect simplicity, where there was not a word too much or too little, and where every word had its effect.

In his ninetieth year, Rogers's memory began to fail in a manner that was painful to his friends. He was no longer able to relate his shortest stories, or welcome his constant companions with his usual complimentary expressions. He began to forget familiar faces, and at last forgot that he had ever been a poet.

On the morning of the 18th of December, 1855, the Tithonus of living poets was taken from among us, in his ninety-third year : he died in his own house, surrounded by the works of art which his fine taste had brought about him.

"He expired," writes Dr. Beattie, who was with him, "at half-past twelve this morning. A more tranquil and placid transition I never beheld. His devoted niece closed his eyes, and his faithful domestics stood weeping round his bed. Some of the attendant circumstances reminded me of Campbell; but *this* was more calm, solemn, and impressive—quite in keeping with the scene in his 'Human Life.'" He rests in his chosen grave in Hornsey churchyard.

Mr. Rogers was a link between the days of Johnson, Burke, and Reynolds, and our own time (1855). He had rambled over St. Anne's Hill with Fox and Grattan. Sheridan addressed to him the last letter he ever wrote, begging for pecuniary assistance, that the blanket on which he was dying might not be torn from his bed by bailiffs; and Rogers answered the call with a remittance of £200. "There is a happy and enviable poet," said Thomas Campbell, one day, on leaving Rogers's house: "he has some four or five thousand pounds a-year, and he gives away fifteen hundred in charity." He enjoyed life, had money, fame, honours, love, and troops of friends. His recipe for long life was "Temperance, the bath and flesh-brush, and *don't fret.*"

He had heard the Duke of York relate how he and his brother George, when young men, were robbed by footpads on Hay Hill, Berkeley Street; he had shaken hands with John Wilkes, dined with Lafayette, Condorcet, &c., at Paris, before the great revolution began, and been present at Warren Hastings' trial in Westminster Hall; he had seen Lady Hamilton go through her "attitudes" before the Prince of Wales, and Lord Nelson spin a teetotum with his *one* hand for the amusement of children.

Mr. Cunningham noted, a few days after the death of our poet: "When Rogers made his appearance as a poet Lord Byron was unborn. When Percy Bysshe Shelley was born, Rogers was in his thirtieth year. When Keats was born, the *Pleasures of Memory* was looked upon as a standard poem—and Keats has been dead thirty-five years! When this century commenced, the man who died in the latter half of the century, had already numbered as many years as Burns and Byron had numbered when they died. Mr. Rogers was born before the following English poets: Scott, Southey, Wordsworth, Coleridge, Byron, Moore, Campbell, Bloomfield, Cunningham, Hogg, James Montgomery, Shelley, Keats, Wilson, Tom Hood, Kirke White, Lamb, Joanna Baillie, Felicia Hemans, L.E.L.; and he outlived them all.

"How fondly" (said Rogers) "the surviving friends of Fox cherished his memory! Many years after his death, I was at a *fête* given by the Duke of Devonshire at Chiswick House. Sir Robert Adair and I wandered about the apartments up and down stairs. 'In which room did Fox expire?' asked Adair. 'In this very room.' Immediately Adair burst into tears with a vehemence of grief such as I hardly ever saw."

SIR JOHN SOANE LAMPOONED.

SIR JOHN SOANE, who bequeathed to the country his museum in Lincoln's Inn Fields, which cost him upwards of £50,000, was the son of a bricklayer, and was born at Reading in 1753; he was errand boy to Dance, the architect, and subsequently his pupil. He rose to great eminence, grew rich and liberal; he gave for Belzoni's elaborate sarcophagus in the Soane Museum, 2000 guineas; paid large sums for art rarities; subscribed £1000 for the Duke of York's monument, was contented with his knighthood, and declined to receive a baronetcy. Yet he was a man of overweening vanity, and was much courted by legacy-hunters, whilst his alienation from his son assisted in raising up many enemies, in addition to those which Soane's remarkable success brought against him. From the latter section may have proceeded the following curious and popular squib of the day, said to have been found under the plates at one of the artistic or academic dinners. It is headed :—

"THE MODERN GOTH.

" Glory to thee, great Artist ! soul of taste !
For mending pigsties where a plank's misplaced :
Whose towering genius plans from deep research
Houses and temples fit for Master Birch.
To grace his shop on that important day,
When huge twelfth-cakes are raised in bright array.
Each pastry pillar shows thy vast design—
Hail ! then, to thee, and all great works of thine.
Come, let me place thee in the foremost rank,
With him whose dulness discomposed the bank ;

[*A line illegible.*]

Thy style shall finish what his style begun.
Thrice happy Wren ! he did not live to see
The dome that's built and beautified by thee.
Oh ! had he lived to see thy blessed work,
To see plaster scored like loins of pork ;
To see the orders in confusion move :

Scrolls fixed below, and pedestals above ;
To see defiance hurled at Rome and Greece,
Old Wren had never left the world in peace.
Look where I will, above, below, is shown
A pure disordered order of thine own ;
Where lines and circles curiously unite,
A base, confounded, compound Composite :
A thing from which, in truth it may be said,
Each lab'ring mason turns abash'd his head ;
Which Holland reprobates, and Dance derides,
Whilst tasteful Wyatt holds his aching sides.
Here crawl, ye spiders ! here, exempt from cares,
Spin your fine webs above the bulls and bears !
Secure from harm enjoy the charnell'd niche :
No maids molest you, for no brooms can reach ;
In silence build from models of your own,
But never imitate the works of Soane !"

Soane is described by his biographer as " one of the vainest
and most self-sufficient of men, who courted praise and adulation from every person or source, but dreaded, and was even
maddened by, anything like impartial and discriminating
criticism." But he grew so disgusted with his flatterers, that
a short time before his death he shut himself up in a house
at Richmond, to get out of the way of their attentions.

CLASSIC EPICURISM.

OLD Lucullus, they say,
Forty cooks had each day,
And Vitellius's meals cost a million ;
But I like what is good,
When or where be my food,
In chop-house or royal pavilion.

At all events, (if enough,)
I most heartily stuff,
And a song at my heart alike rushes,
Tho' I've not fed my lungs
Upon nightingale's tongues,
Nor the brains of goldfinches and thrushes.

From an unpublished song, by CAPTAIN MORRIS.

MRS. PIOZZI.

MRS. PIOZZI'S GOSSIP.

IN a letter written by Mrs. Piozzi in her eightieth year, we find this entertaining specimen of her lively, rattling manner :

"Whilst we were living here" (Weston-super-Mare) "at the hotel, the waiter, with a grin upon his naturally sullen countenance, said, 'Here's a man inquires for Mrs. Piozzi.'—'Bid him come in ;' and, seeing the strange visitant, 'Be pleased to call my maid.' Both entered. 'What's all this?' cried I. 'Edwards !'—' Yes, sure !'—'Why, the poor fellow is half dead, I vow, in a smock-frock, and dirty !'—' Yes, sure !'—'And hungry, too ! and mind what he says, Bessy ; he says he walked hither from Dymerchion, 228 miles ; and slept in the streets of Bath last night, and walked here to-day ! For what ! in the name of heaven? Ask him.'— 'He is stone deaf. He came to see you, he says.'—'See me? why he is blind, high gravel blind, at least ; and one eye quite extinguished.'—'I must get him some meat,' says Bessy ; so she did ; and set what we call a Benjamin's mess before him, which a dapper post-boy snatched away, and left my countryman a living study for Liston, a statue of dirt and despair, reversing Neddy Bray's distress, who eat up other people's food, and this fool lost his own. On close inquiry, the poor witless wanderer had gone to Brynbella upon Midsummer-day, it seems, to claim £2, which, as a superannuated labourer, he tells me I used to pay him annually. Salusbury drove him from the door. 'Ah, Sir John, your good aunt, God bless her ! would not have served me so. Where is the lady that was Mistress of this house?'—with a Welsh howl that naturally enough provoked the present Master. 'Why, she is at Bath ; go look for her, you dog !' And the wretched creature took him literally. So I had to ship him off for Cardiff, which, though the wrong end of our principality, was better for him to be lost in than England, and I hope he got safe home somehow.

* * * * * *

"Which of the Conrads known to historic truth is dramatized, I wonder ! The elder was proclaimed King of the Romans about the year 1220 or 30 ; but would absolutely be Emperor in spite of the Pope ; to annoy whose Italian dominions he drove into the Peninsula, and committed famous cruelties at Naples, Capua, etc., after having behaved beautifully the early part of his life; and so they compared him to Nero. He was poisoned by his brother Manfred, but left a son whom the Neapolitans called Conradino—the little Conrad; who had a great soul, however; set an army on foot at sixteen years of age, in order to recover some of his father's conquests, possessed by Charles of Anjou, who defeated him and his martial cousin, Frederick, at Lago Fucino—and, as they crossed a river to escape, caught both the fugitives; and hapless Conrad lost his short life on a scaffold at eighteen years old. He was a youth of quite consummate beauty, which was the reason our King William the Third used to laugh when German friends and flatterers compared them; because, otherwise, the parallel ran happily enough; the same ardour in battle, the same hostility to Popes; and all at so unripe an age too! But, as Dr. Johnson said to Mr. Thrale, 'O, sir, stop my mistress! if once she begins naming her favourite heroes round, we are undone! I hate historic talk, and when Charles Fox said something to me once about Cataline's conspiracy, I withdrew my attention, and thought about Tom Thumb.' Poor dear Doctor Collier loved it no better. 'My sweet child,' he used to say, 'leave thy historians to moulder on the shelf; I have no hooks in my brains to hang their stories on.' And yet their adoring pupil distracts her latest found friend with it in the year 1811—and all out of her own head, as the children say; for ne'er a book have I. Send me the tragedy if 'tis good for anything, and you can do it without inconvenience. Once again, I wonder much who wrote it! Who acted it last night you have told me; and it was very kindly done; and I am now more easy about *your* health, and more careful of *my own*—that I may the longer enjoy the comfort of being considered as dear Mr. Conway's admiring and faithful friend.   "H. L. P."

THOMAS HOOD.

THIS author, unquestionably a man of genius and great application, was born in 1798, in the Poultry, London, where his father was for many years acting partner in the firm of Vernor, Hood, and Sharpe, extensive booksellers and publishers. Thomas Hood was sent to a school in Token House Yard, in the City, as a day-boarder. The two maiden sisters who kept the school, and with whom Hood took his dinner, had the odd name of Hogsflesh; they had a sensitive brother, who was always addressed as "Mr. H.," and who subsequently became the prototype of Charles Lamb's unsuccessful farce called "Mr. H." Hood was afterwards sent to a preparatory school, and in due course was transferred to a finishing school in the neighbourhood of London, but derived little benefit from either.

Hood thus refers to his clerkship :—

> "Time was when I sat upon a lofty stool,
> At lofty desk, and with a clerkly pen,
> Began each morning at the stroke of ten
> To write in Bell and Co's commercial school,
> In Warnford Court— a shady nook and cool—
> The favourite retreat of merchant men.
> Yet would my quill turn vagrant even then,
> And take stray dips in the Castalian pool :
> Now double-entry,—now a flowery trope,—
> Mingling poetic honey with trade wax ;
> Blogg, Brothers—Milton—Grote and Prescott—Pope—
> Bristles and Hogg—Glyn, Mills, and Halifax—
> Rogers and Towgood—Hemp—the Bard of Hope—
> Barilla—Byron—Tallow—Burns and Flax."

In 1811 Hood's father died, and soon afterwards his elder brother died also. Thomas Hood, then the only remaining son of the widow, she was anxious to have him near her, and recalled him home.

In 1812 his mother sent him to a day-school; his account of which, in his literary reminiscences (*Hood's Own*), is very characteristic :—

"In a house, formerly a suburban seat of the unfortunate Earl of Essex, over a grocer's shop, up two pair of stairs, there was a very select day-school, kept by a decayed Dominie, as he would have been called in his native land. In his better days, when my brother was his pupil, he had been master of one of those wholesale concerns in which so many ignorant men have made fortunes, by favour of high terms, low ushers, gullible parents, and victimized little boys. Small as was our college, its principal maintained his state, and walked gowned and covered. His cap was of faded velvet, of black, or blue, or purple, or sad-green, or, as it seemed, of altogether, with a sad *nuance* of brown; his robe of crimson damask lined with the national tartan. A quaint, carved, high-backed, elbowed article, looking like an *emigré* from a set that had been at home in an aristo-cratic drawing-room under the *ancien régime*, was his professional chair, which, with his desk, was appropriately elevated on a dais some inches above the common floor. From this moral and ma-terial eminence he cast a vigilant yet kindly eye over some dozen of youngsters; for adversity, sharpened by habits of authority, had not soured him, or mingled a single tinge of bile with the peculiar red-streak complexion so common to the wealthier na-tives of the north." .... "In a few months, my education progressed infinitely farther than it had done in as many years under the listless superintendence of B.A. and LL.D. and assist-ants. I picked up *some* Latin, was a tolerable grammarian, and so good a French scholar, that I earned a few guineas—my first literary fee—by revising a new edition of *Paul et Virginie* for the press. Moreover, as an accountant, I could work a *summum bonum*, that is, a good sum."

But his health began to fail, and he was sent in a Scotch smack to Dundee, and consigned to a female relation, who, however, refused to take charge of him; she even re-shipped his luggage, and would have sent him back to London, if Hood had not played her an evasive trick, and frustrated her intentions. He immediately took lodgings for himself at Dundee. He was then fifteen years of age, and seems to have been left entirely at his own disposal. Fortunately, he was not idle, and had no taste for dissipation, but took great delight in reading, as well as in rambling, fishing, and boat-ing. His health gradually improved, and after remaining two years at Dundee, he returned to London. He engaged himself to Mr. Robert Sands, an engraver, his uncle, in order to learn his art, and was afterwards with Le Keux, for the same purpose.

In 1821 Mr. John Scott, then editor of the *London Magazine*, was killed in a duel; the magazine passed to other proprietors, who happened to be Hood's friends, and he was offered the situation of sub-editor. He had published some trifles in the *Dundee Advertiser* and the *Dundee Magazine*, while he remained at that place, which were favourably received, but he had not been stimulated to any further appearance to print. "My vanity," he says, "did not rashly plunge me into authorship, but no sooner was there a legitimate opening than I jumped at it, *à la Grimaldi*, and was speedily behind the scenes."

Hood, while in this situation, became acquainted with several persons who have distinguished themselves in English literature, and who were then contributors to the *London Magazine*, with Lamb, Carey, Proctor, Cunningham, Talfourd, Soane, Bowring, Barton, Hazlitt, Elton, Hartley Coleridge, Horace Smith, Reynolds, Poole, Clare, Benyon, and others. With Lamb, especially, Hood afterwards became on terms of great intimacy, which continued till Lamb's death.

Hood's first publication, in a separate form, was *Odes and Addresses to Great People*, in which he was assisted by his brother-in-law, J. H. Reynolds. It was anonymous—a little thin, mean-looking foolscap sub-octavo of poems, with nothing but wit and humour (what could it want more?) to recommend it. Coleridge was delighted with the work, and taxed Charles Lamb, by letter, with the authorship. Who does not remember, in this little book, the well-timed apostrophe to the great work of Brunel—the Thames Tunnel :—

> "Other great speculations have been nursed,
>   Till want of proceeds laid them on the shelf :
> But thy concern was at the worst,
>   When it began to *liquidate* itself."
>   *Ode to Mr. Brunel.*

The tunnel was again emptied; but the work was now discontinued, for want of funds, for seven years :

> "Well ! Monsieur Brunel,
> How prospers now thy mighty undertaking,
> To join by a hollow way the Bankside friends

Of Rotherhithe and Wapping?
          Never be stopping ;
But poking, groping, in the dark keep making
An archway, underneath the dabs and gudgeons,
For colliermen and pitchy old curmudgeons
To cross the water in inverse proportion,
Walk under steam-boats, under the keel's ridge,
To keep down all extortion,
And without sculls to diddle London Bridge !
In a fresh hunt, a new great Bore to worry,
Thou didst to earth thy human terriers follow,
Hopeful at last, from Middlesex to Surrey,
          To give us the ' view hollow.' "

Whims and Oddities, published in 1826, consisted chiefly of
Hood's contributions to the *London Magazine.* His next work
was in prose, *National Tales,* which was followed by *A Plea
for the Midsummer Fairies,* a serious poem of infinite beauty,
full of fine passages and of promise ; it obtained praise from
the critics, but little favour from the public, and Hood's
experience of the unpleasant truth that—

" Those who live to please must please to live,"

induced him to have recourse again to his lively vein. He
published a second series of the *Whims and Oddities,* and the
third series in 1828. He commenced the *Comic Annual* in
1829, and it continued nine years. It proved very profitable,
as the ledger of the publisher attested ; each annual was a
widely printed volume, with illustrations by Hood himself,
and lightly engraved on wood—the price, 12s.

The *Epping Hunt* appeared next, and excited much mirth
by its comicalities. Hood tells us, " it was penned by an
underling at the Wells, a person more accustomed to riding
than writing," as shown in this epistle :—" Sir,—Abouut the
Hunt. In anser to your Innqueries, their as been a great
falling off latterally, so much so this year that there was
nobody allmost. We did a mear nothing provisionally,
hardly a Bottle extra, which is as proof in Pint. In short
our Hunt may be said to be in the last Stag of a Decline.
Bartholomew Rutt." He next edited an annual called the *Gem,*
which was beautifully illustrated with steel plates, and for
this work he wrote the *Dream of Eugene Aram* (one of the
finest productions of Hood's muse), with this note : " The
late Admiral Burney went to school at an establishment where

the unhappy Eugene Aram was usher subsequent to his crime.   The admiral stated that Aram was generally liked by the boys ; and that he used to discourse to them about *murder* in somewhat of the spirit which is attributed to him in this poem."   The poem is exquisitely written throughout, and is sometimes little less than sublime.

Hood next went to the Continent for the benefit of his health, when in Belgium he published his *Up the Rhine,* constructed on the groundwork of *Humphrey Clinker.*   The work consists of imaginary letters from an hypochondriacal old bachelor, his widowed sister, his nephew, and a servant-maid, who form the imaginary traveller's party.   Each individual writes to a friend in England, and describes the scenes, manners, and circumstances in a vein suitable to the assumed characters.   The nephew's remarks seem to embody the opinions and observations of Hood himself.   The book is full of good sense and humour, as are the woodcuts.

Hood next became editor of the *New Monthly Magazine,* from which he retired in 1843, taking with him his contributions, which were reprinted as *Whimsicalities.*   He still continued to suffer from ill health ; and a letter of this period is dated, " From my bed, 17, Elm Tree Road, St. John's Wood, July 18, 1843."   Early in the year 1831 Hood occupied Lake House, situated near the site of Wansted House, in Essex.   While here he wrote his novel of *Tylney Hall,* which is dated Lake House, Oct. 20, 1834.   Its characters are exuberant with wit and humour, but the plot is defective. Hood left Lake House in 1835.

At the termination of the *Comic Annual,* in 1837, Hood commenced the publication of *Hood's Own* in a series of monthly numbers.   It contained a selection from the volumes of the *Comic Annual,* in prose and verse, with several additions.   A portrait of the author, for which he sat at the request of the publisher, is the frontispiece to the work, and is, as he says himself, a faithful likeness.   The title of his work is " *Hood's Own ; or, Laughter from Year to Year,* being Former Runnings of his Comic Vein, with an Infusion of New Blood for General Circulation."   The entire volume contains about 570 pages, with a multitude of wood-cuts ; and four chapters of " Literary Reminiscences " full of personal interest. In the course of this year, public feeling had been much excited by cases of distress and destitution which came before the London police-magistrates, arising from the excessively low rate of wages paid by dealers in ready-made linen to their workwomen. Taking advantage of a market overstocked with labourers, these tradesmen got their work done for a rate of payment so small that fourteen or fifteen hours' labour were frequently required in order to obtain sixpence ! Hood's sympathy was excited, and the *Song of the Shirt* was the result—"a burst of poetry and indignant passion by which he produced tears almost as irrepressibly as in other cases he produced laughter." The *Song of the Shirt* was, it is said, sent to a comic periodical, but was refused insertion ; it has, however, been sung through the whole length and breadth of the three kingdoms.

Our author's last periodical was *Hood's Magazine*, which he continued to supply with the best of its contributions till within a month of his death. Those who have read the work, and have a taste for wit, humour, and character, will not readily forget his "Schoolmistress Abroad," "My Gardener," and his novel of "Our Family," which was interrupted by his last illness and death ; the last chapters were, in fact, written by him when he was propped up by pillows in bed. Hood had the consolation, a short time before his death, of having a Government pension of £100 a year, which was offered him by Sir Robert Peel, in the following noble and touching letter, Sir Robert knowing of his illness, but not of his imminent danger : " I am more than repaid," writes Peel, "by the personal satisfaction which I have had in doing that for which you return me warm and characteristic acknowledgments. You perhaps think that you are known to one with such multifarious occupations as myself, merely by general reputation as an author ; but I assure you that there can be little which you have written and acknowledged which I have not read, and that there are few who can appreciate and admire more than myself the good sense and good feeling which have taught you to infuse so much fun and merriment into writings correcting folly and exposing absurdities, and yet never trespassing beyond those limits within which wit and facetiousness are not very often confined. You may write on, with the consciousness of independence, as free and unfettered as if no communication had ever passed between us. I am not conferring a private obligation upon you, but am fulfilling the intentions of the Legislature, which has placed at the disposal of the Crown a certain sum (miserable indeed in amount) to be applied to the recognition of public claims on the bounty of the Crown. If you will review the names of those whose claims have been admitted on account of their literary or scientific eminence, you will find an ample confirmation of the truth of my statement. One return, indeed, I ask you— that you will give me the opportunity of making your personal acquaintance."

To this statement in the *Cornhill Magazine* (to which we are indebted for many details in this sketch), are appended the following reflections :—" O sad, marvellous picture of courage, of honesty, of patient endurance, of duty struggling against pain ! How noble Peel's figure is, standing by that sick-bed, how generous his words, how dignified and sincere his compassion ! And the poor dying man, with a heart full of natural gratitude towards his noble benefactor, must turn to him and say—' If it be well to be remembered by a Minister, it is better still not to be forgotten by him in a ' hurly Burleigh !' Can you laugh ? Is not the joke horribly pathetic from the poor dying lips ? As dying Robin Hood must fire a last shot with his bow—as one reads of Catholics on their death-beds putting on a Capuchin dress to go out of the world —here is poor Hood at his last hour putting on his ghastly motley, and uttering one joke more. He dies, however, in dearest love and peace with his children, wife, friends ; to the former especially his whole life had been devoted, and every day showed his fidelity, simplicity, and affection. In going through the record of his most pure, modest, honourable life, and living along with him, you come to trust him thoroughly, and feel that here is a most loyal, affectionate, and upright soul, with whom you have been brought into communion. Can we say as much of all lives of all men of letters ? Here is one at least without guile, without pretension, without scheming, of pure life, to his family and little modest circle of friends tenderly devoted."

Hood, in person, was thin, pale, and delicate. In his temper he was kind and cheerful ; he seems to have imbibed the social and benevolent feeling of his friend Lamb, and he was no less than Lamb a favourite among his friends. His long continued sufferings only stimulated him to amuse himself and others by the exercise of his extraordinary imagination, and, when at last he could no longer bear up against his bodily pains, his complaint was simple, but it indicated a terrible degree of suffering—" I cannot die ; I cannot die !"

* * * * * *

After a lethargy which continued some days, he died, May 3, 1845. He was buried on the 10th of May, in Kensal Green Cemetery.

Hood was a striking exemplification of the truth of the remark that humour and pathos almost invariably go together, and that a writer is rarely eminent for one who is not also capable of the other. Hood was certainly no exception to the rule ; and it is difficult to say at this moment whether the author of "Faithless Sally Brown," and of the "Bridge of Sighs," is most endeared to us by his sparkle and show, often profoundly touching, or, on the other hand, by his pathos, peculiar to himself, often appealing to our deepest sympathies through forms of expression which seem to be leading up to the gay or frivolous, and yet hit their mark in the very root of sadness. "There's not a string attuned to mirth," he says himself, "but has its chord in melancholy," and it seems to have been granted to him to discourse the saddest and the merriest music through a medium attuned to both passions at once, and responsive to either one at the slightest suggestions of fancy or feeling.

Hood's vigilance of observation must have been very great. The appearance of nature, the form and usage of society, great diversity of character, all arts, professions, and trades, lay ready in his mind to supply the demands of his rapid, subtle, and versatile imagination. He had wit of the highest quality, as original and as abundant as Butler's or Cowley's, drawn from as extensive an observation of nature and life, if not from so wide a reach of learning, and combined with richness of humour of which Butler had little, and Cowley none. His humour is frequently as extravagantly broad as that of Rabelais, but he has sometimes the delicate touches of Addison.

As a punster Hood stands alone. His puns do not consist of merely double meanings of words, a low kind of punning of which minds of a low order are capable, but of double meanings of words combined with double meanings of sense, in such a manner as to produce the most extraordinary effects of surprise and admiration. His power of exciting laughter is wonderful, his drollery indescribable, inimitable.

In one double sense Hood's puns were apt to involve another double sense, which, while it surprised and delighted the reader, put him in possession of a new idea, serious or grotesque, as it might happen. Thus, in his "Ode on the

Prospect of Clapham College," where he went to school as a boy, he wonders who keeps the school now—

> " How many ushers he employs,
> How many maids, *to see the boys*
> *Have nothing in their heads.*"

The italics are not Hood's. Instances of this sort will recur in numbers to the memory of readers familiar with his works. Perhaps the fairest notion of his average surface-wit and unpremeditated dry humour, as it seasoned his letters and conversation, may be derived from a list of odd titles to books, which, at the request of the Duke of Devonshire, he supplied to be used as lettering-pieces to sham volumes in a library. We shall quote a few :—

On Cutting Off Heirs with a Shilling. By Barber Beaumont.
Percy Vere. In 40 volumes.
Tadpoles ; or, Tales out of My Own Head.
Malthus's Attack of Infantry.
The Life of Zimmerman. By Himself.
Pygmalion. By Lord Bacon.
Boyle on Steam.
Haughtycultural Remarks on London Pride.
Voltaire, Volney, Volta. 3 vols.
Barrow on the Common Weal.
Campaigns of the Brit. Arm. By one of the German Leg.
Recollections of Bannister. By Lord Stair.
Cursory Remarks on Swearing.
In-i-go on Secret Entrances.

Of all Hood's lighter pieces, if indeed, it can be ranked with them, the " Story of Miss Kilmansegg " is that which affords us the best view of his manysidedness, and of his various merits as a thinker, a teacher, and a writer. It abounds in humour, sometimes broad, sometimes sufficiently grim, and rather recondite. It flashes with wit almost from beginning to end, whilst its moral purpose is of the highest, and its philosophy of the soundest. We laugh with the keenest relish as we read, and are borne along by the wondrous verse and rhythm ; we can but laugh at the whimsical fancies, the oddly-disguised meanings, and the sharp, razor-like thrusts at human vanity and weakness ; but, arrived at the end, our risible muscles relax, the inclination to mirth subsides. As we retrace the history we feel the burden of the profound moral which throughout rides along on the playful metre, and we ponder musingly in sober sadness over many a bitter truth which the minstrel has declared, and even more at the portentous views of a thoroughly worldly life conjured up by his impossible fiction.

For Hood's humorous powers of description, note the sketch of the parents as they are present at the christening :

> " To paint the maternal Kilmansegg
>   The pen of an Eastern Poet would beg,
>   And need an elaborate sonnet ;
>   How she sparkled with gems whenever she stirr'd,
>   And her head niddle-noddled at every word,
>   And seem'd so happy, a Paradise Bird
>   Had nidificated upon it.

> " And Sir Jacob the father strutted and bow'd,
>   And smiled to himself, and laughed aloud,
>   To think of his heiress and daughter ;
>   And then in his pockets he made a grope,
>   And then, in the fulness of joy and hope,
>   Seem'd washing his hands with invisible soap
>   In imperceptible water."

The following passage on early education is striking :

> " According to metaphysical creed,
>   To the earliest books that children read
>   For much good or much bad they are debtors ;
>   But before with their A B C they start,
>   There are things in morals as well as art,
>   That play a very important part—
>   ' Impressions before the letters.'

> " Dame Education begins the pile,
>   Mayhap in the graceful Corinthian style,
>   But alas for the elevation !
>   If the lady's maid, or Gossip the nurse,
>   With a load of rubbish, or something worse,
>   Have made a rotten foundation."

The story of Miss Kilmansegg, as the reader may remember, was written to show the utter worthlessness of mere wealth. It runs throughout its whole course in a veritable Pactolian channel : the verses glitter with gold, and are resonant of the precious metal as they hurry along, fate-driven, as it were, towards the tragical climax. Such a subject suited

Hood exactly, for there scarcely existed a man who cared less about wealth for its own sake, or who felt a heartier contempt for the host of servile worshippers who bow down to it. We extract from this rare story the following appropriate

" MORAL.

"Gold ! Gold ! Gold ! Gold !
    Bright and yellow, hard and cold,
    Molten, graven, hammer'd, and roll'd ;
    Heavy to get, and light to hold ;
    Hoarded, barter'd, bought, and sold,
    Stolen, borrow'd, squander'd, doled ;
    Spurn'd by the young, but hugg'd by the old
    To the very verge of the churchyard mould ;
    Price of many a crime untold ;
    Gold ! Gold ! Gold ! Gold !
    Good or bad a thousand-fold !
        How widely its agencies vary—
    To save—to ruin—to curse—to bless—
    As even its minted coins express,
    Now stamp'd with the image of Good Queen Bess,
        And now of a Bloody Mary."

The moral tendency of Hood's works is excellent. In the indulgence of his spirit of fun he is anything but strait-laced as regards the introduction of images and phrases which a fastidious person might call vulgar or coarse ; but an indecent description, or even allusion, will not easily be found. He is liberal, a warm eulogist as well as a glowing depicter of the good feelings of our nature, and the generous actions which these feelings prompt ; and he is an unsparing satirist of vice, pretensions, and cant, in all their forms.

It is fit that one who wrote for the people with such excellent effect, should be rewarded by public honours ; accordingly, soon after Hood's death, a subscription was raised for the benefit of his widow and children, in addition to the Civil List pension granted by her Majesty the Queen. A monument was likewise raised in honour of Hood, bespeaking, with more than usual significance, the respect for his genius which extended to all classes.

"UP THE RHINE."

Up the Rhine merits more notice than we have yet given it. It is primed with humour throughout, and occasionally set off with poetic feeling and fancy, such as those who are acquainted with Mr. Hood's genius only through the medium of his *Comic Annual*, would scarcely give him the credit of possessing.   Amidst abundance of broad humour, there is much that has point-work of elaborate finish; the satire is keener, yet pleasanter, than usual; and, with all this refinement, there is a due admixture of that homeliness of incident, and that nice discernment of the ridiculous, which are the leading characteristics of Mr. Hood's most popular works.

The framework of the present volume is, literally, a family tour of the Rhine; the party consisting of Uncle Orchard, a hypochondriac of the first water—a very teetotaller in melancholy—and his nephew, Frank Somerville, a bright setting for the old man's gravity; then we have Mrs. Wilmot, a widow, sister of Orchard, luxuriating in green sorrow; which is well set off by the *étourderie* of her communicative "woman," Martha Penny.   The whole is in the form of letters, interspersed with incidental verses, prose legends, &c., commemorating the wonders and the humours of the journey.   Here and there, by the way, we are reminded of the grave and sly shafts of the old man of "the Bubbles from the Brunnen," though, without any approach to imitation, for the only want of originality in Mr. Hood is that he occasionally borrows from himself.   We have not space to follow the narrative of the tour, and so must content ourselves with a few flying snatches.   Here is a lyric of

"ROTTERDAM.

"TO * * * * * *

"I gaze upon a city
   A city new and strange;
Down many a wat'ry vista
   My fancy takes a range;
From side to side I saunter,
   And wonder where I am :—
And can *you* be in England,
   And I at Rotterdam !

"Before me lie dark waters,
   In broad canals and deep,
Whereon the silver moonbeams
   Sleep, restless in their sleep :

A sort of vulgar Venice
Reminds me where I am.—
Yes, yes, you are in England,
And I'm at Rotterdam.

" Tall houses, with quaint gables,
Where frequent windows shine,
And quays that lead to bridges,
And trees in formal line,
And masts of spicy vessels,
From distant Surinam,—
All tell me you're in England,
And I'm at Rotterdam.

" Those sailors, how outlandish
The face and garb of each !
They deal in foreign gestures,
And use a foreign speech ;
A tongue not learned near Isis
Or studied by the Cam,
Declares that you're in England,
But I'm at Rotterdam.

" And now across a market
My doubtful way I trace,
Where stands a solemn statue,
The Genius of the place ;
And to the great Erasmus
I offer my salam,—
Who tells me you're in England,
And I'm at Rotterdam.

" The coffee-room is open,
I mingle with the crowd :
The dominoes are rattling,
The hookahs raise a cloud ;
A flavour, none of Fearon's,
That mingles with my dram,
Reminds me you're in England,
But I'm in Rotterdam.

" Then here it goes, a bumper,—
The toast it shall be mine,
In Schiedam, or in Sherry,
Tokay, or Hock of Rhine,—
It well deserves the brightest
Where sunbeam ever swam,—
'The girl I love in England,'
I drink at Rotterdam."

"In consequence of the sea running so high, we were unable to proceed to Rotterdam by the usual channel ; and were occupied during a great part of the second day in going at half-speed through the canals. Tedious as was this course, it afforded us a sight of some of the characteristic scenery of that very remarkable country called Holland. We had abundant leisure to observe the picturesque craft, with their high cabins, and cabin windows well furnished with flower-pots and frows—in fact, floating houses—while the real houses, scarcely above the water-level, looked like so many family arks that had only gone ashore, and would be got off next tide. These dwellings, of either kind, looked scrupulously clean, and particularly gay ; the houses, indeed, with their bright pea-green doors and shutters, shining, bran new, as if, by common consent, or some clause in their leases, they had all been freshly painted within the last week. But probably they must thus be continually done in oil to keep out the water—the very Dryads, to keep them dry, being favoured with a coat, or, rather, pantaloons, of sky-blue or red, or some smart colour, on their trunks and lower limbs. At times, however, nothing could be seen but the banks, till, perchance, you detected a steeple and a few chimneys, as if a village had been sowed there, and was beginning to come up. The vagaries of the perspective, originating in such an arrangement, were rather amusing. For instance, I saw a ruminating cow apparently chewing the top of a tree, a Quixotic donkey attacking a windmill, and a wonderful horse quietly reposing and dozing with a weathercock growing out of his back. Indeed, it is not extravagant to suppose that a frog, without hopping, often enjoys a bird's-eye view of a neighbouring town. So little was seen of the country, that my aunt, in the simplicity of her heart, inquired seriously, 'Where's Holland ?'"

Next is an extract from one of the uncle's letters :—

"Now I am here, I am not sorry to have had a peep at such a country as Holland ; but being described by so many better hands, in books of travels, besides pictures, I need not enlarge. If you only fancy the very worst country for hunting in the whole world, except for otter-dogs, you will have it exactly. Every highway is a canal ; and as for lanes and bridle-roads, they are nothing but ditches. By consequence, the lives of the natives are spent between keeping out water and letting in liquor, such as schiedam, aniseed, curaçoa, and the like ; for, except for the *damming*, they would be drowned like so many rats, and without the *dramming*, they would be martyrs to ague and rheumatics and the marsh fever. Frank says, the Hollanders are such a cold-blooded people that nothing but their ardent spirits keeps them from breeding back into fishes ; be that as it may, I have certainly seen a Dutch youngster, no bigger than your own little Peter, junior, toss off his glass of *schnapps*, as they call it, as if it was to save him from turning into a sprat. It is only fair to mention, that Dutch water seems meant by Providence for scouring, or scrubbing, or washing, or sailing upon, or any other use in nature, except to drink neat. It costs poor Martha a score of wry faces only to hear it named, for she took one dose of it for want of warning, and it gave her a rattling fit of what she calls the Colliery Morbus."

And now for a specimen of the Penny Correspondence—not postage :—

TO REBECCA PAGE, AT WOODLANDS, NEAR BECKNAM, KENT.

" DEAR BECKY,—This is to say we ar all safe and well, tho' its a wunder, for forrin traveling is like a deceatful luvver, witch don't improve ou acquaintance. Wat haven't I gone thro since my last faver ! Fust morbust by bad Dutch warter, and then frited to death at Nim Again with a false alarm of the Frentch, besides a dreadful could ketched, by leavin my warm bed, and no time to clap on a varsal thing, xcept my best cap. Well, I've give three warnins, and the next, as master says, will be for good, even if I have to advertize for a plaice, but ketch me sayin no objexshuns to go abroad. Not but Missis have had her own trials, but that's between our too selves, for she wouldn't like it to git about that she have had a pitcht battel with a dwarft for a glass of gin. Then there's the batterd brass pale, and the Holland—only think, Becky, of the bewtiful Dutch linnin being confisticated by the Custom-house Cæsars ! It was took up for dutis at the Garman outskirts. But, as I tould the officers, the King of Garmany ortn't to think only of the dutis dew to himself, but of his dutis towards his nabers. The Prushian customs is very bad customs, that's certin. Every thing that's xported into the country must pay by wait, witch naterally falls most heviest on the litest pusses. There's dress. Rich folks can go in spidder nets and gossumers, and fine gorses, but pore peple must ware thick stuffs and gingums, and all sorts of corse and doreable texters, and so the hard workin class cum to be more taxt than the upper orders, with their flimsy habbits. The same with other useful artikels. Wat's a silvur tooth-pick in wait compared with a kitching poker, or a filligree goold watch to an 8-day clock ? Howsomever, the Dutch linnin was confisticated in spite of my teeth, for Master chose to giv up the pint, and he desarves to go without a Shurt for his panes.

" Among other discomfits theres no beds in the vessels up the Rind. So, for too hole days, we have been damp shifted, as they call it, without taking off our close, and, as you may suppose, I am tired of steeming. Our present stop is Colon. They say its a verry old citty, and bilt by the Romans, and sure enuff roman .

noses didn't easily turn up. The native must verry strong oil factories, that's certin. O, Becky, sich sniffs, in spite of my stuft hed ! This mornin it rained cats and dogs, but the heviest showrs cant pourify the place. It's enuff to fumigate a pleg. Won thing is the bad smells obleege strangers to buy the O de Colon, and praps the stench is encourraged on that account. The wust is, wen you want a bottel of the rite sort, there's so manny Farinacious impostors, and Johns and Marius, you don't know witch is him or her."

THE BALLAD-SINGER.

IN A SKETCH AFTER THE MANNER OF BISHOP EARLE.

" The ballad-singer is a town-crier for the advertising of lost tunes. Hunger hath made him a wind instrument ; his want is vocal, and not he. His voice had gone a begging before he took it up, and applied it to the same trade ; it was too strong to hawk mackerel, but was just soft enough for *Robin Adair*. His business is to make popular songs unpopular ; he gives the air, like a weathercock, with many variations. As a key, he has but one—a latch-key for all manner of tunes ; and as they are to pass current amongst the lower sorts of people, he makes his notes like a country banker's, as thick as he can. His notes have a copper sound, for he sounds for copper ; and for the musical divisions he hath no regard, but sings on, like a kettle, without taking any heed of the bars. Before beginning he clears his pipe with gin ; and he is always hoarse from the thorough draft in his throat. He hath but one shake, and that in winter. His voice is flat from flatulence ; and he fetches breath, like a drowning kitten, whenever he can. Notwithstanding all this, his music gains ground, for it walks with him from end to end of the street. He is your only performer that requires not many entreaties for a song ; for he will chant, without asking, to a street cur or a parish post. His only backwardness is to a stave after dinner, seeing that he never dines ; for he sings for bread, and though corn has ears, sings very commonly in vain. As for his country, he is an Englishman, that by his birthright he may sing whether he can or not. To conclude, he is reckoned passable in the city, but is not so good off the stones."

SONNET ON STEAM.

" I wish I livd a Thowsen year Ago
  Wurking for Sober six and seven milers
And duble Stages runnen safe and slo
  The Orsis cum in them days to the bilers
But Now by meens of powers of Steem forces
  A-turning Coches into Smoakey Kettles
The Bilers seem a Cumming to the Orses
  And Helps and naggs Will sune to be out of Vittels
Poor Bruits I wunder How we bee to Liv
  When sutch a change of Orsis is our Faits
No nothink need Be sifted in a Siv
  May them Blowd ingins all Blow up their Grates
And Theaves of Oslers crib the Coles and Giv
  Their Blackgard Hannimuls a Feed of Slaits."

TO GRIMALDI.

Hood wrote this touching " Ode to Joseph Grimaldi,
senior," upon his retirement :—

" Joseph ! they say thou'st left the stage
    To toddle down the hill of life,
And taste the flannell'd ease of age
    Apart from pantomimic strife.
' Retir'd ' (for Young will call it so)—
' The world shut out '—in Pleasant Row.

" And hast thou really washt at last,
    From each white cheek the red half-moon ?
And all thy public clownship cast,
    To play the private pantaloon ?
All youth—all ages—yet to be,
Shall have a heavy miss of thee.

" Thou didst not preach to make us wise—
    Thou hadst no finger in our schooling—
Thou didst not lure us to the skies ;
    Thy simple, simple trade was—Fooling !
And yet, Heav'n knows ! we could—we can
Much ' better spare a better man !'

.   .   .   .   .   .

" But Joseph—everybody's Joe—
    Is gone ; and grieve I will and must !
As Hamlet did for Yorick, so
    Will I for thee (though not yet dust) :
And talk as he did when he missed
The kissing crust, that he had kiss'd !

"Ah, where is now thy rolling head !
　　Thy winking, reeling, *drunken* eyes,
(As old Catullus would have said),
　　Thy oven-mouth, that swallow'd pies—
Enormous hunger—monstrous drowth !
Thy pockets greedy as thy mouth !

"Ah ! where thy ears so often cuff'd !
　　Thy funny, flapping, filching hands !
Thy partridge body always stuff'd
　　With waifs and strays and contrabands !
Thy foot, like Berkeley's Foote—for why ?
'Twas often made to wipe an eye.

"Ah, where thy legs—that witty pair ?
　　For ' great wits jump '—and so did they !
Lord ! how they leap'd in lamp-light air !
　　Caper'd and bounced, and strode away.
That years should tame the legs, alack !
I've seen spring through an almanack !

．　　．　　．　　　．　　　　．　　　　．

" For who, like thee, could ever stride
　　Some dozen paces to the mile !
The motley, medley coach provide ;
　　Or, like Joe Frankenstein, compile
The *vegetable man* complete !
A proper Covent Garden feat.

"Oh, who, like thee, could ever drink,
　　Or eat, swill, swallow—bolt, and choke !
Nod, weep, and hiccup—sneeze, and wink !
　　Thy very yawn was quite a joke !
Though Joseph junior acts not ill,
' There's no Fool like the old Fool ' still !

" Joseph, farewell ! dear, funny Joe !
　　We met with mirth—we part in pain !
For many a long, long year must go
　　Ere fun can see thy like again ;
For Nature does not keep great stores
Of perfect clowns—that are not *boors !*"

In an account of Hood's last sight of Grimaldi, he tells us :
" His whole deportment and conversation impressed me with
the opinion that he was a simple, sensible, warm-hearted
being—such, indeed, as he appears in his *Memoirs*—a Joseph
after Parson Adams's own heart. We shook hands heartily,
parted, and I never saw him again ! He was a rare practical

humourist ; and I never look into *Rabelais,* with its huge-mouthed Gargantua, and his enormous appetite for plenty of links, chitterlings, and puddings, in their season, without thinking that, in Grimaldi and his pantomime, I have lost my best set of illustrations of that literary extravaganza."

In the closing batch of *Literary Reminiscences* there are a sort of " Replies to Correspondents ;" we select the following :—

"Amongst other notable men who came to Colebrook Cottage, I had twice the good fortune of meeting with S. T. Coleridge. The first time he came from Highgate with Mrs. Gilman, to dine with ' Charles and Mary.' What a contrast to Lamb was the full-bodied Poet, with his waving white hair, and his face round, ruddy, and unfurrowed as a holy Friar's ! Apropos to which face, he gave us a humorous description of an unfinished portrait, that served him for a sort of barometer, to indicate the state of his popularity. So sure as his name made any temporary stir, out came the canvas on the easel, and a request from the artist for another sitting : down sank the Original in the public notice, and back went the copy into a corner, till some fresh publication or accident again brought forward the Poet, and then forth came the picture for a few more touches. I sincerely hope it has been finished ! What a benign, smiling face it was ! What a comfortable, respectable figure ! What a model, methought, as I watched and admired the ' Old man eloquent,' for a Christian bishop ! But he was, perhaps, scarcely orthodox enough to be trusted with a mitre. At least, some of his voluntaries would have frightened a common every-day congregation from their propriety. Amongst other matters of discourse, he came to speak of the strange notions some literal-minded persons form of the joys of Heaven : joys they associated with mere temporal things, in which, for his own part, finding no delight in this world, he could find no bliss hereafter without a change in his nature, tantamount to the loss of his personal identity. For instance, he said, there are persons who place the whole angelical beatitude in the possession of a pair of wings to flap about with, like ' a sort of celestial poultry.' After dinner he got up, and began pacing to and fro, with his hands behind his back, talking and walking, as Lamb laughingly hinted, as if qualifying for an itinerant preacher ; now fetching a simile from Loddiges' garden at Hackney, and then flying off for an illustration to the sugar-making in Jamaica. With his fine, flowing voice, it was glorious music, of the 'never-ending, still-beginning kind,' and you did not wish it to end. It was rare flying, as in the Nassau Balloon ; you knew not whither, nor did you care. Like his own bright-eyed Marinere, he had a spell in his voice that would not let you go. To attempt to describe my own feeling afterwards, I had been carried, spiralling, up to heaven by a whirlwind intertwisted with sunbeams, giddy and dazzled, but not displeased, and had then been rained down again with a shower of mundane stocks and stones that battered out of me all recollection of what I had heard, and what I had seen !

"On the second occasion, the author of *Christabel* was accompanied by one of his sons. The Poet, talking and walking as usual, chanced to pursue some argument, which drew from the son, who had not been introduced to me, the remark, 'Ah, that's just like your crying up those foolish *Odes and Addresses.*' Coleridge was highly amused with this mal-apropos, and, without explaining, looked slyly round at me, with the sort of suppressed laugh one may suppose to belong to the Bey of Tittery. The truth was, he felt naturally partial to a book he had attributed in the first instance to the dearest of his friends.

"It may be mentioned here, that instead of feeling 'the infinitesimal of an unpleasance' at being addressed in the *Odes*, the once celebrated Mr. Hunt presented to the authors a bottle of his best Permanent Ink, and the eccentric Dr. Kitchiner sent an invitation to dinner.

"From Colebrooke, Lamb removed to Enfield Chase—a painful operation at all times, for as he feelingly misapplied Wordsworth, 'the *moving* accident was not his trade.' As soon as he was settled, I called upon him, and found him in a bald-looking, yellowish house, with a bit of a garden, and a wasp's nest convanient, as the Irish say, for one stung my pony as he stood at the door. Lamb laughed at the fun, but, as the clown says, the whirligig of time brought round its revenges. He was one day bantering my wife on her dread of wasps, when all at once he uttered a horrible shout—a wounded specimen of the species had slyly crawled up the leg of the table, and stung him in the thumb. I told him it was a refutation well put in, like Smollett's timely snowball. 'Yes,' said he, 'and a stinging commentary on Macbeth—

"'By the pricking of my thumbs,
Something wicked this way comes.'

" There were no pastoral yearnings concerned in this Enfield removal. There is no doubt which of Captain Morris's
Town and Country songs would have been most to Lamb's
taste. ' The sweet, shady side of Pall Mall ' would have carried it hollow. In courtesy to a friend, he would select a
green lane for a ramble, but left to himself, he took the turnpike road as often as otherwise. ' Scott,' says Cunningham,
' was a stout walker.' Lamb was a *porter* one. He calculated
distances, not by Long Measure, but by Ale and Beer Measure. ' Now I have walked a pint.' Many a time I have
accompanied him in these matches against Meux, not without
sharing in the stake, and then, what cheerful and profitable
talk ! For instance, he once delivered to me orally the substance of the ' Essay on the Defect of Imagination in Modern
Artists,' subsequently printed in the *Athenæum*. But besides
the criticism, there were snatches of old poems, golden lines
and sentences culled from rare books, and anecdotes of men
of note. Marry, it was like going a ramble with gentle Izaak
Walton, minus the fishing.

" How many of such pleasant reminiscences revive in my
memory, whilst thinking of him, like secret writing brought
out by the kindly warmth of the fire ! But they must be
deferred to leave me time and space for other attributes—for
example, his charity, in its widest sense, the moderation in
judgment which, as Miller says, is ' the Silken String running
through the Pearl Chain of all Virtues.' If he was intolerant
of anything, it was of Intolerance. He would have been (if
the foundation had existed, save in the fiction of Rabelais)
of the Utopian order of Thelemites, where each man under
scriptural warrant did what seemed good in his own eyes.
He hated evil-speaking, carping, and petty scandal. On one
occasion having slipped out an anecdote, to the discredit of a
literary man, during a very confidential conversation, the next
moment, with an expression of remorse, for having impaired
even my opinion of the party, he bound me solemnly to bury
the story in my own bosom. In another case he characteristically rebuked the backbiting spirit of a censorious neighbour.
Some Mrs. Candour telling him, in expectation of an ill-
natured comment, that Miss * * *, the teacher of the ladies'
school, had married a publican. ' Has she so ?' said Lamb,
' then I'll have my beer there !' "

" On the publication of the *Odes and Addresses*, presentation
copies were sent, at the suggestion of a friend, to Mr. Canning

and Sir Walter Scott. The minister took no notice of the little volume ; but the novelist did, in his usual kind manner. An eccentric friend in writing to me, once made a number of colons, semicolons, &c., at the bottom of the paper, adding—

> " ' And these are my points that I place at the foot
> That you may put stops that I can't stop to put.'

It will surprise no one to observe that the author of *Waverley* had as little leisure for punctuation.

> " ' Sir Walter Scott has to make thankful acknowledgments for the copy of the *Odes to Great People* with which he was favoured, and more particularly for the amusement he has received from the perusal. He wishes the unknown author good health good fortune and whatever other good things can best support and encourage his lively vein of inoffensive and humourist satire.
>
> " '*Abbotsford, Melrose, 4th May.*' "

> " Alas ! what a pity it is that so many good things uttered by poets, and wits, and humorists, at chance times—and they are always the best and brightest, like sparks struck out by Pegasus's own hoof, in a curved line amongst the flints—should be daily and hourly lost to the world for want of a recorder ! But in this Century of Inventions, when a self-acting drawing-paper has been discovered for copying visible objects, who knows but that a future Niepce, or Daguerre, or Fox Talbot, may find out some sort of Boswellish writing-paper to repeat what it hears !
>
> " There are other contributors—poor Hazlitt for instance—whose shades rise up before me. Shall we ever meet any-where again ? Alas ! some are dead, and the rest dispersed, and the days of *social* clubs are over and gone, when the pro-fessors and patrons of literature assembled round the same steaming bowl, and Johnson, always best out of print, ex-claimed, ' Lads ! who's for poonch !' "

We should add that Mr. Hood has left a son who inherits much of the genius of his father, so that in this kindred vein he may go on rejoicing.

BAD SPELLING.*

THERE is a story of a man who borrowed a volume of *Chaucer* from Charles Lamb, and scandalized the gentle Elia in returning it by the confidential remark, " I say, Charley, these old fellows spelt very badly." We do not know what this precision would have said of the lords and ladies of Morayshire a hundred and fifty years ago, for, with few exceptions, they spelt abominably. Even Henrietta, Duchess of Gordon, daughter of the celebrated Earl of Peterborough, who writes most sensibly and affectionately to her " deare freind, Mistress Elizabeth Dunbar," is not immaculate in this respect. She talks of a " gownd," is " asured there will be an opportunity," and speaks of " sum wise and nesessary end." But it is a shame of us even to appear to disparage this excellent lady for what was then such a usual infirmity. Her letters are, perhaps, the most worth reading of any in Captain Dunbar's collection, and her literary criticisms on the books she wishes her " deare freind " to read are especially interesting. The gentlemen were, perhaps, still more careless than the ladies in their spelling. Here are a couple of notes, the latter of which is enough to make a modern salmon-fisher's mouth water :—

" Cloavs, Jnr 29, 1703.
" Affectionat Brother,—Cloavs and I shall met you the morou in the Spinle moore, betwixt 8 and nine in the morning, where ye canot miss good sporte twixt that and the sea. ffaile not to bring ane bottle of brandie along, ffor I asheure you ye will lose the wadger. In the mean time, we drink your health, and am your affectionat brother, " R. DUNBAR.
" To the Laird off Thunderton—Heast, heast."

" Innes, June 25, 5 at night.
" Sir,—You will not (I hope) be displeased when I tell you that Wat. Stronoch, this forenoon, killed *eighteen hundred Salmon and Grilses*. But it is my misfortune that the boat is not

* From the *Times* review of Captain Dunbar's *Letters* (1865).

returned yet from Inverness, and I want salt. Therefore by all
the tyes of friendship send me on your own horses eight barrels of
salt or more. When my boat returns, none, particularly Coxton,
shall want what I have. This in great heast from, dear Archie,
yours, " HARRIE INNES.
" I know not but they may kill as many before 2 in the morning, for till then I have the Raick, and to-morrow the Pott.
These twenty years past such a run was not as has been these
two past days in so short a time, therefore heast, heast ; spare not
horse hyre. I would have sent my own horses, but they are all
in the hill for peatts. Adieu, dear Archie."

Our ancestors seem to have regarded spelling much as we
regard the knowledge of French. It was disgraceful not to
have a smattering of it, but exceptional to have mastered it
thoroughly. When we compare the above notes, which would
not confer much credit on a modern national schoolboy, with a
letter written by Duncan Forbes in 1745, we find ourselves in
quite a different atmosphere. The Lord President is terribly
angry with Elgin justices for winking at smugglers ; but he
writes like a scholar and a man of business. While on the
subject of spelling, we must select from Captain Dunbar's
collection two choice specimens of cacography, a " chereot,"
and " jelorfis." The reader will probably guess that the
former stands for chariot, as cheroots were then unknown,
but we defy him to unravel the latter without the context.
" Jelorfis " is the phonetic utterance of an unlucky wight
who had got into prison for giving a chop to another man's
nose, and stands in his vocabulary for " jailor's fees." There
are several characteristic letters from the celebrated Lord
Lovat, in which his Scotch pawkiness and French courtliness,
no unusual mixture early in the eighteenth century, are
clearly displayed. This singular personage, who may be
described as Nature's outline sketch of a character which she
afterwards elaborated in the Bishop of Autun, but who,
unlike Talleyrand, had the misfortune to die in his stocking-
feet, wrote his letters on gilt-edged paper, enclosed in enve-
lopes, and in these honeyed words addresses the Dunbar of
that day :—
" I am exceeding glad to know that you and your lady are
well, and having inquired at the bearer if you had children, he
tells me that you have a son, which gives me great pleasure, and
I wish you and your lady much joy of him, and that you may
have many more, for they will be the nearest relatives I have of

any Dunbars in the world, except your father's children ; and my relation to you is not at a distance, as you are pleased to call it, it is very near, and I have not such a near relation betwixt Spey and Ness : and you may assure yourself that I will always behave to you and yours as a relation ought to do ; and I beg leave to assure you and your lady of my most affectionate regards, and my Lady Lovat's, and my young ones, your little cousins."

Lord Lovat wrote this letter when he was past seventy. Four years later, Dr. Carlyle, of Inveresk, then a mere youth, met him at Luckie Vint's tavern.   He describes him as a tall, stately man, with a very flat nose, who, after imbibing a goodly quantity of claret, stood up to dance with Miss Kate Vint, the landlady's niece.   Five years later his head fell on the scaffold at Tower Hill. *   Here we may pause to observe a curious instance of traditionary linkage.   Dr. Carlyle died within the first decade of this century, so that many persons still living may have conversed with one who had been in company with a man born early in the reign of Charles II. Lovat was not only fond of flattering other people, but liked to be flattered himself also.   This he accomplished by the simple expedient of sending self-laudatory puffs to the *Edinburgh Courant* and *Mercury,* for the insertion of which paragraphs he paid from half-a-crown to four shillings each.

* For an account of Lord Lovat's execution, see *Century of Anecdote,* vol. i. p. 124.

WORTHIES OF ISLINGTON.

A MERRY wight in verse was Mr. George Daniel, the great collector of rare books, prints, and manuscripts, who lived in Canonbury Square, and died April 2, 1864, in his 75th year, leaving a world of curiosities, the collection of a lifetime, to be dispersed by the hammer of the auctioneer in some ten days.* Daniel loved to group his old neighbours at Merry Islington in humorous verse, such as the following, which he

* Mr. Daniel had collected, during his long and active life, a library of rare books, rich in first folios and first editions of Shakspere; and he possessed the cup made from Shakspere's mulberry-tree at New Place, and which was presented to David Garrick by the corporation of Stratford-upon-Avon at the jubilee. Mr. Daniel had written largely on the drama and cognate subjects, with discrimination and critical acumen, for which his extensive acquaintance with his rare library pre-eminently qualified him. He will be remembered as the author of the "Remarks" prefixed to Cumberland's *Plays*, published many years since. He possessed a rich vein of humour, and in 1830 published the *Modern Dunciad*, a satirical poem, which reached its sixth edition; and in similar vein he printed, in 1852, *Democritus in London*, a poetic drama, with "Notes Festivous" of great piquancy. He also contributed to *Bentley's Miscellany* a series of papers entitled "Merrie England in the Olden Time," reprinted in two volumes, the epigrammatic notes in which bristle with comical conceits. That Mr. Daniel did not hoard his bibliographical wealth will be within the recollection of many readers. He was one of the earliest and most valuable contributors to the "Memorabilia" of the *Illustrated London News*, commenced in that journal in the autumn of 1855; the first treasure being a curious Elizabethan ballad by Tarlton, from the extensive and unique collection of black-letter broadside ballads (seventy in number), in the possession of Mr. Daniel, who acquired these rarities some thirty years previously from a private source. "With the present collection" (printed between the years 1539 and 1597, says Mr. Daniel) "no other may compare for interest, variety, and number. They would almost seem, from their spotless and perfect condition, to have been rolled up, locked up, and entirely forgotten for more than two hundred years." Francis Douce was among those who fully appreciated the interest and value of these black-letter treasures. They were bought by Mr. Lilly, the well-known bookseller and publisher, for 750 guineas, and have been reprinted for him in a handsome volume.

wrote in what may be termed the form of a rhyming direc
tory :—

Who has e'er been at Islington, must surely know
Upper Street, and the cot where lives Upcott the Beau,
Ideal of autograph-maniacs, and his
Round, roguish, good-humoured, and rubicund phiz.

With a bow and a smirk, a bob and a whisk,
Dicky Suet's Ha, ha ! and Jack Bannister's frisk,
He struts virtuoso and figure of fun,
Joe Miller, Tom Hearne, bound by Momus in one.

Although he a right merry bachelor stands,
He has ask'd and obtain'd many ladies' fair *hands* ;
And leading a single, respectable life,
He keeps in his harem *maid, widow,* and *wife !*

His cot, in a corner, quaint, antique, and modest,
Was made to contain of all odd things the oddest ;
Forgotten by Time, and saved out of his wreck
By spectacled old bucks—*veluti in spec !*

Walk in, and the motley miscellany see—
Hannah More and Nell Gwynn *tête-à-tête, vis-à-vis* ;
Saint Dunstan, Sir Jeff ; Guy of Warwick, Old Guy ;
Moll Flanders, Queen Bess ; Mary Tofts, Mrs. Fry ;

Brownrigg and Shipton (remarkable mothers) ;
Turpin, Jack Sheppard ; Hind, Barrington (brothers) ;
Miss Blandy, Miss Canning (the devil's own daughters),
Will Somers, Mull'd-Sacke ; Dusty Bob, Billy Waters ;

Quacks, quakers, dwarfs, giants, mimes, mountebanks, mumpers ;
The Hottentot Venus, and Radical Rumpers ;
Parson Huntingdon's pals, where Old Nick in his niche is,
Their long leather ears, and his short leather breeches ;

Fleet weddings, roundabouts, raree-shows, races ;
Through horse collars clowns cutting comical faces ;
Bubbles on dry land, balloons in the air ;
Jack Frost on the Thames holding Bartlemy Fair ;

Duck-hunters merrily bending the stile, O ;
The ghost of Cock Lane, and the cradle of Shiloh ;
Thimble-rigs, little-goes, Punch at his pranks,
And Members of Parliament free as their franks.

To Evelyn and Pepys, and Johnson and Bozzy,
And Goldsmith and Garrick, and Foote and Piozzi,
I often step in, and say, " How d'ye do ?"
At Autograph Cottage, 102 !

And toast (not in tea—tattle's tipple !) the wight,
The famed caligraphist who taught men to write ;
First dipp'd pen in ink, and his foolscap unfurl'd,
And autograph mania all over the world.

What village can boast, like fair Islington town
Such time-honour'd worthies, such ancient renown ?
Here jolly Queen Bess, after flirting with Leicester,
" Undumpish'd "* herself with Dick Tartleton her jester.

Here gallant gay Essex and burly Lord Burleigh
Sat late at their revels, and came to them early ;
Here honest Sir John took his ease at his inn—
Bardolph's proboscis, and Jack's double chin.

Here Finsbury archers disported and quaff'd,
And Raleigh the brave took his pipe and his draught;
Here the Knight of Saint John pledged the Highbury Monk,
Till both to their pallets reel'd piously drunk.

Here stands the tall relic, old Canonbury Tow'r,
Where Auburn's sweet bard† won the Muse to his bow'r—
The Vandal that pulls thy gray tenements down,
When falls the first stone, may that stone crack his crown !

Thy green pleasant pastures, thy streamlets so clear,
Old classical village ! to Elia‡ were dear !
Rare child of humanity ! oft have we stray'd
On Sir Hugh's pleasant banks in the cool of the shade.

Joy to thy spirit, aquatic Sir Hugh !
To the end of old time shall thy River be New !
Thy head, ancient Parr,§ too, shall not be forgotten;
Nor thine, Virgin (?) Queen,‖ though thy timbers are rotten.

* It was a saying of the time that " Dicke Tarleton could undumpish her majestie at his pleasure ;" that is, dissipate the royal
blue-devils after one of Elizabeth Tudor's wonted paroxysms of con-
cupiscence and ferocity.
† Oliver Goldsmith found a pleasant retreat in a curiously oakpan-
elled apartment, which still bears his name, in this venerable Tower.
Here he put the last hand to his *Traveller* and *Deserted Village* and
composed much of his exquisite *Vicar of Wakefield.*
‡ Charles Lamb lived near Colebrooke Row. His favourite walks
were the banks of the New River and Hornsey. The writer, on
these occasions, was his frequent companion.
§ The Old Parr's Head in Upper Street.
‖ The Old Queen's Head in the Lower Street, now razed to the
ground, was one of the most perfect specimens of ancient domestic
architecture in the kingdom. In this ancient hostelrie it is said Sir
Walter Raleigh "puff'd his pipe." For many years it was the convivial resort of retired citizens and thirsty wayfarers, who, under its
primitive porch, quaffed their genuine nut-brown and indulged in
reminiscences of bygone days. The old oak parlour has been preserved from the wreck, and is well worth a visit from the antiquary.

Thy chronicler, Nelson,* his journey is sped ;
Thy guest, little Quick,† is the quick and the dead ;
The last debt of nature he paid, as all must,
And came, like a gentleman, down with his dust.

Farewell, pious Strachan,‡ and the good shepherd Gaskin,§
Who joined men and maids at the third time of asking ;
A sigh for John Nichols,‖ the loyal and true :
Old worthies, farewell ! now a cup to the *new*.

To Percival's¶ health fill a glass to the brim ;
See Islington's great illustrator in him :
Urbanity, taste, liberality, mind—
No skylights, brave boys, and no heel-taps behind !

A bumper to Knight,** and each honest piscator ;
Disciple of Walton—*carissimus frater !*
May death pass him by when he's throwing his hooks,
And long keep the worms from himself and his books !

Worms but remind us of coffins and knells,
And talking of coffins reminds us of shells,
And talking of shells just reminds us to drink on—
· Health and long life to Conchologist Lincolne !††

The sweet Swan of Avon, his works would you view
In rare *old* editions ?—much better than *new*—

* John Nelson, author of the *History and Antiquities of Islington*, the first edition of which is a valuable work ; the second is waste-paper, some of the most interesting parts being omitted, and the hiatus filled up with low detail and pot-house politics.
† The celebrated comedian, whom George III. used to call "his actor." Quick resided in a small umbrageous cottage in Hornsey Row, Islington, the walls of which, passage and staircases, were covered with Zoffani's paintings of him in his capital characters. He lived to be an octogenarian, and was fond (moderately) of punch, entertaining and merry to the last.
‡ The Rev. George Strachan, D.D., late Vicar of St. Mary, Islington.
§ The Rev. George Gaskin, D.D., late afternoon lecturer of ditto.
‖ John Nichols, Esq., of Highbury, late editor of the *Gentleman's Magazine*.
¶ Richard Percival, jun., Esq., F.S.A., of Highbury, whose highly-curious and interesting collection of drawings and prints for the illustration of Islington may be truly pronounced matchless. Few libraries contain more beautifully-illustrated volumes than this gentleman's.
** William Knight, Esq., F.S.A., of Canonbury ; a choice collector of angling books and missals.
†† Abraham Lincolne, Esq., of Highbury.

Repair to the Black-letter *Prophet*,* and then
He'll show you his *lions*, and cry "Good ye *den!*"

Says Old Father Thames, " I a toast will propose
While every man's goblet is under his nose ;
My old Bridge of London was ready to fall ;
Three cheers for new piers and Squire Jones† of Cream Hall !"

All flesh is grass—so philosophers say—
Then while the sun shines we had better make hay ;
As many more worthies are still to be found,
To part on the square, let us drink them all round.

Noah in his ark had a mighty queer lot ;
And who in *his* ark shall say Upcott has not ?
A bumper toast fill of the best in the island
To Upcott,‡ and Autograph Cottage on dry land !

Canonbury Square. G. D.

---

* "The Prophet?" What meaneth the "metre balladmonger?"
We know not of any other prophet appertaining unto " Old Iseldon,"
save the renowned "Brothers ;" but we *do* know a certain bibliographical wight with a biblical cognomen, who rejoiceth in a bundle
of old black-letter ballads, in sundry tiny dingy tomes of merrie
jestes, songs, garlands, penny-drolleries, and profane stage-playes,
and a goodly row of Shaksperian quartos. Can *this* be "a second
Daniel come to judgment?"

† Richard Lambert Jones, Esq., chairman of the London-Bridge
Committee. The library of the city of London owes much to Mr.
Jones's supervisorship and good taste.

‡ William Upcott, Esq., author of *A Bibliographical Account of
the Principal Books relating to English Topography,* a work of great
industry and research. Mr. Upcott possesses the most marvellous
collection of autographs that was ever brought together by the unwearied research and good luck of one individual. This interesting
treasure ought never to see the auction-room : its proper depository
is the British Museum ; and it will reflect lasting discredit on the
powers that be if it is lost to the country.

WALTER SAVAGE LANDOR.

IN the autumn of 1869 there appeared in the *Times* journal a masterly review of *Walter Savage Landor*, a biography, in two volumes, by John Forster, who, in this work, has done good service to the memory of his friend, and has deserved well of the public. The author and his subject are very fortunate in each other; for never was there a man who so much needed a friend after death as Landor, and his cause could not have fallen to better hands than those to which he bequeathed it, and which accordingly took it up.

We miss not one of Landor's thousand scrapes and quarrels; and, though the constant expression of a wish to tell nothing but the truth tends to create suspicion, we believe the biographer has not withheld any fact of importance. Mr. Forster wanted nothing that might render his work thorough and complete—he had, if anything, too much straw to make his bricks with. He himself knew Landor intimately for thirty years, and has enjoyed the acquaintance of most of the many celebrated persons mentioned in these volumes; and, in addition to all this, Landor, who seems from his youth to have been a most careful preserver of manuscript, left behind him an enormous mass of papers, the accumulation of seventy years, which Mr. Forster has had access to.

The reader of leisure and inclination will find little that will not interest him. He will find that a complete picture of the literary life of more than half this century is presented to him, with a striking and remarkable man for its centre figure; he will read with pleasure letters never before published, written by men whose least writing is a curiosity and a treasure; and he will be able to apprehend correctly the character and genius of a man who in his time excited the wonder and admiration of men whom the world has consented to wonder at and admire.

We recommend every one who can spare the time to read these two volumes, and for the sake of those who cannot do this, we will briefly narrate the story of Landor's long life, and endeavour, as far as space will allow, to determine the place in literature to which his works are justly entitled.

Walter Savage Landor was born at Warwick in the year 1775. His father was a country squire, and also a physician, and his mother an heiress of good family. He was sent to Rugby in his tenth year, where he commenced life with that fierce defiance of all authority which continued to the last his predominant characteristic. He was "removed" from the school "at the suggestion of the head-master," towards whom he had used "an expression not necessary to be repeated here." Before leaving, however, he had distinguished himself by his Latin verses, and had also written some English ones, if we may trust the lines transcribed by him many years afterwards, which are indeed as sweet and perfect in their way as anything he ever wrote. At eighteen, the French Revolution being then at its height, he entered as a commoner at Trinity College, Oxford, where he was soon avoided by many as a "mad Jacobin," and whence he was rusticated, after a year and a half, for firing into the window of one of the Fellows, "whom he hated for his Toryism." His disposition at the very outset of his youth appears to have been as strange and impracticable as it was in later life. He prevaricated to save himself from rustication, and yet would not make the smallest concession to the authorities to enable them to deal leniently with him, which they were anxious to do. The rustication brought about a home quarrel, which was patched up after a great deal of friendly diplomacy ; then an attempt was made to get him into the county militia, which fell through, the officers declaring that if he got a commission they would resign theirs ; and he ultimately settled at Swansea, on an allowance made to him by his father.

Here *Gebir* was written, and published at Warwick in 1798 in the form of a sixpenny pamphlet ; three years previously, however, he had printed, and then suppressed, a small volume of miscellaneous poems. *Gebir* for some time attracted no attention, but about eighteen months after its publication a favourable notice of it appeared in the *Critical Review*, written by Southey ; and then an abusive one in the *Monthly*, to which Landor wrote a furious rejoinder, meaning to add it as a note to the second edition. A friend prevailed on him to suppress it. In 1802, Landor was at Paris, and saw Napoleon make his entrance as First Consul. Fifty years after this an Amer-

ican lady listened to his description of the great Emperor—
"exceedingly handsome then, with a rich olive complexion
and an oval face, youthful as a girl's." Returning to England,
his next published *Poetry by the Author of Gebir* found less
favour with Southey, who also reviewed it. Landor now
lived for some time at Bath, extravagantly it appears, and
continually involved in the most extraordinary love entangle-
ments, but writing a wonderful quantity of letters to newspapers and other matter, a very small proportion of which
ever saw the light. He had not yet seen Southey, but to
this period belongs the commencement of their friendship.

In 1825 his father died, and he succeeded to the family
estates, already lessened by his debts. In 1808 he first met
Southey, and their memorable friendship began in a burst of
mutual admiration, and an offer by Landor to pay for printing the series of mythological poems which Southey had
planned. These two men honestly believed each other and
themselves to be very great poets, and Southey's serene accep-
tance of Landor's frantic adulation of that "series of mythological poems" is sad and strange to read. Mr. Forster pleads
hard for them himself, and may he plead successfully!
Southey's poetry, however, seems to have infected his friend's
spirit with its wild heroism ; for, after receiving the second
consignment of the *Kehama* MS., Landor set off in hot haste
with two Irish gentlemen to help to turn the French out of
Spain. He arrived at Corunna a few months before the Convention of Cintra, and at once gave 10,000 reals "for the
benefit of the unfortunate town of Venturada," and raised and
equipped a troop of volunteers for the Spanish army. Hardly,
however, had he done this, when, without a shadow of right
on his side, he quarrelled with the English envoy, his troop
dispersed, and he returned to England as suddenly as he had
quitted it. Once more at home, he wrote most furiously
upon the Convention, crying out, " O Christ !—this England,
this noble country, that hands so mighty and a heart so
sound should have a face all leprosy, and a head fit for nothing
but the vermin that burrow in it !" and wishing to send " the
hand of Sir Hew Dalrymple to be nailed upon the pillory at
Lisbon, and that of Sir Arthur Wellesley for a like exposition
at Madrid," and finally calling out for " the besom of destruction to sweep the land clean."

In 1809 Landor acquired the Llanthony Abbey estate in
Monmouthshire, a noble old ruin surrounded by picturesque

scenery; it produced everything, as he said, but herbage, corn, and money; and he went down to live there, intending to build a house, to restore the abbey, and to plant a wood of cedars of Lebanon. And now commences a chapter of such troubles and misfortunes as surely no landlord, before or since, ever encountered. Two or three impetuous letters to the Bishop of St. David's, intended to procure the removal of the parish church, ended in nothing, the bishop agreeing with Mr. Landor, but fearing it would be necessary to obtain an act of parliament. Landor then took all his friends by surprise, marrying suddenly "a pretty little girl, of whom he seems literally to have had no other knowledge than that she had more curls on her head than any other girl in Bath," and that she had no fortune, the very thing which determined him to marry her, he writes, in answer to some faint objections raised by his mother on the score of his future wife's poverty. He now took up his abode at Llanthony, living in a comfortless way in a turret, as he describes it, "among ruins and rubbish, and bandboxes and broken chairs;" yet he had a spare bed, and Southey and his wife paid him a welcome and long-promised visit. We pass over a quarrel, arising out of some grand jury business, and a letter to the judge, wherein Landor describes himself in contrast to his fellow jurors as "a man who in everything that elevates the character or adorns the mind would blush at descending to a comparison with the first and wisest among them."

In the beginning of this year, 1812, Southey had negotiated with Mr. Murray the publication of *Count Julian*, but could not prevail upon him to undertake a startling political pamphlet written a few months later. At this period Landor's favourite schemes seem to have been the establishment of Lord Wellington on the throne of Portugal and of a printing press at Llanthony, but these soon evaporated in a general disgust and a wish to become a citizen of France.

Partly through Southey's recommendation, Landor had let his largest farm to a Mr. Betham, whose only qualification for what Southey calls a " farmer-agriculturist," seems to have been some years' service as a petty officer in an East Indiaman. The sequel cannot be better told than in the afflicted landlord's own vigorous English, who writes to his friend as follows :—

" I am in no small tribulation from that Betham of whose family you know something. Hearing a good account of his father from you, and that he was desirous of settling here, I offered the old gentleman my two livings, worth about £270 a year, on the decease of the present incumbents, who were each above seventy. That the son might have a comfortable house and a large farm, I consented to accept the resignation of a lease from an excellent tenant, and to allow him £50 a year for it, which £50, however, Mr. Betham was to pay me—the old tenant liking my security better than his. Mr. Betham neglected to gather in his corn, of which the crop was excellent, and lost at least £200 by this ; he did not thatch his hay, by which he lost £200 more ; and by a series of such conduct as might be expected from a sailor turned farmer, and by living at the rate of £1000 a year, he succeeded in spending his wife's fortune—about £3000. In fifteen months I have received no rent from him, though his rent amounts to above £1100. Although for several months he came uninvited, and passed his evenings in my house ; although his sheep have consumed the produce of my garden and fields and woods, he has had the baseness to threaten to shoot my chickens if they come into his fields. I mention this to show the extreme baseness to which he descends. I offered to put his hedges in repair if he would keep them so—he declined it ; finding it more convenient to pasture his sheep in my meadows, and turning them into bare fallows that they may be forced upon my land by hunger. . . All his brothers—three certainly—have abandoned every visible means of procuring an honest livelihood, and are with him ; although his poor labourers are starving, and he has actually borrowed money from them. He has embezzled the money I allowed for the repairs of the house, because I insisted on no written agreement and relied on his honour. He has discharged me and my gamekeeper from shooting on his farm !"

Yet we find that in the middle of all this, Landor had written a comedy, the *Charitable Dowager*, and a quantity of Latin verse. He determined to give any profits which might accrue to a distressed friend, but does not appear to have been able to secure a publisher. This is one of Landor's extraordinary traits : as well as we can make out, in all his life he never made a penny by his works, and yet he hardly ever omitted to devote the prospective but illusory profits to the relief of a plundered city or the salvation of a ruined family. Meanwhile, affairs at Llanthony gradually grew worse and worse, and at last fell into a state of complete anarchy ; Landor's tenants defied him ; he became entangled in a mesh of actions for libel and other suits ; the Bethams " stood upon gateposts and looked into the dining-room, thrust notices into his hands or face, followed him through his pleasure grounds, and on another occasion aimed a bayonet at the wife of his gamekeeper." They and others surrounded his house at night, rooted up his trees, and mended the roads with the ornamental stones of the abbey; and the end of it all was that the Llanthony vision came to an end, and in May, 1814, Landor left England for France. Half-way across the Channel he quarrelled with and parted from his wife, but she rejoined him soon afterwards at Tours, and they left together for Italy, "after contests with his landlady of the most tremendous description." At Como Landor's first child, a son, was born, but his stay there soon came to an end—this time it was printing some Latin poems obnoxious to the authorities, and he moved southwards. Ultimately, in 1821, six years after leaving England, he settled at Florence, which was to be his home for so long, and where he was at last to die.

To this time belongs some Latin and lesser English poetry, as well as two dramatic pieces sent to Southey, *Inez de Castro* and *Ippolite di Este;* but it is in the year 1822 that we first hear of the *Imaginary Conversations,* and in 1824, after many difficulties and delays, the first two volumes of the series were published, and at last, in his 49th year, Landor won for himself a hearing. Now, too, that he had discovered the strength of his genius, he exercised it with all his might, and those inexhaustible and marvellous dialogues continued to pour from his pen almost to the last of the remaining forty years of his life. But he had not discovered, and never did discover, the way to live at peace with his fellow-creatures. Troubles came as thick upon him as ever, but, passing by some half-dozen very pretty quarrels in as many years, we come to the purchase of the Fiesolan Villa, near Florence, in 1829. Landor seems to have entered his new home full of the happiest anticipations, and for some time lived quietly there with his wife and children, writing and sending to England *Imaginary Conversations,* and poetry, English and Latin, and indulging a mania, recently acquired, for picture-dealing. He soon got together, at a handsome outlay, a number of paintings by the best masters, as he believed, and for many years was a willing victim to the dealers. In 1832 he paid a short visit to England, and in 1835 occurred the final quarrel with his wife, which drove him, alone, back to England again. He now settled down at Bath—his favourite town—and grew old there, but as he was not a man to grow old gracefully, a few words may tell the rest. Suffice it to say, that in 1858, at the age of 83, in spite of the entreaties and warnings of the many friends who, with all his faults, he never lacked through his long life, he published a volume of poems, of which the best that can be said is that it involved him in ruinous actions for libel. Transferring all his property to his eldest son, he left England for Italy, and, after six years full of disgraces and miseries, died at Florence in a lodging taken for him by his friends. We cannot omit almost the last incident related of him, and very strange and touching it is :—

" On the night before the 1st of May, Landor became very restless, as during the year had happened frequently, and at about two o'clock in the morning he rang for Mrs. Wilson (his servant) and insisted on having his room lighted. He then asked for pen, ink, and paper, and the date of the day. Being told that it was the dawn of the 1st of May, he wrote a few lines of verse, and, leaning back, said—' I shall never write again. Put out the lights and draw the curtains.' "

It is impossible to compress a notice of all the writings of a man who wrote almost daily for seventy years, and with such ease that, as he tells us, a thousand lines of *Count Julian* were composed in forty hours.

We are struck in reading this biography with the wonderful consistency of Landor's disposition and character all through his life : from first to last he is the same indomitable Titan, confounding and defying alike all authority, whether good or bad. We cannot trace any gradual formation or development ; he was just as impetuous and unbending at eighteen as he was at eighty. To a powerful and vigorous intellect he united most overweening pride, and what is commonly called conceit became in him sublime through its very excess. It never for an instant occurred to him that Byron, Shelley, or Keats wrote better poetry than himself, and in other matters he was just as positive and persuaded. He must have it all his own way ; he neither brooked nor forgave contradiction ; at a smile, even, " he would rush from the room." " Artigas," he says, " is an amazing general : Europe has seen nothing like him since Sertorius." " It is more than two centuries since a work of the same wealth of genius as Beddoes' *Death's Jest Book* has been given to the world." If this is his praise, his blame, we may be sure, was not more qualified. Byron " deserved damnation" for having written *Don Juan ;* Canning was " a scoundrel ;" and so on. And yet, as we have said, with all this, Landor never lacked friends, and it tells us that under all his ruggedness must have lain very much that was noble.

He was generous in the extreme, giving freely his sympathy and his money, two things which do not always go together. And with regard to his faults, we must remember that they, in a great measure, produced his writings. If he had not felt so fiercely he would never have written so powerfully. Had he hated less, he might have loved less, and we cannot spare one spark of that burning passion and worship for all that is good and great which glows in his pages.

Had his poetry been compounded of his personal feelings and experiences, it would have been more popular in the days in which it was written; but he scorned this sort of popularity as he scorned Byron, who pursued it.

Landor was a hater of kings : tyranny was so odious to him that, writing in his own reckless way, he seemed to countenance tyrannicide. But we must remember that he was a man who never let the sun go down upon his wrath before he wrote, and that his wild politics were the result of boiling hatred of an oppression such as we in these times see little of, but which he had beheld walking abroad in the noonday. But whatever there might be rash and violent in his disposition, there was certainly nothing mean or ignoble. No cause was too weak for him to fight for; he never sided with the strong. because they *were* strong, but was ever fearless to a fault. And he was as proud as he was brave ; though he might often have forwarded his own ambition, he never designed in the least degree to court success. Literary fame was very dear to his heart, yet he could scarcely be induced to speak to a publisher ; and his friends had to manœuvre and negotiate for months before his books could be printed, much less published. To sum up all, as his friend Sir William Napier said of him, "He is an oak with many gnarled branches and queer excrescences, but always an oak."

Let us now turn to his works. *Gebir* and *Count Julian* were in their days accounted great and wonderful poems, but are now almost forgotten. What is the reason, and where is the fault—with the public or with the poems? *Gebir* is undoubtedly in many parts very finely written, but its outlandish nomenclature, its lack of human interest, its uncouth and barbarous fable, will evermore prevent it, as they have prevented it, from becoming popular.

Of the tragedy of *Count Julian*, too, the same may be said ; and it is all tragedy : there is no low music, but always the crash of the full orchestra.

The opposite extreme to Landor's epic and tragic poetry is to be met with in Wordsworth, who is sometimes so very simple that he is insipid, while Landor's high-spiced heroical bowl is too much like medicine, very good for us, no doubt, but "we will take it another time." Of his miscellaneous verse it may be said generally that there is a lack of glow and "go" in it : Landor is too apt to walk barefoot when he is off the stilts.

Mr. Forster, jealous as he is for his friend, may well allow his fame to rest chiefly on his prose writings. In the *Imaginary Conversations* and kindred pieces, there is a wiseness of thought, a felicity of illustration, rare indeed. We know of scarcely any books a man may with more advantage study in his youth and recur to in his riper age than those containing the hundred and fifty *Imaginary Conversations*. He will find there a wonderful range of observation and reflection, and an astonishing wealth of language and imagery. He will see how this English tongue, so rusted and worn in the uses of daily life, turns to a bright and tempered weapon in the hands of a master. As Emerson said of Landor—

"His acquaintance with the English tongue is unsurpassed. He is a master of condensation and suppression, and that in no vulgar way. He knows the wide difference between compression and an obscure elliptical style. Dense writer as he is, he has yet ample room and choice of phrase, and often even a gamesome mood between his valid words. There is no inadequacy or disagreeable contraction in one of his sentences, any more than in a human face, where in a square space of a few inches is found room for every variety of expression,—they are cubes, which will stand firm, place them how or where you will."

ALBERT SMITH.

Versatility is a wonderful passport to success. The faculty of turning from one thing to another at the right moment— that is, when it seems to be profitable or promising—is of wonderful importance in the chances of life. The wisdom of proverbs is not always trustworthy, nor does success colour all things in life. Smith is an instance of ceaseless industry and shrewdness, who studied medicine, then betook himself to write for the press and the stage; and next hit upon a safer venture of roaming among continental wonders, with such success as to concentrate his attention upon devising for the entertainment of the public a means of affording them information upon points of minor interest, but which proved very attractive to all growths. This was accomplished with much pleasantry and at economical cost. Add to this, excellent management, and you have the means by which a man, in a few years, became, with the qualities we have indicated, possessed of a handsome fortune.

Such was Albert Smith, whom we were accustomed to meet at certain periodical festivals held beneath the shade of St. Bride's, Blackfriars, on Christmas eve, New-year's eve, and Twelfth-night; and here to welcome the joyous peals from the adjoining steeple. Smith was usually the life and soul of these gatherings, and here he sang his patter songs until he was hoarse, and told his funny stories until the small hours. He had then scarcely attained his twentieth year, but with exuberance of spirits, despite an unmusical voice, he delighted to amuse the circle around him; and it was plain to see that he was to the manner born for the successful illustration of life and manners. His keenness of observation and easy good humour, his alacrity, hearty good-fellowship, and relish for small amusements, were untiring. What he had seen and felt he represented with great facility and sound judgment. It was a great part of his fun to laugh at romance, to explode fables, to expose shams, and to take the jocularly sensible view of every subject.   He succeeded in pleasing the public because he represented ordinary Englishmen so well, and fell in with so many of their opinions.   There was an irrepressible " go " in all he attempted.   He swam strongly, but it was with the tide.   He used to inform his hearers that he was no scholar, and even took credit for not knowing the learned languages.   Still, he knew how to find his way to the hearts of an English audience, great and small, and rarely do we see a man so well adapting himself to a pursuit suitable to him.

Albert Smith was born May 24, 1816, in the rural village of Chertsey, in Surrey, where figured tiles and tesselated pavements, the remains of the famous Abbey—or the house of Cowley, the poet—had less attraction for Albert than the Saxon curfew (still rung), and its monkish inscriptions, the tradition of which he wrought in his youth into a slight story, entitled *Blanch Heriot.*   Smith was educated at Merchant Taylors' school; studied medicine at the Middlesex Hospital, and became a member of the College of Surgeons in 1838; after which he continued his studies at the Hôtel Dieu and Clamart, in Paris; and, on his return to England, practised with his father as a surgeon, at Chertsey.   He had already appeared as an author, in a pamphlet entitled *Arguments against Phrenology,* in which the leading question propounded was, " Whether the external form of the head correspond to the external surface of the brain."   This *brochure* appeared in 1837, when its author was described as " a rising student in one of our metropolitan hospitals."   His argument extends to some two dozen pages, the most remarkable feature in which is the good-natured satire and quiet humour with which the writer demolishes the theory of the phrenologists. In 1838 Albert communicated a series of sketches in Paris to the *Mirror,* then edited by John Timbs.   In 1839-40, appeared in the *Literary World,* Mr. Smith's " Sketches of Evening Parties," the earliest specimens of the writer's home fun; and in the same work he printed and illustrated a narrative of his " Passage of the Great St. Bernard," the *avant-courier* of his " Ascent of Mont Blanc," which he faithfully describes as a long-cherished hope of his early youth.   About this time he gave a very interesting account of his Mont St. Bernard ascent, illustrated with his own drawings, first at the Literary and Philosophical Institution, in Edward Street, Portman Square, which series of *vivâ voce* sketches of travel excited considerable interest. His "Sketches of Evening Parties" were reproduced in *Punch*, and were reprinted twice or thrice in a separate volume, of which large editions were sold.

In 1842 Mr. Smith translated for the *London Saturday Journal* a *nouvellette*, entitled the *Armourer of Paris ;* and an old Chertsey legend, *Blanch Heriot*, which he afterwards dramatised for the Surrey Theatre—this being his first essay in writing for the stage. Next, a shoal of little shilling books—the natural histories of the "Gent," "Stuck-up People," "The Idler," &c.—which Smith poured forth most rapidly, and the publisher, David Bogue, sold by thousands. Yet the first of these little books lay for six months incomplete at the printer's ; but the author, in addition to the copy-money, was eventually presented by the publisher with a hundred-pound bank-note. Smith was now a fast-rising contributor to the magazines, especially to *Bentley's Miscellany*, which retains to this day George Cruikshank's hilarious design on its wrapper, and which continued to prosper, notwithstanding Mr. Dickens's secession from the editorship. In this miscellany first appeared Albert's *Adventures of Mr. Ledbury*, *The Scattergood Family*, *The Marchioness of Brinvilliers*, and *The Pottleton Legacy*, all of which were re-printed in various forms—from the costly three volumes to the shilling'sworths of railway stalls. The number sold of these novels must have been enormous. Smith also contributed occasionally to *Blackwood's Magazine*, the *Keepsake*, the *Book of Beauty*, and other annuals ; and he was for several years the dramatic critic of the *Illustrated London News*, to which journal he also contributed many columns of pictorial drolleries. He wrote several songs for John Parry ; he could improvise, write prologues and epilogues, and was ever ready to assist with his aid a fellow artist. Meanwhile, he well understood small helps to popularity, the earliest of which was Baugniet's clever portrait of our author drawn on stone. Albert was ever ready with the latest conundrum, and created by his mimicry uproarious delight among a roomful of children. In 1841 he contributed to a journal of light sketches entitled the *Cosmorama ;* and next, to *Punch, or the London Charivari*.

In 1849 he made an excursion to the East, and on his return published *A Month at Constantinople*, and produced his entertainment of travel, "The Overland Mail." Next year he made the ascent of Mont Blanc, upon which perilous journey was founded his entertainment, first given at the Egyptian Hall, Piccadilly, March 15, 1852. His " Mont Blanc" had appeared in January, in *Blackwood's Magazine ;* but the author gave it the form of a personal narrative on the first or " private " night, and the audience consisted of invited guests. Beverley painted some charming scenes of the localities in the Ascent, and a proscenium : all these appurtenances cost the author upwards of a thousand pounds. For this entertainment, which is too well known to require description, in the two seasons 1852 and 1853, there paid for admission 193,754 persons—upwards of £17,000 ! There were 471 representations ; and one morning representation, privately, to Prince Albert, the Prince of Wales, and Prince Alfred, at the Egyptian Hall, June 28, 1852.

Such was the success of the " show." The narrative of the " Ascent " was re-printed from *Blackwood*, for private circulation only. It is, altogether, Albert Smith's best literary work, and has a maturity and finish which will last. The Mont Blanc attracted the Queen to the Egyptian Hall in 1854, and her Majesty was pleased to send Smith a diamond scarf-pin in testimony of her gratification. The Mont Blanc was given in 1855, for the thousandth time. For the third season the exhibition-hall was re-fitted as a Swiss *châlet*, and the galleries as those of Bernese *châlets*. For a new entertainment the author visited China, and made of his experiences " Mont Blanc to China," which was delivered before her Majesty and the royal family, April 14, 1859. Of the entertainment the author wrote a sort of handbook, in which he describes his reception by the Chinese, though at first they were greatly puzzled what to make of him, so tickled were they with his drollery. All the proceeds of his final performance in China were given to the charities, on finding which the Chinese *ai-ayed* with astonishment, and conveyed Albert to the steamer in a handsome sedan-chair, with all the paraphernalia of a celestial procession : music to drive away demons ; flags, with devices setting forth his virtues and talents ; and he embarked amidst fire-crackers, to propitiate the elements for his safe voyage home. He was literally overwhelmed with Chinese *curios*. Of the exhibition-room he gives a most interesting page, describing these presents, which were so many vouchers for the authenticity of the " show." Much of its ordering was due to Albert Smith's brother Arthur, who possessed peculiar tact for management. By the way, we scarcely remember two brothers so devoted to each other's interests. Success does not, however, always bring long life to enjoy it. Smith's career had been a life of hard work, that told upon a system which had no relief from intensity. The wear and tear of entertaining the public is one of the most destructive pursuits a man can follow. The Queen, after hearing his "Mont Blanc," is known to have tenderly expressed her sympathy for the exertion. We remember to have met Smith in Piccadilly, when we promised to dine with him in the following week; and, said he, "I will bring you up to the show afterwards." But his health failed, and the day never came. A few evenings after, we read in the *Sun* newspaper an obituary memoir of our dear friend. This proved to be untrue, but he died a few days after (May, 1860), at Northend, the village wherein resided Foote, the comedian; and where Richardson, the novelist, wrote *Sir Charles Grandison* and *Clarissa Harlowe.*

From the *Saturday Review* we glean the following lively comments upon Mr. Smith's entertainments :—" He has received so much praise that he must be tired of hearing that he is amusing, clever, and entertaining. But we must not let the opportunity pass of alluding to the keenness of observation and the easy good-humour which he constantly displays. In his well-known *Engineer's Story,** there is more than cleverness—there is genuine humour. People go to him to be amused, and he gives them an amusement than which nothing in London is more amusing. He is as good as a play, if by a play we mean the plays to be seen in English theatres of the present day. In their own way these plays are often excellent, and there are comic actors in England who rise high even when tested by a European scale. His mammas all want to foist their daughters on rich simpletons—his young ladies all want to show their ankles—his men are all snobs unable to speak a word of French—his priests all wish a pretty girl to sit by their side. Such people exist—there is no departure from the truths of real life. At the close of Mr. Smith's performance he gives a summary of current politics, in a very laughable song, supposed to embody the contents of *Galignani's Messenger.* His politics are the popular politics, and are drawn straight from the *Times* and *Punch.* He informs us that the East India Directors are a lot of old women, with Mrs. Gamp at their head; that as to

* See the *Engineer's Story,* p. 115.

Reform, 'Pam will put a flower in his mouth and do as he pleases about that and everything else,' and that the only 'clause' wanted is the claws of the British Lion, which will rend the Bengal Tiger. Then Mr. Smith sticks up for his cloth, and the English public like a man who honestly proclaims himself to be what he is. He says of himself that he 'goes into private society—it is dreadfully dull, but he goes.' He does not affect a great position, because he has struck out a very successful and lucrative amusement. If he plumes himself upon anything it is upon making his way abroad, on his good humour, on his power of fraternizing with the 'Mossoos.' The claim to qualities like these, evidently well founded, conciliates the audience. No one can listen to him without feeling sure that, like his curate, he is a very good fellow. On the other hand, he reflects the British taste for grand people. 'There are ten dogs of the St. Bernard breed coming over soon,' he tells us—'eight for me, and two for the Prince of Wales.' Put all these things together—popular politics in their most grotesquely popular form, frankness as to his own pretensions, and a discreet conjunction of the Egyptian Hall and Buckingham Palace—and no one can deny that Mr. Smith knows how to find his way to the hearts of an English audience.

"Probably, also, his audience enjoy the depreciation of themselves and their friends implied in every travelling Englishman being represented as a snob, just as they enjoy the most extravagant depreciation of English government and English armies. But a great part of the amusement which this picture affords is derived from the picture not being quite true. The English do not always show themselves in a favourable light abroad; but then it is a general taste among the English to like travelling. They have money for it, and they have courage for it. Consequently a much more mixed set of people leaves this country every year for the Continent, than moves from any one Continental nation to another. But if we are to judge of a nation by its worst specimens, can it be said that any travelling English are worse than the foreigners of Leicester Square? The ignorance of Englishmen is also much exaggerated. There are many more English who can talk French than French people who can talk English; and if we take the class of persons who go to the higher sort of sights, with a wish to understand and appreciate them—who visit picture galleries or the great cities of Italy—we will venture to say that English visitors have an amount of serviceable knowledge of history, antiquities, art, and literature, which the visitors of no other nation can in the least pretend to rival. It is good fun to hear of Mr. Smith's comical acquaintance, Mr. Brown, a distinguished University man, who introduces such recondite phrases as *magna comitante caterva* into his common conversation, and who has no other means of communicating to a French waiter his wish for mushrooms than by drawing on the wall the likeness of one, to which the waiter responds by bringing an umbrella. But it would be absurd if this were meant for anything but an extravagant caricature.

"The second part of *Mont Blanc* is devoted to an account of Mr. Smith's journey to Naples, and is very amusing. The illustrative views are excellent, and, considering the smallness of the space to be operated on, the success with which the ' Blue Grotto ' and the eruption of Vesuvius are represented, is very remarkable."

EDWARDS THE ENGINEER'S STORY.

The following amusing scene is from Albert Smith's popular entertainment given by him at the Egyptian Hall, 1858 : it is a strange and ludicrous picture of that confusion of narrative which some clever persons would term "undeveloped impressions." With this light artillery, Smith was wont to set his audience in a roar ; and by this and kindred means he did more to laugh people out of their follies than could be effected by graver chastisement of " offending Adam."

"On leaving the beautiful blue grotto of Capri, which Mr. Beverley has just shown you, I missed the little steamer back to Naples, so I got another little boat that sailed to Sorento. There was no one on board that I could ask a question of, except a little boy, and he said—

" ' The engineer is below.'

" ' Well, go fetch him up,' said I. So he went down and he brought up my old friend, Edwards, the engineer of the Austrian Lloyds Company. ' Oh, Edwards,' said I, ' is that you ? Are you all right ?'

" ' Well, Mr. Smith,' he said, ' I wish it *was* all right, and right it would have been but for parties *you* know as well as I do. But it's very warm up here ; you had better come below into the engine-room. I have got some export Allsopp below, and you'll find it nice and cool down there.'

"The day was intensely hot ; there was no air stirring in the

8—2

Bay of Naples, no shade anywhere ; so we went down, and the man was right. He had got his old water-pipe, I never saw him without it ; and we had the beer, and very good it was.

" ' What do you think of that beer, Mr. Smith ?' he said.

" ' Well,' I said, 'it's very good.'

" ' Ah,' he said, 'it's better than the Naples beer, is it not ? We have had some Naples beer here up to the last three weeks ago, and the last time the man brought it I said to him, "Old fellow "—those were my words—" your beer wants another hop in it." He did not understand a word what I said, because he talked such gibberish,—he's a regular idiot of a man.'

" ' Well, I said, 'how have you been getting on, Edwards, since I met you last year ? Have you been getting on well ?'

" ' Well, Mr. Smith, perhaps I *have*, and perhaps I *haven't*, is what I should say to a *stranger* ; but to tell you the truth, if my partner had done the right thing when the time came for him to do it, but he didn't do it at the time he *ought* to do it, I should have got along ; but, as I said to him, " Birds of a feather corrupts good manners." I told him so before,—the time I was *there*—not the time I *wasn't* there,—I found the place warn't no account, and so I told him, because happiness is the best politics. Well, then, *what* does *he do ?*'

" ' Edwards,' I said, 'I think you are a little confused in your story.'

" ' Well, sir, as I told you, *what* does my partner do but he buys a cargo of sulphur and saltpetre that he gets from Messina, and he goes to England, and starts a firework manufactory in the Waterloo Bridge Road ; and there he would not let *me* smoke *my* pipe in his workshop, and that's how we broke friends and parted. Well, he had two or three pitches up with the neighbours, and at last he was blown out of his own house into the second floor opposite ; but he died quite quiet in his bed after all —he went out quite quiet, just like a Catherine-wheel off his pin. Well, the Austrian Lloyds wouldn't do nothing for him, so I got the fireworks, and I was obliged to sell them.'

" ' Well, you got on *then*, surely. That set you all right.'

" ' No, it *didn't* ; for I sold them fireworks to the Surrey Gardens, and up to this day I don't know who's to pay me. Then I was obliged to go in the sulphur and saltpetre works in the docks. It's very different *here* to what it is in the docks. A deal of it comes in bags, but if it comes from Catania it don't come in bags, but bags is the best. Then you put 'em down eighty on a page, double columns, forty on each side, cut off the noughts ; then that's added up at the bottom and carried forward to the next page, and then when you get done, that's carried on two pages over, because *that's* nothing to do with the other ; that's the bags you understand from the commencement, and then that depends upon how it comes over ; sometimes it comes in thousands, sometimes more and sometimes less, and sometimes fractional parts, and very often none at all ; and then you add it all up. But why should I deceive you, Mr. Smith ? I hadn't got the *head* for it, and them as hasn't got the heads for it sometimes runs away— goes away holloaing round the docks and is never heard of, which I was only relieved by going to Hampton Court of a Sunday, because in consequence of this they gives me leave to go to Hampton Court, and there I was going up and down, because what goes up must come down. But as to the name of that boat, Mr. Smith, I couldn't tell you what it was, and till you bring it before the proprietors and see what they owe me for more than three years, the affair can't be done ; with your permission, that's how I was going to put it to you. Let's see, I beg your pardon, what was I a-telling you about last, Mr. Smith ?'

"'Something about Hampton Court.'

"'Well, Mr. Smith, *that* was it. I recollect that place now just as well as if I had never been there, which I never have, Mr. Smith; it was Greenwich, or Richmond, or somewhere else. Hampton Court is where you go and see the palace as was built by Linsey —Cardinal Linsey—Cardinal Linsey-Wolsey, I mean,—but the name's nothing to do with it. The party *you* know was there, and he says to me,—I know that young man, Mr. Smith, as well as I know you ; but if you were to pray and beseech me where he was at this moment I couldn't tell you if my head was on the block. This was what he says to me when he run away with Mrs. Edwards. *No*, Mr. Smith, he *did not*,—that man would no more have done that thing than he would have done *nothing at all*, which was what he generally did. " *Edwards*," he says— that was his observation—he says, " *Edwards*"—he said it *just* like that,—" I did not mean anything one way nor the other," and I *know* he didn't ; but he says " *Edwards*, the Austrian Lloyds has no right to go into the vestry and forbid the banns ; which, Mr. Edwards," says he, " I would tell the Austrian Lloyds Company face to face." That woman kept her bed three years ; which, what's the use of your limbs as long as you're happy. By the natural laws of the Parliament of England that's the way I got to hear of this, Mr. Smith, and that puts me in the position as a fellow-countryman ; and as you've always behaved as a gentleman to me, I'd just take the liberty of asking you what you would do if you were in my place. I wish to do the right thing by you, and if you wish to leave your box you can leave it, and that box would cost you four carlinis in Naples, with a bad lock, and evil communications is the mother of all commandments.'"

Next is a sort of Herodotean account, by Edwards, of the descent of the Queen and Prince Albert to a deep mine in Cornwall :

" I received a letter one evening from Mr. Edwards to say how that Prince Albert was coming to our main the next mor' ing. Thinks I, what can the Prence be a-coming to our main for ? And I cudn't slape for the night for thinking what I shud say to the Prence, and what the Preuce cud say to me. Well, in the morning, sure 'nuff, we saw the chay coming, and who should be in it but the Queen, so well as the Prence ! There was a stone wall between, and the men went to it, and it was down in a mi-nute—in less than no time, and they come on, and the Queen got out of the chay, and ran about in the wet grass like a Billy ! Says she to Mr. Taylor—something, but I don't know what—but says he to me, 'Is it safe for the Queen to go into the main ?' 'Safe,' says I ; 'yes, safe as the Rock of Gibraltar !' So the drams were broft footh, and some straw a throw'd into one, and some green baize after it, and the Queen skipt in like a lamb, and I do believe that I touched her ! She didn't like it tho' when 'twas wet ; but when we cum on as far as we cud to the west load, the Prence took the pick, and he throw'd to like—like a man ! and he got a bit a ore. 'This,' said he, 'is from the west looad,' so I puts 'en into my left pocket ; and then we went to the east looad, so I puts 'en into my right pocket ; and as they were coming out, says the Queen to Mr. Taylor, says she, 'What's that there blue that I do see ?' 'Bliss ye, ma'am,' says he, 'that's the light o' day.' One hundred and twenty miners were ready to cheer 'em as they drove off (all red, like Injins, from the red ore of the main), and we did cheer, to be sure, as never was before."

In the active life of a man so various as Albert Smith, we are not surprised to find aërostation one of his passports to popularity. We do not remember how many ascents he made, but one of them—a most perilous one—was made on July 6, 1847. A fortnight previously, he had written, half in joke, in an account of an ascent in the Nassau balloon, that for further excitement he would next ascend at midnight, with fireworks, without ballast, and the valve closed. He little thought how soon three of these conditions would be realized—the fourth being carried out in an entirely opposite manner. Anxious to see a view of London at a great height, he arranged with Mr. Gypson, the aëronaut, for a seat in his car. The night was uncommonly close and sultry, and scarcely a breath of wind was stirring ; what there was blew slightly from the south-east, and the lightning was flashing about the skies, preluding a terrific thunderstorm. Besides Mr. Gypson and Mr. Coxwell, Smith was to have another companion, and they met in Vauxhall Gardens about eleven o'clock. The fireworks—the frame of which resembled a ery large skeleton drum—were to be hung thirty or forty et below it, and fired from the car by a fusee ; a most dangerous method, by the way, as the neck of the balloon was but a few feet overhead. At last, everything was ready for the start. "We took in," says Smith, "some stores for the trip, as, had it been quite dark, it was the intention of Mr. Gypson to have remained up all night, and, with six or eight bags of sand for ballast, gave the command to ' let go.' The balloon rose with extreme velocity, shooting straight up at once, but turning round as it ascended. The match of the fireworks being lighted, they began to shoot forth cascades of coloured fires, which had a beautiful effect. It is impossible to form the feeblest idea of the appearance of London seen by night from the elevation we had now obtained—as nearly as could be judged from the apparent breadth of the river at the bridges, about 4000 feet. In the obscurity, all traces of houses and enclosures were lost sight of. I can compare it to nothing else than floating over a dark blue and boundless sea, spangled with hundreds of thousands of stars. The stars were the lamps. We could see them stretching over the river at the bridges, edging its banks, forming squares and long parallel lines of light in the streets, and solitary sparks—farther and farther apart, until they were altogether lost in the suburbs. The effect was too bewildering—too novel and extraordinary to allow of any of us even to speak ; we could only gaze on them in rapt and deep attention. The fireworks had commenced at Vauxhall, and we saw the blaze of light above the gardens very distinctly, as well as the exploding rockets ; and a flash of lightning now and then illumined the entire panorama, but too transitorily to catch any of its features. Above us the sky was deeply blue, studded with innumerable stars ; in fact, above, below, and around, we appeared sailing through a galaxy of twinkling points of light, incalculable and interminable. The impression made on my mind in these few minutes will never be effaced ; neither will the scene by which it was speedily followed.

"We were all going up, higher and higher, till we had attained the height of 7000 feet—namely, a mile and a quarter perpendicular—when Mr. Coxwell, who had charge of the valve-line, and was sitting in the hoop of the netting above us, informed Mr. Gypson that the balloon was getting very tense from the extreme rarefaction of the external air at the elevation we had attained. It may be necessary to explain that the top of a balloon is furnished with a ' butterfly valve,' a circular double-flap trap opening downwards by a cord which passes through the interior of the balloon, and closing again with a spring when sufficient gas has escaped, which it really does by reason of its buoyancy.   Mr. Coxwell pulled this line, and immediately afterwards we heard a noise, similar to, but not so loud as, the escape of spare steam in a locomotive ; and the lower part of the balloon collapsed rapidly, and appeared to fly up into the upper portion.   To a cry of alarm from Mr. Gypson, Mr. Coxwell answered, ' The valve is gone ! we are all dead men !' or words to that effect ; and that same instant the balloon began to fall with appalling velocity, the immense mass of loose silk surging and rustling frightfully over our heads, as it flapped to and fro, like the sail of a ship when tacking, between the network and cords by which our car was slung, retreating up away from us more and more into the head of the balloon.

"It was then suggested to throw over everything that might ease the balloon.   I had two bags of sand in my lap, which were cast away directly, and Mr. Coxwell lowered himself from the hoop into the car, when we all began to hunt about amongst our feet for whatever we could find.   Bags of ballast, and bottles of brandy and wine, were instantaneously thrown away ; but no effect was perceptible.   The wind still appeared to be rushing up past us at a fearful rate ; and to add to the horror of these few moments, the expiring fireworks floated on the air, and hung about the cordage of the balloon.   The lightning was playing about us.   We must have been then upwards of a mile from the earth.   The balloon began to oscillate frightfully, and our descent scarcely occupied two minutes.   Our velocity was fearful.   The parallelograms of light, too, formed by the squares, got visibly larger and larger, like an image in a phantasmagoria ; and the oscillation of the balloon began to subside, although the car was still swinging.   I attribute our preservation alone to the fact of the upper netting of the balloon having kept firm, preserving the empty silk in an umbrella-shape, which acted as a parachute.   We now saw the houses, the roofs of which appeared advancing to meet us ; and the next instant, as we dashed on their summits, the words, ' Hold hard !' burst simultaneously from all the party.   We were all directly thrown out of the car, along the ground, amidst the cordage and silk of the balloon, which appeared entirely emptied of gas.   Nobody was seriously hurt.   Torn clothes, smashed hats, and a few grazes and bruises were all the evils that resulted from *a descent of a mile without gas !* and above a mile from the gardens." Thither the aëronauts hastened, and were heartily cheered. Mr. Coxwell attributed the accident to the balloon bursting before the valve-line was touched ; the valve being found unmoved upon subsequently examining the balloon ; and Mr. Coxwell remained on the hoop until the concussion. The first impression of the party was that the valve itself had gone.

The following superb spectacle is described in the "Ascent of Mont Blanc," in *Blackwood :*—

"The sun at length went down behind the Aiguille du Goûté, and then, for two hours, a scene of such wild and wondrous beauty—of such inconceivable and unearthly splendour—burst upon me, that, spell-bound and almost trembling with the emotion its magnificence called forth—with every sense, and feeling, and thought absorbed by its brilliancy, I saw far more than the realization of the most gorgeous visions that opium or *hasheesh* could evoke, accomplished. At first, everything about us—above, around, below—the sky, the mountain, and the lower peaks—appeared one uniform creation of burnished gold, so brightly dazzling that, now our veils were removed, the eye could scarcely bear the splendour. As the twilight gradually crept over the lower world, the glow became still more vivid ; and presently, as the blue mists rose in the valleys, the tops of the higher mountains looked like islands rising from a filmy ocean—an archipelago of gold. By degrees this metallic lustre was softened into tints,—first orange, and then bright, transparent crimson, along the horizon, rising through the different hues, with prismatic regularity, until, immediately above us, the sky was a deep, pure blue, merging towards the east into glowing violet. The snow took its colour from these changes ; and every portion on which the light fell, was soon tinged with pale carmine, of a shade similar to that which snow at times assumes from some imperfectly explained cause, at high elevations—such, indeed, as I had seen, in early summer, upon the Furka and Faulhorn. These beautiful hues grew brighter as the twilight below increased in depth ; and it now came marching up the valley of the glaciers until it reached our resting-place. Higher and higher still, it drove the lovely glory of the sunlight before it, until at last the vast Dôme du Goûté and the summit itself stood out, icelike and grim, in the cold evening air, although the horizon still gleamed with a belt of rosy light.

*   *   *   *   *   *

"The stars had come out, and, looking over the plateau, I soon saw the moonlight lying cold and silvery on the summit, stealing slowly down the very track by which the sunset glories had passed upward and away. But it came so tardily that I knew it would be hours before we derived any actual benefit from the light. One after another the guides fell asleep, until only three or four remained round the embers of the fire, thoughtfully smoking their pipes. And then silence, impressive beyond expression, reigned over our isolated world. Often and often, from Chamouni, I had looked up at evening towards the darkening position of the Grands Mulets, and thought, almost with shuddering, how awful it must be for men to pass the night in such a remote, eternal, and frozen wilderness. And now I was lying there—in the very heart of its icebound and appalling solitude. In such close communion with Nature in her grandest aspect, with no trace of the actual living world beyond the mere speck that our little party formed, the mind was carried far away from its ordinary trains of thought—a solemn emotion of mingled awe and delight, and yet self-perception of abject nothingness, alone rose above every other feeling. A vast untrodden region of cold, and silence, and death, stretched out, far and away from us, on every side; but above, heaven, with its countless, watchful eyes, was over all!"

We conclude with a cento of Smith's pleasantries. The first is a quizzical glance at the scientific taste of the article entitled *Science and the Fairies :—*

"SCIENCE AND THE FAIRIES."

" When Father Time was in his prime,
    Some thousand years ago,
  Ere his beard was long, or his pinions strong,
    Or his locks as white as snow,

" In our merry land there dwelt a band
    Of tiny joyous elves,
  Who owned no order or command
    For any but themselves.

" And each one lived in a *cottage ornée*
   Of these elfin gamesome things,
By the tiger-moth thatched with his plume so gay,
   And glazed with a dragon-fly's wings.

" They danced all night in the moonbeams bright,
   And quaffed their cowslip wine;
Then hid their heads in their moth-down beds
   Ere day began to shine.

" And they revelled long, with their dance and song,
   Till a strange gigantic dame
A visit paid to their forest glade,
   And Science was her name.

" Her lungs were air-pumps of wondrous size ;
   Her breath blew forth a steam ;
And with oxyhydrogen her eyes
   Like meteor sparks did gleam.

" With triple cranks and rackwork neat,
   Her limbs and joints did move ;
And her vital powers were raised to heat
   With a Dr. Arnott's stove.

" The fairies gazed on this fearful sight,
   Then swift through the summer air,
In a dreadful fright they all took flight
   To the realms of my lord knows where.

" They have gone for aye, for since that day
   They no longer in England dwell ;
Lone is the glade and the leafy shade,
   And forsaken each quiet dell.

" And Science still her march keeps on ;
   But since that epoch dread,
Our legends old to their graves have gone,
   And Romance herself has fled."

Albert Smith had a horror of the set mirth of Bacchanalian songs, which he thus satirizes in a sort of burlesque Act of " The Social Parliament," intituled " An Act to amend the Laws relating to the giving of Dinner and Evening Parties :"

" And be it enacted That at all Dinners, public or private, the class of Songs known as ' Bacchanalian' be firmly put down, inasmuch as their usual effect is gloomy and depressing, and not promotive of Festivity ; and that the ' Soul lighting the Beacon of Truth in the Eye' be understood to mean the flushed Face and empty babbling of incipient Drunkenness ; and that ' Wreathing a Bowl with Flowers' be looked upon as an Absurdity, and as difficult to do as 'drowning Care' in it ; and that where there is no Bowl to wreathe, the affair is still more absurd. And that waiters be not rebuked for not knowing how to wreathe a Bowl when told, inasmuch as the only example of one existing in that state is the Glass Globe that holds the Gold Fish in the Filter-shop window, just outside Temple Bar."

Among Smith's contributions to subjects of the day, reported with much " go," we may mention his account of the " Eton Montem :"

"We love the pageantry of the Montem dearly, and we trust the period is far off when refinement and the schoolmaster shall have done their worst, and the holiday shall only be mentioned among the *fasti* of other days."

Circumstances combined to render this Montem, of 1841, far more attractive than it had been for several years. The presence of H.R.H. Prince Albert, for the first time, at its celebration, was one principal source of interest ; at the same time he had rendered himself extremely popular with the Eton scholars. Smith's report is not a mere sketch, but extends to some five closely-printed pages of the *Mirror*.

The *Literary World*, to which we have more than once referred, was not " commercially successful," although it won golden opinions from other journals. Theodore Hook, in the *John Bull*, pronounced it to be " without faults, and its tone to be that which is best suited to good and general society. Upon its discontinuance, my valuable contributor invited me to spend a day with him, a practice not uncommon, we suppose, to commemorate the *loss*. I accordingly went to Chertsey, and a pleasant ramble we had of it, not forgetting our walk to Addlestone, where we purchased a right royally carved oak chair of a curiosity dealer ; which Albert's father somewhat irreverently termed ' antique lumber,' though he, good soul, at the same time, sent me a seal-handle, which he had carved from a pile of old London Bridge !"

LEIGH HUNT.

THIS remarkable *littérateur*, or man of letters, has left his *Autobiography*, which his son tells us will be found less a relation of the events which happened to the writer, than of their impression on himself, and the feelings which they excited, or the ideas which they prompted. This characteristic of the writing is in a great degree a characteristic of the man, and thus the book reflects his own life more than on a first judgment it might be supposed to do. "His whole existence, and his habit of mind, were essentially literary. If it were possible to form any computation of the hours which he expended severally in literary labour and in recreation, after the manner of statistical comparisons, it would be found that the largest portion of his hours was devoted to hard work in the seclusion of the study, and that by far the larger portion of the allotted ' recreation' was devoted to reading, either in the study or in the society of his family.

"The artists knew too little of their sitter to catch the most familiar traits of his aspect. He was rather tall, as straight as an arrow, and looked slenderer than he really was. His hair was black and shining, and slightly inclined to wave; his head was high, his forehead straight and white, his eyes were black and sparkling, his general complexion dark. This is a faithful portrait, in which may be seen much of the reflection, the earnestness, and the affectionate thought that were such leading elements in his character.

"Few men were more attractive 'in society,' whether in a large company or over the fireside. His manners were peculiarly animated; his conversation varied, ranging over a great field of subjects, was moved and called forth by the response of his companion; and he was equally ready for the most lively topics or for the gravest reflections—his expression easily adapting itself to the tone of his companion's mind. With much freedom of manners he combined a spontaneous courtesy that never failed, and a considerateness derived from a ceaseless kindness of heart that invariably fascinated even strangers.

" This tendency to seclusion in the study had a very large and serious influence upon Leigh Hunt's life. It arose, as we have seen, from no dislike to society ; on the contrary, from youth to his very latest days, he preferred to have companions with him ; but it was necessary to be surrounded by his books. He used to ascribe this propensity to his two years' seclusion in prison ; and it is probable that that circumstance did contribute to fasten upon his character what must still have been an inborn tendency ; for it continued through all changes of position. His natural faculties conduced to make him regard all things that came before him chiefly from the intellectual or imaginative point of view.

" Seldom have writers so conscientiously verified all their statements of fact. He could work from early morning till far into midnight, every day, for months together ; and he had been a hard-working man all his life. For the greater part, even his recreation was auxiliary to his work. He had thus acquired a knowledge of authorities most unusual, and had heaps of information ' at his fingers' ends ;' yet he habitually verified even what he knew already, though it should be only for some parenthetical use. No tenderness could shake him from sternly rebuking or opposing where duty bade him do so ; and for a principle he was prepared to sacrifice everything, as he had sacrificed money and liberty. For all his excessive desire not to withhold his sympathy, not to hurt others' feelings, or not to overlook any possible excuse for infirmity, moral as well as physical, he never paltered with his own sincerity. He never swerved from what he believed to be the truth.

" In the course of his long life as a public writer, political and polemical animosities died away, and were succeeded by a broader recognition of common purposes and common endeavours, to which he had not a little contributed. His personal friendships embraced every party ; but through all, the spirit of his opinions, the qualities of his character, the unweariedness of his industry, continued the same."

We have condensed these ably-drawn characteristics from the " Introduction," by his eldest son.

The father of Leigh Hunt was a native of the West Indies, and came from Barbadoes, and afterwards settled in England. He then went into the Church, where he became a very po-

pular preacher of charity sermons; and one of his congregation bequeathed him £500 in testimony of the pleasure and
advantage she had derived from his discourses. But unfortunately he delighted some of his hearers too much over the
table; he was lively and agreeable, and had stories to tell of
lords whom he knew. He might have preached there, and
quoted Horace, and been gentlemanly and generous, and drunk
his claret, and no harm done.

In the pulpit of Bentinck Chapel, Lisson Green, Padding-
ton, Leigh Hunt's mother found her husband officiating. He
published a volume of sermons preached there, in which there
is little but elegance of diction and a graceful morality. His
delivery was the charm; and, to say the truth, he charmed
everybody but the owner of the chapel, who looked upon rent
as by far the most eloquent production of the pulpit. The
speculation ended with the preacher being horribly in debt.
Friends, however, were lavish of their assistance.

The father and mother took breath under the friendly roof
of Mr. West, the painter, who had married her aunt. The aunt
and niece were much of an age, and both fond of books. Mrs.
West, indeed, ultimately became a martyr to them; for the
physician declared that she lost the use of her limbs by sitting
in-doors.

From Newman Street the father went to live in Hampstead
Square, whence he occasionally used to go and preach at Southgate. The then Duke of Chandos had a seat in the neighbourhood of Southgate. "He heard my father preach," (says the
autobiographer), "and was so pleased with him, that he requested him to become tutor to his nephew, Mr. Leigh, which
the preacher did, and he remained with his Grace's family for
several years. The Duke was Master of the Horse, and originated the famous epithet of 'heaven-born minister,' applied
to Mr. Pitt. He was described as a man of great sweetness of
nature and good breeding. He was the grandson of Pope
and Swift's Duke of Chandos. Unfortunately for others, it
might be said of my father what Lady Mary Wortley said of
her kinsman, Henry Fielding, 'that give him his leg of
mutton and bottle of wine, and in the very thick of calamity
he would be happy for the time being.' Too well able to
seize a passing moment of enjoyment, he was always scheming, never performing; always looking forward with some
romantic plan which was sure to succeed, and never put in
practice; he wrote more titles of non-existing books than

Rabelais. I have spoken of the Duke of Chandos, to whose nephew, Mr. Leigh, my father became tutor. Mr. Leigh, who gave me his name, was son' of the duke's sister, Lady Caroline, and died member of parliament. He was one of the kindest and gentlest of men, addicted to those tastes for poetry and sequestered pleasure, which were conspicuous in his son, Lord Leigh; for all which reasons it would seem, and contrary to the usurping qualities in such cases made and provided, he and his family were subjected to one of the most extraordinary charges that a defeated claim ever brought drunken witnesses to set up,— no less than the murder and burial of a set of masons, who were employed in building a bridge, and whose destruction in the act of so doing was to bury both them and a monument which they knew of for ever ! To complete the romance of the tragedy, a lady, the wife of the usurper, presides over the catastrophe. She cries, 'Let go !' while the poor wretches are raising a stone at night-time, amidst a scene of torches and seclusion; and down goes the stone, aided by this tremendous father and son, and crushes the victims of her ambition ! She meant, as Cowley says Goliah did of David,

" ' At once their murder and their monument.'

If a charge of the most awful crimes could be dug up against the memories of such men as Thomson and Shenstone, or of Cowley, or Cowper, or the ' Man of Ross,' it could not have created more laughing astonishment in the minds of those who knew them, than such a charge against the family of the Leighs.

"It is a pleasure to me to know that I was ever born in so sweet a village as Southgate. I first saw the light there on the 19th of October, 1784. It found me cradled, not only in the lap of nature, which I love, but in the midst of truly English scenery, which I love beyond all other. Middlesex, in general, is a scene of trees and meadows, of ' greenery ' and nestling cottages; and Southgate is a prime specimen of Middlesex. It is a place lying out of the way of innovation, therefore it has the pure, sweet air of antiquity about it.

"Southgate lies in a cross-country road, running from Edmonton through Enfield Chase into Hertfordshire. It is in the parish of Edmonton; so that we may fancy the *Merry Devil* of that place still playing his pranks hereabouts, and helping innocent lovers to a wedding, as in the sweet little play attributed to Dryden. For as to any such devils going to a place less harmonious, it is not to be thought possible by good Christians. Furthermore, to show what classical ground is round about Southgate, and how it is associated with the best days of English genius, both old and new, Edmonton is the birthplace of Marlowe, the father of our drama, and of my friend Horne, his congenial celebrator. In Edmonton church-yard lies Charles Lamb; in Highgate churchyard, Coleridge; and in Hampstead have resided Shelley and Keats, to say nothing of Akenside before them, and of Steele, Arbuthnot, and others, before Akenside."

In 1792, Leigh Hunt went to school at Christ's Hospital, or Christ Hospital, as he terms it, "an ultra-sympathizing and timid boy." At this point he glances at the children's books of that day, and had a sort of prophetic notion of *Sandford and Merton*, to which Hunt was ever grateful. He tells us that the sight of boys fighting at school frightened him as something devilish, and affected him to tears; he never fought with a boy but once, and then it was on his own account: but though he beat him he was frightened,. and eagerly sought his good-will. He dared everything, however, from the biggest and strongest boys on other accounts; he could suffer better than act; "for the utmost activity of martyrdom is supported by a certain sense of passiveness."

The old discipline of the Blue Coat School is well described by Hunt, who tells us that he never was a fag to anybody; never made anybody's bed, or cleaned his shoes, or was the boy to get his tea, much less expected to stand as a screen for him before the fire, which Hunt had seen done; "though, upon the whole," he adds, "the boys were very mild governors." The whole of the account of Christ's Hospital, and the masters and boys, is an excellent portion of the book. By the way, one of the Blues (Le Grice, the elder), is said to have produced a little anonymous tract on the *Art of Poking the Fire*, which some persons never learn.

Hunt's note on his leaving Christ's Hospital is very touch-ing; he tells us—"For eight years I had gone bareheaded, save now and then a few inches of pericranium, when the little cap, no larger than a crumpet, was stuck on one side, to the mystification of the old ladies in the streets.

" I then cared as little for the rains as I did for anything else. I had now a vague sense of wordly trouble, and of a great and serious change in my condition; besides which, I had to quit my old cloisters, and my playmates, and long habits of all sorts; so that what was a very happy moment to schoolboys in general, was to me one of the most painful of my life. I surprised my schoolfellows and the master with the melancholy of my tears. I took leave of my books, of my friends, of my seat in the grammar-school, of my good-hearted nurse and her daughter, of my bed, of the cloisters, and of the very pump out of which I had taken so many delicious draughts, as if I should never see them again, though I meant to come every day. The fatal hat was put on; my father was come to fetch me,

> " ' We, hand in hand, with strange new steps and slow,
> Through Holborn took our meditative way.'

" I was then," Hunt says, "first deputy Grecian; and had the honour of going out of the school in the same rank, at the same age, and for the same reason as my friend Charles Lamb. The reason was, that I hesitated in my speech. It was understood that a Grecian was bound to deliver a public speech before he left school, and to go into the church afterwards; and as I could do neither of these things, a Grecian I could not be."

Leigh was then a poet, and his father collected his verses, and published them with a large list of subscribers. He has himself described this volume as a heap of imitations, some of them clever enough for a youth of sixteen, but absolutely worthless in every other respect.

Leigh Hunt made his first great advance towards celebrity as a dramatic critic. He diligently attended the theatres; resolutely refused to form any acquaintance with actors or managers, in order to preserve his independence. His criticisms of the actors of his day are severe, but were accepted by playgoers. His estimate of Mrs. Jordan is more considerate:—"In comedy nature had never been wanting; and there was one comic actress, who was nature herself in one of her most genial forms. This was Mrs. Jordan: who, though she was neither beautiful, nor handsome, nor even pretty, nor accomplished, nor 'a lady,' nor anything conventional or *comme il faut* whatsoever, yet was so pleasant, so cordial, so natural, so full of spirits, so healthily constituted in mind and body, had such a shapely leg withal, so charming a voice, and such a happy and happy-making expression of countenance, that she appeared something superior to all those requirements of acceptability, and to hold a patent from nature herself for our delight and good opinion. It is creditable to the feelings of society in general, that allowances are made for the temptations to which the stage exposes the sex; and in Mrs. Jordan's case these were not diminished by a sense of the like consideration due to princely restrictions, and to the manifest domestic dispositions of more parties than one. But she made even Methodists love her. A touching story is told of her apologizing to a poor man of that persuasion for having relieved him. He had asked her name; and she expressed a hope that he would not feel offended when the name was told him. On hearing it, the honest Methodist shed tears of pity and admiration, and trusted that he could not do wrong in begging a blessing on her head."

Here is a specimen of Leigh Hunt's reading at this period: "Goldsmith enchanted me. I knew no end of repeating passages out of the *Essays* and the *Citizen of the World*—such as the account of the Club, with its Babel of talk; of Beau Tibbs, with his dinner of ox-cheek, which 'his grace was so fond of;' and of the wooden-legged sailor, who regarded those that were lucky enough to have their 'legs shot off' on board king's ships (which entitled them to a penny a day), as being 'born with golden spoons in their mouths.' Then there was his correct, sweet style; the village-painting in his poems; the *Retaliation*, which, though on an artificial subject, seemed to me (as it yet seems) a still more genuine effusion; and, above all, the *Vicar of Wakefield*—with Burchell, whom I adored; and Moses, whom I would rather have been cheated with, than prosper; and the Vicar himself in his cassock, now presenting his 'Treatise against Polygamy' (in the family picture) to his wife, habited as Venus; and now distracted for the loss of his daughter Olivia, who is seduced by the villanous squire. I knew not whether to laugh at him, or cry with him most.

"These, with Fielding and Smollett, Voltaire, Charlotte Smith, Bage, Mrs. Radcliffe, and Augustus La Fontaine, were my favourite prose authors."

In 1805, Hunt's brother John set up a paper called the *News*, in Brydges Street, Leigh writing the theatricals for it. In 1807, he published a volume of *Critical Essays* on London performers, in which appeared much hastily-formed judgment; he particularly erred as to Munden, whose super-abundance of humour and expression he confounded with farce and buffoonery : Charles Lamb taught him better.

In 1808, the brothers Hunt set up the weekly paper, the *Examiner*, named after the *Examiner* of Swift and his brother Tories. Leigh Hunt did not think of their politics; he thought only of their wit and fine writing. Fortunately this incident occupies but a short chapter in the *Autobiography*. Leigh Hunt retired from the *Examiner* in 1808, contrary to the advice of friends, who are not always the best advisers. Some years afterwards, Leigh Hunt had an editorial successor, Mr. Fonblanque, who had all the wit for which he (Leigh) toiled, without making any pretensions to it. He was, in-deed, the genuine successor of the Swifts and Addisons them-selves, profuse of wit even beyond them, with superior poli-tical knowledge. The noble and independent, and at the same time liberal spirit in which the *Examiner* was con-ducted, drew all upon it : it took no side, it stood alone. Nevertheless, it acquired by its honest, plain speaking, sufficient influence to make it troublesome; and, at length, the Government of the day felt the necessity of punishing disinterestedness so glaring, and watched its opportunity. On three successive occasions, the attempt was made, and on each the editors escaped. The *Examiner's* first offence was defending a certain Major Hogan, who accused the Duke of York, as Commander-in-Chief, of favouritism and corruption. The second was the following curious remark :—" Of all monarchs since the Revolution, the successor of George III. will have the finest opportunity of becoming nobly popular." The third was an article against military flogging. These three cases of prosecution were not carried out, but the Government being exasperated by failure, the next blow was severe. This was a libellous attack on the Prince Regent, which Leigh Hunt replied to manfully, in such language against a reigning prince, as received castigation. The punish-ment was cruel; the brothers were fined a thousand pounds, and imprisoned for two years, in separate cells. It is a noble fact in their favour, that, being promised privately a remis-sion of the punishment if they would abstain for the future from unpleasant remarks, John and Leigh Hunt refused the offer. They also declined to allow a generous stranger to pay the fine in their stead.

Among three chapters on " Literary and Political Acquaintances," in the *Autobiography*, are many piquant anecdotes, such as the following :—

" Mr. Blanco White, on his arrival in England, was so anxious a student of the language, that he noted down in a pocket-book every phrase which struck him as remarkable. Observing the words ' Cannon Brewery ' on premises then standing in Knightsbridge, and taking the figure of a cannon which was over them, as the sign of the commodity dealt in, he put it down as a nicety of speech, ' The English *brew* cannon.'

"Another time, seeing maid-servants walking with children in a nursery-garden, he rejoiced in the progeny-loving character of the people among whom he had come, and wrote down, ' Public garden provided for nurses, in which they take the children to walk.'

" This gentleman, who had been called ' Blanco ' in Spain —which was a translation of his family name ' White,' and who afterwards wrote an excellent English book of entertaining letters on the Peninsula, under the Græco-Spanish appellation of Don Leucadio Doblado (White Doubled)—was author of a sonnet which Coleridge pronounced to be the best in the English language. I know not what Mr. Wordsworth said on this judgment. Perhaps he wrote fifty sonnets on the spot to disprove it. And in truth it was a bold sentence, and probably spoken out of a kindly, though not conscious, spirit of exaggeration. The sonnet, nevertheless, is truly beautiful. It is one beginning—

" ' Mysterious night ! when our first parent knew.' "

Leigh Hunt's account of his prison life is very interesting. He was ill when he entered on it, and this illness and want of exercise permanently injured his constitution ; but he passed the time pleasantly enough. He papered his prison-walls with roses, and painted the ceiling like a sky ; he furnished his room with a piano, with bookshelves, with his wife and all his children, and turned a little yard into an arbour of summer loveliness by the help of flowers and paint. Charles Lamb was a daily visitor. Thomas Moore introduced Byron, who afterwards came frequently to dine or chat, and was very courteous to the prisoner. And many other worthies, whom Leigh Hunt had not previously known, on this occasion introduced themselves, among whom were Charles Cowden Clarke, William Hazlitt, and Jeremy Bentham. He lost no old friends, and made many new ones. Shelley, though almost a stranger to him, made him what he calls " a princely offer," and Keats penned a sonnet, which was all he could do:

" WRITTEN ON THE DAY THAT MR. LEIGH HUNT LEFT PRISON.

> " What though, for showing truth to flattered state,
>   Kind Hunt was shut in prison, yet has he,
>   In his immortal spirit, been as free
> As the sky-searching lark, and as elate.
> Minion of grandeur ! think you he did wait ?
>   Think you he nought but prison-walls did see,
>   Till, so unwilling, thou unturn'dst the key ?
> Ah, no ! far happier, nobler was his fate !
> In Spenser's halls he strayed, and bowers fair,
>   Culling enchanted flowers ; and he flew
> With daring Milton through the fields of air ;
>   To regions of his own his genius true
> Took happy flights. Who shall his fame impair,
>   When thou art dead, and all thy wretched crew ?"

Strange persons flitted about the place; and Mr. Leigh Hunt, on taking temporary possession of his garret, was treated with this piece of delicacy, which he never should have thought of finding in a prison. " When I first entered its walls, I had been received by the under-gaoler, a man who seemed an epitome of all that was forbidding in his office. He was short and very thick, and had a hook-nose, a great severe countenance, and a bunch of keys hanging on his arm. A friend stopped short at sight of him, and said, in a melancholy tone, ' And this is the gaoler !'

" Honest old *Cave !* thine outside would have been un-worthy of thee, if upon further acquaintance I had not found it a very hearty outside—ay, and in my eyes, a very good-looking one, and as fit to contain the milk of human kindness that was in thee, as the husk of a cocoa. To show by one specimen the character of this man—I could never prevail on him to accept any acknowledgment of his kindness, greater than a set of tea-things, and a piece or two of old furniture, which I could not well carry away. I had, indeed, the pleasure of leaving him in possession of a room which I had papered ; but this was a thing unexpected, and which neither of us had supposed could be done. Had I been a prince, I would have forced on him a pension; being a journalist, I made him accept an *Examiner* weekly, which he lived for some years to relish his Sunday pipe with."

Mr. Hunt relates that Mr. Holme Sumner, on occasion of a petition from another prisoner, told the House of Commons that his room had a view over the Surrey hills, and that he (Hunt) was very well content with it. Among the magistrates who came to see the prisoners was a good-natured man, Lord Leslie, afterwards Earl of Rothes; he heard them with kindness, and his actions did not belie his countenance. The autobiographer's testimony is correct; a kinder-hearted man than the earl could not be imagined.

A surprise was a garden, which is thus described:—

" There was a little yard outside the room, railed off from another belonging to the neighbouring ward. This yard I shut in with green palings, adorned it with a trellis, bordered it with a thick bed of earth from a nursery, and even contrived to have a grass-plot. The earth I filled with flowers and young trees. There was an apple-tree, from which we managed to get a pudding the second year. As to my flowers, they were allowed to be perfect. Thomas Moore, who came to see me with Lord Byron, told me he had seen no such heart's-ease. I bought the *Parnaso Italiano* while in prison, and used often to think of a passage in it, while looking at this miniature piece of horticulture:—

" 'Mio picciol orto,
A me sei vigna, e campo, e selva, e prato.'—BALDI.
" ' My little garden,
To me thou'rt vineyard, field, and meadow, and wood.'

Here I wrote and read in fine weather, sometimes under an awning. In autumn my trellises were hung with scarlet-runners, which added to the flowery investment. I used to shut my eyes in my arm-chair, and affect to think myself hundreds of miles off.

" The first year of my imprisonment was a long pull uphill, but never was metaphor so literally verified, as by the sensation at the turning of the second. In the first year, all the prospect was that of the one coming; in the second, the days began to be scored off, like those of children at school preparing for a holiday."

Leigh Hunt entered the prison on the 3rd of February, 1813, and left it on the same day two years later. The next most noticeable event of his personal history is his friendship with Shelley. It was by Shelley's inducement that he undertook a journey to Italy, to co-operate with Shelley and Byron in a *Liberal* periodical which they proposed to bring out. The voyage proved a troublesome one. He engaged to embark in September, 1821, he actually embarked on November 16 of that year, and, after narrowly escaping shipwreck with his family, the whole of which he had on board, he was landed at Dartmouth. He embarked again in May, 1822, and reached Italy in June. Before he had been many days in Italy, his friend was drowned, and Byron showed signs of relenting in the matter of the *Liberal*. It was but a short connection, as might have been expected. Byron went to Greece, and Leigh Hunt stayed in Italy till 1825, after which he returned to England.

The chapters on Shelley, Keats, Lamb, and Coleridge are full of pleasant reading. It was during his intimacy with Keats that Leigh Hunt wrote the set of essays that have since become popular under the title of the *Indicator*, "which," says the author, "though it was published in a corner, owing to his want of funds for advertising it, and my ignorance of the best mode of circulating such things, an ignorance so profound, that I was not aware of its very self. Hazlitt and Lamb, and others, were greatly pleased with the *Indicator*. Hazlitt's favourite paper (for they liked it enough to have favourite papers), was the one on *Sleep* ; perhaps because there is a picture in it of a sleeping despot ; though he repeated, with more enthusiasm than he was accustomed to do, the conclusion about the parent and the bride. Lamb preferred the paper on *Coaches and their Horses*, that on the *Deaths of Little Children*, and (I think) the one entitled *Thoughts and Guesses on Human Nature*. Shelley took to the story of the *Fair Revenge ;* and the paper that was most liked by Keats, if I remember, was the one on a hot summer's day, entitled *A Now*. He was with me while I was writing and reading it to him, and contributed one or two of the passages." Keats first published in the *Indicator* his beautiful poem *La Belle Dame sans Merci,* and the dream after reading Dante's *Episode of Paulo and Francesca.*

At Home in England opens with this delightful picture :— Returning from Italy—" In England I was at home ; and in English scenery I found my old friend ' pastoral ' still more pastoral. It was like a breakfast of milk and cream after yesterday's wine. The word itself was more verified : for pastoral comes from pasture ; it implies cattle feeding, rather than vines growing, or even goats browsing ; and here they were in plenty, very different from the stall-fed and rarely seen cattle of Tuscany. The country around was almost all pasture ; and beloved Hampstead was near, with home in its churchyard as well as in its meadows. Again I wandered with transport through

> " ' Each alley green,
> And every bosky bourn from side to side,—
> My daily walks and ancient neighbourhood.'

Only for ' bosky bourn ' you must read the ponds in which Shelley used to sail his boats, and very little brooks unknown to all but the eyes of their lovers. The walk across the fields from Highgate to Hampstead, with ponds on one side, and Caen Wood on the other, used to be (and I hope is still, for I have not seen it for some years) one of the prettiest in England. *Poets'* (vulgarly called Millfield) *Lane* crossed it on the side next Highgate, at the foot of a beautiful slope, which in June was covered with daisies and buttercups ; and at the other end it descended charmingly into the Vale of Health, out of which rose the highest ground in Hampstead. It was in this spot, and in relation to it and about this time (if I may quote my own verses in illustration of what I felt), that I wrote some lines to ' Gipsy June,' apostrophizing that brown and happy month on the delights which I found again in my native country, and on the wrongs done him by the pretension of the month of May.

*　　*　　*　　*

> " ' May, the jade, with her fresh cheek,
> And the love the bards bespeak,—
> May, by coming first in sight,
> Half defrauds thee of thy right,
> For her best is shared by thee
> With a wealthier potency ;
> So that thou dost bring us in
> A sort of May-time masculine,
> Fit for action or for rest,
> As the luxury seems the best,—
> Bearding now the morning breeze,
> Or in love with paths of trees,
> Or disposed full length to lie,
> With a hand-enshaded eye,

On thy warm and golden slopes,
Basker in the buttercups ;
List'ning with nice distant ears
To the shepherd's clapping shears,
Or the next field's laughing play
In the happy wars of hay,
While its perfume breathes all over,
Or the bean comes fine, or clover.
Oh ! could I walk around the earth
With a heart to share my mirth,
With a look to love me ever,
Thoughtful much, but sullen never,
I could be content to see
June and no variety,
Loitering here, and living there,
With a book and frugal fare,
With a finer gipsy time,
And a cuckoo in the clime,
Work at morn and mirth at noon,
And sleep beneath the sacred moon.'

"The pleasantest idea which I can conceive of this world, as far as oneself and one's enjoyments are concerned, is to possess some favourite home in one's native country, and then travel over all the rest of the globe with those whom we love ; always being able to return, if we please ; and ever meeting with new objects, as long as we choose to stay away.   And I suppose this is what the inhabitants of the world will come to, when they have arrived at years of discretion, and railroads will have hastened the maturity."

After his removal to Kensington :—" Here, sometimes in the Gardens, sometimes in the quondam Nightingale-lane of Holland House (now partially diverted), I had the pleasure of composing the *Palfrey*, the scenes of which are partly laid in the place.   Here (with the exception of a short interval at Wimbledon) I wrote, besides reviews and shorter articles, one of the dramatic pieces above mentioned, the criticism on *Imagination and Fancy*, and *Wit and Humour ;* the *Stories from the Italian Poets ;* the *Jar of Honey ;* the criticism on the *Book for a Corner ;* a portion of the *Town* (most of which had been produced long before) ; and lastly, the greater part of the work which the reader is now perusing."

CHIARE, FRESCHE, E DOLCE ACQUE.

THE CELEBRATED CANZONE OF PETRARCH.

" Clear, fresh, and dulcet streams,
  Which the fair shape, who seems
  To me sole woman, haunted at noontide ;
  Bough, gently interknit
  (I sigh to think of it),
  Which formed a rustic chair for her sweet side ;
  And turf, and flowers bright-eyed,
  O'er which her folded gown
  Flowed like an angel's down ;
  And you, O holy air and hushed,
  Where first my heart at her sweet glances gushed ;
  Give ear, give ear, with one consenting,
  To my last words, my last and my lamenting.

" If 'tis my fate below,
  And Heaven will have it so,
  That love must close these dying eyes in tears.
  May my poor dust be laid
  In middle of your shade,
  While my soul, naked, mounts to its own spheres.
  The thought would calm my fears,
  When taking, out of breath,
  The doubtful step of death ;
  For never could my spirit find
  A stiller port after the stormy wind ;
  Nor in more calm abstracted bourne,
  Slip from my travailed flesh, and from my bones outworn.

" Perhaps, some future hour,
  To her accustomed bower
  Might come the untamed, and yet the gentle she ;
  And where she saw me first,
  Might turn with eyes athirst,
  And kinder joy to look again for me ;
  Then, O the charity !
  Seeing betwixt the stones
  The earth that held my bones,
  A sigh for very love at last
  Might ask of Heaven to pardon me the past ;
  And Heaven itself could not say nay,
  As with her gentle veil she wiped the tears away.

" How well I call to mind
  When from those bowers the wind

Shook down upon her bosom flower on flower ;
And there she sat, meek-eyed,
In midst of all that pride,
Sprinkled and blushing through an amorous shower.
Some to her hair paid dower,
And seemed to dress the curls,
Queen-like, with gold and pearls ;
Some, snowing, on her drapery stopped ;
Some on the earth, some on the water dropped ;
While others, fluttering from above,
Seemed wheeling round in pomp, and saying ' Here reigns Love.'

" How often then I said,
Inward, and filled with dread,
' Doubtless this creature came from Paradise !'
For at her look the while,
Her voice, and her sweet smile,
And heavenly air, truth parted from mine eyes :
So that, with long-drawn sighs,
I said, as far from men,
' How came I here—and when ?'
I had forgotten ; and, alas !
Fancied myself in heaven, not where I was ;
And from that time till this, I bear
Such love for the green bower, I cannot rest elsewhere."

The rest of Leigh Hunt's life was passed in literary projects,
in pleasant communing with his numerous literary friends,
among whom were Barry Cornwall, Thomas Carlyle, the
Brownings, and many others, in attempts to live cheerfully
under affliction, and, chief of all, in accumulating book-lore.
His closing years were rendered more happy by an opportune
pension of £200 a year which Lord John Russell obtained
for him. He died on the 28th of August, 1859, and was
buried, according to his wish, in Kensal Green Cemetery.

We must now take a farewell glance at a few of the many
contributions of Leigh Hunt to popular reading. Among
them are Egerton Webbe's epigrams, which he bantered in the
London Journal with the following exquisite imitations. He
has not even forgotten (as the *Journal* observed) the solemn
turn of the heads of the epigrams, " Concerning Flavius "—
" On the same "—" To Antonius concerning Lepidus," &c.,
" nor the ingenious art with which Martial contrives to have
a reason asked him, for what he is bent on explaining." The
banters, it is true, " have this drawback ; that being good
jokes upon bad ones, they cannot possibly convey the same

impression;" but the reader is willing to guess it through the wit.

"Concerning Jones.

Jones eats his lettuces undressed ;
D' you ask the reason ?   'Tis confessed,—
That is the way Jones likes them best."

"To Smith, concerning Thomson.

Smith, Thomson puts no claret on his board ;
D' you ask the reason ?—Thomson can't afford."

"To Gibbs, concerning his Poems.

You ask me if I think your poems good ;
If I could praise your poems, Gibbs,—I would."

"Concerning the Same.

Gibbs says his poems a sensation make ;—
But Gibbs, perhaps, is under a mistake."

"To Thomson, concerning Dixon and Jackson.

How Dixon can with Jackson bear,
You ask me, Thomson, to declare ;—
Thomson, Dixon's Jackson's heir."

Were ever three patronymics jumbled so together, or with such a delightful importance !

In the chapter on Playwriting is related a very gratifying account of the author's *Legend of Florence* being welcomed and successful after it had been rejected at another theatre. After describing the reception of the play in the green-room, the author says : " Finally, to crown all, in every sense of the word, Loyal as well as metaphorical, the Queen did the play the honour of coming to see it twice (to my knowledge)— four times, according to that of Madame Vestris, who ought to have known.   Furthermore, when her Majesty saw it first, she was gracious and good-natured enough to express her approbation of it to the manager in words which she gave him permission to repeat to me; and furthermost of all, some years afterwards she ordered it to be repeated before her at Windsor Castle, thus giving me a local memory in the place, which Surrey himself might have envied, and which Warton would certainly have hung, as a piece of its tapestry, with a sonnet."

Another incident is worth quoting.   Mr. Hunt considered that his sufferings in the cause of Reform, and his career as a man of letters, rendered him not undeserving of a pension. Lord Melbourne in this and the previous reign declined the grant; for Mr. Hunt had twice during the Melbourne administration received grants from the Royal Bounty Fund of two hundred pounds each; once during the reign of King William, and the second after the accession of her Majesty. It subsequently turned out, that Lord Melbourne considered it proper for no man to have a pension given him by one sovereign, who had been condemned in a court of law for opposing another.

The last moments are touchingly described by his son: "When Leigh Hunt went to visit his relative at Putney, he still carried with him his work and the books he more immediately wanted. Although his bodily powers had been giving way, his most conspicuous qualities—his memory for books, and his affection—remained; and when his hair·was white, when his ample chest had grown slender, when the very proportion of his height had visibly lessened, his step was still ready, and his dark eyes brightened at every happy expression, and at every thought of kindness. His death was simply exhaustion: he broke off his work to lie down and repose. So gentle was the final approach, that he scarcely recognized it till the very last, and then it came without terrors. His physical suffering had not been severe; at the latest hour he said that his only 'uneasiness' was failing breath. And that failing breath was used to express his sense of the inexhaustible kindnesses he had received from the family who had been so unexpectedly made his nurses,—to draw from one of his sons, by minute, eager, and searching questions, all that he could learn about the latest vicissitudes and growing hopes of Italy,—to ask the friends and children around him for news of those whom he loved,—and to send love and messages to the absent who loved him."

The spirit of the poet was active and cheerful when he wrote the following set of blithe images in December, 1840, on the birth of the Princess Royal :—

> "Behold where thou dost lie,
> Heeding naught, remote on high !
> Naught of all the news we sing
> Dost thou know, sweet ignorant thing ;
> Naught of planet's love nor people's ;
> Nor dost hear the giddy steeples

Carolling of thee and thine,
As if heaven had rained them wine ;
Nor dost care for all the pains
Of ushers and of chamberlains,
Nor the doctor's learned looks,
Nor the very bishop's books,
Nor the lace thut wraps thy chin,
No, nor for thy rank a pin.
E'en thy father's loving hand
Nowise dost thou understand,
When he makes thee feebly grasp
His finger with a tiny clasp ;
Nor dost thou know thy very mother's
Balmy bosom from another's,
Though thy small blind eyes pursue it ;
Nor the arms that drew thee to it ;
Nor the eyes, that while they fold thee,
Never can enough behold thee !"

MEN COMPARED WITH BEES.

(*From a continuation of the " Indicator.*")

". . It has been thought, that of all animated creation, the bees present the greatest moral likeness to man ; not only because they labour and lay up stores, and live in communities, but because they have a form of government and a monarchy. Virgil immortalized them after a human fashion. A writer in the time of Elizabeth, probably out of compliment to the Virgin Queen, rendered them *dramatis personœ*, and gave them a whole play to themselves. Above all, they have been held up to us, not only as a likeness, but as ' a great moral lesson ;' and this, not merely with regard to the duties of occupation, but the form of their polity. A monarchical government, it is said, is natural to man, because it is an instinct of nature : the very bees have it.

" It may be worth while to inquire a moment into the value of this argument ; not as affecting the right and title of our Sovereign Lord King William the Fourth, but for its own sake, as well as for certain little collateral deductions. And, in the first place, we cannot but remark how unfairly the animal creation are treated, with reference to the purposes of moral example. We degrade or exalt them, as it suits the lesson we desire to inculcate. If we rebuke a drunkard or a sensualist, we think we can say nothing severer to him than to recommend him not to make ' a beast of himself ;' which is very unfair towards the beasts, who are no drunkards, and behave themselves as nature intended. A horse has no habit of drinking; he does not get a red face with it. The stag does not go reeling home to his wives. On the other hand, we are desired to be as faithful as a dog, as bold as a lion, as tender as a dove; as if the qualities denoted by these epithets were not to be found among ourselves. But, above all, the bee is the argument. Is not the honey-bee, we are asked, a wise animal?—We grant it.— 'Doth he not improve each passing hour?"—He is pretty busy, it must be owned—as much occupied at eleven, twelve, and one o'clock, as if his life depended on it.—'Does he not lay up stores?'—He does. —'Is he not social?' 'Does he not live in communities?' There can be no doubt of it.—Well, then, he has a monar-chical government; and does not that clearly show that a monarchy is the instinct of nature? Does it prove, by an unerring rule, that the only form of government in request among the obeyors of instinct, is the only one naturally fitted for man?

"In answering the spirit of this question, we shall not stop to inquire how far it is right as to the letter, or how many different forms of polity are to be found among other animals, such as the crows, the beavers, the monkeys; neither shall we examine how far instinct is superior to reason, nor why the example of man himself is to go for nothing. We will take for granted, that the bee is the wisest animal of all, and that it is a judicious thing to consider his manners and customs, with reference to their adoption by his inferiors, who keep him in hives. This naturally leads us to inquire, whether we could not frame all our systems of life after the same fashion. We are busy, like the bee; we are gregarious, like him; we make provision against a rainy day; we are fond of flowers and the country; we occasionally sting, like him; and we make a great noise about what we do. Now, if we resemble the bee in so many points, and his political instinct is so admirable, let us reflect what we ought to become in other respects, in order to attain to the full benefit of his example.

* * * *

"But we have not yet got half through the wonders, which are to modify human conduct by the example of this wise, industrious, and monarch-loving people. Marvellous changes must be effected, before we have any general preten-sion to resemble them, always excepting in the aristrocratic particular. For instance, the aristocrats of the hive, however unmasculine in their ordinary mode of life, are the only males. The working-classes, like the sovereign, are all females ! How are we to manage this ? We must convert, by one sudden metamorphosis, the whole body of our agricultural and manufacturing population into women ! Mrs. Cobbett must displace her husband, and tell us all about Indian corn. There must be not a man in Nottingham, except the Duke of Newcastle ; and he trembling lest the Queen should send for him. The tailors, bakers, carpenters, gardeners, must all be Mrs. Tailors and Mrs. Bakers. The very name of John Smith must go out. The Directory must be Amazonian. This commonalty of women must also be, at one and the same time, the operatives, the soldiers, the virgins, and the legislators of the country ! They must make all we want, fight all our enemies, and even get up a queen for us when necessary ; for the sovereigns of the hive are often of singular origin, being manufactured ! literally 'made to order,' and that, too, by dint of their eating ! They are fed and stuffed into royalty ! The receipt is, to take any ordinary female bee in its infancy, put it into a royal cradle or cell, and feed it with a certain kind of jelly ; upon which its shape alters into that of sovereignty, and her majesty issues forth, royal by the grace of stomach. This is no fable, as the reader may see on consulting any good history of bees. In general, several queen-bees are made at a time, in case of accidents ; but each, on emerging from her apartment, seeks to destroy the other, and one only remains living in one hive. The others depart at the head of colonies, like Dido.

" To sum up, then, the conditions of human society were it to be remodelled after the example of the bee, let us conclude with drawing a picture of the state of our beloved country, so modified. Imprimis, all our working people would be females, wearing swords, never marrying, and occasionally making queens. They would grapple with their work in a prodigious manner, and make a great noise. Secondly, our aristocracy would be all males, never working, never marrying (except when sent for), always eating or sleeping, and annually having their throats cut. The bee massacre takes place in July ; when, accordingly, all our nobility and gentry would be out of town, with a vengeance ! The women would draw their swords, and hunt and stab them all about the West end, till Brompton and Bayswater would be choked with slain.

" Thirdly, her Majesty the Queen would either succeed to a quiet throne, or, if manufactured, would have to eat a prodigious quantity of jelly in her infancy; and so after growing into proper sovereign condition, would issue forth, and begin her reign either with killing her royal sisters, or leading forth a colony to America or New South Wales. She would then take to husband some noble lord for the space of one calendar hour, and dismissing him to his dulness, proceed to lie in of twelve thousand little royal highnesses in the course of the eight following weeks, with others too numerous to mention; all which princely generation with little exception, would forthwith give up their title, and divide themselves into lords or working-women as it happened; and so the story would go round to the end of the chapter, bustling, working, and massacring :—and here ends the sage example of the monarchy of the bees.

" We must observe, nevertheless, before we conclude, that however ill and tragical the example of the bees may look for human imitation, we are not to suppose that the fact is anything like so melancholy to themselves. Perhaps it is no evil at all, or only so for the moment. The drones, it is true, seem to have no fancy for being massacred : but we have no reason to suppose that they, or any of the rest concerned in this extraordinary instinct, are aware of the matter beforehand; and the same is to be said of the combats between the queen-bees; they appear to be the result of an irresistible impulse, brought about by the sudden pressure of a necessity. Bees appear to be very happy, during far the greater portion of their existence. A modern writer, of whom it is to be lamented that a certain want of refinement stopped short his perceptions, and degraded his philosophy from the finally expedient into what was fugitively so, has a passage on this point, as agreeable as what he is speaking of, 'A bee among the flowers in spring,' says Dr. Paley, 'is one of the cheerfullest objects that can be looked upon. Its life appears to be all enjoyment, *so busy and so pleased.*'"

BOBART, A CHARACTER.

" On returning from town, which I did on the top of an Oxford coach, I was relating a story to the singular person who drove it (Bobart, who had been a collegian), when a man who was sitting behind surprised us with the excess of his laughter.

On asking him the reason, he touched his hat, and said, ' Sir, I'm his footman.' Such are the delicacies of the livery, and the glorifications of their masters, with which they entertain the kitchen.

" This Bobart was a very curious person. I have noticed him in the *Indicator*, in the article on ' coaches.' He was a descendant of a horticultural family, who had been keepers of the Physic Garden, at Oxford, and one of whom palmed a rat upon the learned world for a dragon, by stretching out its skin into wings. Tillimant Bobart (for such was the name of our charioteer) had been at college himself, probably as a sizar ; but having become proprietor of a stage-coach, he thought fit to be his own coachman ; and he received your money and touched his hat like the rest of the fraternity. He had a round, red face, with eyes that stared, and showed the white ; and having become, by long practice, an excellent capper of verses, he was accustomed to have bouts at that pastime with the collegians whom he drove. It was curious to hear him whistle and grunt, and urge on his horses with the other customary euphonics of his tribe, and then see him flash his eye round upon the capping gentleman who sat behind him, and quote his never-failing line out of Virgil or Horace. In the evening (for he only drove his coach half way to London) he divided his solace after his labours between his book and his brandy-and-water ; but I am afraid with a little too much of the brandy, for his end was not happy. There was eccentricity in the family, without anything much to show for it. The Bobart who invented the dragon chuckled over the secret for a long time with a satisfaction that must have cost him many falsehoods ; and the first Bobart that is known used to tag his beard with silver on holidays."

" If female society had not been wanting, I should have longed to reside at an university ; for I have never seen trees, books, and a garden to walk in, but I saw my natural home, provided there was no ' monkery' in it. I have always thought it a brave and great saying of Mohammed,—' There is no monkery in Islam.'

> " ' From women's eyes this doctrine I derive :
> They are the books, the arts, the academies,
> Which show, contain, and nourish all the world.' "

LEIGH HUNT'S MARRIAGE.

This is the first mention that the writer makes of his marriage, and it is a striking example of the manner in which, for various reasons, but principally out of delicacy to living persons, he felt himself bound to pass over, with very slight allusions, the greater part of his personal and private life. In the present instance there was no practical reason for this reserve, unless it was that if the author had entered upon domestic matters, he might, with his almost exaggerated sense of the active obligations which truth-speaking involved, have felt bound to enter into personal questions, and perhaps judgments, which he thought it better to waive. The dominating motives for this characteristic reserve are treated in the closing chapter of the volume.   Leigh Hunt was married in 1809, to Marianne, the daughter of Thomas and Ann Kent.   Mr. Kent had died comparatively young.   His widow had obtained an independent livelihood as a dressmaker, in rather a "high" connection; amongst her acquaintance was the young editor, who fell in love with the eldest daughter, and married her after a long courtship.   The bride was the reverse of handsome, and without accomplishments; but she had a pretty figure, beautiful black hair which reached down to her knees, magnificent eyes, and a very unusual natural turn for plastic art.   She was an active and thrifty housewife, until the curious malady with which she was seized totally undermined her strength. Mrs. Kent, her mother, who had perhaps acquired some harshness of character in a very hard school of adversity, never quite succeeded in retaining the regard of her son-in-law— one reason, perhaps, for the reserve which has been noticed. Mrs. Kent made, indeed, some fearful mistakes in her sternness; but she was really a very kind-hearted woman, only too anxious to please, and faithful in the attachments which she formed, even when disappointed.   She subsequently married Mr. Rowland Hunter, a man of keen observation and simple mind, who survived to a great age, and whose hearty friendship was cordially appreciated by Leigh Hunt as they both advanced in years.   Rowland Hunter was the nephew and successor of Johnson, the well-known bookseller in St. Paul's Churchyard, and the early patron of the poet Cowper.   Johnson acquired celebrity for his success in business, his intelligence, and his peculiar hospitality; and Mr. Hunter continued his custom of keeping open-house weekly for literary men, the friends of literature, and persons of any individual mark. At his house, the young author encountered a great variety of minds, and most unquestionably derived great advantage from the opportunity. His conversation frequently turned upon his recollections of these gatherings, and it was in this house that he formed many of his literary and personal acquaintances.

"A DAY WITH THE READER."

" I projected," says Leigh Hunt, " a poem to be called *A Day with the Reader*. I proposed to invite the reader to breakfast, dine, and sup with me, partly at home, and partly at a country inn, in order to vary the circumstances. It was to be written both gravely and gaily, in an exalted, or in a lowly strain, according to the topics of which it treated. The fragment on Paganini was a part of the exordium :

> " ' So play'd of late to every passing thought,
> With finest change (might I but half as well
> So write !) the pale magician of the bow,' etc.

" I wished to write in the same manner, because Paganini, with his violin, could move both the tears and the laughter of his audience, and (as I have described him doing in the verses) would now give you the notes of birds in trees, and even hens feeding in a farm-yard (which was a corner into which I meant to take my companion), and now melt you into grief and pity, or mystify you with witchcraft, or put you into a state of lofty triumph like a conqueror. That phrase of ' smiting' the chords,—

> " ' He smote ;—and clinging to the serious chords
> With godlike ravishment,' etc.—

was no classical commonplace ; nor, in respect to impression on the mind, was it exaggeration to say, that from a single chord he would fetch out

> " ' The voice of quires, and weight
> Of the built organ.'

" Paganini, the first time I saw and heard him, and the first moment he struck a note, seemed literally to strike it ; to give it a blow. The house was so crammed that, being

among the squeezers in 'standing room' at the side of the pit,
I happened to catch the first sight of his face through the arm
akimbo of a man who was perched up before me, which made
a kind of frame for it; and there, on the stage, in that frame,
as through a perspective glass, were the face, bust, and raised
hand, of the wonderful musician, with his instrument at his
chin, just going to commence, and looking exactly as I have
described him.

> " ' His hand,
> Loading the air with dumb expectancy,
> Suspended, ere it fell, a nation's breath.

> " ' He *smote ;*—and clinging to the serious chords
> With godlike ravishment, drew forth a breath,—
> So deep, so strong, so fervid thick with love,—
> Blissful, yet laden as with twenty prayers,
> That Juno yearn'd with no diviner soul
> To the first burthen of the lips of Jove.

> " ' The exceeding mystery of the loveliness
> Sadden'd delight ; and with his mournful look,
> Dreary and gaunt, hanging his pallid face'
> 'Twixt his dark flowing locks, he almost seem'd,
> To feeble or to melancholy eyes,
> One that had parted with his soul for pride,
> And in the sable secret liv'd forlorn.'

" To show the depth and identicalness of the impression
which he made on everybody, foreign or native, an Italian
who stood near me, said to himself, after a sigh, ' O Dio !' and
this had not been said long, when another person in the same
manner uttered the words, ' O Christ !' Musicians pressed
forward from behind the scenes, to get as close to him as
possible ; and they could not sleep at night for thinking of
him."

DOCTOR MAGINN.

ONE of the finest humorists of the day was William Maginn, a native of Cork, born in 1793.

In *Bentley's Miscellany*, were collected in 1859, several papers, whence is derived the following :

"William Maginn is no more. The bright spirit whose wit was the delight of thousands—whose learning won the admiration of a quarter of a century—whose poetry could win the applause of Byron himself, and whose simplicity and modesty were the charm of all who knew him, is now passed away. The picturesque little village of Walton-on-Thames now contains all that was mortal of one of the most distinguished critics and scholars of the age. He died in his 54th year, August, 1842, leaving a wife and family to lament their irreparable loss."

Born in 1794, the precocity of his talents astonished all who knew him. He entered college in his tenth year, and passed through it with distinction. For a few years he assisted his father in conducting a large academy at Cork; but on the first appearance of *Blackwood's Magazine*, he edited that journal in Edinburgh. Having by his connection with it, and his contributions to the *Quarterly Review*, fully established his name as a writer of first-rate ability, he came to London, and was soon appointed to the joint editorship of the *Standard*, with the amiable and learned Dr. Giffard. On the establishment of *Bentley's Miscellany*, Maginn became a contributor to its pages; and to him the public are indebted for the able series of articles entitled the *Shakspeare Papers*.

The following sketch of Maginn, as he appeared about this period, was drawn by Dr. Macnish, better known by the name of the *Modern Pythagorean* :—

"I dined to-day at the Salopian with Dr. Maginn. He is a most remarkable fellow. His flow of ideas is incredibly quick, and his articulation is so r e pid, that it is difficult to follow him.

He is altogether a person of vast acuteness, celerity of apprehension, and indefatigable activity both of body and mind. He is about my own height, but I could allow him an inch round the chest. His forehead is very finely developed, his organ of language and ideality large, and his reasoning faculties excellent. His hair is quite gray, though he does not look more than forty. I imagined he was much older-looking, and that he wore a wig. While conversing, his eye is never for a moment at rest ; in fact, his whole body is in motion, and he keeps scrawling grotesque figures upon the paper before him, and rubbing them out again as fast as he draws them. He and Giffard, are, as you know, joint editors of the *Standard.*

" I had some queer chat with O'Doherty. I did not measure Maginn's chest, but I examined his head. He has a very fine development of the intellectual power, especially ideality and wit, which are both unusually large. His language is also large, and he has much firmness and distinctiveness, which better accounts for the satirical bent of his genius. That beautiful tale, the *City of the Demons,* he informed me, he wrote quite off-hand. He writes with vast rapidity. He speaks French, Italian, and German fluently ; these, together with a first-rate knowledge of Latin, Greek, and English, make him master of six languages, so that you can allow him one. He is altogether a most remarkable man. Indeed, I consider him quite equal to Swift, and, had his genius, like Swift's, been concentrated in separate works, instead of being squandered with wasteful prodigality in newspapers and magazines, I have no doubt it would have been considered equally original and wonderful. He was much tickled with the apotheosis which I recited to him. I told him you were a master of seven languages. Had you been present, I would have confined your abilities to a smaller number, lest he should have taken into his head to try you with the other. The letter-press of the *Gallery of Literary Portraits* he hit off at a moment's notice."

Dr. Moir of Musselburgh, the distinguished poet, says :

" In a portion, and no inconsiderable one, of the literary world, Dr. Maginn is known, *par excellence,* as *the Doctor,* in the same way as Professor Wilson is recognised as *the Professor.* By every one capable of judging, the powers of Dr. Maginn are acknowledged to be of the highest order, from the *City of the Demons,* the *Man in the Bell, Colonel Pride,* the *Shakspeare Papers* and many other things, posterity will be able to appreciate him."

Such was William Maginn. It is, to be sure, enviable praise to be associated with so brilliant a name as Swift ; but, much as we admire the writings of the Dean, we must in justice say that they are far short of those of Maginn, for Swift was morose and cynical and austere, Maginn was kind and gentle and child-like. Swift's whole conversation was irony or sarcasm; Maginn's was entirely genial and anecdotical, and free from bitterness.

A Correspondent describes Maginn in the zenith of his glory—which radiated from *John Bull* or sent forth a rich stream of light from the pages of *Fraser*. "His conversation was careless and off-hand, and but for the impediment of speech, would have the charm of a rich comedy. His choice of words was such as I have rarely met with in any of my contemporaries; for, in my days, it had become the vogue to corrupt English in many ways, to bring down your subject by homely, if not coarse phrases, and to neglect all those adjuncts to reasoning and to wit which a true sense of our language affords."

Two years hence our Correspondent describes Maginn as greatly changed. "His hair was now very thin, and scattered over an anxious brow; the sweet mildness of his eye was gone, his speech was more faltering than ever; many moments elapsed before he could utter a word, a natural defect was heightened by nervous debility, and the approach of his last fatal disease. Still, broken up and impaired as he was, there were genuine bursts of humour, a scholar-like nicety of expression; above all, a humbled and, perhaps, chastened spirit was apparent. We had a day of talk of the sterling and standard writers of England; themes fitted for the Augustan age flowed freely. Swift, was, perhaps, the model of Maginn, certainly, he was the object of his adoration; and, as he aptly quoted him, true Irish humour played upon the features of the modern satirist.

* * * * * *

"I saw Maginn no more. I was not surprised when I learned that slow disease had wasted his limbs and brought him to the brink of the grave, but had left his intellect bright and clear to the last. That was a wonderful mind which could stand the wear and tear to which poor Maginn subjected it. His last thoughts, as they are recorded, were of Literature and of Homer.

"How like a dream it now seems, to suppose Maginn, the soul and centre of a certain circle, who hung upon his appearance, and adulated his talents! And now, how the memory of his brief, feverish existence has passed away, revived only by the accents of compassion, or adduced to point a moral. How completely was his fame limited to a certain circle! How un-English was his reputation—how non-European his celebrity!

"When I last saw Maginn I knew him not; his manner was unobtrusive; the circle who stood around him had scarcely heard his name. He stood behind, in a retired part of the room. Unseen he went away—no one missed him. I cannot close this sketch better than by appending the following exquisite lines, which illustrate the versatile genius of Dr. Maginn :—

"'THE MOCKINGS OF THE SOLDIERS.

"'FROM ST. MATTHEW.

" ' Plant a crown upon His head,
　　Royal robe around Him spread ;
　　See that His imperial hand
　　Grasps as fit the sceptral wand :
　　Then before Him bending low,
　　As become His subjects, bow ;
　　Fenced within our armed ring,
　　Hail Him, hail Him, as our King !

" ' Plaited was of thorns the crown,
　　Trooper's cloak was royal gown ;
　　If His passive hand, indeed,
　　Grasp'd a sceptre, 'twas a reed.
　　He was bound to feel and hear
　　Deeds of shame and words of jeer ;
　　For He whom king in jest they call
　　Was a doomed captive scorned by all.

" ' But the brightest crown of gold,
　　Of the robe of rarest fold,
　　Or the sceptre which the mine
　　Of Golconda makes to shine,
　　Of the lowliest homage given
　　By all mankind under heaven,
　　Were prized by Him no more than scorn,
　　Sceptre of reed or crown of thorn.

" ' Of the stars His crown is made,
　　In the sun He is array'd,
　　He, the lightning of the spheres
　　As a flaming sceptre bears :
　　Bend in rapture before Him
　　Ranks of glowing seraphim ;
　　And we, who spurn'd Him, trembling stay
　　The judgment of His coming day.' "

In the *Dublin University Magazine*, January, 1844, is an elaborate paper, interweaving a few biographical memoranda of Maginn, with some critical observations on his writings. The whole paper is a very meritorious contribution, but is far beyond our grasp.

"We beheld," says the author, "far off in the distance, the works of Maginn (a goodly collection of octavos), taking their place beside those of Swift and Lucian, referred to as authorities in the canons of criticism, and translation, and historical anecdote, or consulted for their wit and humour. But, on further experience, it was found that to carry out our wish was of too Elysian a nature to be gratified." The author then says :—"There is scarcely a single point in which we contemplate the intellectual character of Maginn, that we are not struck with admiration, with reverence, and regard. As a poet, he has left behind him writings realizing the lineaments of poetry in all their lustre. As a scholar, he was, perhaps, the most universal of his time, no subject being unknown to him, or beyond the reach of his reading; for, more various in his learning than Voltaire, far more profound and elegant than Johnson; he was rivalled, perhaps, only by Peter Bayle, or that erudite old man, James Roche, of Cork. As a political writer, he was once pronounced by no mean authority, to be ' the greatest in the world,' and, although perfection in that attainment is scarcely worth the ambition of a lofty mind, it would be hard to name any author of our time, except Sydney Smith, who was at once so witty, so philosophical, so elegant and earnest in political discourses.

"As a conversationalist, he was known for the liveliness of his fancy, the diversity of his anecdotes, the richness and felicity of his illustrations, the depth and shrewdness of his truths, the readiness of his repartee, the utter absence of any thing like dictation to those who came to listen and to be instructed. Lastly, as a man, he possessed the most childlike gentleness and simplicity, the greatest modesty, the warmest heart, the most benevolent hand, with the most scanty means. From faults he was not free, from wild irregularities he was not exempt. But genius is seldom perfect. The rock upon which Steele and Burns split, the sole blot upon Addison, the only stigma upon Charles Lamb, that which exiled Fox from the cabinet of England, and reduced Sheridan to poverty and shame,—was the ruin, too, of William Maginn. But let us draw over it the veil of charity, and remember that he was a man!

"Originality, the distinctive attribute of genius, he possessed in no ordinary degree ; and whether we examine his criticisms or his maxims, grave or gay, his translations or his songs, his tales or his humorous compositions, we shall find that to no one preceding writer is he much indebted for his mode of thought and style. He resembles Aristophanes, or Lucian, or Rabelais, more, perhaps, than any modern author. He has the same keen and delicate raillery, the withering sarcasm, the strange and humorous incident, the quaint learning, tho bitter scorn of quackery or imposture, the grave and laughable irony, the profound and condensed philosophy of the above illustrious triad ; but the grossness and obscenity, the loose and depraved sentiments, the utter defiance of modesty and decorum, which their ordinary imitators substitute for wit and wisdom, he did not possess in the slightest degree. Even Swift has not equalled him in sarcasm, though in the power of irony he may be entitled to more praise, as having preceded Maginn.

"Read any subject on which the Doctor has written, although his view of it is different from other men—an eccentric or a satirical one, for instance—he still clothes it with such new light, he illuminates it so brilliantly from the golden lamp of his own intellect, and displays such admirable common sense in all he says, that the reader will derive from his odd, hasty, but masterly delineations, a more perfect idea of the matter in question, than from the most profound and laboured, and even learned disquisitions of others. Read, for example, his famous essay on Dr. Farmer's *Learning of Shakspeare*, and his still more famous papers on Southey's strange performance, *The Doctor*. In the latter there is more fire, more philosophy, and more beauty, in a small compass, than in the Laureate's five volumes, so that, if ever any man after Rousseau was entitled to Sir William Jones's eloquent summary of that fine genius ' whose pen, formed to elucidate all the arts, had the property of spreading light before it on the darkest subject, as if he had written with phosphorus on the sides of a cavern,' most assuredly that man was William Maginn.

"As a scholar he has been compared to Porson, whom, however, he did not approach. But few men possessed a more deeply founded acquaintance with the standard writers of Greece and Rome, or a more extensive knowledge of the best authors in the modern Continental languages ; and this wealth

of erudition it was which enabled him so beautifully to
decorate those papers which he composed the quickest, and
make them, in the words of Thucydides, ' treasures for all
posterity, rather than exercises for present and temporary
perusal.' His fine knowledge of the Greek is best demon-
strated by his admirable and witty translations from Lucian ;
and his *Homeric Ballads,* which, for antique dignity and faithfulness, are unsurpassed by any versions in our language, and
carry his name down to all time with that of Pope. Those
who wish to know *what* and *how* Homer wrote, must read
Maginn—those who seek to be delighted with the *Iliad,* must
peruse Pope.

" Perhaps the English language does not contain anything
more terse or noble than his *Soldier Boy;* it is worth a
hundred Irish melodies, and a thousand Oriental romances.
To this may be added his third part of *Christabel,* which is a
more spirited and weird-like conclusion than the author himself might have drawn, and perhaps it was a consciousness
that he could not excel this finale of the Doctor, which prevented Coleridge from attempting the completion. As a paro-
dist he was inimitable—perhaps the greatest that ever lived.

" His conversation was an outpouring of the gorgeous stores
wherewith his mind was laden, and flowed on, like the
storied Pactolus, all golden. Many a happy hour has the
writer of this sketch listened to Maginn as, with head leaning back in a huge arm-chair, and eye lighted up beneath
his eloquent forehead and light, flowing hair, he spoke the
words of brightness and wisdom ; recapitulating the many
anecdotes of Scott and Hogg, and Coleridge and Hook, with
which his memory was thickly enamelled.

" When the elegant Aristophanes sought to express, by
metaphor, the rapture with which he listened to one of the
most eloquent speakers of old, he declared to him that he
had *spoken roses.* But the words of Maginn were of a higher
mould, of a richer texture, of a greater worth ; for all he said
was distinguished more for value than for tinsel ; and he
thought with Burke, that the jewel of conversation is its
tendency to the useful, and carelessness of the gaudy. And
we do not know any other famous conversationalist, to whom
the beautiful passage, in which Wilberforce alludes to Burke's
discourse, applies with more perfect justness : ' Like the
fated object of the fairy's favours, whenever he opened his
mouth, pearls and diamonds dropped from him.'

"From Maginn's candour, much of his excellence was derived. The leaders which he wrote for the newspapers were usually finished in half an hour, or perhaps less; but the inventive understanding that dictated them, the terseness, darting, like sturdy oak trees, in every sentence, the sparkle of wit, or the thrust of sarcasm—these gave value to the article, and atone for its haste. The writings on which he bestowed most care were the *Homeric Ballads*; and for the last few years, he was seldom without a copy of the *Iliad* and *Odyssey*, in his room, or on his bed. For these translations, he felt indeed almost an enthusiasm. As we have mentioned Homer, it may be added that he was a constant student of the Bible, and would pore over its sublime pages for hours. He preferred the Old Testament to the New, and was most partial to Isaiah, whom he called one of the grandest of poets."

Such is a brief character of Maginn.

The Doctor is stated to have first met with Mr. Blackwood in this manner. He had already contributed to his *Magazine* several biting papers, which had excited a considerable ferment both in Edinburgh and Cork; but the intercourse between him and his publisher had as yet been wholly epistolary, the latter not even knowing the name of his correspondent. Determined now to have an interview with Mr. Blackwood, Maginn set out for Edinburgh, where he arrived on a Sunday evening, and on the ensuing forenoon he presented himself in the shop in Princes Street, where the following conversation took place. It must be observed, in passing, that Mr. Blackwood had received numerous furious communications, more especially from Ireland, demanding the name of the writer of the obnoxious articles, and he now believed this was a visit from one of them to obtain redress *in propriâ personâ*.

"You are Mr. Blackwood, I presume?"

"I am."

"I have rather an unpleasant business, then, with you regarding some things which have appeared in your magazine. They are so and so," (mentioning them); "would you be so kind as to give me the name of the author?"

"That requires consideration, and I must first be satisfied that——"

"Your correspondent resides in Cork, doesn't he? You need not make any mystery about that."

"I decline at present giving information on that head,

before I know more of your business—of your purpose—and who you are."

" You are very shy, sir. I thought you corresponded with Mr. Scott, of Cork " (the assumed name which he had used).

" I beg to decline giving any information on that subject."

" If you don't know him, then, perhaps you *could* know your own handwriting " (drawing forth a bundle of letters from his pocket). " You need not deny your correspondence with that gentleman—I am that gentleman."

Fraser's Magazine was commenced in February, 1830. The publisher, Mr. Fraser, is said never to have recovered from the beating so severely inflicted by Messrs. Grantley and Craven Berkeley, 3rd August, 1836, in consequence of an article which appeared in the magazine written by Dr. Maginn—the trial consequent upon which violent proceedings took place in the December following. A duel was fought by Mr. Grantley Berkeley and Dr. Maginn. Three shots were exchanged without effect, and the parties were withdrawn from the ground by their respective seconds.

Amongst the other papers contributed to Blackwood by Dr. Maginn was the story of the " Man in the Bell," which was quoted by Lord Brougham in one of his speeches in the House of Lords. It appeared in the November number for 1821, and was founded on the adventure of a singular character in the belfry of the Cathedral of Cork (Maginn's native city), a writing-master, named Fitzgerald, who published in 1783 a rude chronicle of events, entitled the *Cork Remembrancer*, now not to be procured.

Among the pleasantries of this wit and scholar was the following, which he wrote to one of his pupils, to inquire after a missing lexicon, as follows :—" Dowden !!! Schleusner? Maginn —" which he expounded,

" Dowden, my thrice admired ;
Query, have you Schleusner ?
I, Maginn, am minus of it."

In the dwelling and sponging-house of the sheriff's officer, Hemp, in Shire Lane, Temple Bar, Theodore Hook, while under arrest for a defalcation as Treasurer of the Mauritius, made the acquaintance of Dr. Maginn, who had come over from Cork to assist in *John Bull*. He was Hook's nightly visitor; and two spirits of closer kindred could not have met. Hook left Shire Lane in April, 1834, after a banquet, for which he improvised a song, in the chorus not sparing himself :—

" Let him hang with a curse—this atrocious, pernicious
  Scoundrel, that entered the till at Mauritius."

Hook was then removed to the rules of the King's Bench (Temple Place), where he worked hard, in addition to the editorship of *John Bull*, in founding his profitable fame.

It is not generally known that Dr. Maginn wrote for Knight and Lacy, the publishers in Paternoster Row, a novel embodying the strange story of the Polstead Murder of 1828, under the title of the *Red Barn*, by which the publishers cleared many hundreds of pounds.

Amid the melancholy instances of genius and talent impeded and finally extinguished by the want of ordinary prudence and circumspection of conduct, Dr. Maginn is lamentably conspicuous. Possessed of one of the most versatile of minds, which enabled him to pass with the utmost ease from grave to gay, from the rollicking fun of the " Story without a Tail," and " Bob Burke's Duel," to the studies and delicate discrimination of the *Shakspeare Papers*, and the classic eloquence of the *Homeric Ballads*, he yet found himself incompetent to the proper husbanding and turning to account of these gifts, and after enduring the last miseries of a debtor's prison, fell a victim soon afterwards to consumption.

Having previously passed with distinguished reputation through a course of study at Trinity College, Dublin, he continued to discharge the duties of this office with much credit for some years till he abandoned it to devote himself entirely to a literary life. Some of his first essays were trifles and *jeux d'esprit*, written in connection with a literary society in Cork, of which he was a member. They excited a good deal of local attention. In 1816, he obtained the degree of LL.D., and soon after became a contributor to the *Literary Gazette*, then under the management of Mr. William Jerdan, who says that Maginn was in the habit of sending him " a perfect shower of varieties ; classic paraphrases, anecdotes, illustrations of famous ancient authors, displaying a vast acquaintance with and fine appreciation of them." It is principally, however, with *Blackwood's* and *Fraser's Magazines* that his name is associated, being a contributor to the former almost from its commencement, whilst the latter owed mainly its existence to him, being projected by him in company with Mr. Hugh Fraser, to whom he supplied nearly all the letter-press of the celebrated " Gallery of Portraits." One of his articles, a review of the novel *Berkeley Castle*, led to a duel with the Hon. Grantley Berkeley, which, after three rounds of shots had been exchanged without doing further damage than grazing the heel of Dr. Maginn's boot and the collar of Mr. Berkeley's coat, ended in the parties quitting the ground, on the interference of the seconds, without speaking a word, or making any explanation.

Notwithstanding the many sources of livelihood which our author's prolific and versatile genius opened up to him, his improvident habits kept him constantly in difficulties, which at last so thickened upon him, that he repeatedly became the inmate of a jail ; and in the spring of 1842, the misery and depression of spirits which he had undergone, terminated in a rapid decline. In the vain hope of re-establishing his health, he retired from London to Walton-on-Thames, where, however, his disease gradually gained strength; his frame wasted to a shadow ; and in the month of August, 1842, he expired. To the last he retained almost undiminished his wonderful flow of humour and animal spirits, and talked and jested with his friends as far as his reduced strength and emaciated frame would permit. He complained bitterly of the neglect with which he had been treated by his party (the Tories) ; and there can be no doubt that, to a certain extent, the reproach was well founded, though the generosity of Sir Robert Peel was liberally displayed a few days before Maginn's death, on his unfortunate situation being brought under the notice of the premier.

Maginn's character presents much of the conventional characteristics of the Irishman—warm-hearted, generous, and impulsive, freely imparting of his substance to his friends in their need, and as readily borrowing from them to supply his wants in his own. The reckless conviviality of his nature disposed him not unfrequently to excesses which ultimately shattered and destroyed his constitution. Such a vein, how-ever, of bonhomie and real kindliness of heart was perfectly irresistible. His conversation is described as a jumble of incongruous subjects, theology, politics, and general literature, all cemented together in an overpowering style of drollery, which, however, not unfrequently left the listeners at a loss whether to surrender themselves unconditionally to the influence of the ludicrous or admire the great common sense and profound vein of philosophy conspicuous in all his remarks. The ease and rapidity with which he wrote were astonishing. Jumping out of bed, he would seat himself in his shirt at his desk, and run off in an hour one of his brilliant papers for *Blackwood* or *Fraser*. Not unfrequently, it must be added, he composed with the pen in one hand and a glass of brandy-and-water in the other. Much of what he wrote was necessarily of an ephemeral character, and his works will therefore, probably, in a succeeding generation, be comparatively little read, whilst his memory, like that of Foote, is preserved as that of a brilliant wit and conversationalist. Yet he was far from being a mere droll or after-dinner talker. His *Shakspeare Papers* contain some of the most delicately appreciative touches which have ever been presented on the subject of our great national dramatist; and his *Homeric Ballads* fairly rival in vigour and classic genius the *Lays of Ancient Rome* of Macaulay.

On Dr. Maginn the following epitaph was written by his friend, John Gibson Lockhart :—

" WALTON-ON-THAMES, AUGUST, 1842.

" Here, early to bed, lies kind WILLIAM MAGINN,
　Who, with genius, wit, learning, life's trophies to win,
　Had neither great lord nor rich cit of his kin,
　Nor discretion to set himself up as to tin ;
　So, his portion soon spent, like the poor heir of Lynn—
　He turned author ere yet there was beard on his chin,
　And, whoever was out, or whoever was in,
　For your Tories his fine Irish brains he would spin ;
　Who received prose and rhyme with a promising grin—
　'Go ahead, you queer fish, and more power to your fin,'
　But to save from starvation stirred never a pin.
　Light for long was his heart, though his breeches were thin,
　Else his acting for certain was equal to Quin ;
　But at last he was beat, and sought help of the bin
　(All the same to the Doctor, from claret to gin),
　Which led swiftly to jail and consumption therein.
　It was much, when the bones rattled loose in the skin,
　He got leave to die here, out of Babylon's din.
　Barring drink and the girls, I ne'er heard a sin :
　Many worse, better few, than bright, broken Maginn."

" Dr. Maginn, in his younger days, deeply pondering on the fleeting nature of the beauties of modern compositions, and the frail transitory efforts of all living forms of speech, had a notion of recovering these charming things from inevitable decay, and announced himself to the public as a poetical *Embalmer.* He printed a proposal for wrapping up in the imperishable folios of Greek and Latin, with sundry spices of his own, the songs and ballads of these islands, which, in a few centuries, will be unintelligible to posterity. He had already commenced operating on ' Black-eyed Susan,' and had cleverly disembowelled ' Alley Croaker,' both of which made excellent classic mummies. ' Wapping Old Stairs,' in his Latin translation, seemed to be the veritable *Gradus ad Parnassum ;* and his Greek version of ' 'Twas in Trafalgar's Bay,' beat all Æschylus ever sung about Salamis. What became of the project, and why the Doctor gave it up, we cannot tell ; he is an unaccountable character. But while we regret this embalming plan should have been abandoned, we are free to confess that, in our opinion, ' Old King Cole,' in Hebrew, was his best effort. It was equal to Solomon in all his glory."—*Reliques of Father Prout.*

WILLIAM MAKEPEACE THACKERAY.

TOWARDS the close of the year 1863, this popular and original writer was taken from us, under circumstances which intensified the public grief for the loss at the season when thousands were enjoying the delights afforded by his genius; seldom has our great festival been so saddened by popular sorrow in the darkness which for us and all who knew him overshadowed this festive season. It was not of the great author and the brilliant wit that we thought most; it was of the warm-hearted, simple-minded gentleman, honest in all his ways, in all his words, full of charity in his utmost satire, and ready to give even when he had little to spare.

The prominent incidents of a literary man's life are not numerous, and there have been published so many memoirs of Mr. Thackeray in biographical dictionaries. He was descended from Dr. Thackeray, who was for some time Head Master at Harrow, and introduced there the Eton system. His father was in the Civil Service of the East India Company, and he was born at Calcutta, in 1811. He was sent to England in his seventh year, when, the ship having touched at St. Helena, he saw Napoleon. He has himself described the incident. "My black servant took me a walk over paths and hills till we passed a garden, where we saw a man walking. 'That is Bonaparte,' said the black; 'he eats three sheep every day, and all the children he can lay his hands on.'" On reaching England, as soon as his age admitted, he was sent to the Charterhouse School. Of his residence at that venerable seat of education, he retained a kindly recollection throughout the remainder of his life, and has more than once made loving reference to the old monastery of the Carthusians. He afterwards graduated at the University of Cambridge, which he left without taking a degree. At this time his passion was to acquire fame as a painter, and he worked hard to lay the foundation of his future fame in that direction. Among other efforts made for that purpose he proceeded to Rome, where he resided for some time studying the works of the great masters. He also lived for some time at Weimar with the same view, and in the course of his residence he made the acquaintance of Goethe. His wonderful pictorial genius, however, was not fated to find its fitting implement in the painting-brush or on canvas ; in spite of his most assiduous endeavours, he was not able to overcome the technical difficulties of the art, and the only traces of his early studies that remained in after years were to be found in those droll and often grotesque sketches that were used to illustrate his own writings ; indeed, the rival claims of literature began very early to exercise a distracting influence upon his studies, and as far back as 1837 he occasionally addressed a contribution to the *Times*, under the editorship of Barnes. His connection with newspaper literature was further strengthened by an engagement on the *Constitutional*, a daily paper which was started about that time, but which had a short-lived existence.

An introduction to the editor of *Fraser's Magazine* opened up to him more genial occupation. He contributed a number of papers on his favourite subject of art, besides various reviews. It was not long, however, before he struck out a new path for himself in a series of social sketches, in which he first developed that keen, penetrating satire, that power of penetrating beneath the disguises of conventional life, which he afterwards worked out more fully in his various novels, and on which his fame will permanently rest. His favourite signature in the magazine was " Michael Angelo Titmarsh," a pseudonym which he wore long after it served to conceal him, which he adopted in many of his other writings, and which, in fact, he never wholly abandoned till he exchanged it for his later one of *Pendennis*. Among the works of a more complete form which he published under the earlier title may be mentioned his *Irish Sketch Book* and his *Journey from Cornhill to Grand Cairo*, in each of which the beaten routine of the ground over which he travels is broken up and rendered picturesque by his overflowing humour and his keen, biting, but genial satire. For a time he was one of the contributors to *Punch*, and his *Fitzjeames' Diary*, satirizing the extravagances of the railway mania, and his *Snob Papers*, are among the most amusing that have ever appeared in the pages of our facetious contemporary. The former series was in some measure a mere continuation of the *Plush Papers* that had previously appeared in *Fraser's Magazine*, and in both Mr. Thackeray showed an extraordinary facility in copying the modes of thought, the broken sentences, the illogical and inconsequent argument, and the capricious spelling of the half-educated hangers-on of gentility; and which, when taken in connection with the somewhat similar imitations of a Frenchman translating his Paris thoughts into English language, may be regarded as marvels of literary ingenuity.

A variety of circumstances brought him into the world of letters and of journalism when he contributed to the *Times*. He contributed to other periodicals, wrote various books of travel, and worked for the publishers, any that came to him, as a barrister takes his brief from any respectable attorney. The mass of work which he got through in this way was very great, but much of it is interesting only as the early practice of one who before long rose to be a master of English. On the whole, as we look back upon these writings, we do not think that if his fame at that time was unequal to his merits, the public were much to blame. The very high opinion which his friends entertained of him must have been due more to personal intercourse than to his published works.

It was not until 1846 that Mr. Thackeray fairly showed to the world what was in him. Then began to be published, in monthly numbers, the story of *Vanity Fair*. It took London by surprise—the picture was so true, the satire was so trenchant, the style was so finished. It is difficult to say which of these three works is the best—*Vanity Fair*, *Henry Esmond*, or *The Newcomes*. Men of letters may give their preference to the second of these, which is indeed the most finished of all his works. But there is a vigour in the first-mentioned, and a matured beauty in the last, which to the throng of readers will be more attractive. At first reading, *Vanity Fair* has given to many an impression that the author is too cynical. There was no man less ill-natured than Mr. Thackeray, and, if anybody doubts this, we refer him to *The Newcomes*, and ask whether that book could be written by any but a most kind-hearted man. We believe that one of the greatest miseries which Mr. Thackeray had to endure grew out of the sense that he, one of the kindest of men, was regarded as an ill-natured cynic.

The first to follow in Mr. Dickens's wake was Mr. Thackeray. It is said that his *Vanity Fair* was declined by an eminent publishing firm ; and when the early numbers, clad in their prime yellow covers, and illustrated with the quaint figures, first made their appearance, they excited little attention.* It was not long, however, before Becky Sharpe began to fascinate the public, as she fascinated all with whom she came in contact in the novel. Month by month the serial grew in favour ; the early numbers, which had fallen almost still-born from the press, were eagerly inquired after, and long before the story was brought to a close, the public recognised that they were in possession of a genius of deeper and keener insight, though it might be of narrower range, than Mr. Dickens himself. From that time the fame of Mr. Thackeray was established, and he ever after moved full in the public eye. For several years subsequently the novel reading public might always calculate upon the monthly instalment of a novel from the pen either of Dickens or Thackeray ; for, though by an agreement between them, written or otherwise, the one reposed while the other published, the twin luminaries were never long together both absent from the sky. The practice continued till the fashion changed, and both authors addressed their widely extended audiences from other vantage grounds. Mr. Thackeray's first departure from the monthly serial was in the case of his *Esmond*, which was published complete in a three-volume novel, and which is by many persons regarded as the best of his works. It is certainly a wonderful production, not only revivifying the wits and heroes of the golden days of Queen Anne, by describing through them the habits and manners of the period, but even going so far as to reproduce the style, language, and mode of thought of Addison and Steele. This reproduction of the language, manners, and modes of thought of a bygone period is no doubt highly successful ; but for originality and freshness of observation we do not believe he ever produced anything equal to *Vanity Fair*. It was the fountain from whence all his other works were drawn. In all his subsequent works his best

* It is understood that the sale of *Vanity Fair*, in shilling parts, did not exceed 7000 ; nor did it reach any great number until *Vanity Fair* was completed in a large volume.

characters are little better than reproductions of Becky Sharpe, the Marquis of Steyne, the Crowleys, Sir George Osborne, and Major Dobbin.

If Dickens led the way in the monthly publication of his tales, Thackeray was the first to charm the public in addressing his thoughts to them by the living voice. He addressed his "Lectures on the English Humourists" to brilliant audiences in Willis's Rooms, and the success which the experiment obtained in the metropolis was but the herald of the favour with which they were afterwards received in the principal English towns. These were followed by a series of lectures on the Georgian Era, which Thackeray crossed the Atlantic to deliver in the United States. These lectures, it is hardly necessary to state, were not very complimentary to the four monarchs whose lives and characters he depicted; and he incurred some obloquy at the time in this country for having gone, as it were, to uncover his country's nakedness before hostile critics, who were sure to gloat with malicious delight over the exposure. At all events, the lecturer himself was received by our Transatlantic kindred with great favour. The fruit of his tour in the States was soon afterwards apparent in his novel of the *Virginians*.

In 1860 Messrs. Smith and Elder commenced the *Cornhill Magazine*; and the announcement that Mr. Thackeray had undertaken the editorship gave it at once a start and a standing-place in popular favour which it might otherwise have taken years to attain. He was not only the editor, but one of the principal writers, the first number opening with a portion of a tale by him, under the title of *Lovel the Widower*. The work, as it proceeded, however, did not come gratefully to the author, and he brought it to an abrupt ending, commencing soon afterwards a work of higher pretensions, and, as it proved, the last of his works, *Philip on his Way in the World*. In addition there were the pleasant, gossiping *Roundabout Papers*, light, graceful comments on the current topics of the day, overflowing with kindly humour, and straying into all pleasant literary bypaths. He subsequently gave up the editorship of the magazine, but he contributed an occasional *Roundabout Paper* to the last.

Of the publishers' house, No. 65, Cornhill, we have this lively record:—"Our storehouse being in Cornhill," explains its first editor, W. M. Thackeray, in a letter to a friend form-

ing the preface to the first number, " we date and name our
magazine from its place of publication." Father Prout (F.
Mahoney) contributed an inaugural ode on the occasion, in
which he gaily rallies the editor :—

> " There's corn in Egypt still
> (Pilgrim from Cairo to Cornhill) ;"

and advises him—

> ——" as to those
> Who bring their lumbering verse or ponderous prose
> To where good SMITH and ELDER
> Have so long held their
> Well-garnish'd Cornhill storehouse—
> Bid them not bore us,
> Tell them instead
> To take their load next street, the Hall of Lead."

Thackeray himself alludes to the house in the first of his
Roundabout Papers :—" I had occasion," he says, " to pass a
week in the autumn in the little old town of Coire or Chur,
in the Grisons, where lies buried that very ancient British
king, saint, and martyr, Lucius, who founded the church of
St. Peter which stands opposite the house No. 65, Cornhill."
After describing the statue of the saint, he remarks—" From
what I may call his peculiar position with regard to No. 65,
Cornhill, I beheld this figure of St. Lucius with more interest
than I should have bestowed upon personages who, hierarchi-
cally, are, I dare say, his superiors."

Mr. Thackeray once put in a claim for senatorial honours.
He had delivered a course of lectures at Oxford, where he was
received with great enthusiasm, and about the time a vacancy
occurred in the representation. He was pitched upon by a
section of the Liberal party as their candidate, and at their
request he contested the city ; but we suspect not very heartily,
and certainly the cause of English politics lost nothing, if it
did not gain much, in his defeat by the Chancellor of
the Duchy of Lancaster. Still, the canvas was unpromising,
as was our impression in seeing the candidate soliciting the
suffrages in the city of Oxford.

DEATH OF MR. THACKERAY.

The first announcement of Mr. Thackeray's illness was in these touching words:—" Suddenly, one of our greatest literary men has departed.   Never more shall the fine head of Mr. Thackeray, with its mass of silvery hair, be seen towering among us.   Within two days ago he might have been seen at his club, radiant and buoyant with glee.   Yesterday morning he was found dead in his bed.   With all his high spirits he did not seem well; he complained of illness; but he was often ill, and he laughed off his present attack.   He said that he was about to undergo some treatment which would work a perfect cure in his system, and so he made light of his malady.   He was suffering from two distinct complaints, one of which now wrought his death.   More than a dozen years before, while he was writing *Pendennis*, it will be remembered that the publication of that work was stopped by his serious illness.   He was brought to death's door, and he was saved from death by Dr. Elliotson, to whom, in gratitude, he dedicated the novel when he lived to finish it.   But ever since that ailment he had been subject every month or six weeks to attacks of sickness, attended with violent retching.   He was congratulating himself the day before on the failure of his old enemy to return, and then he checked himself, as if he ought not to be too sure of a release from his plague.   On the next morning the complaint returned, and he was in great suffering all day.   He was no better in the evening, and his servant, about the time of leaving him for the night, proposed to sit up with him.   This he declined.   He was heard moving about midnight, and he must have died between two or three in the morning of December 24.   His medical attendants attribute his death to effusion on the brain.   They add that he had a very large brain, weighing no less than $58\frac{1}{2}$ oz.   He thus died of the complaint which seemed to trouble him least.   He died full of strength and rejoicing, full of plans and hopes ; he was congratulating himself on having finished four numbers of a new novel ; he had the manuscript in his pocket, and with a boyish frankness showed the last pages to a friend, asking him to read them and see what he could make of them.   When he had completed four numbers more he said he would subject himself to the skill of a very clever surgeon, and be no more an invalid.   In the fulness of his powers he fell before a complaint which gave him no alarm."—(*Times.*)

Mr. Thackeray desired to be interred in the simplest manner at Kensal-green. He was laid in a brick-built grave beside one of his children, and his family affections were so strong that we believe it would have been a positive pain to him if, when he was alive, he could have looked forward to being separated from his children in the tomb. Those who were nearest to him, and whom he loved best of all in the world, were so much in his mind that even in the presence of casual acquaintances whom he saw only at one or other of his clubs he could not choose but let out somewhat of the strong feeling which stirred within his heart for those who were as the light of his eyes. It was one of the simplest and most winning traits of his character ; and by those who could not help knowing what he felt in this way no more touching sight could be witnessed than that of his two young daughters, veiled in crape, advancing from the crowd that pressed about the grave, taking a last sad look at the coffin, and then suddenly turning away. These are reasons why Mr. Thackeray should be buried in his own ground at Kensal-green.

The funeral procession left the private residence of the deceased, at Kensington, shortly before eleven o'clock, and arrived at the cemetery about noon. There was but one mourning coach, and in this and the succeeding carriage, which was the private one of the deceased, were seated the Rev. F. St. John Thackeray and Mr. James Rodd, cousins of the deceased ; Captain Shaw, his brother-in-law ; and the Hon. R. Curzon. The remaining carriages were those of Mr. Martin Thackeray, General Low, Lord Gardner, Sir W. Frazer, Hon. R. Curzon, Earl Granville, Mr. Macaulay, Q.C., Sir James Colville, and Mr. Bradbury.

A vast concourse of his friends were enabled to surround his grave, and pay him the last honour. Mr. Thackeray had the gift of associating with a wonderful variety of persons ; to be in his company was, in the case of most persons, to be entirely at ease with him. Among the great throng of mourners were noticeable nearly all the foremost men of letters and artists of the day, some of them having travelled far to be present on the sad occasion. Only a few of Mr. Thackeray's most intimate friends were expressly invited to the funeral. The hundreds on hundreds who attended came of their own accord to bear witness to the worth of a dear friend and a much admired man ; and of all these we venture to refer to but one name—that of Mr. Charles Dickens. We do so, because he is the author most frequently remembered in connection with Mr. Thackeray, and because he has sometimes been regarded as a rival. In fact, there can be no rivalry between these two great novelists, and any special comparison between them must proceed on superficial grounds.

The funeral service was read, in a solemn and impressive manner, by the chaplain of the cemetery, the Rev. Charles Stuart. When the coffin was placed in the little chapel of the burial-ground, a strong desire was manifested by nearly every one to enter the building; but the space inside was soon occupied, as far as it could be conveniently.

After the conclusion of the first part of the service, the mass of those present proceeded to the grave, which is in a quiet spot on the left side of the cemetery, and not far from the entrance-gate.

The numbers present amounted to nearly a thousand. The scene at the grave, both during and after the ceremony of interment, was extremely affecting. The silence was profound, and every countenance bespoke a deep sense of grief.

The coffin, which was exceedingly plain, bore upon it the following inscription :—

WILLIAM MAKEPEACE THACKERAY,
ESQ.,
DIED 24TH DECEMBER,
1863,
AGED 52 YEARS.

Among the mourners were Mr. Dickens, Mr. Tom Taylor, Mr. Shirley Brooks, Mr. Mark Lemon (the editor of the famous periodical in which was laid the foundation of Mr. Thackeray's fame), Mr. John Leech (a fellow-pupil and friend), Mr. Tenniel, Mr. Horace Mayhew—in short, the whole staff of the contributors to *Punch ;* Mr. Robert Browning (the poet), Mr. Anthony Trollope, Mr. Theodore Martin, Mr. John Hollingshead, Mr. G. H. Lewes, Mr. Dallas, Dr. W. Russell, Sir James Carmichael, Mr. H. Cole, C.B., Mr. Robert Bell, Mr. O'Neill, R.A., Mr. Creswick, R.A., Mr. George Cruikshank, Archdeacon Hale, Mr. E. Pigott, M. Louis Blanc, Mr. Herman Merivale, Rev. W. Brookfield, Baron Marochetti, A.R.A., Rev. William Mitchell, Mr. Russell Sturgis, Mr. George Smith, Mr. Charles Collins, Mr. Palgrave Simpson, Mr. Henry Thompson, Mr. Seymour Hayden, Mr. F. Fladgate, Mr. Reeves Traer, Mr. Henry Reeve, Mr. F. Elliot,

Mr. W. Richmond, A.R.A., Mr. John Millais, A.R.A., Mr. Richard Doyle, Mr. Valentine Princep, Sir William Alexander, Mr. Richard Redgrave, R.A., &c.

In the corridor at the Charterhouse is a tablet to Thackeray; and among the memorials of eminent Carthusians is preserved the iron bedstead upon which he slept at Charterhouse.

SALE OF THE EFFECTS OF THE LATE MR. THACKERAY.

The following are some of the curiosities and other effects of Mr. Thackeray, the sale of which took place, by Messrs. Christie and Manson, on the premises, 2, Palace Green, Kensington, the handsome house built in the Queen Anne style. Of porcelain, Dresden and Sévres, many brought very large prices—for instance, four dinner-services realized the aggregate amount of £69 10s.; two Sévres sauceboats, £9. The pictures, water-colour drawings, and engravings were only twenty-five. The first picture put up was by De Troye, painted in commemoration of the Peace of Utrecht, £18. An exquisite painting by Boucher, designed as a circular centre-piece for a ceiling, subject "Two Cupids sporting," fetched £25 10s. A charming little picture, by J. F. Herring (1855), "A Partridge and Young in a Corn Field," realized £21. An elegant composition by Watteau, entitled, "A Conversation Champêtre," was sold for £10 5s. A charming painting by Van Loo, "The Portrait of a Lady," a work of great beauty, and exquisite colour and finish, after an eager competition, was knocked down at £25 10s. A picture, by J. Leslie, "A Roman Peasant Boy, with a Water Bottle and Dog at his side," fetched £20 10s. "A View on the North Eske," by G. Stanfield (1852), brought £16 15s. "A Sketch Portrait of the late Duke of Wellington," by J. Ward (1830), apparently unfinished, was sold for £8 15s. There were three pictures which attracted some attention, one by Begyn, "An Italian River Scene," with sheep and goats feeding, and a woman and child reposing at the foot of a tree, sold for £8 15s. "A View of the Low Countries," by E. Van der Velde, with an encampment of Spanish troops, general's staff, sold for £10; and one by J. Mytens (1655), "A Girl," and painted in landscape, a beautifully finished painting, sold for £15 15s. The remaining pictures were not remarkable, though all were very good examples of their respective schools.

The plated and silver articles comprised the usual appurtenances of the table, many of them of exquisite workmanship, which may be estimated from the fact that one salver (silver) fetched £2 10s. an ounce. Two articles deserve also especial notice. An oval inkstand, with chased claw feet and engraved open-work border, two glasses with silver tops, taper candlestick and extinguisher, with an inscription, "To William M. Thackeray, from an obliged friend, Nov. 16th, 1851 ;" and a magnificent fluted punch bowl, with waved edge, chased with scroll and foliage, and with lion-mask handles, and inscribed, "From the Publishers to the Author of *Vanity Fair* and *Pendennis.*" This latter was knocked down at £2 3s. an ounce. The sale extended to three days.

SOCIAL AND LITERARY CHARACTER.

" Mr. Thackeray's age was but fifty-two, and he seemed a man large, vigorous, and cheerful, with yet a quarter of a century of life in him. There were some parts of his character that never felt the touch of his years, and these were tenderly remembered at many a Christmas fireside. There was to the last in him the sensibility of a child's generous heart, that time had not sheathed against light touches of pleasure and pain. His sympathy was prompt and keen ; but the same quick feeling made him also over-sensitive to the small annoyances that men usually learn to take for granted as but one form of the friction that belongs to movements of all kinds. He was sensitive to his sensitiveness, and did in his writings what thousands of men do in their lives, shrouded an over tender heart in a transparent veil of cynicism. Often he seemed to his readers to be trifling or nervously obtruding himself into his story when he was but shrinking from the full discovery of his own simple intensity of feeling. In his most polished works, *Vanity Fair, Esmond,* or the *Newcomes* —in which last book the affected cynicism, that, after all, could not strike deeper than into the mere surface of things, is set aside, and more nearly than in any other of his works discharge is made of the whole true mind of William Makepeace Thackeray—in these his masterpieces there is nothing better, nothing more absolutely genuine and perfect in its way than the pure spirit of frolic in some of his comic rhymes. He could play with his ' Pleaseman X.' very much as a happy child plays with a toy; and how freely and delightfully the strength of his wit flowed into the child's pantomime tale of *The Rose and the Ring*. It is not now the time for taking exact measure of the genius of the true writer we have lost. What sort of hold it took upon the English mind and heart his countrymen knew by the sad and gentle words that to the last connected the sense of his loss in almost every household with the great English festival of lovingkindness. There are men who, appealing to widely-spread forms of ignorance or prejudice, have more readers than Mr. Thackeray; and yet the loss of one of these writers on the eve of Christmas would have struck home nowhere beyond the private circle of his friends. Whatever the extent or limit of his genius, Mr. Thackeray found the way to the great generous English heart. And the chief secret of his power was the simple strength of sympathy within him, that he might flinch from expressing fully, but that was none the less the very soul of his successful work. Quickly impressible, his mind was raw to a rough touch; but the same quality gave all the force of its truth to his writing, all the lively graces to his style. That part of him which was the mere blind he put up at the inconveniently large window in his breast, degenerated into formula: and there were some who might be pardoned for becoming weary at the repetition of old patterns of sarcasm at the skin-deep vanities of life. But the eye was a dull one that could not look through this muslin work into a mind that, so to speak, was always keeping Christmas, although half ashamed to be known at the clubs as guilty of so much indulgence in the luxuries of kindly fellowship, and so continual an enjoyment of the purest side of life. Whatever little feuds may have gathered about Mr. Thackeray's public life lay lightly on the surface of the minds that chanced to be in contest with him. They could be thrown off in a moment, at the first shock of the news that he was dead. In the course of his active career there are few of his literary brethren with whom he had not been brought into contact. He worked much and variously; many and various also were his friends. To some of the worthiest in the land he was joined in friendship that had endured throughout the lifetime of a generation, and there were very humble rooms in London where there were tears for him whose left hand did not know what his right hand had done in silent charity.

"Thackeray had a rarer distinction than that of being a

great writer : he was a classical one. He was the greatest
master of English prose which the century has produced.
There may have been men of greater genius than he ; there
may have been more forcible writers than he ; but no one
has approached him in the command of polished idiomatic
English in all its varieties, in flexibility and richness and
finish of style. At first this was not fully understood ; but
now it is seen more and more clearly every year ; and Thackeray's English, notwithstanding the liberties which he sometimes took with it, is coming to be regarded as the model
English. We may say of him, as Johnson said of another,
the most classical writer of the last century, ' Whoever
wishes to attain an English style, familiar but not coarse, and
elegant but not ostentatious, must give his days and nights
to the volumes of Thackeray.' "—From the *Examiner*.

"VANITY FAIR,"

Says Mr. Nassau Senior, in his clever *Essays on Fiction*, "appears
to me by far the best, the fullest of natural and amusing
incident, and of characters with bold and firm outlines, and
fine and consistent outline. It is called ' A Novel without a
Hero,' and certainly, if hero or heroine be a person fitted to
attract the affection or to rouse the admiration of the reader
—if he or she is to be reverenced or to be adored—there is
none such in *Vanity Fair*. There are, however, two marked
figures which so far act the part of heroines as to be the
props on which the whole name of the narrative is suspended
—the centres which give to the plot the amount of unity
which it possesses. These, of course, are Amelia and Becky.
Their outward circumstances have much similarity. Each is
born in middle life ; they are educated at the same school ;
each marries, and at the same time, a military man ; each
loses her husband, though not by similar causes, and is left
with a single boy ; each struggles with poverty, and each
withdraws at the end of the story in affluence. An ordinary
writer would have found it difficult to keep distinct characters so similar in their fortunes. In Mr. Thackeray's there
the resemblance ends. In every other respect, they are not
merely different but contradicted. One is the representation
of virtue without intellect, the other that of intellect without
virtue. One has no head, the other no heart.

" There are few passages in the work more highly finished

than the interview between Sedley after his bankruptcy, with his old *protégé*, Captain Dobbin :—

" ' " I am very glad to see you, Captain Dobbin. Sir," said he, after a skulking look at his visitor, "how is the worthy alderman, and my lady, your excellent mother, sir ?" He looked round at the waiter, as he said "My lady," as much as to say, "Hark ye, I have friends still, and persons of rank and reputation, too." "My wife will be very happy to see her ladyship. I've a very kind letter here from your father, sir, and beg my respectful compliments to him. Lady D—— will find us to be in rather a smaller house than we are accustomed to receive our friends in ; but it's snug, and the change of air does good to my daughter, who was suffering in town rather —you remember little Emmy, sir ?—yes, suffering a great deal." The old gentleman's eyes were wandering as he spoke, and he was thinking of something else, as he sat thrumming on his papers, and fumbling at the worn red tape.

" ' " You're a military man," he went on ; " I ask you, Bill Dobbin, could any man have speculated upon the return of that Corsican scoundrel from Elba ? When the allied sovereigns were here last year, and we gave 'em that dinner in the City, sir, and we saw the temple of concord, and the fireworks, and the Chinese bridge in St. James's Park, could any sensible man suppose that peace wasn't really concluded, after we'd actually sung *Te Deum* for it, sir ? I ask you, William, could I suppose that the Emperor of Austria was a damned traitor—a traitor, and nothing more ; I don't mince words—a double-faced, infernal traitor and schemer, who meant to have his son-in-law back all along ? And I say that the escape of Boney from Elba was a damned imposition and plot, sir, in which half the powers of Europe were concerned, to bring the funds down and to ruin the country. That's why I'm here, William. That's why my name's in the *Gazette*. Why, sir, because I trusted the Emperor of Russia and the Prince Regent. Look here. Look at my papers. Look what the funds were on the 1st of March—what the French fives when I bought for the account—and what they are at now. There was collusion, sir, or that villain never would have escaped. Where was the English Commissioner who allowed him to get away ? He ought to be shot, sir,— brought to a court-martial, and shot, by Jove !"

" ' " We're going to hunt Becky out, sir," Dobbin said, rather alarmed at the fury of the old man, the veins of whose forehead began to swell, and who sat drumming his papers with his clenched fist. "We're going to hunt him out, sir—the Duke's in Belgium already, and we expect marching orders every day?"

"'"Give him no quarter. Bring back the villain's head, sir. Shoot the coward down, sir," Sedley roared. "I'd enlist, myself, by —— ; but I'm a broken old man—ruined by that damned scoundrel—and by a quarrel—and by a parcel of swindling thieves in this country whom I made, sir, and who are rolling in their carriages now."'

"Mr. Sedley is merely contemptible. His wife is equally contemptible, but, having a stronger will, is also odious. Mr. Thackeray has delightfully sketched her whole character in the scene in which she quarrels with Amelia for exclaiming that her child shall not be poisoned with Daffy's Elixir.

"'Till the termination of her natural life, this breach between Mrs. Sedley and her daughter was never thoroughly mended ; the quarrel gave the elder lady numberless advantages, which she did not fail to turn to account with female ingenuity and perseverance. For instance, she scarcely spoke to Amelia for many weeks afterwards. She warned the domestics not to touch the child, as Mrs. Osborn might be offended. She asked her daughter to see and satisfy herself that there was no poison prepared in the little daily messes that were concocted for Georgy. When neighbours asked after the boy's health, she referred them pointedly to Mrs. Osborn. She never ventured to ask whether the baby was well or not. *She* would not touch the child, although he was her grandson, and her own precious darling, for she was not used to children, and might kill it.'"

Mr. Senior, at the close of his extracts, apologises : "Our defence is, that we have been reviewing one of the most remarkable books of the age—a work which is sure of immortality as ninety-nine hundreds of modern novels are sure of annihilation."

A LESSON IN COOKERY.

"There occurs in Mr. Thackeray's *Lecture on Steele* a passage which" (says Mr. Senior) "leads us to suspect that he had not studied with the attention that his great office requires, all the works of the authors whom he is criticising. He treats the dinner, in the *Polite Conversation,* as a specimen of the habits of the time.

"'Fancy' (he says) 'the moral condition of that society in which a lady of fashion provided a great shoulder of veal, a sirloin, a goose, hare, rabbit, chickens, partridges, black-puddings, and a ham, for a dinner for eight Christians. What could have been the condition of that polite world in which people openly ate goose after almond pudding, and took their soup in the middle of dinner?'

"Now, the great Simon Wagstaff, in the preface to his immortal work, has answered all this by anticipation.

"'Some' (he says) 'will perhaps object that when I bring my company to dinner I mention too great a variety of dishes, not consistent with the art of cookery, or proper for the season of the year, and *part of the first course is mingled with the second*; and a failure in politeness by introducing a black-pudding to a lord's table, and at a great entertainment. But if I had omitted the black-pudding, what would have become of that exquisite reason given by Miss Notable for not eating it? The world, perhaps, might have lost it for ever, and I should have been justly answerable. I cannot but hope that such hypercritical readers will please to consider that my business was to make so full and complete a body of refined sayings, as compact as I could, only taking care to produce them in the most natural and probable manner, in order to allure my readers into the very substance and marrow of this most admirable and necessary art.'"

ENGLISH HUMOURISTS.

"Mr. Thackeray's natural tendency was towards comedy, or rather towards satire. He

"'Shines in exposing knaves and painting fools.'

But his favourite amusement is the unmasking hypocrisy. He delights to show the selfishness of kindness, the pride of humility, the consciousness of simplicity.

"As a satirist, Mr. Thackeray is as indulgent to his real as he is severe towards his imaginary characters. He treats, indeed, Congreve with superciliousness, and Sterne with contempt almost amounting to disgust, and trembles before the awful phantom of Swift; but embraces all the other spirits that he calls up—Addison, Steele, Prior, Gay, Pope, Hogarth, Smollett, Fielding, and Goldsmith—with the cordiality of a brother of the craft.

" In his first lecture, Mr. Thackeray professes to point out
this common quality of the humorous writer, who, he says,
' besides appealing to your sense of ridicule, professes to
awaken and direct your love, your pity, your kindness—your
scorn for untruth, pretension, imposture—your tenderness for
the weak, the poor, the oppressed, the unhappy.   To the best
of his means and ability he comments on all the ordinary
actions and passions of life almost.   He takes upon himself to
be the week-day preacher, so to speak.

" Nor " (says Mr. Senior) " is it difficult to say what moral
writer does not come within so capacious a definition as this ?
At the head of the humourists of the eighteenth century we
should have to put Johnson, Horace Walpole, and Cowper ;
for never were men who commented more diligently on all
the ordinary actions and passions of life, and their comments
were deeply tinged with the wisdom resembling absurdity,
and the absurdity resembling wisdom, to which we give the
name of Humour.   Little new was to be said about Swift
after Johnson and Scott ; or about Addison, after Johnson and
Macaulay ; but we are glad to see a whole lecture given to
Steele, to whose biography less attention has been paid than
his amusing chequered character, and the great share which
he occupies in our earlier English literature deserve."

ETHIOPIAN MINSTRELS.

" When humour joins with rhythm and music, and appears
in songs" (says Thackeray), " its influence is irresistible ; its
charities are countless ; it stirs the feelings to love, peace,
friendship, as scarce any mortal agent can.   The songs of
Béranger are hymns of love and tenderness.   I have seen
great whiskered Frenchmen warbling the ' Bonne Vielle,'
the ' Soldats au paus, au paus,' with tears rolling down their
moustaches.   At a Burns festival, I have seen Scotchmen
singing Burns, while the drops twinkled on their furrowed
cheeks, while each rough hand was flung out to grasp its
neighbour's, while early scenes and sacred recollections, and
dear and delightful memories of the past came rushing back
at the sound of the familiar words and music, and the softened
heart was full of love and friendship and home.   Humour !
if tears are the alms of gentle spirits, and may be counted, as
sure they may, among the sweetest of life's charities, of that
kindly sensibility, and sweet and sudden emotion, which

exhibits itself at the eyes, I know no such provocative as humour; it is an irresistible sympathiser; it surprises you into compassion; you are laughing and disarmed, and suddenly forced into tears. I heard a humorous balladist not long since, a minstrel with wool on his head and an ultra-Ethiopian complexion, who performed a negro ballad, that I confess moistened these spectacles in a most unexpected manner. I have gazed at dozens of tragedy queens, dying on the stage, and expiring in appropriate blank verse, and I never wanted to wipe them. They have looked up, with deep respect, be it said, at many scores of clergymen in pulpits, and without being dimmed; and behold a vagabond, with a corked face and a banjo, sings a little song, strikes a wild note which sets the whole heart thrilling with happy humour! Humour is the mistress of tears; she knows the way to the *fons lachrymarum*, strikes in dry and rugged places with her enchanting wand, and bids the fountain gush and sparkle. She has refreshed myriads more from her natural spring than ever tragedy has watered from her pompous old urn."

THACKERAY'S CHARACTER OF GEORGE THE FOURTH.

"With a slate and a piece of chalk" (said Thackeray), "I could at this very desk perform a recognisable likeness of George IV. And yet, after reading of him in scores of volumes, hunting him through old magazines and newspapers, you will find nothing but a coat and wig, and the mask smiling below it— nothing but a great simulacrum. His sires and grandsires were men with individualities; they had steady loves and hatreds; one knew what they would do under given circumstances. The sailor-king who succeeded him was a man; and the Duke of York, his brother, was a man—a big, burly, jolly, cursing, courageous man. But this George was but a bow and a grin; he was all outside a tailor's work—fine cocked-hat, nutty-brown wig, coat, huge black stock, under-waistcoats, more under-waistcoats, and then nothing—a royal mummy." The lecturer said he had once thought it would be good sport to hunt him down, but he would be ashamed to summon a full field, and then hunt such poor game. He spent £10,000 a year for the coats on his back; and the sums given him by the nation were past counting. He spent an income of £66,000, £70,000, £100,000, £120,000 a year—

the nation was continually paying debts for him of £180,000 or £650,000—besides granting mysterious foreign loans, the proceeds of which this man pocketed. He was so lovely to look upon that he was described as Prince Florizel. He and his brother-king, Louis d'Artois—who subsequently, driven away by his people, had to seek shelter in Holyrood—shared between them the title of "the First Gentlemen of Europe." It was, of course, a point of loyalty to accord the title to George in this country. It was Walter Scott who was his champion—who rallied all Scotland to him, laying about him with his claymore on all his enemies. The House of Brunswick had no such two defenders as Samuel Johnson and Walter Scott. The dreadful dulness of papa's Court at Windsor, however, was such as would have made scapegraces of any princes. But his brothers, after sowing their wild oats and spending their youth in riotous living, settled down into quiet if not good men. But throughout, Prince Florizel was the same. He signalized his entrance into life by an act worthy of him—he invented a new shoe-buckle, an inch long and five inches broad, which covered almost the whole instep, and reached down to the ground on either side—a sweet invention, lovely and useful as the prince on whose foot it sparkled. His natural companions were dandies and parasites, French ballet-dancers, French cooks, horse-jockeys, boxers, china, jewel, and gimcrack-merchants. Fox, and Pitt, and Burke, and Sheridan were sometimes his guests, but what had they in common with their host of Carlton House? His opinions on anything but the best pattern for a waistcoat, or the sauce for a partridge, were not worth anything.

THE HEROINE OF ESMOND.

"We are always ordered to admire the beauty of a heroine" (says Mr. Senior), "but if we obey, it is usually on the act of faith. The description is so vague, that we are forced to take her charm on trust. But Mr. Thackeray's portrait of Beatrix is so animated and so individualised, that it affects the imagination as if it were painted in colours instead of words.

"She was a brown beauty; that is, her eyes, hair, and eyebrows and eyelashes were dark; her hair curling with rich undulations, and waving over her shoulders; but her complexion was as dazzling white as snow in sunshine, except her cheeks, which were a bright red, and her lips, which were of a still deeper crimson. Her mouth and chin, they said, were too large and full, and so they might be for a goddess in marble, but not for a woman whose eyes were fire, whose look was love, whose voice was the sweetest love song, whose shape was perfect symmetry, health, decision, activity; whose foot, as it planted itself on the ground, was firm but flexible, and whose motion, whether rapid or slow, was always perfect grace, agile as a nymph, lofty as a queen—now melting, now imperious, now sarcastic, there was no single movement of hers but was beautiful. As he thinks of her, he who writes feels young again, and remembers a paragon.

"Beatrix is the only character that interests; but there are many that amuse. All of them, indeed, amuse; for, except when he is playing with a doll which he wants to dress up as a good heroine, Mr. Thackeray can produce nothing that is not amusing."

HOMAGE TO WOMEN.

" "It was Steele" (says Mr. Thackeray, in one of the most pleasing pages of his *Lectures*) "who first began to pay a manly homage to the goodness and understanding, as well as the tenderness and beauty of woman. In his comedies, the heroes do not rant and rave about the divine beauties of Gloriana or Statira, as the characters were made to do in the chivalry romances and the high-flown dramas just going out of vogue; but Steele admires women's virtue, acknowledges their sense, and adores their purity and beauty, with an ardour and strength which should win the good will of all women to their hearty and respectful champion. What can be more delightful than the following:—

" ' As to the pursuits after affection and esteem, the fair sex are happy in this particular, that with them the one is much more nearly related to the other than in men. The love of a woman is inseparable from some esteem of her; and as she is naturally the object of affection, the woman who has your esteem has also some degree of your love. A man that dotes on a woman for her beauty, will whisper his friend, " That creature has a great deal of wit when you are well acquainted with her." And if you examine the bottom of your esteem for a woman, you will find you have a greater opinion of her beauty than anybody else. As to us men, I design to pass most of my time with the facetious Harry Bickerstaff: but William Bickerstaff, the most prudent man of our family, shall be my executor.'—*Tatler*, No. 206."

DICK STEELE AT CHARTERHOUSE.

The Duke of Ormond, the patron of Steele's father, was one of the governors of the old school of Charterhouse, near Smithfield, where, as soon after his father's death as he could be entered, Richard Steele was sent as gown-boy. Respecting him the following entries exist in the books of the Charter-house ; for which information Dr. Steele is indebted to the kindness of the present principal of that institution :—" Nov. 17ᵗʰ, 1684, Richard Steel, admitted for the Duke of Ormond" (*i.e.*, nominated by him) ; "aged 13 years, on 12ᵗʰ March last ;" and " Nov. 1ˢᵗ, 1869, Richard Steel elected to the University." (Here we see the name has not a final *e*.)

Mr. Thackeray, who was himself educated upon this noble institution, has speculatively sketched Steele's school-boy life. He says, in *English Humourists* :— .

" I am afraid no good report could be given by his masters and ushers of that thick-set, square-faced, black-eyed, soft-hearted little Irish boy. He was very idle. He was whipped deservedly a great number of times. Though he had very good parts of his own, he got other boys to do his lessons for him, and only took just as much trouble as should enable him to scuffle through his exercises, and by good fortune escape the flogging-block. One hundred and fifty years after, I have myself inspected, but only as an amateur, that instrument of righteous torture still existing, and in occasional use, in a secluded private apartment of the old Charterhouse School ; and have no doubt it is the very counter-part, if not the ancient and interesting machine itself, at which poor Dick Steele submitted himself to the tormentors.

"Besides being very kind, lazy, and good-natured, the boy went invariably into debt with the tart-woman ; ran out of bounds, and entered into pecuniary, or rather promissory, engage-ments with the neighbouring lollipop vendors and piemen— exhibited an early fondness for drinking mum and sack, and bor-rowed from all his comrades who had money to lend."

The writer admits that he has " no sort of authority for the statements here made of Steele's early life ;" but he reasons upon the child being father of the man ; adding, " If man and boy resembled each other, Dick Steele, the schoolboy, must have been one of the most generous, good-for-nothing, amiable little creatures that ever conjugated the word *tupto*, I beat, *tuptomai*, I am whipped, in any school in Great Britain." There is, however, presumptive evidence that Steele was not so bad a boy as here sketched—from his ready scholarship of after years, as well as from the kind expressions long inter-changed between him and its old head-master, Dr. Ellis, he may be assumed to have passed fairly through the school.

VANITY FAIR.—BECKY.—THE CRAWLEYS.

Becky is the character among all that Mr. Thackeray has drawn, which has received the most applause. She has no affectation, no piety, no disinterested benevolence. She is, indeed, perfectly selfish. She wants all the virtues which are to be exercised for the benefit of others. She has neither justice nor veracity. She treats mankind as mankind treats brutes—as mere sources of utility or amusement, as instruments or playthings, or prey. But many of the self-regarding virtues she possesses in a high degree. She has great industry, prudence, decision, courage, and self-reliance. . . As might be expected in a person of her good sense and self-control, she is a mistress of the smaller virtues—good temper and good-nature; she always wishes to please, because it is only by pleasing that she can subjugate. She is not resentful nor spiteful, because she despises all around her too much to waste anger on them, and because she knows that petty injuries are generally repaid with interest. · Her estimate of herself is not far from the truth. She is visiting a sober country house, in which she formerly lived as governess :—

"One day followed another, and the ladies of the house passed their lives in those calm pursuits and amusements which satisfy country ladies. Rebecca sang Handel and Haydn to the family of evenings, and essayed in a large piece of worsted work, as if she had been born to the business, and as if this kind of life was to continue with her until she should sink to the grave in a polite old age, leaving regrets and a great quantity of consols behind her, as if there were not cares and duns, schemes, shifts, and poverty waiting outside the park gates to pounce upon her when she issued into the world again.

"'It isn't difficult to be a country gentleman's wife,' Rebecca thought; 'I think I could be a good woman if I had five thousand a year. I could dawdle into the nursery and count the apricots on the wall. I could water plants in a greenhouse, and pick off dead leaves from the geraniums; I could ask old women about their rheumatisms, and order half-a-crown's worth of soup for the poor; I shouldn't miss it

much out of five thousand a year. I could go to church
and keep awake in the great family pew ; or go to sleep behind the curtains, and with my veil down, if I only had
practice. I could pay everybody if I had but the money.'

"The old haunts, the old fields and woods, the copses,
ponds, and gardens, the rooms of the old house where she had
spent a couple of years, seven years ago, were all carefully
revisited by her. She had been young then, or comparatively
so, for she forgot the time when she ever was young, but she
remembered her thoughts and feelings seven years back, and
contrasted them with those which she had at present, now
that she had seen the world, and lived with great people, and
raised herself beyond her original humble station.

"'I have passed away because I have brains,' Becky
thought, ' and almost all the rest of the world are fools. I
could not go back and consort with those people now, whom
I used to meet at my father's studio. Lords come up to my
door with stars and garters, instead of poor artists with screws
of tobacco in their pockets. I have a gentleman for a husband, and an earl's daughter for a sister, in the house where I
was little better than a servant a few years ago. But I am
much better to do now in the world than I was when I was
the poor painter's daughter, and wheedled the grocer round
the corner for sugar and tea. Suppose I had married Francis,
who was so fond of me, I couldn't have been much poorer
than I am now. Heigho ! I wish I could exchange my position in society, and all my relations, for a snug sum in the
three per cent. consols !' For so it was that Becky fell into
the vanity of human affairs, and it was in these securities
that the world would have liked to cast anchor."

The game which poor Becky plays is, from its outset, almost
a hopeless one ; it is to rise in the world without money, or
birth, or connections, or friends. She begins it at seventeen ;
the orphan penniless daughter of a drunken, unsuccessful
painter and a French opera girl. Received as a French
teacher in Miss Pinkerton's school, bored by the pompous
vanity of the mistress, the silly chat and scandal and quarrels
of the girls, and the frigid, empty correctness of the gover-
nesses, she forms harsher habits of unsympathising self-
existence. She fights her way to be a governess in Sir
Pitt Crawley's family ; and by a mixture of wheedling, coax-
ing, flattering, and rallying (described with as much humour
as it is conceived), hooks, and plays with, and at last lands,

her first spoil—Captain Rawdon Crawley. Her prize, however, resembles the gold paid by the magician in the *Arabian Nights*, which turned to leaves in the receiver's purse. Crawley's aunt, disgusted by his match, burns a will under which he was to have inherited £50,000, and Becky finds that all she has gained is a good-natured husband, overwhelmed with debt, with no property but his commission in the Life Guards, and no knowledge except of whist, piquette, and billiards. With her usually good sense, she makes the most of her unpromising cards—goes with the regiment to Brussels—turns the general commanding the division into her slave—provides victims for the admirable play of her husband—and makes him the happiest of mortals.

"How the Crawleys got the money which was spent upon the entertainments with which they treated the polite world, was a mystery which gave rise to some conversation at the time, and probably added zest to these little festivities. Who knows what stories were or were not told of our dear and innocent friend? Certain it is, that if she had all the money which she was said to have begged or borrowed or stolen, she might have capitalised and been honest for life, whereas—but this is advancing matters. The truth is that, by economy and good management—by a sparing use of ready money, and by paying scarcely anybody—people can manage, for a time at least, to make a great show with very little means; and it is our belief, that Becky's much-talked-of parties, which were not, after all that was said, very numerous, cost this lady very little more than the wax candles which lighted the walls. Stillbrook supplied her with game and fruit in abundance. Lord Steyne's cellar was at her disposal, and that excellent nobleman's famous cooks presided over her little kitchen, or sent by my lord's order the rarest delicacies from their own. I protest it is quite shameful in the world to abuse a simple creature, as people of her time abuse Becky, and I warn the public against believing one-tenth of the stories against her."

THACKERAY'S TALES AND NOVELS.

The first contributions he made to literature under a distinctive name were the tales, criticisms, and descriptive sketches which appeared in *Fraser's Magazine* under the pseudonyms of Michael Angelo Titmarsh, and George Fitz-

Boodle, Esq. The keen observation, delicate irony, and refined style of these magazine papers attracted the notice of
readers like the late John Sterling, who predicted the author's
future fame, but left the mass of devourers of monthly literature unconscious of extraordinary merit. The first of his
works which appeared in a separate form were *The Paris
Sketch Book* (1840), and *The Second Funeral of Napoleon*, and
The Chronicles of a Dream in metre, published together
(1841). But neither these, nor *The Irish Sketch Book* (1843),
made a permanent impression on the public, which, so faithful
to old friends, was in this case slow to discover unaided
merit. Some of Mr. Thackeray's best smaller pieces, as " The
Hoggarty Diamond " and " Barry Lyndon," appeared in
Fraser. Passing over some small occasional and Christmas
books, *Notes of a Journey from Cornhill to Grand Cairo* (1846),
Mrs. Perkins's Ball (1847), *Dr. Birch and his Young Friends*
(1849), we come to *Pendennis*, the portraiture of a man of
unpleasant character, notwithstanding his sense of conventional honour, whom Mr. Thackeray invited the world,
" knowing how mean the best of us is," to receive with
charity, " with all his faults and shortcomings, who does not
claim to be a hero, but only a man and a brother." It was
in *Pendennis* that critics first discovered the tendency, which
has since been frequently charged on Mr. Thackeray, and
traced in nearly all his writings, to dwell by preference on
the dark and unlovely side of human character, and hold up
the petty and ignoble side of all things while overlooking the
goodness that exists in the world. The charge first took a
serious form in a criticism of *The Kickleburys on the Rhine*,
Mr. Thackeray's Christmas book in 1859, and provoked an
exceedingly caustic reply, prefixed to a second edition of
the volume, which delighted the most brilliant audiences
which have honoured a literary man in these days, and have
since been numbered with his published works. In 1852
The History of Henry Esmond, Esq., was given to the world.
As an achievement of literary art this has usually been considered the greatest of the author's performances, but if the
test of literature is the interest it excites, *Esmond* has been
surpassed by many of the author's works which exhibits less
technical skill. The nobler tone of this work may be considered either as a refutation of the censures founded on the
features of *Pendennis*, or as an improvement suggested by the
taste of the public, expressed through the medium of adverse

criticism. *The Newcomes*, published in 1855, revealed a deeper pathos than any of Mr. Thackeray's previous novels, and showed that the author could when he pleased give us pictures of moral beauty and loveliness. The success of the "Lectures on the English Humourists," and the tendency of the historical studies evident in *Esmond*, led Mr. Thackeray to prepare a series of lectures on "The Four Georges," which he first delivered in the United States. The subject was not favourable to the display of the author's more genial qualities; very little that is good could be said of the Georges. Yet where in English literature shall we find anything more solemn and affecting than his picture of the affliction of the old king, the last of that name?

MR. M. A. TITMARSH.

Titmarsh is a very lively, pleasant fellow; just such a *compagnon de voyage* as we should be glad to fall in with on our next trip to Paris. He has a very nice perception of the ridiculous, and a talent for raillery which would have delighted even the great Lord Shaftesbury, who maintains that nothing is proof against raillery but what is honest and just. Now, Mr. Titmarsh flies at the weak points of English and French alike, and lashes their dishonesty and injustice with a freedom of wit and humour which is truly amusing. But he is no caricaturist. He is, we rejoice to add, a grateful man; in proof of which we quote his Dedication to a person, who, though vulgarly termed a fraction of humanity, is an important helpmate in enabling any one to cut a figure in this great world. Here is the proof :

"*Dedicatory Letter to M. Aretz, tailor, &c. 27, Rue Richelieu, Paris.*

"SIR,—It becomes every man in his station to acknowledge and praise virtue wheresoever he may find it, and to point it out for the admiration and example of his fellow men.

"Some months since, when you presented to the writer of these pages a small account for coats and pantaloons manufactured by you, and when you were met by a statement from your creditor, that an immediate settlement of your bill would be extremely inconvenient to him; your reply was, 'Mon Dieu, sir, let not that annoy you; if you want money, as a gentleman often does in a strange country, I have a thousand-franc note at my house which is quite at your service.'

"History or experience, sir, makes us acquainted with so few actions that can be compared to yours—an offer lik‹ this from a stranger and a tailor seems to me so astonishir.g —that you must pardon me for thus making your virtue public, and acquainting the English nation with your merit and your name. Let me add, sir, that you live on the first floor; that your‧cloths and fit are excellent, and your charges moderate and just ; and, as a humble tribute of my admiration, permit me to lay these volumes at your feet. Your obliged, faithful servant,

"M. A. TITMARSH."

THE PLUSH PAPERS.

The *Yellowplush Papers,* the reader need scarcely be told, first appeared in *Fraser's Magazine ;* no matter, for they deserve a second and a third reading, they are so life-like and laughter moving. So, reader, do not spurn a literary footman of Mr. Yellowplush's distinction ; he is, be assured, a very faithful chronicler of his ladies and gentlemen, for he was "some time footman in many genteel families," from all of whom he received an excellent character for honesty and sobriety. Besides, we would ask, who can so well recount the private histories of "their betters" as their servants, and who are so fit to become their biographers. True it is that all are not equally gifted : Yellowplush may not, like Dodsley, be a " Muse in Livery," nor be mistaken by his maxims for Lord Chesterfield ; nor may he, in these degenerate days, meet with such a Mæcenas as Pope ; but, be assured that this said Yellowplush is a shrewd painter of human follies, whether he sketches Miss Shum's husband, skims " The Diary of George IV." chronicles the doings of Mr. Deuceace, or turns critic next, and strips the literary jackdaw of his borrowed feathers and falsely earned fame. Some of his critiques, by the way, will give vanity the jaundice, and make her sons take the tinge of the reviewer's livery. Here is a pair of portraits : " Well, being a Whig, it's the fashion as you know, to receive littery pipple ; and accordingly, at dinner t'other day, whose name do you think I had to hollar out on the fust landing place about a wick ago ? After several dukes and markises had been enounced, a very gentill fly drives up to our door, and out steps two gentlemen. One was a paily and wore spectickles, a wig, and a white neckcloth, the other was slim, with a hook nose, a pail face, a small waist, a pair of falling shoulders, a tight coat, and a catarack of black sattin tumbling out of his busum, and falling into a gilt velvet weskit. The little genlmn settled his wigg, and pulled out his ribbinns; the younger one fluffed the dust off his shoes, looked at his wiskers in a little pockitglass, settled his crevatt; and they both mounted upstairs." The book is embellished with three accurate portraits of the authors, supposed to be marching hand in hand, and just on the brink of immortality.

THE SECOND FUNERAL OF NAPOLEON.

In 1841, Mr. Thackeray published a narrative of this grand ceremony, in *Three Letters addressed to Miss Smith, of London;* and *The Chronicle of the Drums.* 1. The first letter detailed the disinterment of Napoleon at St. Helena. 2. The voyage from St. Helena to Paris. 3. *The Funeral Ceremony.* The little square book is illustrated with effective wood-engravings, copied from the French. Here is the descriptive letterpress of the latter scene:

" The church began to fill apace, and you saw that the hour of the ceremony was drawing near.

" Imprimis came men with lighted staves, and set fire to at least ten thousand of wax candles that were hanging in brilliant chandeliers in various parts of the chapel. Curtains were dropped over the upper windows as these illuminations were effected, and the church was left only to the funeral light of the spermaceti. To the right was the dome, round the cavity of which sparkling lamps were set that designed the shape of it brilliantly against the darkness. In the midst, and where the altar used to stand, rose the catafalque. And why not? Who is god here but Napoleon? and in him the sceptics have already ceased to believe, but the people does still somewhat. He and Louis XIV. divide the worship of the place between them.

" As for the catafalque, the best that I can say for it is that it is really a noble and imposing-looking edifice, with tall pillars supporting a grand dome, with innumerable escutcheons, standards, and allusions, military and funereal; a great eagle, of course, tops the whole; tripods burning spirits of wine stand round this kind of dead-man's throne, and as we saw it (by peering over the heads of our neighbours in the front rank), it looked, in the midst of the black concave, and under the effect of half-a-thousand flashing cross-lights, properly grand and tall. The effect of the whole chapel, however (to speak the jargon of the painting-room), was spoiled by being *cut up*; there were too many objects for the eye to rest upon. The ten thousand wax candles, for instance, in their numberless twinkling chandeliers, the raw *tranchant* colours of the new banners, wreaths, bees, N's, and other emblems, dotting the place all over, and incessantly puzzling, or rather *bothering*, the beholder.

" High over head, in a sort of mist, with the glare of their original colours worn down by dust and time, hung long rows of dim, ghostly-looking standards captured in old days from the enemy. They were, I thought, the best and most solemn part of the show.

" To suppose that the people were bound to be solemn during this ceremony is to exact from them something quite needless and unnatural. The very fact of a squeeze dissipates all solemnity. One great crowd is always, as I imagine, pretty much like another: in the course of the last few years I have seen three; that attending the coronation of our present sovereign, that which went to see Courvoisier hanged, and this which witnessed the Napoleon ceremony. The people so assembled for hours together are jocular rather than solemn, seeking to pass away the weary time with the best amusements that will offer. There was, to be sure, in all the scenes above alluded to, just one moment—one particular moment—when the universal people feels a shock, and is for that second serious.

" But except for that second of time, I declare I saw no seriousness here beyond that of *ennui*. The church began to fill with personages of all ranks and conditions. First, opposite our seats, came a company of fat grenadiers of the National Guard, who presently, at the word of command, put their muskets down against benches and wainscots, until the arrival of the procession.

" For seven hours these men formed the object of the most anxious solicitude of all the ladies and gentlemen seated on our benches. They began to stamp their feet, for the cold was atrocious, and we were frozen as we sate. Some of them fell to blowing their fingers, one executed a kind of dance, such as one sees often here in cold weather: the individual jumps repeatedly upon one leg and kicks out the other violently, meanwhile his hands are flapping across his chest. Some fellows opened their cartouche-boxes, and from them drew eatables of various kinds. You can't think how curious we were to know the qualities of the same *Tiens, ce gros qui mange une cuisse de volatille !' 'Il a du jambon, celui là.'* 'I should like some too,' growls an Englishman, 'for I hadn't a morsel of breakfast,' and so on. This is the way, my dear, that we see Napoleon buried.

"Did you ever see a chicken escape from a clown, in a pantomime, and hop over into the pit, or amongst the fiddlers ? and have you not heard the shrieks of enthusiastic laughter that the wondrous incident occasions ? We had our chicken, of course ; there is never a public crowd without one. A poor unhappy woman, in a greasy plaid-cloak, with a battered, rose-coloured plush bonnet, was seen taking her place among the stalls allotted to the grandees. *'Voyez donc l'Anglaise,'* said everybody, and it was too true. You could swear that the wretch was an Englishwoman—a bonnet was never made or worn so in any other country. Half an hour's delightful amusement did this lady give us all : she was whisked from seat to seat by the huissiers, and at every change of place woke a peal of laughter. I was glad, however, at the end of the day, to see the old pink bonnet over a very comfortable seat, which somebody had not claimed, and she had kept.

"Are not these remarkable incidents ? The next wonder we saw was the arrival of a set of tottering old invalids, who took their places under us, with drawn sabres. Then came a superb drum-major, a handsome, smiling, good-humoured giant of a man, his breeches astonishingly embroidered with silver lace. Him a dozen little drummer-boys followed. 'The little darlings !' all the ladies cried out in a breath : they were, indeed, pretty little fellows, and came and stood close under us ; the huge drum-major smiled over his little red-capped flock, and for many hours, in the most perfect contentment, twiddled his moustachios, and played with the tassels of his cane.

"Now the company began to arrive thicker and thicker. A whole covey of *conseillers d'état* came in, in blue coats, embroidered with blue silk ; then came a crowd of lawyers, in toques and caps, among whom were sundry venerable judges, in scarlet, purple velvet, and ermine—a kind of Bajazet costume. Look there ! there is the Turkish ambassador, in his red cap, turning his solemn brown face about, and looking preternaturally wise.   The Deputies walk in a body.   Guizot is not there; he passed by just now, in full ministerial costume.   Presently, little Thiers saunters back.   What a clear, broad, sharp-eyed face the fellow has, with his gray hair cut down so demure! A servant passes, pushing through the crowd a shabby wheel-chair. It has just brought old Monçey, the Governor of the Invalides, the honest old man who defended Paris so stoutly in 1814.   He has been very ill, and is worn down almost by infirmities; but in his illness he was perpetually asking—'Doctor, shall I live till the 15th?   Give me till then, and I die contented.'   One can't help believing that the old man's wish is honest, however one may doubt the piety of another illustrious marshal who once carried a candle before Charles X., in a procession, and has been this morning to Neuilly, to kneel and pray at the foot of Napoleon's coffin.   He might have said his prayers at home, to be sure; but don't let us ask too much; that kind of reserve is not a Frenchman's characteristic.

   "Bang, bang!   At about half-past two a dull sound of cannonading was heard without the church, and signals took place between the commandant of the Invalides, of the National Guards, and the big drum-major.   Looking to their troop (the fat nationals were shuffling into line again), the two commandants uttered, as nearly as I could catch them, the following words:—

   "'Harrum—Hump!'

   "At once all the national bayonets were on the present, and the sabres of the old invalids up.   The big drum-major looked round at the children, who began very slowly and solemnly on their drums, rub-dub-dub—rub-dub-dub—(count two between each)—rub-dub-dub; and a great procession of priests came down from the altar.

   "First, there was a tall, handsome cross-bearer, bearing a long gold cross, of which the front was turned towards his grace the archbishop.   Then came a double row of about sixteen incense-boys, dressed in white surplices: the first boy about six years old, the last with whiskers and of the height of man.   Then followed a regiment of priests, in black tippets and white gowns; they had blacks hoods, like the moon when she is at her third quarter, wherewith those who were bald (many were, and fat too) covered themselves. All the reverend men held their heads meekly down, and affected to be reading in their breviaries.

"After the priests came some bishops of the neighbouring districts, in purple, with crosses sparkling on their episcopal bosoms.

"Then came, after more priests, a set of men whom I have never seen before—a kind of ghostly heralds, young and handsome men, some of them, in stiff tabards of black and silver, their eyes to the ground, their hands placed at right angles with their chests.

"Then came two gentlemen bearing remarkable tall candle-sticks with candles of corresponding size. One was burning brightly, but the wind (that chartered libertine) had blown out the other, which nevertheless kept its place in the procession. I wondered to myself whether the rev. gent. who carried the extinguished candle felt disgusted, humiliated, mortified, perfectly conscious that the eyes of many thousands of people were bent upon that bit of refractory wax. We all of us looked at it with intense interest.

"Another cross-bearer, behind whom came a gentleman carrying an instrument like a bedroom candlestick.

"His Grandeur Monseigneur Affre, Archbishop of Paris—he was in black and white, his eyes were cast to the earth, his hands were together at right angles on his chest, on his hands were black gloves, on the black gloves sparkled the sacred episcopal—what do I say?—archiepiscopal ring. On his head was the mitre. It is unlike the godly coronet that figures upon the coach-panels of our own right reverend bench. The archbishop's mitre may be about a yard high, formed within probably of consecrated pasteboard; it is without covered by a sort of watered silk of white and silver. On the two peaks at the top of the mitre are two very little spangled tassels that frisk and twinkle about in a very agreeable manner.

"Monseigneur stood opposite to us for some time, when I had the opportunity to note the above remarkable phenomena. He stood opposite me for some time, keeping his eyes steadily on the ground, his hands before him, a small clerical train following after. Why didn't they move? There was the National Guard keeping on presenting arms, the little drummers going on rub-dub-dub—rub-dub-dub—in the same steady slow way, and the procession never moved an inch—there was evidently, to use an elegant phrase, a hitch somewhere.

" (Enter a fat priest, who bustles up to the drum-major.)

" Fat Priest.—Taisez-vous.

" Little Drummers.—Rub-dub-dub — rub-dub-dub — rub-dub-dub, &c.

" Drum-Major.—Qu'est-ce donc ?

" Fat Priest.—Taisez-vous, vous dis-je, ce n'est pas le corps. Il n'arrivera pas pour une heure.

" The little drums were instantly hushed, the procession turned to the right-about, and walked back to the altar again, the blown-out candle that had been on the near side of us before was now on the off side, the National Guards set down their muskets and began at the sandwiches again. We had to wait an hour and a half at least before the great procession arrived. The guns without went on booming all the while at intervals ; and as we heard each, the audience gave a kind of ' ah-ah-ah !' such as you hear when the rockets go up at Vauxhall.

" At last the real procession came.

" Then the drums began to beat as formerly, the nationals to get under arms, the clergymen were sent for, and went, and presently—yes, there was the tall cross-bearer at the head of the procession, and they came *back* !

" They chanted something in a weak, snuffling, lugubrious manner, to the melancholy bray of a serpent.

" Crash ! however, Mr. Habeneck and the fiddlers in the organ-loft pealed out a wild shrill march, which stopped the reverend gentlemen ; and in the midst of this music,

" And of a great trampling of feet and clattering,

" And of a great crowd of generals and officers in fine clothes,

" With the Prince de Joinville marching quickly at the head of the procession,

" And while everybody's heart was thumping as hard as possible,

" Napoleon's coffin passed.

" It was done in an instant. A box, covered with a great red cross—a dingy-looking cross lying on the top of it—seamen on one side, and invalids on the other ; they had passed in an instant and were up the aisle.

" A faint snuffling sound as before was heard from the officiating priests, but we knew of nothing more. It is said that old Louis Philippe was standing at the catafalque, whither the Prince de Joinville advanced, and said, 'Sire, I bring you the body of the Emperor Napoleon.'

" Louis Philippe answered, ' I receive it in the name of France.' Bertrand put on the body the most glorious, victorious sword that ever has been forged since the apt descendants of the first murderer learned how to hammer steel, and the coffin was placed in the temple prepared for it.

" The six hundred singers and the fiddlers now commenced the playing and singing of a piece of music ; and a part of the crew of the Belle Poule skipped into the places that had been kept for them under us, and listened to the music, chewing tobacco. While the actors and fiddlers were going on, most of the spirits-of-wine lamps or altars went out.

" When we arrived in the open air, we passed through the court of the Invalides, where thousands of people had been assembled, but where the benches were now quite bare. Then we came on to the terrace before the place : the old soldiers were firing off the great guns, which made a dreadful stunning noise, and frightened some of us, who did not care to pass before the cannon and be knocked down even by the wadding. The guns were fired in honour of the king, who was going home by a back door. All the forty thousand people who covered the great stands before the Hotel had gone away too. The imperial barge had been dragged up the river, and was lying lonely along the quay, examined by some few shivering people on the shore.

" It was five o'clock when we reached home ; the stars were shining keenly out of the frosty sky, and Françoise told me that dinner was just ready.

" In this manner, my dear Miss Smith, the great Napoleon was buried. Farewell."

The Funeral Ceremony is followed by *The Chronicle of the Drum,* which closes with these stanzas :

" Ah, gentle, tender, lady mine,
    The winter wind blows cold and shrill,
  Come, fill me one more glass of wine,
    And give the silly fools their fill.

" And what care we for war and wrack,
    How kings and heroes rise and fall ?
Look yonder, in his coffin black,
    There lies the greatest of them all !

" To pluck him down, and keep him up,
    Died many million human souls :
'Tis twelve o'clock, and time to sup,
    Bid Mary heap the fire with coals.

" He captured many thousand guns ;
    He wrote " The Great" before his name ;
And dying, only left his sons
    The recollection of his shame.

" Though more than half the world was his,
    He died without a rood his own ;
And borrowed from his enemies
    Six foot of ground to lie upon.

" He fought a thousand glorious wars,
    And more than half the world was his,
And somewhere, now in yonder stars,
    Can tell, mayhap, what greatness is."

SMOLLETT'S " HUMPHRY CLINKER."

" ' Humphry Clinker,' " says Mr. Thackeray (in his admirable lectures on English humourists), " is, I do believe, the most laughable story that has ever been written since the goodly art of novel-writing began. This verdict is in accordance with the general opinion, and it may be added that not only is the humour of the book finer and clearer than in any of Smollett's former novels, but the style is also more mellow, and the whole conception deeper and happier. There is a harsher power in some parts of ' Peregrine Pickle ;' but, if any one of Smollett's novels is entitled to a permanent place among the English classics, it is ' Humphry Clinker.' Coming after the ' Adventures of an Atom,' it is a biographical curiosity and we can only account for the more genial spirit which it shows as compared with that savage performance, by supposing that, in the quiet of his Italian retirement, the author had regained something of serenity and resignation.

Looking back, in this state of comparative composure, on the preceding three or four years of his life, we can conceive him dwelling with a melancholy self-irony on their various reminiscences, and resolving then to cast them into the shape of a novel. . . . In carrying out this scheme, Smollett had more than the usual pleasure which an author feels in a story of his own making. An exile on the Italian coast, he repeated in imagination, as he wrote, his recent visit to his native land ; fancied himself walking once more, in the person of Mathew Bramble, in the High Street of Edinburgh ; posting thence with Jerry to Glasgow, and there shaking hands with Moore and his other Glasgow acquaintances ; and finally, as the goal of his ideal journey, domiciled again in his cousin's house, amid the oak-woods of Cameron, in the heart of scenery to him the loveliest in the world. The Scotticism of ' Humphry Clinker' is unmistakable. The best parts of the book are unquestionably those describing the Scotch portion of the tour, and these are written with an accuracy as to places, persons, and names, which shows that it was Smollett's intention in the book to enlighten the English ignorance as to the state of the northern part of the island, and beat down by facts as well as laugh down by jests the international rancour still prevailing. How patriotically, for example, he speaks of Edinburgh as a ' hot-bed of genius,' enumerating eminent contemporary names in proof of the representation ; and with what satisfaction, in passing through Glasgow, he introduces Glassford, the great merchant, as a proof of the enterprise of the place, and his old master, Dr. Gordon, as a proof of its public spirit ! With what care, too, is the character of Lesmahago drawn, as a type at once of the good and the bad, the excellent and the absurd, in the Scottish national temper. Scott's Dugald Dalgetty is not a better character than Smollett's Lesmahago."

HOGARTH'S "LONDON APPRENTICES."

"We give the moral of the famous story of ' Industry and Idleness,' from Hogarth's ' London Apprentices.'

"Fair-haired Frank Goodchild smiles at his work, whilst naughty Tom Idle snores over his loom. Frank reads the edifying ballads of Whittington and the London 'Prentice, whilst that reprobate Tom Idle prefers Moll Flanders, and drinks hugely of beer. Frank goes to church of a Sunday, and warbles hymns from the gallery; while Tom lies on a tombstone outside playing at halfpenny-under-the-hat with street blackguards, and is deservedly caned by the beadle. Frank is made overseer of the business, while Tom is sent to sea. Frank is taken into partnership, and marries his master's daughter, sends out broken victuals to the poor, and listens, in his nightcap and gown, with the lovely Mrs. Goodchild by his side, to the nuptial music of the City bands and the marrow-bones and cleavers; whilst idle Tom, returned from sea, shudders in a garret lest the officers are coming to take him for picking pockets. The Worshipful Francis Goodchild, Esq., becomes Sheriff of London, and partakes of the most splendid dinners which money can purchase or aldermen devour; whilst poor Tom is taken up in a night-cellar, with that one-eyed and disreputable accomplice who first taught him to play chuck-farthing on a Sunday. What happens next? Tom is brought up before the justice of his country, in the person of Mr. Alderman Goodchild, who weeps as he recognises his old brother 'prentice as Tom's one-eyed friend peaches on him, and the clerk makes out the poor rogue's ticket for Newgate. Then the end comes. Tom goes to Tyburn in a cart with a coffin in it; whilst the Right Honourable Francis Goodchild, Lord Mayor of London, proceeds to his Mansion-house in his gilt coach with four footmen and a sword-bearer, whilst the companies of London march in the august procession, whilst the train-bands of the City fire their pieces and get drunk in his honour, and oh! crowning delight and glory of all, whilst his Majesty the king looks out from his royal balcony, with his ribbon on his breast and his Queen and his star by his side, at the corner house of St. Paul's-churchyard, where the toy-shop now is. In that last plate of the 'London Apprentices' in which the apotheosis of the Right Honourable Francis Goodchild is drawn, a ragged fellow is represented in the corner of the simple kindly piece, offering for sale a broadside purporting to contain an account of the appearance of the ghost of Tom Idle, executed at Tyburn."

CHARLES DICKENS.

THE story of the life of Charles Dickens, the most original novelist of our own times, in the opening portions of his career, may soon be told, especially when we take into account the many gifted pens which have written upon his genius, in epitomising the early stages, youthful traits appertaining to his years, and not to his disposition. "Careless observers," remarks a writer in the *Quarterly Review*, Jan. 1872, "frequently mistake the attributes of childhood for the bent of the particular child, and are severe in foibles, which are as certain to be shed with time as the first set of teeth. Sometimes a circumstance belongs jointly to the era of life and the customs of the generation. The young contemporaries of Dickens resembled their successors in seasoning their talk and letters with familiar expressions for which no authority can be found in *Johnson's Dictionary*. The usage breaks out in the early letters of Dickens, and in a few years it ceases. Such passing habits are the conventional practice of a period, and do not throw any light upon the taste of the individual. 'I am no more ashamed,' said Southey, 'of having been a republican than of having been a boy,' and the lively remark has a wide application. Characters would often be absolutely falsified if we were to judge them by the grave belief or playful adversity which is born of the time, and died with it."

Charles Dickens, the son of John Dickens, a clerk in the Navy Pay Office, was born at Landport in Portsea, February 7, 1812. The duties of his father's office obliged him frequently to change his residence, and much of the future novelist's infancy was spent at Portsmouth; he was removed to London when Charles was two years old, and, when he was

between four and five, to Chatham.   The lad was taught
English and a little Latin by his mother ; was next sent to a
day school kept by a mistress ; and at the age of seven, to an
academy kept by a Baptist minister.   Though a circumstance
slight in itself, it may interest some readers to be informed
that his schoolmaster there was the late Rev. William Giles,
F.R.A.S., latterly of Chester.   As an evidence of his kindly
disposition, it may be mentioned that, some years ago, when
such fame as he had acquired would cause most men to forget
their former old associations, Dickens joined some other old
scholars in the presentation of a service of plate to Mr. Giles,
accompanied by a most gratifying testimonial of regard, to
which he had attached his well-known bold autograph.   A
gentleman, who was ten years Mr. Giles's junior, was at school
at the same time with Dickens, there being only two years
difference in their ages.   He used often to speak of the
marked geniality of Dickens's character as a boy, and of his
proficiency in all boyish sports, such as cricket, &c.

The incidents of this period are chronicled with sufficient
particularity, when we are told that the little scholar, when
about four years old, " cried daily to climb some steps in
Rome Lane, Chatham, in order to reach a dame's school,
which was held in an apartment over a shop."

When Dickens's father was removed from Chatham to
Somerset House, his little son's schooling came to an end.
His genius had been put upon the proper track, and in the
particulars which constituted his peculiar distinction for his
future eminence proceeded without a pause.

An extraordinary stretch of memory is related of Dickens's
early childhood — in his manhood, he remembered the scenes
he had left when he was two years old.   It is true that Dr.
Johnson's memory extended to two years and a half ; but of
particular events the Doctor did not know whether he remembered the thing, *or the talk of it.* Dickens's habit of observation was singularly keen. Before he was taken from Chatham,
he noted " with ceaseless watchfulness, the virtues, foibles,
and oddities of the people around him."   Indeed, he made
the eccentricities of mankind his study.

Dickens's education suited his natural gifts. He depended for
nearly the whole of his amusement upon reading, principally
drawn from his father's book-shelf, and as the books which an
author loved to read are a matter of interest to the readers
of his biography, we are not surprised to find his favourite

authors to have been the masterpieces of fiction, Smollett, Goldsmith, and Defoe ; the *Arabian Nights, Don Quixote*, and *Gil Blas ;* the essays of Addison and Johnson, and the collection of farces edited by Mrs. Inchbald. The church, the barn, the alehouse of Cheltenham, and its environs, appeared in his fancy to be the very scene of the adventures told in *Tom Jones, Peregrine Pickle*, and *Roderick Random.* The books which were the companions of his play-hours came to the aid of his precocious observation, and rendered it more precocious still. Thus, he acquired a second education, in this apprenticeship to authorship. He looked at the people amongst whom he lived through the searching eyes of De Foe, and Fielding, and Smollett, and Cervantes. "He could not," says the *Quarterly Reviewer*, "comprehend all their profound and subtle traits ; but they taught him to see both further and deeper. In this process he did more than extend his knowledge of human nature. In blending the fictions of his favourite novelists with the localities and facts of his personal history he was learning to use the materials he had accumulated. He was daily constructing miniature romances, composed in part of his own experience, and in part of the stories which had captivated his imagination. There could be no more effectual method than this intermixture to teach him the mature skill of his predecessors. Their style alone would have made invaluable instructors, for most of his authors were models of easy, pure, vigorous, or graceful English." Thus far his education turned out propitious.

The next stage was beset with care ; but proved probationary, and advantageous. Dickens, the father, the government clerk, had six children, and was of improvident habits, and much in debt ; and at the date of his return to London, entered into a composition with his creditors. His income was, consequently, reduced, and he was compelled to take a lower rented house in Baynham Street, Camden Town ; a washer-woman lived next door, and a Bow Street officer lived over the way. Among such neighbours Charles lost his companionship, and his occupation was to clean his father's boots, to go errands, and to take charge of his brothers and sisters. But he was cut off from his scholarly associates, and lost his opportunity of study. "What would I have given," said Charles, "if I had anything to give, to have been taught something anywhere." Still, the education of the would-be novelist went on ; and among his delights was a visit to

London, in company with any elder, in a walk through St.
Giles's, which, even at this early period, impressed him, and
led him afterwards, when his powers of observation were more
matured, to exclaim : "What wild visions of prodigies of
wickedness, want, and beggary arose in my mind out of that
place !" He thus saw some of the worst sides of London life,
which made him long the more to be sent to school. About
this time he took much interest in writing sketches of queer
people with whom he came in contact ; one of these was an
eccentric old barber, in Soho, who "was never tired of reviewing the events of the last war, and especially of detecting
Napoleon's mistakes, and rearranging his whole life for him
on a plan of his own,"—with that fondness which even early
youth delights in. Another contributor of oddity was a deaf
old charwoman, in the Baynham Street lodging, who excelled
in making delicious hashes with walnut ketchup.

At length the time came when, his father earning nothing,
his mother exerted herself to set up a girl's boarding-school,
at No. 4, Gower Street North, where a brass plate notified,
"Mrs. Dickens' Establishment." "I left at a great many
other doors," writes her son, "a great many circulars, calling
attention to the merits of the establishment ; yet nobody ever
came to school, nor do I recollect that anybody ever proposed
to come, or that the least preparation was made to receive
anybody." This scheme having failed to brighten the hopes
of the family, fresh debts were contracted, knocks at the door
were more frequent, and the clerk was thrown into the Marshalsea prison. In this new "house of care," he told his son
to "take warning, and to observe that if a man had twenty
pounds a year, and spent nineteen pounds, nineteen shillings,
and sixpence, he would be happy ; but a shilling spent the
other way would make him wretched." "The debtor," says
Mr. Forster, in his *Life of Charles Dickens*, "understood this
obvious truth as well before his troubles as when he pointed
the moral with his own example. Men usually err from
weakness, and not from ignorance, and expect their children
to be wiser for the knowledge which has been of no service
to themselves."

As the father of the family was removed to the Marshalsea,
Charles had to sell the "family library" we have just described, and to pawn all that could be pledged ; and, at last,
there was nothing left except a few chairs, a kitchen table, and
some bedding. "Thus they encamped, as it were, in the two

parlours of the empty house, and lived there night and day."

While John Dickens continued an inmate of the Marshalsea, an employment was found for Charles, by these fortuitous circumstances: "A sister of his mother had a step-son, James Lamert. Two Warrens, Robert and Jonathan, each claimed a property in the method of compounding Warren's blacking. Robert had succeeded in getting the chief custom of the public, and the rival establishment of Jonathan, which languished for want of capital, was sold to George Lamert, the cousin and brother-in-law of James." The blacking manufacture appears to have been *ab incepto* a competitive prize; and in this case it bettered the prospects of George Lamert, who was appointed manager of the above manufactory. He offered to give young Dickens work at a salary of six or seven shillings a week; and the lad, at some ten years of age, sat down to earn his livelihood by tying covers over the paste blacking-pots, and affixing a printed label. When his mother joined his father in the Marshalsea, a lodging was hired for Charles. His anguish at this change was extreme. "The misery," he says, "it was to my young heart to believe that, day by day, what I had learned and thought, and delighted in, and raised my fancy and emulation up by, was passing away from me, never to be brought back any more, cannot be written."

The blacking premises were in Old Hungerford Market. For two horrible years of degradation, borne in sickness and in sorrow, heroically for duty's sake, the world seemed pitiless to him. "My father and mother," he says, "could hardly have been more satisfied if I had been twenty years of age, distinguished at a grammar-school, and going to Cambridge."

He went to the Royal Academy of Music, to see his sister, who was a pupil there, receive a prize, and the effect it had upon him was a striking evidence of the extent to which his position preyed upon his mind. "I could not bear," he says, "to think of myself, beyond the reach of all such honourable emulation and success. The tears ran down my face. I felt as if my heart were rent. I prayed when I went to bed that night to be lifted out of the humiliation and neglect in which I was. I never had suffered so much before."

As a relief to his blacking business, Charles continued to add to his portraits from the inmates of the prison. From among the associations of the blacking factory he brought away Fagin and Mr. Sweedlepipe. There was now a gather-

ing of the Dickenses in the Marshalsea. Mr. Dickens had
retired from his official duties on a pension; his wife and
children shared his apartment; and " in every respect but
elbow-room, the family," as Dickens said to Mr. Forster,
" lived more comfortably in prison than they had done for a
long time out of it." Still, Charles was only an occasional
visitor. He felt acutely the exclusion from the domestic
circle, and the desolation of returning from his work to a
blank. A back attic was hired for him in the neighbourhood
of the Marshalsea, and he breakfasted and supped every day
at his " home." What he saw in the Marshalsea was good
material for him : he got his mother to tell him all she heard
of the respective histories of the motley population, and he
pieced out the hints from his own imagination. He scanned
each debtor separately with the inquisitive eyes that saw the
manners in his face; "he marked the peculiarities of dress,
of gait, of voice, of language; he discriminated the weak-
nesses which were comical, and the sadder traits which were
pathetic." He was present to see the debtors pass one by
one through a small room, where they affixed their names to a
petition to the King, for a grant to drink his Majesty's health
on his birth-day; and in testimony of his boyish intenseness
of observation, and his consequent tenacity of memory, he
says, " When I look with my mind's eye into the Fleet Prison
during Mr. Pickwick's incarceration, I wonder whether half-
a-dozen men were wanting from the Marshalsea crowd that
came filing in again." So it was that the varied forms of
society in which he was constrained to mingle went filing on
before him, and have since " come filing in again" for the
delight of multitudes.

We now return to the *Quarterly Review* :

" In due time Mr. Dickens took the benefit of the Insolvent
Debtors' Act, and was released from the Marshalsea. The
liberation of Charles followed at no great interval. Mr.
Dickens was dissatisfied with something in the treatment of his
son, and wrote an angry letter to the manager of the blacking
business. James Lamert thought the letter insulting, and
told the lad that, since he was the theme of the outrage, he
must leave the establishment. His mother interceded with
her step-nephew, soothed his irritation, and obtained permission for her son to return. There was a division between
husband and wife on the occasion. 'My father said I should

go back no more, and I should go to school. I do not write resentfully or angrily, for I know how all these things have worked together to make me what I am, but I never afterwards forgot, I never shall forget, I never can forget, that my mother was warm for my being sent back.' The spirit which pervades the comment of Dickens exhibits the least amiable phase of a character that commonly overflowed with kindness and generosity. The question had two sides; Dickens saw one, and his mother the other. Whoever may have been to blame, the family were always in distress. In Gower Street, they sometimes had not enough to eat; the mother's first thought was for the physical wants of her household; the earnings of Charles were an important addition to their means, and she probably considered that his education might be postponed till their poverty had abated. The master-passion of the boy was for the improvement of his mind. He sighed, before all things, to be extricated from the miserable occupation of tying paper over pots, and he perceived that nothing beyond wiser economy was needed to accomplish the end. His was the sounder view, but what was not sound was his inability to allow for the prudential calculations of a mother, whose children were not strangers to the pinchings of hunger, and his too sensitive recollection, at the height of his fame, when every obstacle had been subdued, of a mistaken opinion delivered a quarter of a century before."

Charles Dickens was dismissed from the blacking manufactory in 1824, when he was about twelve years old. Shortly afterwards, he was sent by his father to the academy of Mr. Jones, a Welshman, in the Hampstead Road, one of an ignorant and irascible tribe, who flogged boys unmercifully for not understanding perplexities which the master was incompetent to deal with. The type of school which will live in the novels of Dickens when the reality is gone, would be enough to tell us that he had been under the Creakles of his generation. Much was suffered in such places, and little learned. Dickens had the luck to escape the suffering : he was only a day-pupil, and there was a wholesome fear of tales being carried home to the parents. He did not learn Greek and Latin, which favoured his impunity from corporal punishment.

Two surviving school-fellows, who have written their recollections of him at Jones's academy, agree that even in the commercial department he was not distinguished. " I cannot recall anything," says Mr. Thomas, " that then indicated he would hereafter become a literary celebrity," and Dr. Danson says that his mastery of the English language must have been acquired by long and patient study after he left. The slender promise he gave may be gathered from the fact that the coincidence of name never suggested to Dr. Danson that the famous novelist could be his old intimate at the academy, and he did not suspect the identity till he read in *Household Words* a paper entitled " Our School," in which the establishment of Mr. Jones was the basis of a sketch intentionally heightened by the fancy of the author. " The aspect Dickens presented to his playmates was merely that of a handsome, curly-headed, healthy boy, who having outgrown his original delicacy of constitution, and enjoying more than an average share of animal spirits, entered with glee into the sports and tricks of the hour."

Dickens remained for a couple of years at Mr. Jones's academy, and on leaving in 1826, was sent, for a short period, to a second school. In 1827 he became a clerk in a solicitor's office, and kept to the calling till November, 1828. He was not articled and had no intention of practising the law; he was only hired to keep accounts, and do formal work; he studied, not law, but lawyers, and no class yielded him a richer harvest. On leaving the attorney's office, he determined to do something better. His father had mastered the intricacies of short-hand, and was a reporter of parliamentary debates; his son determined to follow his example. Up to nine years of age he was tied to the rules of school, at the manufactory he had to observe the long and punctual hours of labouring men; for two years and a half he was again subjected to the rigid laws of school, and for two years more to an equally rigid attendance at his office; the vast proportion of what is best in his writings is derived from what he had seen or undergone in childhood, boyhood, and dawning manhood; his deficiency was in his acquaintance with books, which he had read but little.

Dickens now determined to qualify himself to be a first-rate reporter : no amount of skill in taking down words will enable a reporter to render speeches correctly unless he can follow the sense. To learn something of what accomplished men know is an essential auxiliary in recording what they say, concurrently with the practice of the short-hand symbols ; Dickens, therefore, became a constant reader at the British

Museum. His progress in both undertakings was singularly rapid. He was skilled enough in short-hand at the end of eighteen months to obtain professional employment. Time did not permit him to run the immense circuit of literature. He was strongest in fiction and travels, and not having gleaned his opinions of books through books, his judgment of them had a charming directness and independence; and of book knowledge, Dickens often said to Mr. Forster, this was the most productive season of his life. The library of Dickens was the living book of mankind. He was, before all, an observer, and he had little more to ask of books, than to teach him how to shape his native ideas. Dickens had abundance of excellent English at his command, and a clear and fluent style, but the want of a chaste taste in passages of his composition betrayed that he had not lingered long enough over the highest literature to get thoroughly imbued with its austere refinements. While Dickens was studying at the British Museum, and mastering short-hand—he was in love. " The attachment," he says, " excluded every other idea from my mind for four years, at a time when four years are equal to four times four. A determination to overcome all the difficulties fairly lifted me up into that newspaper life, and floated me away over a hundred men's heads." Of the causes which prevent the course of love from running smooth, Shakspeare omits the commonest—the want of money. Before Dickens was in a position to give the object of his admiration a suitable home, the lovers were separated, and he did not again set eyes upon the lady for five and twenty years. The first effect of the meeting was to agitate his mind with the memory of his youthful emotions; the second effect was to make him smile at the disproportionate homage which had intoxicated him before. He had shadowed forth his early passion in the love of David Copperfield for Dora, and shortly after he had renewed his acquaintance with the inspirer of the four years' enthusiasm, he commenced in the Flora of *Little Dorrit*, the companion picture of a middle-aged woman, who, seen by her former admirer, appears to his sober, riper judgment a commonplace person whom he had strangely invested with illusive charms. The contrast is often true, and not less true than it is often fallacious.

Dickens commenced reporting in the middle of 1830, and continued in the profession till the middle of 1836. He was employed at the outset in the courts of law, where he studied in an attorney's office, and in 1831 attained the highest grade of his difficult art, and entered the gallery of the Houses of Parliament.

It was at first intended that young Charles should be sent to an attorney's office ; but he had literary tastes, and eventually was permitted by his father to exchange the law for a post as one of the reporters on the staff of the *True Sun*. When Parliament was not sitting, he often made journeys into the country, to report the speeches at public meetings. Railroads there were not, and he had often to post back at the rate of fifteen miles an hour, that a report might be in time for the morning paper, and having the palm of his hand for a desk, he transcribed his notes for the printer by the light of a dark lantern, as he was whirled along in a gallop in a chaise and four. This work was beset with all sorts of perils, and he was known to relate to Mr. Forster, that he had " to change for all sorts of breakages fifty times in a journey, such being the ordinary results of the pace which we went at. There never was anybody connected with a newspaper who, in the same space of time, had so much express and post-chaise experience as I have." Yet, he exulted in the work, there never was such a short-hand writer ; and Dickens ascribed much of his after success in authorship to the wholesome training of severe newspaper work. It required close application, and ready execution. " His alert mind " (says the *Quarterly Reviewer*) " moved quickly, seldom loitering over his business, and his facility, which did not exclude unwearied efforts after excellence, was of inestimable value in a long series of fictions, written month by month, as they were published, or at most with only a number or two of manuscript in advance."

Our author subsequently transferred his services to the *Morning Chronicle*, then under Mr. John Black, who accepted and inserted in the evening edition of his journal the first fruits of the pen of Charles Dickens—those *Sketches of English Life and Character* which were afterwards reprinted and published in a collective form under the title of *Sketches by Boz*, in 1836, and the following year. For these *Sketches* Dickens received the sum of £150, but when his fame rose, he purchased the copyright of the *Sketches* for the sum of £2500. Dickens had been three years and a half a reporter, when in 1833, at the age of twenty-two, he contributed to the *Monthly Magazine* the earliest of the above *Sketches*. The series was then continued in the *Evening Chronicle*, adapted to the morning paper, to which these *Sketches* at once attracte d notice, and the public looked with something more than curiosity for the time when the successful author should throw off his mask and proclaim himself to the world. To adopt the phrase of an epigram which appeared in the *Carthusian,*

> " Who the Dickens ' Boz ' could be
> Puzzled many a learned elf ;
> But time unveiled the mystery,
> And ' Boz ' appeared as Dickens' self."

Dickens was reporter, and his salary was raised from five to seven guineas a-week, on account of his extra contributions. Captain Holland, the *littérateur,* during his editorship of the *Monthly Magazine,* consigned one of the above papers to " the rejected " basket, from which limbo it was rescued by a dropper-in, whose attention was drawn to the somewhat mystical signature of Charles Dickens appended to it. The paper proved to be the " Bloomsbury Christening," one of the raciest of the author's early sketches, and familiar to playgoers.

Almost simultaneously with these *Sketches,* in 1835 appeared a comic opera from Dickens's pen, entitled the *Village Coquettes,* an operatic burlette, the music by John Hullah.

About this time Dickens began to assume the name of " Boz," which is stated to have originated as follows :—A fellow-passenger with Mr. Dickens in the *Britannia* steam-ship, across the Atlantic, inquired of the author the origin of his signature " Boz." Mr. Dickens replied that he had a little brother who resembled so much the Moses in the *Vicar of Wakefield,* that he used to call him Moses also ; but a younger girl, who could not then articulate plainly, was in the habit of calling him Bozie or Boz. This simple circumstance made him assume that name in the first article he risked to the public, and therefore he continued the name, as the first effort was approved of.

Pickwick, the hero of his first novel, was called after a coach proprietor, whose name being painted on the door of numerous coaches, was familiar to everybody. An accidental association had, probably, recommended it to Dickens. The coach proprietor was Moses Pickwick, and the jesting uses to which Dickens had long put The Moses, coupled with the jingling oddity of the word Pickwick, induced him to appropriate the second half of the name.

The graphic power of describing the ordinary scenes of common life, especially in their more ludicrous aspects, did not escape the notice of Messrs. Chapman and Hall, then of the Strand, but now of Piccadilly, and they accordingly requested " Boz " to write for them a serial story in monthly parts ; the result was the publication of the *Posthumous Papers of the Pickwick Club.*   It is said that a portion of the rough outline of the work was the result of a suggestion thrown out by Mr. Hall, one of the firm above-mentioned ; but be that as it may, the subject was treated by " Boz " in a manner at once so easy, so graphic, and so natural, and yet with such a flow of genuine humour, that the author found himself raised almost to the highest literary fame.   Illustrated at first by poor Seymour, and afterwards by Mr. Hablot K. Brown (" Phiz "), the *Pickwick Papers* found an enormous sale from their first appearance, and Mr. Charles Dickens presented himself to the world as their author in 1838.

The great success of *Pickwick* naturally led to offers being made to Mr. Dickens by the London publishers ; but the author wisely consulted his own reputation, and confined himself to the production of *Nicholas Nickleby* in a similar style and form.   The work was written to expose in detail the cruelties which were practised upon orphans and other neglected children at small and cheap schools, where the sum charged for the board of hungry and growing lads, with everything included, ranges from £16 to £20 a year.   Mr. Dickens tells us, in the preface to this book, as it stands republished in the collective edition of his works, that it was the result of a personal visit of inspection paid by himself to some nameless " Dotheboys' Hall " amid the wolds of Yorkshire ; and the reader who has carefully studied it will with difficulty be persuaded that Mr. Squeers and Mr. John Browdie are not taken from living examples.   The work was published in 1839.

The disappearance from our newspapers of strings of " Education " advertisements of schools, with low tariff, in Yorkshire, shows the effect of satiric humour in correcting abuses of our own time.   The dietary of a school in Yorkshire, barmecide breakfasts and dinners, was often held up *in terrorem* to refractory boys, who heard the threat of " I'll send you to Yorkshire," with fear and trembling.   Mr. Dickens gives an admirable exposure of this Spartan system in his tale of *Nicholas Nickleby,* in the preface to which he says :—

"I cannot call to mind now how I came to hear about Yorkshire schools, when I was not a very robust child, sitting in bye places, near Rochester Castle, with a head full of Partridge, Strap, Tom Pipes, and Sancho Panza; but I know that my first impressions of them were picked up at that time, and that they were, somehow or other, connected with a suppurated abscess that some boy had come home with in consequence of his Yorkshire guide, philosopher, and friend having ripped it open with an inky penknife."

Before the book was written, Mr. Dickens went into Yorkshire to look for a school in which the imaginary boy of an imaginary widow might be put away until the thawing of a tardy compassion in that widow's imaginary friends. Then some stern realities were seen; and we are told also, in the preface, of a supper with a real John Browdie, whose answer as to the search for a cheap Yorkshire schoolmaster was, "Dom'd if ar can gang to bed and not tellee, for weedur's sak', to keep the lattle boy from a' sike scoundrels, while there's a harse to hoold in a' London, or a goother to lie asleep in!"

To our thinking, one of the most attractive sketches in this work is the following passage upon the culture of flowers in London :—

"A fine morning, Mr. Linkinwater," said Nicholas, entering the office.

"Ah!" replied Tim, "talk of the country, indeed! What do you think of this now for a day—a London day—eh?"

"It's a little clearer out of town," said Nicholas.

"Clearer!" echoed Tim Linkinwater. "You should see it from my bedroom window."

"You should see it from *mine*," replied Nicholas, with a smile.

"Pooh! pooh!" said Tim Linkinwater, "don't tell me. Country!" (Bow was quite a rustic place to Tim.) "Nonsense. What can you get in the country but new-laid eggs and flowers? I can buy new-laid eggs in Leadenhall Market any morning before breakfast; and as to flowers, it's worth a run upstairs to smell my mignonette, or to see the double-wallflower in the back-attic window, at No. 6, in the court."

"There is a double-wallflower at No. 6, in the court, is there?" said Nicholas.

"Yes, is there," replied Tim, "and planted in a cracked jug, without a spout. There were hyacinths there this last spring, blossoming in——but you'll laugh at that, of course."

"At what?"

"At their blossoming in old blacking-bottles," said Tim.

"Not I, indeed," returned Nicholas.

Tim looked wistfully at him for a moment, as if he were encouraged by the tone of this reply to be more communicative on the subject : and sticking behind his ear a pen that he had been making, and shutting up his knife with a sharp click, said,.

"They belong to a sickly bed-ridden hump-backed boy, and seem to be the only pleasures, Mr. Nickleby, of his sad existence. How many years is it," said Tim, pondering, "since I first noticed him quite a little child, dragging himself about on a pair of tiny crutches? Well! well! not many ; but though they would appear nothing, if I thought of other things, they seem a long, long time, when I think of him. It is a sad thing," said Tim, breaking off, " to see a little deformed child sitting apart from other children, who are active and merry, watching the games he is denied the power to share in. He made my heart ache very often."

"It is a good heart," said Nicholas, " that disentangles itself from the close avocations of every day, to heed such things. You were saying—"

"That the flowers belonged to this poor boy," said Tim, "that's all. When it is fine weather, and he can crawl out of bed, he draws a chair close to the window, and sits there looking at them, and arranging them all day long. We used to nod at first, and then we came to speak. Formerly, when I called to him of a morning, and asked him how he was, he would smile, and say, ' Better ;' but now he shakes his head, and only bends more closely over his old plants. It must be dull to watch the dark house-tops and the flying clouds for so many months ; but he is very patient."

"Is there nobody in the house to cheer or help him ?" asked Nicholas.

"His father lives there, I believe," replied Tim, " and other people too ; but no one seems to care much for the poor sickly cripple. I have asked him very often if I can do nothing for him ; his answer is always the same,—' Nothing.' His voice has grown weak of late, but I can see that he makes the old reply. He can't leave his bed now, so they have moved it close beside the window, and there he lies all day : now looking at the sky, and now at his flowers, which he still makes shift to trim and water with his own thin hands. At night, when he sees my candle, he draws back his curtain, and leaves it so till I am in bed. It seems such company to him to know that I am there, that I often sit at my window for an hour and more, that he may see I am still awake ; and sometimes I get up in the night to look at the dull melancholy light in his little room, and wonder whether he is awake or sleeping.

"The night will not be long coming," said Tim, " when he will sleep and never wake again on earth. We have never so much as shaken hands in all our lives ; and yet I shall miss him like an old friend. Are there any country flowers that could interest me like these, do you think ? Or do you suppose that the withering of a hundred kinds of the choicest flowers that blow, called by the hardest Latin names that were ever invented, would give me one fraction of the pain that I shall feel when these old jugs and bottles are swept away as lumber ? Country !" cried Tim, with a contemptuous emphasis ; "don't you know that I couldn't have such a court under my bedroom window anywhere but in London ?"

With which inquiry, Tim turned his back, and pretending to be absorbed in his accounts, took an opportunity of hastily wiping his eyes when he supposed Nicholas was looking another way.

On January 1, 1837, Dickens entered into an engagement with Mr. Bentley to edit a monthly magazine, with the title of *Bentley's Miscellany*, which soon became very popular, illustrated, as it was, by George Cruikshank, and started by Dickens with *Oliver Twist*, which is generally esteemed his best work ; though the tragic power of some of its scenes are condemned by delicate readers. *Oliver Twist* lets the reader into the secrets of life as it was, and, perhaps, still is, to be found too often in workhouses and in the "slums" of London, for the delineation of which localities of the metropolis this work is remarkable. When finished it was republished as a novel in three volumes, and in that shape, too, enjoyed an extensive sale. That infamous rookery of the dangerous classes, which extended northward, parallel with the Fleet ditch, is thus sketched in 1837 :—

"Near to the spot on which Snow Hill and Holborn meet, there opens, upon the right hand as you come out of the City, a narrow and dismal alley leading to Saffron Hill. In its filthy shops are exposed for sale huge bunches of pocket-handkerchiefs of all sizes and patterns—for here reside the traders who purchase them from pickpockets. Hundreds of these handkerchiefs hang dangling from pegs outside the windows, or flaunting from the door-posts ; and the shelves within are piled with them. Confined as the limits of Field Lane are, it has its barber, its coffee-shop, its beer-shop, and its fried-fish warehouse. It is a commercial colony of itself—the emporium of petty larceny, visited, at early morning and setting-in of dusk, by silent merchants, who traffic in dark back-parlours, and go as strangely as they come. Here the clothesman, the shoe-vamper, and the rag-merchant display their goods as sign-boards to the petty thief ; and stores of old iron and bones, and heaps of mildewy fragments of woollen-stuff and linen, rust and rot in the grimy cellars."

We have a distinct recollection of young persons being

cautioned against the villanies of back-parlours in this empo-rium of petty larceny.

Here is a locality more tortuous :—" As John Dawkins objected to entering London before nightfall, it was nearly eleven o'clock when they reached the turnpike at Islington. They crossed from the Angel into St. John's Road, struck down the small street which terminates at Sadler's Wells Theatre, through Exmouth Street and Coppice Row, down the little court by the side of the workhouse, across the classic ground which once bore the name of Hockly-in-the-Hole, hence into Little Saffron Hill, and so into Saffron Hill the Great," &c.

In the following year, Mr. Dickens undertook the produc-tion of a collection of stories in weekly numbers. The series was entitled *Master Humphrey's Clock*, and it contained, among other tales, those since republished under the names of *The Old Curiosity Shop*—famous for its touching episode of " Little Nell,"—and of *Barnaby Rudge*, which carries the reader back to the days of the Gordon riots.

About the time of the publication of *Master Humphrey's Clock* appeared his *Memoirs of Joseph Grimaldi*, the celebrated clown, almost his only production which deals with plain prose of facts. The materials of this work were woven by Mr. Dickens into a popular narrative, but it was never re-ceived as a work of his execution; although a late reprint of it was edited by Mr. Charles Whitehead.

After completing *Master Humphrey's Clock*, Mr. Dickens visited America. On his return, in 1842, he published the materials which he had collected in the United States, under the title *American Notes for General Circulation*. Many of its statements, however, were controverted by American writers, in a book entitled *Change for American Notes*. Mr. Dickens, however, received corrections of his *Notes* with courtesy from correspondents.

In 1844 he published *Martin Chuzzlewit* in numbers, like *Pickwick* and *Nicholas Nickleby*, and in the summer of the same year visited Italy and Rome. An account of much that he saw and heard in this tour, he gave afterwards to the world in the columns of the *Daily News*, of which he became the first editor. He wrote the prospectus of the *Daily News*, with much tact and judgment, and concluded with this as-surance :—

' "Entering on this adventure of a new daily journal in a spirit of honourable competition and hope of public usefulness, we seek, in our new station, at once to preserve our own self-respect, and to be respected for ourselves and for it, by our readers. Therefore we beg them to receive, in this our first number, the assurance that no recognition or interchange of trade abuse, by us, shall be the destruction of either sentiment; and that we intend proceeding on our way, and theirs, without stooping to any such flowers by the road side."

Its first number appeared on January 1st, 1846; but after a few months Mr. Dickens withdrew from the editorship, and returned to his former line of humorous serial publications, varying, however, their monthly appearance with occasional stories of a more strictly imaginative cast, called "Christmas Books." Of these, the first, *A Christmas Carol*, was published so far back as 1843; the second, the *Chimes*, appeared at Christmas, 1845; the third, the *Cricket on the Hearth*, followed in 1846; the fourth, the *Battle of Life*, in 1847; and the fifth, the *Haunted Man and the Ghost's Bargain*, in 1848. These Christmas books were of unequal merit: neither of them reached the popularity of the first—the *Christmas Carol*.

A curious anecdote is related of the attractiveness of Dickens's books: "Mr. Davy, who accompanied Colonel Chest ney up the Euphrates, had been in the service of Mehemet Ali Pasha. *Pickwick* happening to reach Davy while he was at Damascus, he read a part of it to the Pasha, who was so delighted with it that Davy was, on one occasion, summoned to him in the middle of the night, to finish the reading of some part in which they had been interrupted. Mr. Davy read, in Egypt, upon another occasion, some passages from these unrivalled papers to a blind Englishman, who was in such ecstasy with what he heard, that he exclaimed that he was almost thankful he could not see he was in a foreign country, for that, while he listened, he felt completely as though he were again in England."

A sound divine of the last century observes: "Men are more ambitious to display the abilities of the head than to cultivate the good qualities of the heart." Charles Dickens thus points to an error of this class: "Men talk of Nature as an abstract thing, and lose sight of Nature as they do so. They charge upon Nature matters with which she has not the smallest connection, and for which she is in no way responsible." This is one of those happy quips of world-knowledge to be found in the later writings of Charles Dickens, and which bade fair to outlive the gossamer of his genius.

Among Dickens's early works was the *Child's History of England*, a book intended for early readers, but disfigured by many crudely-formed opinions, which became adopted in schools under the guidance of tutors but little qualified for the teaching of youth. Mr. Forster has shown that "there was always some grave central purpose in the mind of Dickens which was the axis upon which the amusement revolved, and without dwelling upon the obvious questions which are recognized by all the world, he has pointed out the wealth of other excellences which were likely to be overlooked."

Besides the works already named, Mr. Dickens has published *Dealings with the Firm of Dombey and Son*, the *History of David Copperfield, Bleak House, Little Dorrit, A Tale of Two Cities, Our Mutual Friend*, the *Uncommercial Traveller, Great Expectations*, and last of all, the *Mystery of Edwin Drood*, of which only three numbers appeared.

In 1850 Mr. Dickens projected a cheap weekly periodical, which he called *Household Words*, and which was published by Messrs. Bradbury and Evans; but difficulties having arisen between author and publishers, it was discontinued in 1859, and Mr. Dickens commenced in its stead its successor, *All the Year Round*, which he continued to conduct to the last. Both works were characterized by a life-like spirit of observation and well-timed spirit : the presiding genius was Charles Dickens, but the co-operation of able hands was easily recognized.

Mr. Dickens was an accomplished amateur performer, and often took part in private theatricals for charitable objects. Of late years he had frequently appeared before the public as a "reader" of the most popular portions of his own works, of which he showed himself to be a most vivid and dramatic interpreter. He retired from this work in March, 1860, when his reputation stood at its highest. His renderings of his best creations, both humorous and pathetic, of his most stirring scenes and warmest pictures of life, will not readily be forgotten. Men and women, persons and places, we knew all before in the brilliant pages of his novels; but the characters lived with a new life, and the scenes took the shape of reality in the readings of the master.

In the summer of 1841, during a short tour in Scotland, Mr. Dickens being tired of sight-seeing and other turmoil, wrote to his friend Mr. Forster, "The moral of all this is that there is no place like home, and that I thank God most heartily for having given me a quiet spirit, and a heart that won't hold many people;" but "travel created an appetite for home, and home for travel." The truth of this alternation became evident : he exchanged novel-writing for a visit to America. He sailed from Liverpool January 3rd, 1842, and from New York, back, on June 7th. His journey through America was a triumphal progress, but inconveniences greatly proponderated, as he thus characteristically tells us : " I can do nothing that I want to do," he wrote to Mr. Forster from New York, " go nowhere where I want to go, and see nothing that I want to see. If I turn into the street I am followed by a multitude. If I stay at home the house becomes with callers like a fair. If I visit a public institution with only one friend, the directors come down incontinently, waylay me in the yard, and address me in a long speech. I go to a party in the evening, and am so enclosed and hemmed about by people, stand where I will, that I am exhausted for want of air. I dine out, and have to talk about everything to everybody. I go to church for quiet, and there is a violent rush to the neighbourhood of the pew I sit in, and the clergyman preaches at me. I take my seat in a railway car, and the very conductor won't let me alone : I get out at a station, and can't drink a glass of water without having a hundred people looking down my throat when I open my mouth to swallow."

By these disagreeables exaltation was quelled. Dickens offended the editors of newspapers by advocating international copyright, they pronounced him to be a mere "mercenary scoundrel;" and he grew tired of the social homage. "I really think," he said, "my face has acquired a fixed expression of sadness from the continual and unmitigated boredom I endure." In spite of the scramble to look at him, and shake hands with him, there was a national insensibility to the chief characteristics of his genius. "I should think," he wrote, "there is not on the face of the earth a people so entirely destitute of humour, vivacity, or the capacity of enjoyment. I am quite serious when I say that I have not heard a hearty laugh these six weeks, except my own, nor have I seen a merry face on any shoulders but on a black man's." Even if every one around him had been as great humourists as himself, the pleasure of endless formal receptions must necessarily have been in a sense of their weariness.

He, on his part, was not formed for exhibition before assemblies agape for dazzling display. " I must confess to a considerable disappointment in the personal of my idol," wrote a young lady after talking with him at a party at Cincinnati. " I felt that his throne was shaken, although it never could be destroyed." He was too natural to be a king to such exacting subjects. The efforts to amuse, which were unpleasing to his intimate associates, fulfilled their purpose with strangers who were anxious for specimens of conversation in keeping with his fame. This occasional concession to popular expectation was impossible to Dickens. He was inclined to reserve in large companies, and any deliberate attempt to draw him out only caused him to retire more resolutely within himself. On his second visit to America, in 1868, he and his admirers understood each other better, and they parted with increased respect on both sides.

Mr. Dickens, in bidding his last audience farewell, consoled them with the promise that his retirement would be devoted all the more to his original and higher art. His words have scarcely had time to allow of their fulfilment in the way and in the degree in which, doubtless, he hoped to be able to fulfil them. It may be well here to place on record his parting speech on the occasion of his last reading at St. James's Hall :—

"Ladies and Gentlemen,—It would be worse than idle, it would be hypocritical and unfeeling, if I were to disguise that I close this episode in my life with feelings of very considerable pain. For some fifteen years in this hall and in many kindred places, I have had the honour of presenting my own cherished ideas before you, for your recognition ; and, in closely observing your reception of them, have enjoyed an amount of artistic delight and enjoyment which, perhaps, it is given to few men to know. In this task, and in every other I have ever undertaken, as a faithful servant of the public, always imbued with a sense of duty to them, and always striving to do his best, I have been uniformly cheered by the readiest response, the most generous sympathy, and the most stimulating support. Nevertheless, I have thought it well, at the full flood-tide of your favour, to retire upon those older associations between us which date from much further back than these, and henceforth devote myself exclusively to the art that first brought us together. Ladies and Gentlemen, in but two short weeks from this time I hope that you may enter, in your own homes, on a new series of readings at which my assistance will be indispensable, but from these garish lights I vanish now for evermore, with one heartfelt, grateful, respectful, and affectionate farewell."

While *Pickwick* charms us with its broad humour, it is in *Nicholas Nickleby* and *Oliver Twist* that the power of Charles Dickens's pathos shows itself. In those two works he evinced a sympathy for the poor, the suffering, and the oppressed, which took all hearts by storm. This power of sympathy it was, no doubt, which has made his name a household word in English homes. How many a phase of cruelty and wrong his pen exposed, and how often he stirred others to try at least to lessen the amount of evil and of suffering which must be ever abroad in the world, will never be fully known. There was always a lesson beneath his mirth.

The sad event of Mr. Dickens's death caused a thrill of sorrow, as well as surprise. On Wednesday evening, June 5th, 1870, he was seized with a fit at his residence, Gadshill Place, Higham, near Rochester, between six and seven o'clock, while at dinner. Mr. Stephen Steele, a surgeon at Strood, was sent for, and promptly arrived. He found Mr. Dickens in a very dangerous state, and remained with him for some hours. A physician was summoned from London yesterday morning, and Mr. Steele was also in attendance. Unfortunately, there was no improvement in the patient. In the afternoon Mr. Steele was again summoned from Strood. The reports in the after part of the day were discouraging, and shortly after six o'clock the great novelist expired.

There is no one, we are sure, of the men of the present day whose name will live longer in the memories of English readers, or will be more thoroughly identified with the English language, than the inimitable author of *Pickwick*.

It only remains for us to add that he married in 1838 a daughter of Mr. George Hogarth, a musical writer of eminence in his day, and a man of high literary attainments—who was formerly the friend and law agent of Sir Walter Scott, and well known in private life to Jeffrey, Cockburn, and the other literary celebrities who adorned the society of Edinburgh some forty or fifty years ago.

THE GRAVE OF DICKENS.

The grave is in Poets' Corner, at the foot of Handel's, the head of Sheridan's, and between Lord Macaulay and Cumberland, the dramatic poet. A few feet removed, and near to the side of Dickens, but towards his feet, lie Johnson and Garrick, while near them repose the remains of Campbell. The statue of Addison and the bust of Thackeray overlook the grave at its head ; Shakspeare's monument is not far from its foot, and Goldsmith's monument is on the left.

The *Times* says :—" We congratulate the Dean of Westminster on his ready sympathy with the public feeling. He has found a grave for Dickens by the side of Macaulay, close to Handel, Johnson, Garrick, and Campbell, under the shadow of the monuments of Thackeray, Addison, Goldsmith, and Shakspeare. The man, the company, and the place are alike worthy of each other. It was said of old to be the work of dramatic writers ' to purify the passions,' and nothing could better describe the office of modern novelists. So far, at least, as this world is concerned, no profession can assert a higher aim than thus to make us more simple, more pure, and more true ; and, as the Bishop of Manchester said the other evening, the work of the great novelist was but in harmony with the work of the Church. Many a great statesman who has been borne with pomp to the Abbey had less opportunity for benefiting his country and his race than the novelist who has been quietly laid in Poets' Corner ; but, whatever the powers of the divines, or the statesmen, or the men of learning who crowd that national shrine, none used their talents with greater faithfulness or greater reverence than Charles Dickens."

The *Daily Telegraph* says :—" We have given Dickens a grave where the best and greatest among our dead are laid, because the best and greatest do generally receive such homage ; and it is, moreover, becoming and useful to have enriched the Santa Croce of England with ' all that can die ' of a writer who, with so much humour, so wide a knowledge of humanity, and so sweet an eloquence, never penned an ignoble or impure line. This was done no less for our sake than for his, because, as he made his own greatness, so, being dead, he could have taken care of it by his own tombstone ; for, we repeat it, the place where his body rested could want no previous history and no associations ; it must have become, by reason of that single grave, such as Stratford-upon-Avon is—a burial-place consecrated for ever, and to all the world, by a single presence and a single inscription. It is better, nevertheless, to have him resting among his peers, the first and greatest children of Britain; and better still to have laid him there in the simplicity and modesty which he preferred and desired."

THE FUNERAL OF CHARLES DICKENS.

The burial of Mr. Charles Dickens in Westminster Abbey afforded profound satisfaction to the public mind; and the extreme privacy with which the mournful ceremony was conducted made a deep and lasting impression. The great novelist shrewdly secured his remains from being made the subject of an absurd display by a provision of his will, which had the additional beneficial effect of ensuring to those nearest and dearest to him the opportunity of committing his body to the dust amidst the sanctity of their private sorrow, unobserved and undisturbed. His last utterance, coming, as it were, from the grave itself, is in strict accordance with his long-cherished opinion that funerals, as commonly conducted in this country, were hideous blemishes on our code of social manners. The people who were shocked by Mr. Dickens, when he scoffed aloud at some hypocrisy, bigotry, or knavery, we fear were very much shocked that he should have detested the forms of genteel burial, and should have been entombed in Westminster Abbey without a procession of coaches and a choral service. The executors, with the sanction of the Dean and Chapter of Rochester, erected to his memory in Rochester Cathedral a handsome brass tablet on the wall of the south-west transept, under the monument to Richard Watts, a local benefactor. The tablet records the dates of the birth and death of the deceased, that he is buried in Westminster Abbey, and that the tablet is erected " to connect his memory with the scenes in which his earliest and his latest years were passed, and with the associations of Rochester Cathedral and its neighbourhood, which extended over all his life."

WILL OF CHARLES DICKENS.

(*Dated May* 11*th,* 1869.)

" I emphatically direct that I be buried in an inexpensive, unostentatious, and strictly private manner, that no public announcement be made of the time or place of my burial, that at the utmost not more than three plain mourning coaches be employed, and that those who attend my funeral wear no scarf, cloak, black bow, long hatband, or other such revolting absurdity. I direct that my name be inscribed in plain English letters on my tomb, without the addition of ' Mr.' or ' Esquire.' I conjure my friends on no account to make me the subject of any monument, memorial, or testimonial whatever. I rest my claims to the remembrance of my country upon my published works, and to the remembrance of my friends upon their experience of me; in addition thereto, I commit my soul to the mercy of God, through our Lord and Saviour Jesus Christ, and I exhort my dear children to try to guide themselves by the teaching of the New Testament in its broad spirit, and to put no faith in any man's narrow construction of its letter here or there."

IN MEMORIAM.—CHARLES DICKENS.

The whole Weekly Press mourned the death of Charles Dickens. We have space for only a few passages from many eloquent and touching tributes to his memory.

Not only the English nation, says the *Saturday Review,* but all nations and people that speak or understand the English tongue, will hear with the profoundest regret of the death of the great novelist; and no writer can undertake the melancholy task of noticing the loss we have sustained without feeling how large a blank is made by the sudden death of an author whose compositions have furnished one of the chief sources of intellectual wealth to this generation. The language of Mr. Dickens has become part of the language of every class and rank of his countrymen.

The *Spectator* says that the greatest humourist whom England ever produced —— Shakespeare himself certainly not excepted — is gone. Mr. Dickens taught us by his humour, as nothing else could have taught us, how full to overflowing what is called "vulgar" life is of all the human qualities, good and evil, which make up the interest of human existence. His delight in the grotesque has done far more than ever Mr. John Stuart Mill by any philosophical defence of liberty could do, to make us tolerant towards individual eccentricity of almost every shade, and even to teach us to pet it with something like parental fondness. And he has given a greater impulse than any man of his generation to that righteous hatred of caste-feeling and class-cruelty which more and more distinguishes modern society, though he did not quite rise perhaps to that "enthusiasm of humanity" which some regard as the essence of Christianity itself.

The *John Bull* finds it impossible to regard his death in any other light than that of a national loss. "Very often he took a different view from ourselves on questions of the first moment, whether ecclesiastical or political, but it is impossible not to feel that many men, with more professions of religion, have done infinitely less to exalt the tone of morality in their generation than the humorous author of the *Pickwick Papers*. His deep love of honesty, his hatred of hypocrisy, and his bold denunciation of shams, will ever command the respect of Englishmen; while his deep love of domestic life, his tender pathos in describing scenes of sorrow, will show that the keen satirist had a tender heart, and that, if he could wing from his bow an arrow venomed with just indignation, he could also write with the spirit of one who had a 'love passing the love of woman.' So proudly, and yet gently, we lay Charles Dickens to his rest. He has won the national heart, and, like Horace of old, we welcome even the friendly scourge of his satire.

"'Tangit et admissus circum præcordia ludit.'

When we gather again around the Christmas hearth, and read once more the genial lessons of charity hidden beneath the surface of his Christmas tales, we may not irreverently apply to the great satirist, the words of Holy Scripture—'He being dead yet speaketh.'"

The *Press and St. James's Chronicle*, in the death of Mr. Charles Dickens, points to a blank in the intellect and in the social existence of this country. Death has removed one whose genial nature and whose great descriptive powers bridged the chasm that events and the progress of civilization, in the materialistic sense of the term, had left gaping between the wealthier and more industrious classes of society. Mr. Dickens understood all classes, except the highest ; and they were all the more apt to become his pupils, because he had the good sense to abstain from attempting to depict a phase of society with which he was not thoroughly familiar.

The *Era* remarks that in Mr. Dickens's death the loss is a national one, and is felt] by all classes to be so. " His rank among the authors of fiction has long been settled, nor will the verdict be disturbed. No man has made so much mark upon the social character of his time. The names of scores of his personages have become typical, and his humour caused a re-casting of the comic tone of his age. It may be permitted to this journal to remember that he was ever a devoted lover of the higher drama, that he was a histrionic artist of rare ability, and that he was ever the actor's best and warmest friend."

EARLY WRITINGS OF DICKENS.

Some thirty years ago there appeared in the *Quarterly Review,* No. 127, in a review of *Oliver Twist,* an exposition of the true character and tendency of the writings of Dickens *at that date.* They are plentifully sprinkled with home truths, and passages selected as fairly as possible, with the view of showing both sides of the writer's view of the genius of Dickens ; for, though justice be here and there very hardly dealt, the whole paper may be taken as the best estimate then formed of the blemishes and merits of this very popular author, it being always borne in mind that the extent of public favour is but a very uncertain test of its leading worth.

"Life in London," as revealed in the pages of Dickens, opens a new world to thousands born and bred in the same city, whose palaces overshadow their cellars, for the one half lives without knowing how the other half dies ; in fact, the region about Saffron Hill is less known than the *Oxford Tracts ;* the inhabitants are still more strange ; they are as human, at least to all appearance, as the Esquimaux or Russians. Secure in their own right, they really enjoy Boz ; they have none of the vulgarity of the class who cut human nature unless perfectly *comme-il-faut.*

. Boz's works are a sign of the times, their periodical return excites more interest than that of Halley's comet. They, like good sermons, contribute to our moral health, for mirth, cakes, ale, and ginger, hot in the mouth, do us good.

The works of Boz came out in numbers, suited to this age of division of labour, cheap, and not too long—double merits. Boz is the only *work* which the superficial acres of type called newspapers leave the human race time to peruse. His popularity is unbounded—not that that of itself is a test of either honesty or talent. Boz fills the print-shops—Boz furnishes subjects to playwrights and farce-writers; he is the play himself, now that brutes feed where Garrick trod. The strength of Boz consists in his originality, in his observation of character, his humour—on which he never dwells. He leaves a good thing alone, like curaçoa, and does not dilute it; wit, which is not taught in Gower Street, drops out of his mouth as naturally as pearls and diamonds in the fairy tale; the vein is rich, racy, sparkling, and good-natured—never savage, sarcastic, malevolent, nor misanthropic; always well placed and directed against the odious, against purse-proud insolence, and the abuse of brief authority. Boz never ridicules the poor, the humble, the ill-used; he spares to real sorrow "the bitterest insult of a scornful jest;" his sympathies are on the right side and carry his readers with him. Though dealing with the dregs of society, he is never indelicate, indecent, nor irreligious; he never approves or countenances the gross, the immoral, or offensive: he but holds these vices up in a pillory, as a warning of the disgrace of criminal excess. Boz, like the bee, buzzes amid honey without clogging his wings; he handles pitch charmingly; the tips of the thumb and forefinger of the cigaresque señoras of Paraguay are infinitely more discoloured. He tells a tale of real crushing misery in plain, and therefore most effective language; he never *then* indulges in false sentimentality, or mawkish, far-fetched verbiage. Fagin, Sikes, and the dog especially, are always in their proper and natural places, always speaking, barking, and acting exactly as they ought to have done, and, as far as we are able to judge, with every appearance of truth. Boz sketches localities, particularly in London, with marvellous effect; he concentrates with the power of a camera lucida. Born with an organic bump for distinct observation of men and things, he sees with the eye, and writes with the pen of an artist—we mean with artistical skill, and not as artists write. He translates nature and life. The identical landscape or occurrence, when reduced on one sheet, will interest and astonish those who had before seen with eyes that saw not, and heard with ears that heard not, on whom previously the general incident had produced no definite effect. Boz sets before us in a strong light the water-standing orphan's eye, the condemned prisoner, the iron entering into his soul. This individuality arrests, for our feelings for human suffering in the aggregate are vague, erratic, and undefined.

His "gentle and genteel folks" are unendurable; they are devoid of the grace, repose, and ease of good society; a something between Cheltenham and New York. They and their extreme propriety of ill-bred good-breeding are (at least we hope so) altogether the misconceptions of our author's uninitiated imagination, mystified by the inanities of the kid-glove novelists. Boz is, nevertheless, never vulgar when treating on subjects which are avowedly vulgar. He deals truly with human nature, which never can degrade; he takes up everything, good, bad, or indifferent, which he works up into a rich alluvial deposit. He is natural, and that never can be ridiculous. He is never guilty of the two common extremes of second-rate authors—the one a pretension of intimate acquaintance with the inner life of Grosvenor Square—the other an affected ignorance of the doings, and a sneering at bad dinners, of Bloomsbury—he leaves that for people to whom such dinners would be an unusual feast.

Boz is regius professor of slang, that expression of the mother-wit, the low humour of the lower classes, their Sanscrit, their hitherto unknown tongue, which, in the present phase of society and politics, seems likely to become the idiom of England. Where drabs, house-breakers, and tavern-spouting patriots play the first-fiddle, they can only speak the language which expresses their ideas and habits. In order fully to enjoy their force, we must know the conventional value of these symbols of ideas, although we do not understand the lingo like Boz, who has it at his fingers'-ends. We are amused with the comicality, in spite of our repugnance that the decent veil over human guilt and infirmities should be withdrawn; we grieve that the deformity of nakedness should not only be exhibited to the rising generation, but rendered agreeable by the undeniable drollery; a coarse transcript would not be tolerated.

Boz's plot is devoid of art. This, a fault in comedy, is pardonable in tragedy—where persons, not events, excite. We foresee the thunder-cloud over Œdipus and the Master of Ravenswood without decrease of interest, which is not diminished even on re-perusal, by our perfect knowledge of the catastrophe; but Boz must remember that he is not in the high tragedy line, which deals more in the expression of elevated persons and thoughts, in an elevated manner, than in the mere contrast of situations and events, and make a better story the next time. He should also avoid, in future, all attempts at pure pathos—on which he never ventures without reminding us of Sterne, and of his own immense inferiority to that master. Let him stick to his native vein of the *seriocomic*, and blend humour with pathos. He shines in this: his fun sets off his horrors as effectually as a Frenchman's gravity in a quadrille does his levity in an *emeute*, or a massacre.

HISTORY OF "PICKWICK."

From the *Athenæum* :—" As the author of the ' Pickwick Papers' (and of one or two books), I send you a few facts, and no comments, having reference to a letter signed ' R. Seymour,' which in your editorial discretion you published last week. Mr. Seymour, the artist, never originated, suggested, or in any way had to do with, save as illustrator of what I devised, an incident, a character (except the sporting tastes of Mr. Winkle), a name, a phrase, or a word, to be found in the ' Pickwick Papers.' I never saw Mr. Seymour's handwriting, I believe, in my life. I never even saw Mr. Seymour but once in my life, and that was within eight and forty hours of his untimely death. Two persons, both still living, were present on that short occasion. Mr. Seymour died when only the first twenty-four printed pages of the ' Pickwick Papers ' were published; I think before the next three or four pages were completely written; I am sure before one subsequent line of the book was invented. In the Preface to the Cheap Edition of the ' Pickwick Papers,' published in October, 1847, I thus described the origin of that work :—' I was a young man of three and twenty, when the present publishers, attracted by some pieces I was at that time writing in the *Morning Chronicle* newspaper (of which one series has lately been collected and published in two volumes, illustrated by my esteemed friend Mr. George Cruikshank), waited upon me to propose a something that should be published in shilling numbers—then only known to me, or, I believe, to anybody else, by a dim recollection of certain interminable novels in that form, which used, some five and twenty years ago, to be carried about the country by pedlars,

and over some of which I remember to have shed innumerable tears, before I served my apprenticeship to Life. . . .
The idea propounded to me was that the monthly something
should be a vehicle for certain plates to be executed by Mr.
Seymour, and there was a notion, either on the part of that
admirable humorous artist, or of my visitor (I forget which),
that a ' Nimrod Club,' the members of which were to go out
shooting, fishing, and so forth, and getting themselves into
difficulties through their want of dexterity, would be the
best means of introducing these. I objected, on consideration, that although born partly bred in the country I was no
great sportsman, except in regard of all kinds of locomotion;
that the idea was not novel, and had been already much
used; that it would be infinitely better for the plates to arise
naturally out of the text; and that I should like to take my
own way, with a freer range of English scenes and people,
and was afraid I should ultimately do so in any case, whatever course I might prescribe to myself at starting. My
views being deferred to, I thought of Mr. Pickwick, and
wrote the first number, from the proof sheets of which Mr.
Seymour made his drawing of the Club, and that happy portrait of its founder, by which he is always recognized, and
which may be said to have made him a reality. I connected
Mr. Pickwick with a club, because of the original suggestion,
and I put in Mr. Winkle expressly for the use of Mr. Seymour. We started with a number of twenty-four pages
instead of thirty-two, and four illustrations in lieu of a couple.
Mr. Seymour's sudden and lamented death before the second
number was published, brought about a quick decision upon
a point already in agitation; the number became one of
thirty-two pages with two illustrations, and remained so to
the end.' In July, 1849, some incoherent assertions made
by the widow of Mr. Seymour, in the course of certain endeavours of hers to raise money, induced me to address a
letter to Mr. Edward Chapman, then the only surviving
business-partner in the original firm of Chapman and Hall,
who first published the ' Pickwick Papers,' requesting him to
inform me in writing whether the foregoing statement was
correct. In Mr. Chapman's confirmatory answer, immediately
written, he reminded me that I had given Mr. Seymour more
credit than was his due. ' As this letter is to be historical,'
he wrote, ' I may as well claim what little belongs to me in
the matter, and that is, the figure of Pickwick. Seymour's

first sketch,' made from the proof of my first chapter, ' was of a long, thin man. The present immortal one he made from my description of a friend of mine at Richmond.' "

CHARACTERS IN NOVELS.

" Although thousands have already written the epitaph of Charles Dickens, and all have been emulous to do his memory honour, it seems as though the surprise and shock of his death had not yet passed away. No warning rumour had floated about ; no hints of a decaying constitution ; certainly no evidence in his latest works of any eclipse passing over that ardent and brilliant mind. The blow fell in a moment, and we are but now beginning to realise the nature and degree of the general loss. The band of English writers without Charles Dickens among them—*All the Year Round* with his name obliterated from the title—society without his presence—it actually appears a dream ! Such a friendship had been established between him and his fellow-men ; so familiar his creations that they had added, literally, scores of words to the language ; so indelible the impression of his character-painting, that it formed a gallery of pictures in every mind. And the poetry of his style had entered into many a favourite song which will be sung in a sad spirit for the future. We all had an affection for him, a pride in his genius, a rejoicing in his success ; he was so true, so single-hearted, so simply a man of letters, who loved his art, and never dishonoured it by an hypocrisy or an impurity. The promise of a new book by him stirred the public mind with deep anticipations of pleasure, so vividly was it remembered how delighting he could be in all his moods, what strength and truth of human interest in his stories and radiance in his manner of telling them, what justice in his distributions of destiny among the personages of his dramas ; how intense his contempt could be when it had to deal with meanness of spirit and vulgar pretensions, and how glowing his sympathy with the most child-like of innocent enjoyments. Without suggesting in any other sense a comparison, we may say that there was a touch of Shakespeare in Charles Dickens, in that he took his colour with equal art from every source alike—millionnaire and beggar, the high-bred and the base, the high-fashioned and the population of the London cellarage, soft drawing-room luxury and the interiors of Newgate and the Marshalsea, my lady's chamber and the slums. The incense of the country-side, the salt of the sea, the smoke of the cities, and the peace of lonely hamlets, came and went upon his canvas as though all had been similarly familiar to him.   But though idyllic in taste, he never elaborated his landscapes ; though an incomparable master of pathos, he interspersed it gently among lighter passages, relieving the imagination, as it were, from time to time —though he drew ruffians, assassins, hangmen, and others, lowest among the low, he would not brutalise his volumes by any ribaldry of theirs ; and hence, notwithstanding the strange visits made by him into regions of squalor and crime, whatever he wrote was readable by the very youngest and purest.

" Moreover, his humour, while occasionally grotesque, was invariably untainting ; he borrowed nothing from the gross satirists of former days ; indeed, it was a distinguishing attribute of Charles Dickens that he was supremely original ; he had no models except the men and women around him— no teacher except the life of the epoch in which his fame rose to a height so transcendent.   There is only one Dombey, one Paul, one Captain Cuttle.   Romance presents us with no second Quilp, or Toots, or Gubby.   Little Nelly wanders to her grave alone, and poor Dora, in the whole round of fictitious girls, is without a companion.   Thus again, with the scenes and manners chosen—the infamous abuses of law and administration, the disgraces of systems now rapidly vanishing ; the sufferings of the poor at the hands of their appointed guardians ; the ignorance and depravity of their children in an enlightened age, and a cloud of other social scandals which he undoubtedly helped to clear away.   Another generation may not quite appreciate the humours of Dotheboys' Hall, the pomposities of the Board and Mr. Bumble in the town where Master Oliver Twist acquired his earliest experience ; the horrible processes of Chancery in the colossal case of Jarndyce v. Jarndyce ; the cruelties and corruptions witnessed by Mr. Dorrit in his imprisonment, or the imbecilities of the Circumlocution Office, though that has some vitality in it still ; but there is the reality and animation of Dutch-work about these pictures, and the novelist, in fact, preserved in one form, so that posterity might at least understand them, the very institutions which he was assisting to destroy in another.   And besides, his narratives were so enchaining that the shiftings of scenery will always intensify the action of the play.   The mysteries of Barnaby Rudge, Lady Deadlock, and Hannon, the great dust contractor ; the pastoral charm that

follows a child from the *Old Curiosity Shop*, among the villages
and fields ; the unprecedented adventures of the Pickwickian
party ; the incomparable comedy of Toots, and Guppy, and
Chadband, and Mrs. Gamp, and Mrs. Jellaby, and Mantalini,
and Turveydrop—not even to mention the younger and the
elder Weller, and the not less inimitable Paul Dombey, and
Ham, and the outcast boy that died in the Children's Hospital,
and the sad sweet funeral of Little Nelly, possess fascinations of
their own apart from time or place, or any public purpose which
the writer may have had in his mind. Admiration is hardly
the term expressing the feeling they must inspire : it is rather
gratitude ; it is a sort of intellectual love ; Charles Dickens
was the daily companion of myriads—in their solitude, in
their sickness, on their travels anywhere and everywhere, and
his passing away is mourned with a grief which successive
years, in our generation at least, will not diminish, because
his voice will be missed, and the gifts from his pen, and the
influence that made him precious to literature. Moreover,
this, our latest and our heaviest loss, brings back the memory
of that brilliant band which once encircled him—Thackeray,
Leech, Leman, Frank Stone, Douglas Jerrold, Gilbert
A'Beckett, and the rest. Dickens, by far the hardest worker
of the whole phalanx, thought over his novels, and wrote them
with the most concentrated care—never slovenly, never heed-
less, invariably studying them from the first to the last line,
as works of art, which he designed, not for a season, but for
many a decade to come.

"And he had his reward. Though dying prematurely, with
his genius bright and his energies unrelaxed, he lived to see
his works raised to a high and permanent place in English
literature, to hear them spoken of by strangers wherever he
went, to find them in the princely mansions and on the humblest of bookstalls, to know that the reading of them, unless
by a few sour eccentrics, was regarded as indispensable, as
supplying an element in the staple stock of conversation ; and
to meet, wherever he went, far or near, for their sake, hosts
upon hosts of friends, with the widest doors of welcome and
the loudest acclaim of praise. He died, and there was an universal outbreak of sorrow ; not an invidious syllable has
broken the harmony of this generous lament ; the Sovereign
has sent a message of even affectionate condolence to his
children ; and every pleasant anecdote, every winning trait,
and every fragment of kindly reminiscence connected with

him has been, in these few days since he was taken away, listened to as with a personal and wistful interest. Such a manifestation is deserving of record ; but it was due to the writer, who, with such a versatility and prodigality of genius, commanding every mood of the human mind, a master of tears and laughter, an exquisite poet, and a subtle satirist, who painted low life like Teniers, and landscape like Claude, sorrow like Dolce, and pleasure like Watteau, did not once take advantage of his power and fame to check an aspirant toiling far behind him on his own path, or wound any one by unscrupulous caricature, or indulge his wondrous wit beyond the point at which the most innocent girl might innocently enjoy it. Qualities like these are rare, even in the literature of our own day. They prove the existence in the man possessing them, of a deep and delicate conscience, a fine moral dignity, a sense of responsibility to his readers, a love of literature in its purest shape, and a mind which, while exuberant with all varieties of laughter-moving fancies, would never condescend to put his sparkling, pungent, magical pen to an ignoble use. Such a man we had in Charles Dickens while he was among us."—From the *Standard* journal.

DICKENS AT GADSHILL.

ONE summer's day—ah, saddest eighth of June !—
　My brooding heart, my very soul descries
Around a châlet, in a grove at noon,
　Dream children from the flowering earth arise.

So hushed (like death !) the calm, sequestered scene,
　One notes with eye, not ear, the fitful breeze,
Thro' sunlit branches, flickering gold and green
　About yon Swiss roof nestling 'mid the trees.

Like faithful wanderers seen returning home,
　Like magnets trembling truthful to the north,
To this one spot on all the world they roam
　Again they throng, round him who called them forth.

No shadowy semblance theirs of human life,
　Ideal shapes of visionary birth ;
They breathe, they move with vital force more rife
　Than fleeting, fleshly forms that people earth.

The Angel-Child, the Guardian Guide of Age,
　With soul as pure as all the tears we shed
When swimming eyes first read on blotted page
　"Dear, gentle, patient, noble Nell was dead."

The fading boy, the blossom nipped in bud,
 Whose infant grace had oft the quaintest air,
Who questioned voices in the ocean flood,
 Whose looks of love were sad as tones of prayer,

Till passed, like sigh in sleep, his parting breath,
 And o'er the couch where lay the gentle Paul,
Naught stirred above "the old, old fashion, Death"—
 Naught save "the golden ripple on the wall !"

The sweet Child-Wife, the darling of a heart
 Whose tenderest chords that solemn eve were riven,
When Dora's doom was told with speechless art—
 "That mute appeal, that finger raised to heaven !"

The little cripple with the active crutch,
 At thought of whom the mother's eyes grew dim,
Sighing, as fell the black work from her touch,
 It was "the colour—Ah, poor Tiny Tim !"

The stripling frail, who, dying with a kiss,
 A child at heart, a man but to the sight !
Poor Rick ! began the world again—not this,
 Ah no, "not this—the world that sets this right."

And orphan Johnny, his lost home afar,
 An infant waif on awful billows hurl'd,
No mother clinging to it, floats, frail spar,
 O'er that dark sea that rolls round all the world."

Around the sunlit châlet where, within,
 Dreams the great Dreamer 'neath the shadowing trees,
From flowering earth, fresh dews of love to win,
 Dream-children rise in lovely forms like these.

No spectral shades for glimpses of the moon,
 But radiant shapes in calm of summer-day,
They come unbidden to his haunts, at noon,
 Down the bright path they went—to point the way.

These haunts the aptest symbols of a life
 That loved the pleasaunce winter ne'er bereaves
Of verdure, in those grand old cedars rife
 Crowned with a lasting glory of Green Leaves.

And yonder, basking in the golden air,
 Luring his thoughts where'er his glance may roam,
Cinctured by blossoms in a garden fair,
 The dear, familiar roof-beams of his home.

Between that home and this secluded haunt
 Flows the broad highway, symbol here again
That alien to his hearth no tread of want
 Or toil was held, or ever passed in vain.

O Friend ! O Brother ! dearer to my heart
  Than ev'n thy loving frendship could discern,
Thy thoughts, thy dreams were of our lives a part,
  Thy genius love, not merely fame, could earn.

Affection, admiration, honour, praise,
  Innocent laughter and ennobling tears,
Are thine by right, not through mere length of days,
  A loftier life, in never-ending years.

C. K., in the Athenæum.

CHARLES DICKENS'S SPEECHES.*

We may confidently presume that there are few English
or American readers who will not welcome the appearance of
the book before us. "It has often been observed," says Mr.
Dickens in one of the speeches now in our hands in a collected form, "that you cannot judge of an author's personal
character from his writings." And truly it is dreary to remember how many writers whose works abound in fine moral sentiments and "noble thoughts ably expressed" require, in
order that we may fully appreciate their books, that a veil be
drawn over their lives and personal characters. Few authors
are heroes to their valets de chambre. But it is precisely
because the great man who has left us was so truly and consistently great "in soul and action," that his writings are what
they are to all of us, and that we look for the same charm in
his speeches and private letters as in his books. As he wrote
he lived. The deep and noble views of life and human
nature which will be a possession for the ages yet to come, in
the pages of David Copperfield or the Old Curiosity Shop, were
dear to the author's heart, and were the ground of his actions
and conduct through life. The unaffected simplicity which
gives their charm to the stories to which every Christmas we
looked forward, imparted its fragrance to the daily deeds and
the occasional speeches of Mr. Dickens. The book before us
contains a report of Mr. Dickens's speeches from 1841 to the
last he ever uttered in public, prefaced by an introduction
briefly reviewing the author's life, with an historical survey
of his works, and concludes with a few specimens of his
private letters and poetic compositions. In the introduction

* "The Speeches of Charles Dickens, now First Collected." (John
Camden Hotten.)

the compiler brings the great writer before us. Few things are more difficult than to introduce so well known a man. In such a case the duty of the writer is to give us a few facts connecting the various incidents of his author's life with each other, and to supply any pieces of information bearing on the subject likely to be less known to the generality of readers, troubling us as little as possible with his own private opinions upon such of his author's works as are so well known and so highly appreciated as to require, in Bishop Hall's words, "nothing but age to make them classical."

This is what the compiler has succeeded in doing in the present instance. The public will assuredly thank him for bringing under notice some passages of those chapters subsequently omitted in one of Mr. Dickens's earlier works, where " the two Wellers " were once more introduced. How interesting, too, that extract from Professor Wilson's speech in 1841, expressing his appreciation of Dickens's powers and success. If we take this speech, together with the noble tribute paid to the genius of Dickens by the Dean of Westminster in his funeral sermon, as echoing the consistent opinion of all his countrymen to the character of that genius during nearly thirty years, we shall feel that there is little left to add to them.

The same earnest, practical sympathy found in the life and writings of Dickens is not wanting in his speeches ; and as much may also be said of his powers as a humourist. Many men of lively and sparkling wit, like Hood, have been, in private life, melancholy and depressed ; but the fund of humour, the power of seeing the comic side of human life and human nature which delights us in *Bleak House* or *Pickwick*, imparted an air of pleasantry to nearly every one of the author's public addresses, and infused gaiety into his private conversations. But that which, perhaps more than anything else, secures the sympathy of his readers, is the fact that, in delineating the tragic side of human life—however intense his perception of the sorrows and sufferings of his fellow-men —it never drives him to a state of scepticism or despair.

" Hope and a renovation without end "

is ever before him. The constant presence of a higher Power turning evil into good, and causing earth's wildernesses to become fruitful fields, supports him and nerves him, as his speeches alone everywhere testify, to an untiring and not hopeless effort to raise, by word and deed, the fallen and the trodden down, and makes him, through all his endeavours, trust in and follow the example of Him "who" (he says) "took the highest knowledge into the humblest places, and whose great system comprehended all mankind." In the speech delivered at the Free Trade Hall, Manchester, in 1858, Mr. Dickens humorously describes the ordinary run of public speeches as

"Vying with the other in the two qualities of having little or nothing to do with the matter in hand, and of being always addressed to any audience in the wide world rather than the audience to which it was delivered."

Mr. Dickens's own speeches are certainly free from this fault, all of them breathing warm, affectionate, and manly sympathy with his fellow-man, and alike in this, that they all express his yearning desire to benefit his race. They all of them occupy themselves directly and scrupulously with the matter in hand. One great advantage undoubtedly is that they give us here and there a glimpse of the speaker's opinion upon certain subjects not directly treated of in his writings. In politics he was certainly a Liberal, and one would be inclined to say a Democratic Liberal. He states his political creed thus :—

"My faith in the people governing is, on the whole, infinitesimal ; my faith in the People governed is, on the whole, illimitable."

Dickens appears to have been a little too much of a modern metaphysical politician, and speaks of "the wishes of the people" with implicit faith, as though "the people" ever wished anything but what a small, intelligent, and influential minority for the time being taught them to wish. We get, too, an expression of cordial sympathy with the full development of Mr. Mill's doctrine about the capabilities of women, expressed in Dickens's very latest speech, delivered May 2, 1870.

But the great charm of Dickens is that in his noble view of man and his earnest efforts for the good of mankind he is hindered by no party narrowness. He rises above it. In one of his speeches he calls party "for the most part an irrational sort of thing," and he possesses the rare gift of combining all the energy of a party man with a genius too comprehensive to become sectarian. A man of letters, especially, should always rise above " party spirit." One other point we will notice as well illustrated by the book before us. Dickens possessed, in a high degree, that un-English quality which Mr. Matthew Arnold calls "urbanity of style." He never expresses himself with fierceness even when he feels the most, or without discrimination even where his convictions are deepest. His heart is deep, but his mind is evenly balanced ; his feelings strong, but his intellect discerning. For instance, to a man who believed, as Dickens did, that ignorance is the cause of vice, and that liberal education, widely extended, is a matter of the utmost importance, no saying could be more hateful than the adage, " Knowledge is a dangerous thing." Yet he does not lash himself into fury about it. Observe the temperate and graceful style of the following :—

" For the same reason I rigidly abstain from putting together any of the shattered fragments of that poor clay image of a parrot, which was once always saying, without knowing why, or what it meant, that knowledge was a dangerous thing. I should as soon think of piecing together the mutilated remains of any wretched Hindoo who has been blown from an English gun. Both, creatures of the past, have been—as my friend Mr. Carlyle vigorously has it—' blasted into space ;' and there, as to this world, is an end of them."

On much the same subject he is confronted with a like Philistinish weapon, but how calmly and in how self-possessed a manner he wards off the blow :—

" Why, when I hear such cruel absurdities gravely reiterated, I do sometimes begin to doubt whether the parrots of society are not more pernicious to its interests than its birds of prey."

We might give many such instances from these speeches, but we content ourselves with one more. It was in 1855, the obstinate and unyielding nature of the then House of Commons as to the passing of such measures as Mr. Dickens longed to see for the benefit of his fellow-men might have excused some British vehemence and invective, but in contrast to what we might have looked for read this :—

" I will merely put it to the experience of everybody here, whether the House of Commons is not occasionally a little hard of hearing, a little dim of sight, a little slow of understanding, and whether, in short, it is not in a sufficiently invalided state to require close watching, and the occasional application of sharp stimulants ; and whether it is not capable of considerable improvements ? "

We now take leave of the author and the compiler, only thanking the latter for giving us a fresh opportunity of studying, and a fresh pleasure in contemplating the great genius, the lofty aims, the noble nature, and consistent character of our great countryman.—From the *Echo* journal.

CHARLES DICKENS AND WASHINGTON IRVING.

We have received a copy of correspondence which will be read with interest as showing the friendship which existed between these two distinguished authors.   The intercourse between them commenced in 1841, when Mr. Irving was in his fifty-eighth year, and Mr. Dickens had attained precisely half that number of years—twenty-nine.   The American took the lead, and wrote a letter expressing his heartfelt delight with the writings of the Englishman and his yearnings toward him.   The reply was minute, impetuously kind, and eminently characteristic. " There is no man in the world," said Mr. Dickens, " who would have given me the heartfelt pleasure you have. . . . There is no living writer, and there are very few among the dead, whose approbation I should feel so proud to earn.   And with everything you have written upon my shelves, and in my thoughts, and in my heart of hearts, I may honestly and truly say so.   If you could know how earnestly I write this, you would be glad to read it, as I hope you will be, faintly guessing at the warmth of the hand I *autobiographically* hold out to you over the broad Atlantic. . . . I have been so accustomed to associate you with my pleasantest and happiest thoughts and with my leisure hours, that I rush at once into full confidence with you, and fall, as it were naturally, and by the very laws of gravity, into your open arms. . . . I cannot thank you enough for your cordial and generous praise, or tell you what deep and lasting gratification it has given me."

After the two authors had met face to face, and Mr. Irving had been appointed American Minister to Spain, Mr. Dickens wrote to him :—" What pleasure I have had in seeing and talking with you I will not attempt to say. I shall never forget it as long as I live. What *would* I give if we could have but a quiet week together ! Spain is a lazy place, and its climate an indolent one. But if you ever have leisure under its sunny skies to think of a man who loves you, and holds communion with your spirit oftener, perhaps, than any other person alive—leisure from listlessness, I mean—and will write to me in London, you will give me an inexpressible amount of pleasure."

The following letter was written by Mr. Dickens, during his last visit to America, to Mr. Charles Lanman, of Georgetown :—

" 'Washington, Feb. 5, 1868.

" ' My dear Sir,—Allow me to thank you most cordially for your kind letter and for its accompanying books. I have a particular love for books of travel, and shall wander into the *Wilds of America* with great interest. I have also received your charming sketch with great pleasure and admiration. Let me thank you for it heartily. As a beautiful suggestion of nature, associated with this country, it shall have a quiet place on the walls of my house as long as I live.

" ' Your reference to my dear friend, Washington Irving, renews the vivid impressions re-awakened in my mind at Baltimore the other day. I saw his fine face for the last time in that city. He came there from New York, to pass a day or two with me before I went westward, and they were made among the most memorable of my life by his delightful fancy and genial humour. Some unknown admirer of his books and mine sent to the hotel a most enormous mint-julep, wreathed with flowers. We sat, one on either side of it, with great solemnity (it filled a respectable sized round table), but the solemnity was of a very short duration. It was quite an enchanted julep, and carried us among innumerable people and places that we both knew. The julep held out far into the night, and my memory never saw him afterwards otherwise than as bending over it with his straw with an attempted gravity (after an anecdote involving some wonderfully droll and delicate observation of character), and then, as his eye caught mine, melting into that captivating laugh of his, which was the brightest and best I have ever heard.

" ' Dear Sir, with many thanks, faithfully yours,

" ' CHARLES DICKENS.' "

AN EXECUTION.

One of the most powerful pieces of writing by Charles Dickens is his description of the execution of the murderers, the Mannings, at Horsemonger Lane, on the morning of November 13, 1849 :—

" I went there" (says Dickens) " with the intention of observing the crowd gathered to behold it, and I had excellent opportunities of doing it, at intervals, all through the night, and continuously from daybreak until after the spectacle was over.

"I believe that a sight so inconceivably awful as the wickedness and levity of the immense crowd collected at that execution could be imagined by no man, and could be presented by no heathen land under the sun. The horrors of the gibbet and of the crime which brought the wretched murderers to it, faded in my mind before the atrocious bearing, looks, and language of the assembled spectators. When I came upon the scene at midnight, the *shrillness* of the cries and howls that were raised from time to time, denoting that they came from a concourse of boys and girls already assembled in the best places, made my blood run cold. As the night went on, screeching, and laughing, and yelling in strong chorus of parodies on negro melodies, with substitutions of 'Mrs. Manning' for 'Susannah,' and the like, were added to these. When the day dawned, thieves, low prostitutes, and vagabonds of every kind flocked on to the ground, with every variety of offensive and foul behaviour, fightings, faintings, whistlings, imitations of Punch, brutal jokes, tumultuous demonstrations of indecent delight when swooning women were dragged out of the crowd by the police with their dresses disordered, gave a new zest to the general entertainment. When the sun rose brightly—as it did—it gilded thousands upon thousands of upturned faces, so inexpressibly odious in their brutal mirth or callousness, that a man had cause to be ashamed of the shape he wore, and to shrink from himself as fashioned in the image of the devil. When the two miserable creatures who attracted all this ghastly sight about them were turned quivering into the air, there was no more emotion, no more pity, no more thought that two immortal souls had gone to judgment, no more restraint in any of the previous obscenities, than if the name of Christ had never been heard in this world, and there were no belief among men but that they perished like the beasts.

"I have seen, habitually, some of the worst sources of contamination and corruption in this country, and I think there are not many phases of London life that could surprise me. I am solemnly convinced that nothing that ingenuity could devise to be done in this city, in the same compass of time, could work such ruin as one public execution, and I stand astounded and appalled by the wickedness it exhibits.

I do not believe that any community can prosper where such a scene of horror and demoralization as was witnessed this morning outside Horsemonger Lane is presented at the very doors of good citizens, and is passed by, unknown or forgotten."

THE INSOLVENT DEBTORS' COURT.

One of the most felicitous of the sketches of the life of London, which Mr. Charles Dickens has written, is that of the Insolvent Debtors' Court, in his *Pickwick Papers*, 1837. It has no exaggeration or caricature, but is an admirable piece of quiet humour ; and it is a remarkable instance of the author's humour, being exercised without any appearance of effort, or overstrained effect. The Court here sketched exists no longer but in our humourist's sketch :—

" In a lofty room, badly lighted, and worse ventilated, situate in Portugal Street, Lincoln's Inn Fields, there is, nearly the whole year round, one, two, three, or four gentlemen in wigs, as the case may be, with little writing-desks before them, constructed after the fashion of those used by the judges of the land, barring the French-polish ; a box of barristers on their right hand, an enclosure of insolvent debtors on their left ; and an inclined plane of most especially dirty faces in their front. These gentlemen are the Commissioners of the Insolvent Court, and the place in which they sit is the Insolvent Court itself.

" It is, and has been, time out of mind, the remarkable fate of this Court to be somehow or other held and understood by the general consent of all the destitute, shabby-genteel people in London as their common resort, a place of daily refuge. It is always full. The steams of beer and spirits perpetually ascend to the ceiling, and being condensed by the heat, roll down the walls like rain. There are more old suits of clothes in it at one time than will be offered for sale in all Houndsditch for a twelvemonth ; and more unwashed skins and grizzly beards than all the pumps and shaving-shops between Tyburn and Whitechapel could render decent between sunrise and sunset.

" It must not be supposed that any of these people have the least shadow of business in, or the remotest connection with, the place they so indefatigably attend. If they had, it would be no matter of surprise, and the singularity of the thing would cease at once. Some of them sleep during the

16—2

greater part of the sitting ; others carry small portable dinners wrapped in pocket-handkerchiefs, or sticking out of their worn-out pockets, and munch and listen with equal relish ; but no one among them was ever known to have the slightest personal regard in any case that was ever brought forward. Whatever they do, there they sit from the first moment to the last. When it is heavy, rainy weather, they all come in wet through ; and at such times the vapours of the Court are like those of a fungus-pit.

"A casual visitor might suppose this place to be a temple dedicated to the Genius of Seediness. There is not a messenger or process-server attached to it who wears a coat that was made for him ; not a tolerably fresh or wholesome-looking man in the whole establishment, except a little white, appled-headed tipstaff, and even he, like an ill-conditioned cherry preserved in brandy, seems to have artificially dried and withered up into a state of preservation, to which he can lay no natural claim. The very barristers' wigs are ill-powdered, and their curls lack crispness.

"But the attorneys, who sit at a bare large table below the Commissioners, are, after all, the greatest curiosities. The professional establishment of the more opulent of these gentlemen consists of a blue bag and a boy, generally a youth of the Jewish persuasion. They have no fixed offices, their legal business being transacted in the parlours of public-houses, or the yards of prisons, whither they repair in crowds, and canvass for customers, after the manner of omnibus cads. They are of a greeny and mildewed appearance ; and if they can be said to have any vices at all, perhaps drinking and cheating are the most conspicuous among them. Their residences are usually on the outskirts of the 'Rules,' chiefly lying within a circle of one mile from the obelisk in St. George's Fields. Their looks are not prepossessing, and their manners are peculiar."

In the grounds at Gadshill is preserved a châlet, which was presented a few years since to Mr. Dickens by a Swiss admirer. It is erected opposite the house in the shrubbery, and approached by a tunnel underneath the turnpike road. This châlet, embosomed in some very fine trees, is placed upon an eminence commanding a noble view of the mouth of the Thames and the opposite coast of Essex. It was a favourite retreat of Charles Dickens, and here he passed the morning and afternoon of his last day upon earth !

On one occasion Charles Dickens was upholding the theory that whatever trials or difficulties might stand in a man's path, there is always something to be thankful for. "Let me, in proof thereof," said Dickens, "relate a story. Two men were to be hanged at Newgate for murder. The morning arrived; the hour approached; the bell of St. Sepulchre's began to toll; the convicts were pinioned; the procession was formed; it advanced to the fatal beam; the ropes were adjusted around the poor men's necks; there were thousands of motley sight-seers of both sexes, of all ages, men, women, and children, in front of the scaffold; when, just at that second of time, a bull which was being driven to Smithfield, broke its rope and charged the mob right and left, scattering people everywhere with its horns, whereupon one of the condemned men turned to his equally unfortunate companion, and quietly observed, 'I say, Jack, it's a good thing we ain't in that crowd.'"

THE LAST PAGE.

In the last novel which Mr. Dickens ever completed, and in the last paragraph of its last page, he wrote words which now possess a remarkable interest :—

"On Friday, *the ninth of June*, in the present year (1865), Mr. and Mrs. Boffin (in their manuscript dress of receiving Mr. and Mrs. Lammle at breakfast) were on the South-Eastern Railway with me in a terribly-destructive accident. When I had done what I could to help others, I climbed back into my carriage—nearly turned over a viaduct, and caught aslant upon the turn—to extricate the worthy couple. They were much soiled, but otherwise unhurt. The same happy result attended Miss Bella Wilfer on her wedding-day, and Mr. Riderhood inspecting Bradley Headstone's red neckerchief as he lay asleep. I remember with devout thankfulness that I can never be much nearer parting company with my readers for ever than I was then, until there shall be written against my life the two words with which I have this day closed this book—THE END."

It is now strange to observe that just five years later, on the very same day of the very same month, THE END came, and the reader will probably be impressed with Mr. Dickens's own account of its first approach in the spring of the year :—

"Once upon a time (no matter when), I was engaged in a

pursuit (no matter what), which could be transacted by myself alone, in which I could have no help, which imposed a
constant strain on the attention, memory, observation, and
physical powers, and which involved an almost fabulous
amount of change of place and rapid railway travelling.   I
had followed this pursuit through an exceptionally trying
winter in an always trying climate, and had resumed it in
England after but a brief repose.   Thus it came to be pro-
longed until at length—and, as it seemed, all of a sudden—
it so wore me out that I could not rely, with my usual cheerful confidence, upon myself to achieve the constantly recurring task, and began to feel (for the first time in my life)
giddy, jarred, shaken, faint, uncertain of voice and sight, and
tread and touch, and dull of spirit.   The medical advice I
sought within a few hours was given in two words, ' Instant
rest.'   Being accustomed to observe myself as curiously as if
I were another man, and knowing the advice to meet my
only need, I instantly halted in the pursuit of which I speak,
and rested.

   " My intention was to interpose, as it were, a fly-leaf in the
book of my life, in which nothing should be written from
without for a brief season of a few weeks.   But some very
singular experiences recorded themselves on this same fly-leaf,
and I am going to relate them literally.   I repeat the word,
literally.

   " My first odd experience was of the remarkable coincidence
between my case, in the general mind, and one Mr. Merdle's
as I find it recorded in a work of fiction called *Little Dorrit*.
To be sure, Mr. Merdle was a swindler, forger, and thief, and
my calling had been of a less harmful (and less remunerative)
nature, but it was all one for that.

   " Here is Mr. Merdle's case :—

   " At first he was dead of all the diseases that ever were
known, and of several brand-new maladies invented with the
speed of Light to meet the demand of the occasion.   He had
concealed a dropsy from infancy ; he had inherited a large
estate of water on the chest from his grandfather ; he had had
an operation performed upon him every morning of his life
for eighteen years ; he had been subject to the explosion of
important veins in his body after the manner of fireworks, he
had something the matter with his lungs, he had had something the matter with his heart, he had had something the
matter with his brain.   Five hundred people who sat down to

breakfast entirely uninformed on the subject believed before they had done breakfast that they privately and personally knew Physician to have said to Mr. Merdle, 'You must expect to go out some day like the snuff of a candle;' and that they knew Mr. Merdle to have said to Physician, 'A man can die but once.' By about eleven o'clock in the forenoon, something the matter with the brain became the favourite theory against the field; and by twelve the something had been distinctly ascertained to be 'Pressure.'

" Pressure was so entirely satisfactory to the public mind and seemed to make every one so comfortable, that it might have lasted all day but for Bar's having taken the real state of the case into Court at half-past nine. Pressure, however, so far from being overthrown by the discovery, became a greater favourite than ever. There was a general moralizing upon Pressure, in every street. All the people who had tried to make money and had not been able to do it, said, ' There you were !' You no sooner began to devote yourself to the pursuit of wealth than you got Pressure. The idle people improved the occasion in a similar manner. ' See,' said they, ' what you brought yourself to by work, work, work.' You persisted in working, you overdid it. Pressure came on, and you were done for !' This consideration was very potent in many quarters, but nowhere more so than among the young clerks and partners who had never been in the slightest danger of overdoing it. These, one and all, declared, quite piously, that they hoped they would never forget the warning as long as they lived, and that their conduct might be so regulated as to keep off Pressure, and preserve them, a comfort to their friends, for many years.

" Just my case—if I had only known it—when I was quietly basking in the sunshine in my Kentish meadow !

" But while I so rested, thankfully recovering every hour, I had experience more odd than this. I had experiences of spiritual conceit, for which, as giving me a new warning against that curse of mankind, I shall always feel grateful to the supposition that I was too far gone to protest against playing sick lion to any stray donkey with an itching hoof. All sorts of people seemed to become vicariously religious at my expense. I received the most uncompromising warning that I was a heathen; on the conclusive authority of a field preacher, who, like the most of his ignorant and vain and daring class, could not construct a tolerable sentence in his native tongue or pen a fair letter. This inspired individual called me to order roundly, and knew in the freest and easiest way where I was going to, and what would become of me if I failed to fashion myself on his bright example, and was on terms of blasphemous confidence with the Heavenly Host. He was in the secrets of my heart and in the lowest soundings of my soul—he!—and could read the depths of my nature better than his A B C, and could turn me inside out, like his own clammy glove. But what is far more extraordinary than this—for such dirty water as this could alone be drawn from such a shallow and muddy source—I found from the information of a beneficed clergyman, of whom I never heard and whom I never saw, that I had not, as I rather supposed I had, lived a life of some reading, contemplation, and inquiry; that I had not studied, as I rather supposed I had, to inculcate some Christian lessons in books; that I had never tried, as I rather supposed I had, to turn a child or two tenderly towards the knowledge and love of our Saviour; that I had never had, as I rather supposed I had had, departed friends, or stood beside open graves; but that I had lived a life of ‘uninterrupted prosperity,’ and that I needed this ‘check, overmuch,’ and that the way to turn it to account was to read these sermons and these poems enclosed, and written and issued by my correspondent! I beg it may be understood that I relate facts of my own uncommercial experience, and no vain imaginings. The documents in proof lie near my hand.

“Another odd entry on the fly-leaf, of a more entertaining character, was the wonderful persistency with which kind sympathizers assumed that I had injuriously coupled with the so suddenly relinquished pursuit, those personal habits of mine most obviously incompatible with it, and most plainly impossible of being maintained, along with it. As, all that exercise, all that cold bathing, all that wind and weather, all that uphill training—all that everything else, say, which is usually carried about by express trains in a portmanteau and hat-box, and partaken of under a flaming row of gaslights in the company of two thousand people. This assuming of a whole case against all fact and likelihood struck me as particularly droll, and was an oddity of which I certainly had had no adequate experience in life until I turned that curious fly-leaf.

“My old acquaintances the begging-letter writers came out

on the fly-leaf, very piously indeed. They were glad, at such a serious crisis, to afford me another opportunity of sending that Post-office order. I needn't make it a pound, as previously insisted on—ten shillings might ease my mind. And Heaven forbid that they should refuse, at such an insignificant figure, to take a weight off the memory of an erring fellow-creature! One gentleman, of an artistic turn (and copiously illustrating the books of the Mendicity Society), thought it might soothe my conscience in the tender respect of gifts misused, if I would immediately cash up in aid of his lowly talent for original design—as a specimen of which he enclosed me a work of art which I recognized as a tracing from a woodcut originally published in the late Mrs. Trollope's book on America, forty or fifty years ago. The number of people who were prepared to live long years after me, untiring benefactors to their species, for fifty pound a piece down, was astonishing. Also, of those who wanted bank notes for stiff penitential amounts, to give away—not to keep, on any account.

"Divers wonderful medicines and machines insinuated recommendations of themselves into the fly-leaf that was to have been so blank. It was specially observable that every prescriber, whether in a moral or physical direction, knew me thoroughly—knew me from head to heel, in and out, through and through, upside down. I was a glass piece of general property, and everybody was on the most surprisingly intimate terms with me. A few public institutions had complimentary perceptions of corners in my mind, of which, after considerable self-examination, I have not discovered any indication. Neat little printed forms were addressed to those corners, beginning with the words, ' I give and bequeath.'

" Will it seem exaggerative to state my belief that the most honest, the most modest, and the least vainglorious of all the records upon this strange fly-leaf, was a letter from the self-deceived discoverer of the recondite secret ' How to live four hundred or five hundred years?' Doubtless it will seem so, yet the statement is not exaggerative by any means, but is made in my serious and sincere conviction. With this, and with a laugh at the rest that shall not be cynical, I turn the fly-leaf, and go on again."

DEAN STANLEY ON CHARLES DICKENS.

The announcement that Dean Stanley intended to make Charles Dickens and his works the subject of his sermon in Westminster Abbey, brought together a very large congregation to the afternoon service, and some time before three o'clock the choir and transepts were filled to overflowing, as well as the seats in the Sacrarium. At the end of the Third Collect the Dean was conducted to the pulpit, and took his text from the Gospel of the day, the Parable of the Rich Man and Lazarus, which, he observed, was most appropriate to the occasion, and chimed in admirably with the service performed within those walls on the previous Tuesday—the funeral of " that gifted being who for years had delighted and instructed the generation to which he belonged." He showed that the story of Dives and Lazarus formed something more than an ordinary " parable," and that, in spite of both the one and the other being " as purely imaginary beings as Hamlet or Shylock," it was a " tale of real life, so real that we can hardly believe it to be fiction, and not an actual history." "The Bible, then," urged the preacher, "sanctions this mode of teaching, which has been in a special sense God's gift to our own age. In various ages," he continued, " this gift has assumed various forms, the divine flame of poetry, the far-reaching page of science, the searching analysis of philosophy, the glorious page of history, the stirring eloquence of preacher or orator, the grave address of moralist or divine—all these we have had in ages past, and to some extent we have them still ; but no age has developed like this the gift of speaking in parables, of teaching by fiction." " Poetry," he continued, " may kindle a loftier fire, the drama may rivet the attention more firmly, science may open a wider horizon, and philosophy may touch a deeper spring, but no works are so penetrating or so persuasive, enter so many houses, or attract so many readers, as the romance or novel of modern times." And in proportion as the good novel is the best, so is the bad novel the worst of instructors ; but the work of the successful novelist, if pure in style, elevating in thought, and true in its sentiment, is the best of blessings to the Christian home, which the bad writer would debase and defile. In the writings of Charles Dickens it is clearly shown that " it is possible to move both old and young to laughter without the use of a single expression which could defile the purest or shock the most sensitive;" he taught a lesson to the world that it is possible to jest without the introduction of depraving scenes or the use of unseemly and filthy jokes. "So thought and so wrote, not only the genial and loving humourist whom we mourn, but Walter Scott and Jane Austen and Elizabeth Gaskell and William Thackeray." But, he urged, there was something even higher than this to be learnt in the writings of Charles Dickens, and which it was well to speak of in the House of God and beside that new-laid grave. "In that long series of stirring tales, now closed, there was a palpably serious truth—might he not say a Christian and Evangelical truth?—of which we all needed much to be reminded, and of which in his own way he was the special teacher. In spite of the Oriental imagery with which it is surrounded, the Gospel tells us, and the departed writer did but re-echo the truth, that the Rich Man and Lazarus lived very near and close to each other; he showed us, in his own dramatic and sympathetic manner, how close that lesson lay at the gates of the upper and wealthier classes of modern English society in this age of wide-spread civilization and luxury." The Poor Man had but one name given him in the parable, but in the writings of Charles Dickens he bore many names and wore many forms; now coming to us in the type of the forlorn outcast, now in that of the workhouse child struggling towards the good amid an atmosphere of cruelty, injustice, and vice. "We have need, then," he continued, "of such a teacher to remind us of one great lesson of life, the duty of sympathy with the poor and the weak, with the absent, and with those who cannot speak for themselves. And it is because this susceptibility, this gift of sympathy is so rare, that we ought to value it highly where we meet it, and to reckon it as a gift from God." . . . "As the Rich Man was made to see and to feel Lazarus at his gate, so our departed instructor taught us to realize as brought into very near contact with ourselves the suffering inmates of the workhouse, the neglected children in the dens and dark corners of the streets of our great cities, the starved and ill-used boy in remote schools far from the observation of the world at large. All of these must have felt that a new ray of sunshine was poured by his writings on their dark existence, and a new interest awakened outside in their forlorn and desolate lot. In him an unknown friend pleaded their cause with a voice which rang through the palaces of the rich and great, as well as through the cottages of the poor; and by him these gaunt figures and strange faces, though in a slightly exaggerated form, were made to stand and speak face to face with those who, up to that time, had doubted their existence." And, further, the same faithful hand which thus depicted the sufferings of the Poor Man, drew also pictures of that unselfish kindness, that kindly patience, that tender thoughtfulness, that sympathy for the weak and helpless which often underlie a rough exterior. When the little workhouse boy wins his way, pure and undefiled, through the mazes of wickedness, into a happy home; when the little orphan girl brings thoughts of heaven into the hearts of all around her, and is as the very gift of God to those whose desolate life she cheers, there is a lesson taught which none can read and learn without being the better for it. In fact, he laboured to tell us the very old, old story, that even in the very worst and most hardened of mankind there is some soft and tender point, and, what is more, a soul worth being touched and reached and rescued and regenerated. He helped to blot out the hard line which too often severs class from class, and made Englishmen feel more as one family than they had felt before. Therefore, it was felt that he had not lived in vain, or been laid in vain here in this sacred house, which is the home and the heart of the English nation." There was, of course, to be learnt from the text one further great and fearful lesson—the solemn weight and burden of individual responsibility of each man to his Maker for the life that he has led, and the use which he has made of the talents vouchsafed to him. This lesson was brought very close to those fourteen mourners and the handful of other persons who were gathered a few days before in the silence and stillness of that vast empty church around the grave of the great novelist. But he would not dwell long on this lesson, nor would he add there any eulogy on the dead, further than to remark that his grave, already strewed with flowers, would henceforth be a sacred spot both with the New World, as well as with the Old, as that of the representative of the literature, not of this island only, but of all who speak our English tongue.

PROFESSOR JOWETT, M.A., ON CHARLES DICKENS.

At the special Sunday evening service at Westminster Abbey, the Rev. B. Jowett, Professor of Greek at Oxford, alluded as follows to the death of Mr. Charles Dickens. After referring to men of genius who had previously departed, the reverend gentleman proceeded : " I have already detained you too long, and yet I do not like to conclude without saying one word more—that word has been in the hearts and on the tongues of most of us during the past week. We know that we cannot leave the grave of a departed friend without taking a last look, and we like to think of the rays of the setting sun upon his resting-place. He whom we now mourn was the friend of mankind, a philanthropist in the true sense, the friend of youth, the friend of the poor ; the enemy of every form of meanness and oppression. I am not going to attempt to draw a portrait of him. Men of genius are different from what we suppose them to be ; they have greater pleasures and greater pains, greater affections and greater temptations than the generality of mankind, and they can never be altogether understood by their fellow-men. We do not wish to intrude upon them, or analyze their lives and characters. They are extraordinary persons, and we cannot prescribe to them what they should be. But we feel that a light has gone out, the world is darker to us when they depart. There are so very few of them that we cannot afford to lose them one by one, and we look vainly round for others who may supply their places. And he whose loss we now mourn occupied a greater space than any other writer in the minds of Englishmen during the last thirty-five years. We read him, talked about him, acted him ; we laughed with him, we were aroused by him to a consciousness of the misery of others, and to a pathetic interest in human life. The workhouse child, the cripple, the half-clothed and half-starved inhabitant of a debtors' prison, found a way to his heart, and through the exertions of his genius, touched our hearts also. Works of fiction would be intolerable if they attempted to be sermons directly to instruct us ; but indirectly they are great instructors of this world, and we can hardly exaggerate the debt of gratitude which is due to a writer who has led us to sympathize with these good, true, sincere, honest English characters of ordinary life, and to laugh at the egotism, the hypocrisy, the false respectability of religious professors and others. To another great humourist who lies in this church, the words have been applied that the gaiety of nations was eclipsed by his death. But of him who has been recently taken I would rather say, in humbler language, that no one was ever so much beloved, or so much mourned. Men seem to have lost, not a great writer only, but one whom they had personally known. And so we bid him farewell."

THE FRENCH PRESS ON CHARLES DICKENS.

The news of Mr. Charles Dickens's death was received by the Paris papers with expressions of deep regret, and most of them have noticed the career and writings of our great novelist. While all admit the purity and humour of his works, it is evident that their appreciation of them is not so high as that entertained here or in the United States—a fact which is not surprising, seeing the difference between the genius of the two nations, and the imperfect manner in which Mr. Dickens's works have been translated into French. By several papers Dickens is compared with Balzac, but of course with a difference. The *Liberté* observes that "with both writers keen observation was the ruling faculty; both excelled in observation and in description; both enabled us to regard their creations as living persons, by minutely picturing even the least objects surrounding them; both were equally conspicuous for producing truth in fiction. But we must add that Balzac was not Dickens, nor was Dickens Balzac. Both being original by nature, each followed the ideas of his epoch, and reflected the habits of his country. There is an analogy between them, but no resemblance. The dreamy element, the fanciful note, as with Hoffman and Nodier, was more strong in Dickens; the tendencies of the thinker were strongest in Balzac." The *Patrie* remarks that Dickens differed from Balzac, "and it is his good fortune in not sharing Balzac's discontent, his bitterness, or his constant waspish misanthropy. Balzac looked upon society from his own point of view, and, not finding it satisfactory, condemned society. Dickens, on the contrary, saw the world as it is, without hatred and without admiration, being more ready to laugh at its defects than to weep over its vices. He was more philosophical with his British phlegm, for he amused, and occasionally improved those whom Balzac discouraged and embittered. His lively, but profound pictures of English society are a perfect representation of the nineteenth century ; for, as with all great writers, he enlarged the scene, and his principal characters might have lived in any part of Europe. It is by reason of this extensive observation, and this elevation of view, that Charles Dickens will take rank with Walter Scott, and above Thackeray, Lytton, and other English writers of great talent, but who possessed not that which Dickens, like Shakspeare and Molière, possessed— genius." The *Temps* admires the humour and truth of Dickens's books, and describes him as a literary counterpart of Hogarth, but objects to his inclination to describe hideous and painful scenes, and ignoble characters. It is disposed to think that the comic writings of Dickens prove him to have been rather light-hearted than witty. The *Figaro* observes that Dickens had an advantage over Balzac in " that perfectly British quality —that mixture of sentiment and gaiety which constitutes the ' humour' of English literature." The *Gaulois* notices the clear insight into character, the love of children, the tender sympathy towards the suffering, and the compassion for the weak and oppressed that are the striking characteristics of Dickens's writings. In the same paper, M. Paul Féval gives an account of his first acquaintance and subsequent friendship with Dickens, of whom he speaks with admiration and affection. One observation he quotes as having been made to him by his illustrious English friend, that " Balzac and many other authors are marked as if criticism had upon them the effect of an attack of small-pox. They become gloomy and dispirited like jaded horses. They are too egotistical ; the prickings of the flies of journalism make them nervous and ill-natured. For myself, I have been spoilt in a contrary sense. I have been praised more than I deserve." " He was wrong," adds M. Paul Féval, " but he told no falsehood. Nothing in him was false, not even his modesty."

RELIQUES OF FATHER PROUT.

FRANCIS MAHONY, late P.P. of Watergrasshill, who also rejoiced in the *nom de plume* of *Father Prout*, was born in Ireland about 1805, but left that country at an early age, for the Jesuit College in France, and the University of Rome. Returning from Italy in clerical orders, a short experience of their Irish exercise seems to have decided him to adopt literature as a profession. Uniting in an eminent degree ripe scholarship, a ready pen, and a racy style, he was, under the name of Father Prout, gladly enrolled amongst the band of able men who, in the hey-day of Dr. Maginn, contributed to *Fraser's Magazine.* The papers from his pen, re-published in *Fraser*, 1836, had been long out of print. The new edition (Bohn, 1860), was next stereotyped, and illustrated, with admirable etchings by D. Maclise, R.A. In 1870, another edition was published (Bell and Daldy), with a preface, which we shall presently notice.

Mahony was also one of the earliest and most sparkling writers in *Bentley's Miscellany*, in 1837 ; subsequently, he spent some years in travelling through Hungary, Asia Minor, Greece, and Egypt, and has written several books ; but his chief literary labours were devoted to the columns of the newspapers. He undertook, at the request of Charles Dickens, in 1847, the Roman Correspondence of the *Daily News ;* and contributed to the columns of that journal, a series of papers, full of sparkling wit and zeal for the cause of Italy. These were collected and published by Bentley (1849), under the title of *Facts and Figures* from Italy. He was examined by the Parliamentary Committee on the Mortmain Laws in 1851, principally as it regarded their effect in the Roman States, disclosing some curious particulars respecting the general management of that territory. On the staff of the *Globe* newspaper, his pen was easily recognizable ; and latterly his department was continental politics, and his habitat Paris.

Mahony, in the preface already named, and dated Paris, Nov. 20, 1859, thus agreeably characterises the *Reliques :*—

" Oliver Goldsmith, in his green youth, aspired to be the rural pastor of some village Auburn ; and in after-life gave embodiment to his earlier fancies in a Vicar of Wakefield. But his Dr. Primrose had immense advantages over Dr. Prout. The olive-branches that sprang from the vicar's roof-tree, if they divided, certainly enhanced the interest felt in his character ; while the lone incumbent of Watergrasshill was thrown on his own resources for any chance of enlisting sympathy. The ' great defender of monogamy ' could buy a wedding-gown, send his boy Mores to the fair, set out in pursuit of his lost daughter, get into debt and jail ; exploits which the kindly author felt he could have himself achieved. Prout's misogamy debarred him from these stirring social incidents : he had nothing left for it but to talk and write, and occasionally ' intone ' a genial song.

" From such utterances the mind and feelings of the man have to be distilled. It requires no great palæontological acumen to perceive that he belonged to a class of mortals, now quite gone out of Irish existence, like the elk and wolf-dog ; and it has been a main object in this book out of his ' relics ' to ' restore ' him for purposes of comparative anatomy.

" It will be noticed that the Father's rambles are not limited by any barrier of caste, or coat, or coterie ; his soul is multilateral, his talk multifarious, yet free, it is hoped, from garrulity, and decidedly exempt from credulity. He seems to have had a shrewd eye for scanning Humbug, and it is well for him (and for others) that he has vacated his parish in due course of nature. He would have stoutly resisted in Ireland the late attempted process of Italian Cullenization. For though he patronized the effort of Lord Kingston to naturalize in Munster the silkworm from that peninsula (see his version of good Bishop Vida's *Bombices*, page 523), mere caterpillars, snails, and slimy crawlers, he would have put his foot on.

" From Florence the poet Browning has sent for this edition some lines lately found in the Euganeian hills, traced on a marble slab that covered the bones of Pietro d' Abano, held in his old age to be an astrologer, of which epitaph the poet has supplied this vernacular rendering *verbatim*—

> " ' Studying my cyphers with the compass,
> I find I shall soon be under the daisy ;
> Because of my lore folks make such a rumpus,
> That every dull dog is thereat *unaisy.*'

" Browning's attempt suggests a word or two on Prout's own theory of translation, as largely exemplified in this volume. The only perfect reproduction of a couplet in a different idiom occurred in A.D. 1170, when the Archbishop of York sent a salmon to the chronicler of Malmesbury, with request for a receipt in verse, which was handed to bearer in duplicate—

> " ' Mittitur in disco mihi piscis ab archiepisco-
> -Po non ponetur nisi potus. Pol! mihi detur.'

> " ' I'm sent a fyshe, in a dyshe, by the archbish-
> -Bop, is not put here. Egad! he sent noe beere.'

" Sense, rhythm, point, and even pun are here miraculously reproduced. Prout did his best to rival him of Malmesbury, but he held that in the clear failure of one language to elicit from its repertory an exact equivalent, it becomes not only proper but imperative (on the law principle of *Cestui apres* in case of trusts) to fall back on an approximate word or idea of kindred import, the interchange in vocabulary showing at times even a balance in favour of the substitute, as happens in the ordinary course of barter on the markets of the world. He quite abhorred the clumsy servility of adhering to the letter while allowing the spirit to evaporate ; a mere verbal echo, distorted by natural anfractu-osities, gives back neither the tone nor quality of the original voice ; while the ease and curious felicity of the primitive utter-ance is marred by awkwardness and effort ; spontaneity of song being the quintessence.

" Modest distrust of his own power to please deterred Prout from obtruding much of his personal musings ; he preferred chewing the cud of classic fancies, or otherwise approved and substantial stuff ; delighting to invest with new and varied forms what had long gained universal recognition. He had strict notions as to what really constitute the *Belles Lettres*. Brilliancy of thought, depth of remark, pathos of sentiment, sprightliness of wit, vigour and aptitude of style, with *some* scholarship, were requisites for his notice, or claim to be held in his esteem a literary man. It is useless to add how much of recent growth, and how many pretenders to that title he would have eschewed.

" A word as to the Etchings of D. Maclise, R.A. This great artist in his boyhood knew Prout, and has fixed his true features in enduring copper. The only reliable outline of Sir Walter Scott, as he appeared in plain clothes, and without ideal halo, may be seen at page 54, where he ' kisses the Blarney Stone,' on his visit to Prout in the summer of 1825. Tom Moore, equally *en deshabille*, can be recognized by all who knew him, perpetrat-ing one of his ' rogueries,' at page 150. The painter's own slim and then youthful figure is doing homage to L.E.L. on a moonlit bank at page 229, while the ' garret' of Béranger, page 299, the ' night before Larry's execution,' page 367, and ' Mandarins robing Venus in silk,' page 533, are specimens of French, Irish and Chinese humanity.

"But it is his great cartoon of writers in *Fraser*, anno 1835 (*front.*), that will most interest coming generations. The banquet was no fiction, but a frequent fact in Regent Street, 212. Dr. Maginn in the chair, addressing the staff contributors, has on his right Barry Cornwall (Proctor), Robert Southey, Percival Bankes, Thackeray, Churchill, Serjeant Murphy, Macnish, Ainsworth, Coleridge, Hogg, Galt, Dunlop, and Jerdan. Fraser is croupier, having on his right Crofton Croker, Lockhart, Theodore Hook, Sir David Brewster, Dr. Moir (Delta), Tom Carlyle, Count D'Orsay (talking to Allan Cunningham), Sir Egerton Brydges ; Rev. G. R. Gleig, Chaplain of Chelsea Hospital ; Rev. F. Mahony, Rev Edward Irving (of the unknown tongues), a frequent writer in *Fraser*, and a frequenter in his sanctum, where ' oft of a stilly night ' he quaffed Glenlivat with the learned editor."

In his preface to the first edition of the *Reliques*, the author (Oliver Yorke) states :

"In giving utterance to regret, we do not insinuate that the present production of the lamented writer is unfinished or abortive : on the contrary, our interest prompts us to pronounce it complete, as far as it goes. Prout, as an author, will be found what he was in the flesh—' *totus teres atque rotundus.*' Still, a suitable introduction, furnished by a kindred genius, would in our idea be ornamental. The Pantheon of republican Rome, perfect in its simplicity, yet derived a supplementary grace from the portico superadded by Agrippa.

"Much meditating on the materials that fill ' the chest,' and daily more impressed with the merit of our author, we thought it a pity that his wisdom should be suffered to evaporate in magazine squibs. What impression could, in sooth, be made on the public mind by such desultory explosions ? Never on the dense mass of readers can isolated random shots produce the effect of a regular *feu de peloton.* For this reason we have arranged in one volume his files of mental musketry, to secure a simultaneous discharge. The hint, perhaps, of right belongs to the ingenious Fieschi (1835).

"We have left prefixed to each paper such introductory comments as at the time we indulged in, with reference to contemporary occurrences—and, on looking back, we find we have been on some occasions historical, on others prophetical, on some perhaps rhapsodical. This latter charge we hereby ' confess and avoid,' pleading the advice and example of Pliny the Younger : ' *Ipsa varietate,*' are his words, ' *tentamus efficere ut alia aliis, quædam fortasse omnibus placeant.*' This would appear to constitute the whole theory of miscellaneous writing.

"We have hitherto had considerable difficulty in establishing,

17—2

to the satisfaction of refractory critics, the fact of our author's
death. People absurdly persist in holding him in the light of a
living writer : hence a sad waste of wholesome advice, which, if
judiciously expended on some reclaimable sinner, would, no doubt,
fructify in due season. In his case 'tis a dead loss—Prout is a
literary mummy ! Folks should look to this : Lazarus will not
come forth to listen to their strictures ; neither, should they
happen to be in a complimentary mood, will Samuel arise at the
witchery of commendation.

" Objects of art and virtu lose considerably by not being viewed
in their proper light ; and the common noonday effulgence is not
the fittest for the right contemplation of certain *capi d' opera*.
Canova, we know, preferred the midnight taper. Let, therefore,
' *ut fruaris reliquiis* ' (*Phæd.* lib. i. fab. 22), the dim penumbra
of a sepulchral lamp shed its solemn influence over the page of
Prout, and alone preside at its perusal.

" Posthumous authorship possesses infinite advantages ; and
nothing so truly serves a book as the author's removal from the
sphere or hemisphere of his readers. The *Memoirs of Captain
Rock* were rendered doubly interesting by being dated from
Sidney Cove. Byron wrote from Venice with increased effect.
Nor can we at all sympathise with the exiled Ovid's plaintive
utterance, ' *Sine me, liber, ibis in urbem.*' His absence from
town, he must have known, was a right good thing for his
publisher under ' the pillars.' But though distance be useful,
death is unquestionably better. Far off, an author is respected ;
dead, he is beloved. *Extinctus amabitur.*"

But how shall we give the reader any idea of the rich variety
of grotesque humour which these 600 closely-printed pages present to the reader, commencing with " An Apology for Lent,"
and closing with Father Prout's translation of "Life's a Bubble?"
The vignette, by the way, is Maclise's " First Planting the
Potato in Ireland," in the letter-press to which, curious it is to
read, " To Sir Walter Raleigh no monument has yet been
erected, and nothing has been done to repair the injustice of
his contemporaries. His head was rolled from the scaffold
on Tower Hill ; * and though he has fed with his discovery
more families, and given a greater impulse to population, than
any other benefactor of mankind, no testimonial exists to
commemorate his benefaction." It appears that Prout ate of
the pancake, and that its effects proved fatal. A Latin elegy
was composed by the most learned of the order, Father
Magrath. That elegy is subjoined, as a record of Prout's

* It will, however, be remembered that Raleigh was beheaded in
Old Palace Yard !

genuine worth, and as a specimen of *Leonine verse*, which is translated :

"Sweet upland ! where, like hermit old, in peace sojourn'd
   This priest devout ;
Mark where beneath thy verdant sod lie deep inurn'd
   The bones of Prout !
Nor deck with monumental shrine or tapering column
   His place of rest,
Whose soul, above earth's homage, meek yet solemn,
   Sits 'mid the blest.
Much was he prized, much loved ; his stern rebuke
   O'erawed sheep-stealers ;
And rogues fear'd more the good man's single look
   Than forty Peelers.
He's gone ; and discord soon I ween will visit
   The land with quarrels ;
And the foul demon vex with stills illicit
   The village morals.
No fatal chance could happen more to cross
   The public wishes ;
And all the neighbourhood deplores his loss,
   Except the fishes ;
For he kept Lent most strict, and pickled herring
   Preferred to gammon.
Grim Death has broke his angling-rod ; his berring
   Delights the salmon.
No more can he hook up carp, eel, or trout,
   For fasting pittance,—
Arts which Saint Peter loved, whose gate to Prout
   Gave prompt admittance.
Mourn not, but verdantly let shamrocks keep
   His sainted dust ;
The bad man's death it well becomes to weep,—
   Not so the just."

The next Relique is "A Plea for Pilgrimages." There stands near the village of Blarney, an old castle of the M'Carthy family, rising abruptly from a bold cliff, at the foot of which rolls an inconsiderable stream, the fond and frequent witness of Prout's angling propensities. The well-wooded demesne, an extensive lake, a romantic cavern, and an artificial wilderness of rocks, belongs to the family of Jeffreys, which boast in the Dowager Countess of Glengall a most distinguished scion, her ladyship's mother having been immortalized under the title of "Lady Jeffers," with the other natural curiosities produced by this celebrated spot, in that never-sufficiently-to-be encored song, "The Groves of Blarney." But neither the stream, nor the lake, nor the castle, nor the village (a sad ruin! which, but for the recent establishment of a spinning-factory by some patriotic Corkonian, would be swept away altogether, or possessed by the owls as a grant from Sultan Mahmoud);— none of these picturesque objects has earned such notoriety for "the Groves" as a certain stone, of a basaltic kind, rather unusual in the district, placed on the pinnacle of the main tower, and endowed with the property of communicating to the happy tongue that comes in contact with its polished surface the gift of gentle insinuating speech, with soft talk in all its ramifications, whether employed in vows and promises light as air, ἔπεα πτερόεντα, such as lead captive the female heart; or elaborate mystification of a grosser grain, such as may do for the House of Commons; all summed up and characterized by the mysterious term Blarney.

To Crofton Croker belongs the merit of elucidating this obscure tradition. It appears that in 1602, when the Spaniards were exciting our chieftains to harass the English authorities, Cormac M'Dermot Carthy held, among other dependencies, the castle of Blarney, and had concluded an armistice with the lord-president, on condition of surrendering this fort to an English garrison. Day after day did his lordship look for the fulfilment of the compact; while the Irish Pozzo di Borgo, as loath to part with his stronghold as Russia to relinquish the Dardanelles, kept protocolising with soft promises and delusive delays, until at last Carew became the laughing-stock of Elizabeth's ministers, and "Blarney-talk" proverbial.

Prout's theory on this subject might have remained dormant for ages, and perhaps been ultimately lost to the world at large, were it not for an event which occurred in the summer of 1825. The occurrence about to be commemorated was, in truth, one of the first magnitude, and well calculated, from its importance, to form an epoch in the Annals of the Parish. It was the arrival of Sir Walter Scott at Blarney, towards the end of the month of July.

Years have now rolled away, the "Ariosto of the North" is dead, and our ancient constitution has since fallen under the hoofs of the Whigs; quenched is many a beacon-light in Church and State—Prout himself is no more; and plentiful indications tell us we are come upon evil days: but still may we be allowed to feel a pleasurable, though somewhat saddened emotion, while we revert to that intellectual meeting, and bid memory go back in "dream sublime" to the glorious exhibition of Prout's mental powers. It was, in sooth, a great day for old Ireland; a greater still for Blarney; but, greatest of all, it dawned, Prout, on thee! Then it was that thy light was taken from under its sacerdotal bushel, and placed conspicuously before a man fit to appreciate the effulgence of so brilliant a luminary—a light which we, who pen these words in sorrow, alas! shall never gaze on more!—a light

> "That ne'er shall shine again
> On Blarney's stream!"

That day it illumined the "cave," the "shady walks," and the "sweet rock-close," and sent its gladdening beam into the gloomiest vaults of the ancient fort; for all the recondite recesses of the castle were explored in succession by the distinguished poet and the learned priest, and Prout held a candle to Scott.

We read with interest, in the historian Polybius, the account of Hannibal's interview with Scipio on the plains of Zama; and often have we, in our schoolboy days of unsophisticated feeling, sympathised with Ovid, when he told us that he only got a glimpse of Virgil; but Scott basked for a whole summer's day in the blaze of Prout's wit, and witnessed the coruscations of his learning. The great Marius is said never to have appeared to such advantage as when seated on the ruins of Carthage: with equal dignity Prout sat on the Blarney stone, amid ruins of kindred glory. Zeno taught in the "porch;" Plato loved to mourn alone on the bold jutting promontory of Cape Sunium; Socrates, bent on finding Truth, "in sylvis Academi quærere verum," sought her among the bowers of Academus; Prout courted the same coy nymph, and wooed her in the "groves of Blarney."

"On the eve of that memorable day I was sitting on a stool in the priest's parlour, poking the turf fire, while Prout, who had been angling all day, sat nodding over his '*breviary*,' and, according to my calculation, ought to be at the last psalm of vespers, when a loud official knock, not usual on that bleak hill, bespoke the presence of no ordinary personage. Accordingly, the 'wicket, opening with a latch,' ushered in a messenger clad in the livery of the ancient and loyal corporation of Cork, who announced himself as the bearer of a despatch from the mansion-house to his reverence; and, handing it with that deferential awe which even his masters felt for the incumbent of Watergrasshill, immediately withdrew.   The letter ran thus :—

"'*Council Chambers, July* 24, 1825.
"'VERY REVEREND DOCTOR PROUT,
        "'Cork harbours within its walls the illustrious author of "Waverley." On receiving the freedom of our ancient city, which we presented to him (as usual towards distinguished strangers) in a box carved out of a chip of the Blarney stone, he expressed his determination to visit the old block itself.   As he will, therefore, be in your neighbourhood to-morrow, and as no one is better able to do the honours than you (our burgesses being sadly deficient in learning, as you and I well know), your attendance on the celebrated poet is requested by your old friend and foster-brother,
                    "'GEORGE KNAPP, *Mayor.*'

" The republic of letters has great reason to complain of Dr. Maginn, for his non-fulfilment of a positive pledge to publish 'a great historical work' on the mayors of Cork.   Owing to this desideratum in the annals of the empire, I am compelled to bring into notice thus abruptly the most respectable civic worthy that has worn the cocked hat and chain since the days of John Walters, who boldly proclaimed Perkin Warbeck, in the reign of Henry VII., in the market-place of that beautiful city.   Knapp's virtues and talents did not, like those of Donna Inez, deserve to be called

            "' Classic all,
    Nor lay they chiefly in the mathematical,'

for his favourite pursuit during the canicule of 1825, was the extermination of mad dogs ; and so vigorously did he urge the carnage during the summer of his mayoralty, that some thought he wished to eclipse the exploit of St. Patrick in destroying the breed altogether, as the saint did that of toads. A Cork poet, the laureate of the mansion-house, has celebrated Knapp's prowess in a didactic composition, entitled *Dog-Killing, a Poem*, in which the mayor is likened to Apollo in the Grecian camp before Troy, in the opening of the *Iliad.*"

KISSING THE BLARNEY STONE.

The wonders of the castle, the cave, and lake were speedily

gone over, and we shift the scene to the tabernacle of Father
Prout, on Watergrasshill, where, round a small table, sat
Scott, Knapp, and Prout—a triumvirate of critics never
equalled.   The papers fell into my hands when the table was
cleared for the subsequent repast, and thus I am able to submit to the world's decision what these three could not decide,
viz., *which* is the *original* version of the " Groves of Blarney."
At the moment of going to press with the Doric, the Vulgate,
and Gallic texts in juxtaposition with the supposed original
(Corcagian) a fifth candidate for priority starts up, the Italic,
said to be sung by Garibaldi in bivouac amid the woods
over Lake Como, May 25, 1859.

The next Relique is " The Carousal," much beyond our
limits, as are " Dean Swift's Madness," and the " Rogueries
of Tom Moore."   From " the Prout Papers " we quote.   A
profane French sophist has attributed Noah's escape from the
Flood to a sad partiality :

> " To have drown'd an old chap,
>   Such a friend to ' the tap,'
> The flood would have felt compunction :
>   Noah owed his escape
>   To his love for the grape ;
> And his ' ark ' was an empty puncheon."

The illustrious Queen Anne, who, like our own Regina,
encouraged literature and patronized wit, was thus calumniated
after death, when her statue was put up with its back to
Paul's Church, and its face towards that celebrated corner
of the churchyard, which in those days was a brandy-shop.

SCOTT.

There is certainly somewhat of Grecian simplicity in the
old song itself ; and if Pindar had been an Irishman, I think
he would have celebrated this favourite haunt in a style not
very different from Millikin's classic rhapsody.

PROUT.

Millikin, the reputed author of that song, was but a simple
translator from the Greek original.   Indeed, I have discovered,
when abroad, in the library of Cardinal Mazarin, an old
Greek manuscript, which, after diligent examination, I am
convinced must be the oldest and " princeps editio " of the
song.   I begged to be allowed to copy it, in order that I

might compare it with the ancient Latin or Vulgate translation which is preserved in the Brera at Milan ; and from a strict and minute comparison with that, and with the Norman-French copy which is appended to Doomsday-book, and the Celtic-Irish fragment preserved by Crofton Croker (rejecting as spurious the Arabic, Armenian, and Chaldaic stanzas on the same subject, to be found in the collection of the Royal Asiatic Society), I have come to the conclusion that the Greeks were the undoubted original contrivers of that splendid ode ; though whether we ascribe it to Tyrtæus or Callimachus will depend on future evidence ; and perhaps, Sir Walter, *you* would give me your opinion, as I have copies of all the versions I allude to at my dwelling on the hill.

SCOTT.

I cannot boast, learned father, of much νους in Hellenistic matters ; but should find myself quite at home in the Gaelic and Norman-French, to inspect which I shall with pleasure accompany you : so here I kiss the stone !

Not a word is requisite to commend this charming volume of rich fancy and exquisite learning to every reader.

> " Through flowery paths
> Skilled to guide youth, in haunts where learning dwells,
> They fill'd with honey'd lore their cloistered cells."

From " the literature of *Prout*, the Jesuit," we quote the massacre this month by a brutal populace in Madrid of fourteen Jesuits, in the hall of their college of St. Isidore, which has drawn somewhat of notice, if not of sympathy, to this singular order of literati, whom we never fail, for the last three hundred years, to find mixed up with every political disturbance. There is a certain species of bird well known to ornithologists, but better still to mariners, which is sure to make its appearance in stormy weather—so constantly indeed, as to induce among the sailors (*durum genus*) a belief that it is *the fowl* that has raised the tempest. Leaving this knotty point to be settled by Dr. Lardner in his " Cyclopædia," at the article of " Mother Carey's chickens," we cannot help observing, meantime, that since the days of the French League under Henri Trois, to the late final expulsion of the *branche aînée* (an event which has marked the commencement

of Regina's accession to the throne of literature), as well in
the revolutions of Portugal as in the vicissitudes of Venice,
in the revocation of the edict of Nantz, in the expulsion of
James II., in the severance of the Low Countries from Spain,
in the invasion of Africa by Don Sebastian, in the Scotch
rebellion of '45, in the conquest of China by the Tartars, in
all the Irish rebellions, from Father Salmeron in 1561, and
Father Archer (for whom see " Pacata Hibernia "), to that
anonymous Jesuit who (according to Sir Harcourt Lees) threw
the bottle at the Lord Lieutenant in the Dublin theatre some
years ago—there is always one of this ill-fated society found
in the thick of the confusion—

> " And whether for good, or whether for ill,
>   It is not mine to say ;
> But still to the house of Amundeville
>   He abideth night and day !

> " When an heir is born, he is heard to mourn,
>   And when ought is to befall
> That ancient line, in the pale *moonshine*
>   He walks from hall to hall."—BYRON.

However, notwithstanding the various and manifold com-
motions which these Jesuits have confessedly kicked up in
the kingdoms of Europe and the commonwealth of Christen-
dom, we, Oliver Yorke, must admit that they have not
deserved ill of the *Republic of Letters ;* and therefore do we
decidedly set our face against the Madrid process of knocking
out their brains ; for, in our view of things, the *pineal gland*
and the *cerebellum* are not kept in such a high state of cultivation in Spain as to render superfluous a few colleges and
professors of the *literæ humaniores.* George Knapp, the vigilant mayor of Cork, was, no doubt, greatly to be applauded
for demolishing with his civic club the mad dogs which
infested his native town ; and he would have won immortal
laurels if he had furthermore cleared that beautiful city of the
idlers, gossips, and cynics who therein abound ; but it was a
great mistake of the Madrid folks to apply the club to the
learned skulls of the few literati they possessed. We are
inclined to think (though full of respect for Robert Southey's
opinion) that, after all, Roderick was *not* the last of the Goths
in Spain.

When the Cossacks got into Paris in 1814, their first
exploit was to eat up all the tallow candles of the conquered

metropolis, and to drink the train oil out of the lamps, so as to leave the " Boulevards " in Cimmerian darkness.　By mur-dering the schoolmasters, it would seem that the partisans of Queen Christina would have no great objection to a similar municipal arrangement for Madrid.　But all this is a matter of national taste ; and as *our* gracious Regina is no party to " the quadruple alliance," she has determined to adhere to her fixed system of non-intervention.

Meantime, the public will peruse with some curiosity a paper from Father Prout, concerning his old masters in litera-ture.　We suspect that on this occasion sentimental gratitude has begotten a sort of " drop serene " in his eye, for he only winks at the rogueries of the Jesuits ; nor does he redden for them the gridiron on which he gently roasts Dr. Lardner and Tom Moore.　But the great merit of the essay is, that the composer evidently had opportunities of a thorough knowledge of his subject—a matter of rare occurrence, and therefore quite refreshing.　He appears, indeed, to be fully aware of his vantage-ground : hence the tone of confidence, and the firm, unhesitating tenour of his assertions.　This is what we like to see.　A chancellor of England who rarely got drunk, Sir Thomas More, has left this bit of advice to folks in general :—

> Wise men alwaye
> affirme and say
> 　that tis best for a man
> diligently
> for to apply
> 　to the business he can,
> and in no wyse
> to enterprise
> 　　　another facultie.
> A simple hatter
> should not go smatter
> 　in philosophie ;
> nor ought a peddlar
> become a meddlar
> 　in theologie.*

Acting on this principle, how gladly would we open our columns to a treatise by our particular friend, Marie Taglioni, on the philosophy of *hops !*—how cheerfully would we wel-come an essay on *heavy wet* from the pen of Dr. Wade, or of Jack Reeve, or any other similarly qualified Chevalier de Malte !　We should not object to a tract on gin from Charley Pearson ; nor would we exclude Lord Althorp's thick notions on "*flummery*," or Lord Brougham's XXX. ideas on that

---

* See this excellent didactic poem printed at length in the elabo-rate preface to Dr. Johnson's Dictionary.　It is entitled, " A merrie Jest, how a Sarjeant would learn to play y* Frere ; by Maister Thomas More, in hys youthe."

mild alcohol which, for the sake of peace and quietness, we shall call "*tea*." Who would not listen with attention to Irving on a matter of "unknown tongues," or to O'Brien on "Round Towers?" Verily it belongeth to old Benjamin Franklin to write scientifically on the *paratonnère ;* and his contemporary, Talleyrand, has a paramount claim to lecture on the *weather-cock.*

> "Sumite materiam vestris qui scribitis æquam
> Viribus."

Turning finally to thee, O Prout! truly great was thy love of frolic, but still more remarkable thy wisdom. Thou wert a most rare combination of Socrates and Sancho Panza, of Scarron and the venerable Bede! What would we not have given to have cracked a bottle with thee in thy hut on Watergrasshill, partaking of thy hospitable "herring," and imbibing thy deep flood of knowledge with the plenitude of thy "Medoc?" Nothing gloomy, narrow, or pharisaical, ever entered into thy composition—"In wit, a man; simplicity, a child." The wrinkled brow of antiquity softened into smiles for thee; and the Muses must have marked thee in thy cradle for their own. Such is the perfume that breathes from thy chest of posthumous elucubrations, conveying a sweet fragrance to the keen nostrils of criticism, and recalling the funeral oration of the old woman in Phædrus over her emptied flagon—

> "O suavis anima! quale te dicam bonum
> Antehàc fuisse, tales cùm sint reliquiæ."

OLIVER YORKE.

Regent Street, 1st Sept., 1834.

FROM "THE SONGS OF FRANCE."

ON WINE, WAR, WOMEN, WOODEN SHOES, PHILOSOPHY, FROGS, AND FREE TRADE.

> "Cool shade is summer's haunt, fireside November's ;
> The red red rose then yields to glowing embers :
> Etchings by Dan Maclise then place before us !
> Drawings of Cork ! to aid Prout's Gallic chorus."

O. Y.

In this gloomy month our brethren of the "broad sheet," resigned to the anticipated casualties of the season, keep by them, in stereotype, announcements which never fail to be put in requisition, viz., "Death by Drowning," "Extraordinary Fog," "Melancholy Suicide," "Felo de se," with doleful headings borrowed from Young's "Night Thoughts," Ovid's "Tristia," Hervey on Tombs, and Zimmerman on Solitude. There is much punctuality in this recurrence of the national dismals. Long ago, Guy Faux considerately selected the fifth of November for despatching the stupid and unreformed senators of Great Britain : so cold and comfortless a month being the most acceptable, he thought, that could be chosen for warming their honourable house with a few seasonable fagots and barrels of gunpowder. Philanthropic citizen ! Neither he nor Sir William Congreve, of rocket celebrity—nor Friar Bacon, the original concocter of "villanous saltpetre"—nor Parson Malthus, the patentee of the "preventive check"—nor Dean Swift, the author of "A Modest Proposal for turning into Salt Provisions the Offspring of the Irish Poor"—nor Brougham, the originator of the new *reform* in the poor laws—nor Mr. O'Connell, the Belisarius of the poor-box, and the stanch opponent of any provision for his half-starved tributaries—will ever meet their reward in this world, nor even be appreciated or understood by their blind and ungrateful fellow-countrymen. Happily, however, for some of the above-mentioned worthies, there is a warm *corner* reserved, if not in Westminster Abbey, most certainly in "another place ;" where alone (God forgive us !), we incline to think, their merits can be suitably acknowledged.

Sorrowful, indeed, would be the condition of mankind, if, in addition to other sources of sublunary desolation over which we have no control, Father Prout were, like the sun, to obnubilate his disk, and withdraw the light of his countenance from a disconsolate world :

"Caput obscurâ nitidum ferrugine texit,
    Impiaque æternam timuerunt sæcula noctem."

Then, indeed, would unmitigated darkness thicken the already "palpable" obscure ; dulness place another pad-"Lock on the human understanding," and knowledge be at one grand entrance fairly shut out. But such "disastrous twilight" shall not befall our planet, as long as there is MS. in "the chest" or shot in the locker. Generations yet unborn shall walk in the blaze of Prout's wisdom, and the learned of

our own day shall still continue to light the pipe of knowledge at the focus of this luminary. So essential do we deem
the continuance of his essays to the happiness of our contemporaries, that were we (*quod Deus avertat !*) to put a stop to
our accustomed issues of " Prout paper," forgeries would
instantly get into circulation ; a false paper currency would
be attempted ; there would arise ψευδο-Prouts : but they would
deceive no one, much less *the elect.* Farina of Cologne is
obliged to caution the public, in the envelope of his long
bottles, against spurious distillations of his wonderful water :
" Rowland," of Hatton Garden, finds more than one " Oliver "
vending a counterfeit " Macassar." We give notice, that no
" Prout paper " is the *real* thing unless with label signed
" OLIVER YORKE." There is a Bridgewater Treatise in circulation, said to be from the pen of one Dr. Prout ; 'tis a sheer
hoax. An *artist* has also taken up the name ; but he must
be an impostor, not known on Watergrasshill. Owing to the
law of celibacy, " the Father " can have left behind him no
children, or posterity whatever ; therefore, none but himself
can hope to be his parallel. We are perfectly aware that he
may have " nephews," and other collateral descendants ; for
we admit the truth of that celebrated placard, or lampoon,
stuck on Pasquin's statue in the reign of Pope Borghese
(Paul IV.) :

" Cùm factor rerum privaret semine clerum,
 In Satanæ votum successit turba *nepotum !*"—*i.e.,*

" Of bantlings when our clergymen were freed from having bevies,
 There next arose, a crowd of woes, a multitude of *nevies !*"

But should any audacious thief attempt to palm himself as a
son of this venerable pastor, let him look sharp ; for Terry
Callaghan, who is now in the London police (through the
patronage of Feargus O'Connor), will quickly collar the
ruffian in the most inaccessible garret of Grub Street : to
profane so respectable a signature, the fellow must be what
Terry calls " a bad mimber intirely ;" what we English call
a " jail-bird."

We have to acknowledge the receipt of a communication,
referring to our " Songs of France," from the pen of the facetious knight, Sir Charles Wetherell. Great men's peculiarities
attract no small share of public attention : thus, *ex. gr.*, Napo-

leon's method of plunging his fore-finger and thumb into his waistcoat pocket, in lieu of a snuff-box, was the subject of much European commentary; and one of the twelve Cæsars was nicknamed Caligula from a peculiar sort of Wellington boot which he happened to fancy.

Whatever may be the failings and errors of our poet, due to the disastrous days on which his youth has fallen, there is discernible in his writings the predominant character of his mind—frankness, single-heartedness, and candour. It is impossible not to entertain a friendly feeling towards such a man; and I am not surprised to learn that he is cherished by the French people with a fervency akin to idolatry. *He* is no tuft-hunter, nor Whigling sycophant, nor trafficker in his merchandise of song. Neither has he sought to convert his patriotism into an engine for picking the pockets of the poor. *He* has set up no pretensions to nobility; although he could no doubt trump up a story of Norman ancestry, and convert some old farm-house on the sea-coast into an "abbey." It is not with the affectation of a swindling demagogue, but with the heartfelt cordiality of one of themselves, that he glories in belonging to *the people.* What poet but Béranger ever thought of commemorating *the garret* where he spent his earlier days?

LE GRENIER DE BERANGER.

Je reviens voir l'asyle où ma jeunesse
  De la misère a subi les leçons :
J'avais vingt ans, une folle maitresse,
  De francs amis, et l'amour des
    chansons :
Bravant le monde, et les sots, et les
    sages,
  Sans avenir, riche de mon printems,
Leste et joyeux, je montais six étages—
Dans un grenier qu'on est bien à vingt
    ans !

C'est un grenier, point ne veux qu'on
  l'ignore :
  Là fut mon lit, bien chétif et bien
    dur ;
Là fut ma table ; et je retrouve encore
  Trois pieds d'un vers charbonnés
    sur le mur.

THE GARRET OF BERANGER.

Oh ! it was here that Love his
    gifts bestowed
  On youth's wild age !
Gladly once more I seek my
    youth's abode,
  In pilgrimage :
Here my young mistress with
    her poet dared
  Reckless to dwell :
She was sixteen, I twenty, and
    we shared
  This attic cell.

Yes, 'twas in a garret ! be it
    known to all,
  Here was Love's shrine :
There read, in charcoal traced
    along the wall,
  Th' unfinished line—

Apparaissez, plaisirs de mon bel âge,
  Que d'un coup d'œil a fustigé le
    tems !
Vingt fois pour vous j'ai mis ma mon-
    tre en gage—
  Dans un grenier qu'on est bien à
    vingt ans !

Here was the board where kin-
    dred hearts would blend.
  The Jew can tell
How oft I pawned my watch,
    to feast a friend
  In attic cell !

Lisette ici doit surtout apparaître,
  Vive, jolie, avec un frais chapeau ;
Déjà sa main à l'étroite fenêtre
  Suspend son schale en guise de ri-
    deau :
Sa robe aussi va parer ma couchette—
  Respecte, Amour ! ses plis longs et
    flottans :
J'ai su depuis qui payait sa toilette—
  Dans un grenier qu'on est bien à
    vingt ans !

O ! my Lisette's fair form could
    I recall
  With fairy wand !
There she would blind the win-
    dow with her shawl—
  Bashful, yet fond !
What though from whom she
    got her dress I've since
  Learnt but too well,
Still in those days I envied not
    a prince
  In attic cell !

A table un jour, jour de grande rich-
    esse,
  De mes amis les voix brillaient en
    chœur,
Quand jusqu'ici monte un cri d'alé-
    gresse,
  Qu'à Marengo Bonaparte est vain-
    queur !
Le canon gronde—un autre chant
    commence—
  Nous célébrons tant de faits éclatans;
Les rois jamais n'envahiront la
    France—
  Dans un grenier qu'on est bien à
    vingt ans !

Here the glad tidings on our
    banquet burst,
  Mid the bright bowls :
Yes, it was here Marengo's
    triumph first
  Kindled our souls !
Bronze cannon roared ; France
    with redoubled might
  Felt her heart swell !
Proudly we drank our Consul's
    health that night
  In attic cell !

Quittons ce toit, où ma raison s'en-
    ivre—
  Oh, qu'ils sont loin ces jours si re-
    grettés !
J'échangerai ce qu'il me reste à vivre
  Contre un des jours qu'ici Dieu m'a
    comptés,
Pour rêver gloire, amour, plaisir, folie,
  Pour dépenser sa vie en peu d'in-
    stans,
D'un long espoir pour la voir em-
    bellie—
  Dans un grenier qu'on est bien à
    vingt ans !

Dreams of my joyful youth !
    I'd freely give,
  Ere my life's close,
All the dull days I'm destined
    yet to live,
  For one of those !
Where shall I now find rap-
    tures that were felt,
  Joys that befell,
And hopes that dawned at
    twenty, when I dwelt
  In attic cell ?

Nothing can offer a more ludicrous image to the dispassionate observer of passing transactions, than the assumption of radical politics by some men whose essential nature is thoroughly imbued with contempt for the mob, while they are straining every nerve to secure its sweet voices. I could name many who *assume* such sentiments respecting the distinctions of hereditary rank in this country, yet would feel very acutely the deprivation of the rank and name they bear, or an inquiry into the devious and questionable title by which they retain them. The efforts they make to conceal their private feelings before the multitude recall a hint addressed to some "republicans who paraded the streets of Paris in 1793 :

> " Mais enfoncez dans vos culottes
> Le bout de linge qui pend !
> On dira que les patriotes
> Ont déployé le ' drapeau blanc.' "

Autobiography is the rage. John Galt, the Ettrick Hogg, the English Opium-eater, Sir Egerton Brydges, Jack Ketch, Grant-Thorburn, and sundry other personages, have lately adorned this department of our literature. In his song, the "Tailor and the Fairy," Béranger has acquitted himself of a task indispensable in modern authors.

THE SONGS OF HORACE.

" When Alba warred with Rome for some disputed frontier farms,
Three Horaces gained fatherland ascendancy in arms ;
A single-handed champion now amid the lyric throng,
ONE of the name stands forth to claim supremacy in song."

BARRY CORNWALL.

When the celebrated lame poet, Paddy Kelly, had the honour of being introduced to George the Fourth, on that monarch's *Mulgravising* visit to Dublin (an honour extended to several other distinguished natives, such as Falvey the sweep, Jack Lawless the orator, Daniel Donnelly the boxer, and another Daniel, who of late years has practised a more profitable system of *boxing*), his Majesty expressed himself desirous of personally witnessing an exhibition of the bard's extemporaneous talent, having heard many marvellous accounts of the facility with which his genius was wont to vent itself in unpremeditated verse. The Hibernian *improvisatore* forth-

with launched out into a dithyramb, of which the burden
appeared to be a panegyric on Byron and Scott, whose praises
he sang in terms of fervid eulogy; winding up with what
certainly seemed to his illustrious auditor a somewhat abrupt
and startling conclusion, viz. :

> "'Twould take a Byron and a Scott, I tell ye,
> Rolled up in one, to make a PAT O'KELLY !"

Doubtless such *was* the honest conviction of the Irish
rhapsodist; and if so, he had an undeniable right to put his
opinion on record, and publish it to the world. Are we not,
every week, favoured by some hebdomadal Longinus with *his*
peculiar and private ideas on the sublime; of which the last
new tragedy, or the latest volume of verse (blank or otherwise),
is pronounced the finest model? What remedy can the public
have against the practice of such imposition? None whatever,
until some scientific man shall achieve for literature what has
been done for the dairy, and invent a critical "lactometer," by
which the exact density of milk and water poetry may be
clearly and undeniably ascertained. At present, indeed, so
variable seems the standard of poetical merit, that we begin to
believe true what Edmund Burke says of taste among the
moderns; that "its essence is of too ethereal a nature for us
ever to hope it will submit to bear the chains of definition."

All this he has found supereminently in the canonized
object of these running commentaries. He stands not alone
in hailing therein Horace as prince of all lyric poets of every
age and clime. In so doing, he merely bows to the general
verdict of mankind.

Prout always paid deference to time-honoured reputations.
Great was, hence, his veneration for the "venerable Bede;"
and, notwithstanding the absence of all tangible evidences,
most vigorously did he admire the "admirable Crichton."
In Aristotle he persisted to recognise the great master-mind of
metaphysics; he scouted the transcendentalism of Kant:
sufficient for him was the cosmogony of Moses; he laughed
to scorn the conjectures of geology.*

This reminds us of the "astounding discovery" with which

---

* At this period the difficulty of reconciling geology with
Genesis was yet rife, and Colburn, Dean of York, was applauded
in his denunciations of Dr. Buckland, subsequently Dean of
Westminster.

18—2

Dr. Buckland is reported to have lately electrified the Bristolians. Ephraim Jenkinson's ghost must have heard with jealousy, on the banks of the Styx, the shouts of applause which echoed the doctor's assertion on the banks of the Avon, that the world had already lasted "millions of years;" that "a new version of Genesis" would be shortly required, since a new light "had been thrown on Hebrew scholarship!" The doctor's declaration is very properly described as the only "original fact" elicited at the meeting. What fun! to hear a mite in the cavity of a Gloucester cheese gravely reasoning on the streaks (or strata) of red and yellow, and finally concluding, all things duly considered, that the invoice of the farmer who made it bears a wrong date, and that the process of fabricating the cheese in question must have been begun as long ago, at least, as the days of the heptarchy!

There is often more strict logic, and more downright common sense, in a poet's view of nature and her works, than in the gravest and most elaborate mystifications of *soi-disant* philosophy. We shall, therefore, hesitate not to place in contraposition to this Bucklandish theory the ideas of Chateaubriand on this subject, leaving to any dispassionate thinker to say on which side reason and analogy preponderate. "They tell us," says the author of the *Génie du Christianisme*, whose exact words we cannot remember at this time of the evening, "that the earth is an old toothless hag, bearing in every feature the traces of caducity; and that six thousand years are not enough to account for the hidden marks of age discoverable to the eyes of Science:—but has it never occurred to them, that, in producing this globe for the dwelling of man, it may have suited Providence to create all its component parts in the stage of full maturity, just as Adam himself was called into being at the full age of manhood, without passing through the preparatory process of infancy, boyhood, or youth? When God planted the soil of Paradise, think ye that the oak of a hundred years' growth was wanting to shed its mighty shadow over our first parents? or are we to believe that every tree was a mere shrub, just emerging from the ground? Was the lion, whom Milton describes so graphically as

> "Pawing to get free
> His hinder parts,

nothing but a new-born cub? I do not believe it.

After the Reliques of various countries, teeming with classic imagery and *verve,* follow two songs :

THE LADYE OF LEE.

There's a being bright, whose beams
Light my days and gild my dreams,
Till my life all sunshine seems—'tis the ladye of Lee.

Oh ! the joy that Beauty brings,
While her merry laughter rings,
And her voice of silver sings—how she loves but me !

There's a grace in every limb,
There's a charm in every whim,
And the diamond cannot dim—the dazzling of her e'e ;

But there's a light amid
All the lustre of her lid,
That from the crowd is hid—and only I can see.

'Tis the glance by which is shown
That she loves but me alone ;
That she is all mine own—this ladye of Lee.

Then say, can it be wrong,
If the burden of my song
Be, how fondly I'll belong to this ladye of Lee ?

LIFE, A BUBBLE.—A BIRD'S-EYE VIEW THEREOF.

Down comes rain-drop, bubble follows :
  On the house-top one by one
Flock the synagogue of swallows,
  Met to vote that autumn's gone.

There are hundreds of them sitting,
  Met to vote in unison ;
They resolve on general flitting.
  "I'm for Athens off," says one.

" Every year my place is filled in
  Plinth of pillared Parthenon,
Where a ball has struck the building,
  Shot from Turk's besieging gun."

"As for me, I've got my chamber
   O'er a Smyrna coffee-shop,
Where his beadroll, made of amber,
   Hadji counts, and sips a drop."

"I prefer Palmyra's scantlings,
   Architraves of lone Baalbec,
Perched on which I feed my bantlings
   As they ope their bonnie beak."

While the last, to tell her plan, says,
   "On the second cataract
I've a statue of old Ramses,
   And his neck is nicely crack'd."

Globe, 20th Sept.   F. M.

The "Groves of Blarney" have been commemorated by the
Greek poets many centuries before the Christian era.

APPENDIX.

DEAN SWIFT.

"THE WONDER OF ALL THE WONDERS THAT THE WORLD EVER WONDERED AT."

UNDER the title of *Horæ Subsecivæ*, by Dr. West, of Dublin, appeared the following amusing trifle :—

" Among Swift's works, we find a *jeu a'esprit*, entitled the 'Wonder of all the Wonders that the World ever Wondered at,' and purporting to be an advertisement of a conjurer. There is an amusing one of the same kind by a very humorous German writer, George Christopher Lichtenberg, which, as his works are not much known here, is perhaps worth translating. The occasion on which it was written was the following : In the year 1777, a celebrated conjurer of those days arrived at Göttingen. Lichtenburg, for some reason or other, did not wish him to exhibit there ; and, accordingly, before the other had time even to announce his arrival, he wrote this advertisement, in his name, and had it printed and posted over the town. The whole was the work of one night. The result was, that the real Simon Pure decamped next morning without beat of drum, and never appeared in Göttingen again. Lichtenberg had spent some time in England, and understood the language perfectly, so that he may have seen Swift's paper. Still, even granting that he took the hint from him, it must be allowed he has improved on it not a little, and displayed not only more delicacy, which, indeed, was easy enough, but more wit also.

" ' Notice.

" ' The admirers of supernatural Physics are hereby informed that the far-famed magician, Philadelphus Philadelphia (the same that is mentioned by Cardanus, in his book *De Naturâ Supernaturali*, where he is styled " the envied of Heaven and Hell "), arrived here a few days ago by the mail, although it would have been just as easy for him to come through the air, seeing that he is the person who, in the year 1842, in the public market at Venice, threw a ball of cord into the clouds, and climbed upon it into the air till he got out of sight. On the 9th of January, of the present year, he will commence at the Merchants' Hall, publico-privately, to exhibit his one-dollar tricks, and continue weekly to improve them, till he comes to his five-hundred-guinea tricks ; amongst which last are some which, without boasting, excel the wonderful itself, nay are, as one may say, absolutely impossible.

" ' He has had the honour of performing with the greatest possible approbation before all the potentates, high and low, of the four quarters of the world ; and even in the fifth, a few weeks ago, before her Majesty Queen Oberea, at Otaheite.

" ' He is to be seen every day, except on Mondays and Thursdays, when he is employed in clearing the heads of the honourable members of the Congress of his countrymen at Philadelphia ; and at all hours, except from eleven to twelve in the forenoon, when he is engaged at Constantinople ; and from twelve to one, when he is at his dinner.

" ' The following are some of his common one-dollar tricks ; and they are selected, not as being the best of them, but as they can be described in the fewest words :—

" ' 1. Without leaving the room, he takes the weather-cock off St. James's Church, and sets it on St. John's, and *vice versâ*. After a few minutes he puts them back again in their proper places. N.B. All this without a magnet, by mere sleight of hand.

" ' 2. He takes two ladies, and sets them on their heads on a table, with their legs up ; he then gives them a blow, and they immediately begin to spin like tops with incredible velocity, without breach either of their head-dress by the pressure, or of decorum by the falling of their petticoats, to the very great satisfaction of all present.

" ' 3. He takes three ounces of the best arsenic, boils it in a gallon of milk, and gives it to the ladies to drink. As soon as they begin to get sick, he gives them two or three spoonfuls of melted lead, and they go away in high spirits.

" ' 4. He takes a hatchet, and knocks a gentleman on the head with it, so that he falls dead on the floor. When there, he gives a second blow, whereupon the gentleman immediately gets up as well as ever, and generally asks what music that was.

" ' 5. He draws three or four ladies' teeth, makes the company shake them well together in a bag, and then puts them into a little cannon, which he fires at the aforesaid ladies' heads, and they find their teeth white and sound in their places again.

" ' 6. A metaphysical trick, otherwise commonly called πᾶν, *metaphysica*, whereby he shows that a thing can actually be and not be at the same time. It requires great preparation and cost, and is shown so low as a dollar, solely in honour of the University.

" ' 7. He takes all the watches, rings, and other ornaments of the company, and even money if they wish, and gives every one a receipt for his property. He then puts them all in a trunk, and brings them off to Cassel. In a week after, each person tears his receipt, and that moment finds whatever he gave in his hands again. He has made a great deal of money by this trick.

" ' N.B. During this week, he performs in the top room at the Merchants' Hall ; but after that, up in the air over the pump in the market-place ; for whoever does not pay, will not see.' "

FIELDING, THE NOVELIST.

In the *Times* of July 2, 1840, Fielding, " one of the greatest humourists in our language," found an able apologist and indulgent critic, who has sketched the novelist's character so vigorously, that we are induced to travel somewhat " out of the record," and quote its substance. It occurs, we should explain, in a notice of an edition of Fielding's works, with a Memoir, by Thomas Roscoe, to the merits of which the reviewer does ample justice. Having stated that the biographer rescues Fielding's memory from the attacks which rivals, poetasters, and fine gentlemen have made upon it, the reviewer proceeds :—

" Great were his errors, doubtless, and low his tastes. We fear very much that he did even worse, in the course of his hard life, than what Walpole has described of him ; viz., banqueting with three Irishmen and a blind man, on some cold mutton and a bone of ham, in one plate ; but this, we take it, is the cause of quarrel with him—that he ate mutton with three low Irishmen and a blind beggar : if he had eaten it off a clean cloth with persons of quality, we should not have heard so much of his vices. It is that vulgar, dirty cloth which shocks the world so much, and that horrid low company—not the mutton. The public of our day need scarcely be warned that, if they are to pass an hour with Fielding, they will find him continually in such low company; those, therefore, who are excessively squeamish and genteel will scornfully keep away from him ; those who have a mind to forgive a little coarseness, for the sake of one of the honestest, manliest, kindest companions in the world, cannot, as we fancy, find a better than Fielding, or get so much true wit and shrewdness from any other writer of our language.

" ' With regard to personal appearance,' says his biographer, ' Fielding was strongly built, robust, and in height rather exceeding six feet. He was possessed of rare conversational powers and wit. A nobleman, who had known Pope, Swift,

and the wits of that famous *clique*, declared that Harry Fielding surpassed them all.   He loved all manly sports; kept.
hounds and horses in the brief days of his prosperity ; and.
signalized himself by the driving of that coach to which he
has attributed, in *Amelia*, so many of the misfortunes of poor
Booth.   At nineteen, with his annuity, " that any one might
pay who would," he came upon the town, and lived jovially
upon his wits.   Now with lords and gentlemen of fashion
over their wine ; now with the Lady Bettys and Sir Harrys
of Garrick's company—often with other inhabitants of Covent Garden, not even so reputable as the latter—we see in
what a school the poor fellow was bred, and can account for
many of the errors of his works, and their author.'

" He and Hogarth, between them, have given us a strange
notion of the society of those days.   Walpole's *Letters*, for
all their cold elegance, are not a whit more moral than those
rude, coarse pictures of the former artists.   Lord Chesterfield's
model of a man is more polite, but not so honest as Tom
Jones, or as poor Will Booth with his ' chairman's shoulders,
and calves like a porter.'   Little Walpole, with his thin
shanks and weak stomach, who is always at his tea and pa-
nada, and flustered by a couple of glasses of burgundy, does.
not debauch like a stalwart sinner of six feet and as many
bottles ; who can drink anything, from *clos vougeot* to old tom,
and drink it in any company too ; but he has his little genteel
sins in his little genteel society ; and he and his countesses can
snigger over naughty stories, and cry ' fie ' at George Selwyn's
last, and be just as wicked as Henry Fielding in his tavern-
chair, carousing with Heaven knows whom.

" The world does not tolerate now such satire as that of
Hogarth and Fielding ; and the world, no doubt, is right in
a great part of its squeamishness ; for it is good to pretend to
the virtue of chastity, even though we do not possess it ;
nay, the very restraint which the hypocrisy lays on a man is
not unapt, in some instances, to profit him.   But any man
who has walked through Regent Street of a night, or has
been behind the scenes of the Opera, or has even been to a
theatre, and looked up to that delectable part of the house—
the second tier of boxes—must know that the *Rake's* and *Har-
lot's Progress* is still by no means concluded, and will see the
same parts acted by young swaggering dandies in macintoshes
or pilot coats, and charming syrens in the last new *mode* from
Paris, as were played a hundred years since by pretty fellows

in laced hats and bob wigs, and madams in stiff hoops and brocades. The same vice exists, only we don't speak about it; the same things are done, but we don't call them by their names. Here lies the chief immorality of Fielding, as we take it. As for Hogarth, he has passed into a tradition; we allow him and Shakspeare to take liberties in conversation that we would not permit to any other man. It is wise that the public modesty should be so prudish as it is : that writers should be forced to chasten their humour, and, when it would play with points of life and character which are essentially immoral, that they should be compelled, by the general outcry of incensed public propriety, to be silent altogether. But an impartial observer, who gets some little of his knowledge of men from books, and some more from personal examination of them, knows pretty well that Fielding's men and Hogarth's, are Dickens's and Cruikshanks', drawn with ten times more skill and force, only the latter humourists dare not talk of what the elder discussed honestly.

" Let us, then, not accuse Fielding of immorality, but simply admit that his age was more free-spoken than ours, and accuse it of the fault (such as it is), rather than him. But there is a great deal of good on the other hand, which is to be found in the writings of this great man, of virtue so wise and practical, that the man of the world cannot read it and imitate it too much. He gives a strong, real picture of human life ; and the virtues which he exhibits shine out, by their contrasts, with the vices which he paints so faithfully, as they never could have done if the latter had not been depicted as well as the former. He tries to give you, as far as he knows it, the whole truth about human nature : the good and the evil of his characters are both practical. *Tom Jones'* sins and his faults are described with a curious accuracy ; but then follows the repentance which comes out of his very sins, and that, surely, is moral and touching. Booth goes astray (we do verily believe that many persons, even in these days, are not altogether pure), but how good his remorse is ! Are persons, who profess to take the likeness of human nature, to make an accurate portrait? This is such a hard question, that, think what we will, we shall not venture to say what we think. Perhaps it is better to do as Hannibal's painter did, and draw only that side of the face which has not the blind eye. Fielding attacked it in full. Let the reader, according to his taste, select the artist who shall give a likeness of him, or only half a likeness.

" Young Harry Fielding, six feet high, and twenty years of age, ready for a row, or a bottle, or what else you please, was a young fellow upon town, with very loose morals indeed, and never seems to have thought of much beyond the pleasure of living and being jolly. A number of his errors must be attributed to his excessive and boisterous bodily health. But he was an honest-hearted fellow, with affections as tender and simple as ever dwelt in the bosom of any man ; and if, in the heyday of his spirits, and the prodigal outpouring of his jovial good humour, he could give a hand to many ' a lad and lass ' whom the squeamish world would turn its back on (indeed, there was a virtue in his benevolence ; but we dare not express our sympathies now for poor Doll Tearsheet, and honest Mistress Quickly)—if he led a sad riotous life, and mixed with many a bad woman in his time, his heart was pure, and he knew a good one when he found her. He married, and (though Sir Walter Scott speaks rather slightingly of the novel in which Fielding has painted his first wife), the picture of Amelia, in the story of that name, is (in the writer's humble opinion) the most beautiful and delicious description of a character that is to be found in any writer, not excepting Shakspeare. It is a wonder how old Richardson, girded at as he had been by the reckless satirist—how Richardson, the author of *Pamela*, could have been so blinded by anger and pique as not to have seen the merits of his rival's exquisite performance.

" Amelia was in her grave when poor Fielding drew this delightful portrait of her : but, with all his faults, and extravagances, and vagaries, it is not hard to see how such a gentle, generous, loving creature as Fielding was, must have been loved and prized by her. She had a little fortune of her own, and he, at this time, inherited a small one from his mother. He carried her to the country ; and, like a wise, prudent Henry Fielding as he was, who, having lived upon nothing very jovially for some years, thought £5000 or £6000 an endless wealth, he kept horses and hounds, flung his doors open, and lived with the best of his county. When he had spent his little fortune, and saw that there was nothing for it but to work, he came to London, applied himself fiercely to the law, seized upon his pen again, never lost heart for a moment, and, be sure, loved his poor Amelia as tenderly as ever he had done. It is a pity that he did not live on his income, that is certain ; it is a pity that he had not been born a lord, or a thrifty stock-broker at the very least ; but we should not have had *Joseph Andrews* if this had been the case ; and, indeed, it is probable that Amelia liked him quite as well after his ruin, as she would have done had he been as rich as Rothschild.

" The biographers agree that he would have been very successful at the bar, but for certain circumstances. These ugly circumstances always fall in the way of men of Fielding's genius : for, though he amassed a considerable quantity of law, was reputed to be a good speaker, and had a great wit, and a knowledge of human nature, which might serve him in excellent stead, it is to be remarked that those, without a certain degree of patience and conduct, will not insure a man's triumph at the bar ; and so Fielding never rose to be a Lord Chancellor, or even a judge. They say he used to come home from a supper-party, and, after tying a wet cloth round his head, would begin to read as stoutly as the soberest man in either of the Temples. This is very probable ; but there are still better ways of keeping the head cool, which the author of *Tom Jones* seems to have neglected. In short, he had ruined his constitution ; had acquired habits that his resolution could not break through ; and was paying, with gout and a number of other ills, the price of his debaucheries as a young adventurer on the town, and his dissipations as a country gentleman.

" His days of trouble had now begun in earnest ; and, indeed, he met them like a man. He wrote incessantly for the periodical works of the day ; issued pamphlets ; made translations ; published journals and criticisms ; turned his hand, in a word, to any work that offered ; and lived as best he might. This indiscriminate literary labour, which obliges a man to scatter his intellects upon so many trifles, and to provide weekly varieties as sets-off against the inevitable weekly butcher's bills, has been the ruin of many a man of talent since Fielding's time ; and it was lucky for the world, and for him, that, at a time of life when his powers were at the highest, he procured a place which kept him beyond the reach of weekly want, and enabled him to gather his great intellect together, and produce the greatest satire, and two of the most complete romances, in our language.

" Let us remark, as a strong proof of the natural honesty of the man, the exquisite art of these performances, the care with which the situations are elaborated, and the noble, manly language corrected. When Harry Fielding was writing for the week's bread, we find style and sentiment both care-less, and plots hastily worked off. How could he do other-wise? Mr. Snap, the bailiff, was waiting with a writ with-out—his wife and the little ones asking wistfully for bread within. Away, with all its imperfections on its head, the play or the pamphlet must go. Indeed, he would have been no honest man had he kept them longer on his hands, with such urgent demands upon him as he had.

"But as soon as he is put out of the reach of this base kind of want, his whole style changes; and, instead of the reck-less and slovenly hack-writer, we have one of the most minute and careful artists that ever lived. Dr. Beattie gave his testimony to the merit of *Tom Jones*. Moral or immoral, let any man examine this romance as a work of art merely, and it must strike him as the most astonishing production of human ingenuity. There is not an incident, ever so trifling, but advances the story, grows out of former incidents, and is connected with the whole. Such a literary *providence*, if we may use such a word, is not to be seen in any other work of fiction. You might cut out half of *Don Quixote*, or add, transpose, or alter any given romance of Walter Scott, and neither would suffer. *Roderick Random*, and heroes of that sort, run through a series of adventures, at the end of which the fiddles are brought, and there is a marriage. But the his-tory of *Tom Jones* connects the very first page with the very last, and it is marvellous to think how the author could have built and carried all this structure in his brain, as he must have done, before he began to put it to paper.

"For his vices and imprudence no man paid more dearly: ruined fortune, and all the shifts and meanness consequent upon extravagance, ruined health, and the miseries attendant on it, were the punishment that he paid for his errors: they dogged his whole life, and hunted him in the prime of years to his grave. Want, sorrow, and pain subdued his body at last; but his great and noble humour rode buoyant over them all, and his frank and manly philosophy overcame them. His generous attachment to his family comforted him to the last; and, though all the labours of the poor fellow were only sufficient to keep him and them in a bare competence, yet, it must be remembered, to his credit, that he left behind him a friend, who valued him so much as to provide for the family that he had left destitute, and to place them beyond the reach of want. It is some credit to a man to have been the friend of Ralph Allen ; and Fielding, before his death, raised a monument to his friend, a great deal more lasting than bronze or marble, placing his figure in the romance of *Tom Jones*, under the name of Alworthy. ' There is a day, sir,' says Fielding, in one of his dedications to Mr. Allen, ' which no man in the kingdom can think of without fear, but yourself — the day of your death.' Can there be a finer compliment ? nor was Fielding the man to pay it to one who he thought was undeserving of it.

" Never do Fielding's courage, cheerfulness, and affection forsake him ; up to the last days of his life he is labouring for his children. He dies, and is beholden to the admiration of a foreigner, Monsieur de Meyrionnet, French consul at Lisbon, for a decent grave and tombstone. There he lies sleeping after life's fitful fever. No more care, no more duns, no more racking pain, no more wild midnight orgies and jovial laughter. Of the women who are weeping for him a pious friend takes care. Here, indeed, it seems as if his sorrows ended ; and one hopes and fancies that the poor but noble fellow's spirit is, at last, pure and serene."

" The best of the lectures is," says Mr. Senior,* " we think, that on Fielding ; and we are delighted to read Mr. Thackeray's bold and cordial and discriminating praise of this great, but, we fear, somewhat neglected, artist ; a moralist from whom the generation that is now passing away, imbibed a heartier contempt for meanness and duplicity, and a heartier sympathy with courage, frankness, and manliness, than, we fear, are to be acquired from the more decorous narratives which form the mental food of their successors."

FREDERICK THE GREAT.

Mr. Carlyle, in his admirable *Life*, gives the following whole-length portrait of the hero : " About four score years ago, there used to be seen sauntering on the terraces of Sans-Souci, for a short time in the afternoon, or you might have met him elsewhere at an earlier hour, riding or driving in a rapid business manner on the open roads, or through the scraggy woods and avenues of that intricate, amphibious Potsdam region, a highly-interesting, lean, little old man, of alert, though slightly stooping, figure, whose name among strangers was King Friedrich the Second, or Frederick the Great of Prussia, and at

* In his clever *Essays on Fiction*.

home among the common people, who much loved and esteemed
him, was *Vater Fritz*—Father Fred—a name of familiarity
which had not bred contempt in that instance. He is a king
every inch of him, though without the trappings of a king.
Presents himself in a Spartan simplicity of vesture : no crown
but an old military cocked-hat—generally old, or trampled and
kneeded into absolute softness, if new ; no sceptre but one
like Agamemnon's, a walking-stick cut from the woods, which
serves also as a riding-stick (with which he hits the horse ' between the ears,' say authors) ; and for royal robes, a mere soldier's blue coat with red facings, coat likely to be old, and sure
to have a good deal of Spanish snuff on the breast of it ; rest
of the apparel dim, unobtrusive in colour or cut, ending in
high, over-knee military boots, which may be brushed (and, I
hope, kept soft with an underhand suspicion of oil), but are
not permitted to be blackened or varnished ; Day and Martin
with their soot-pots forbidden to approach.

" The man is, not of godlike physiognomy any more than of
imposing stature or costume ; close-shut mouth with thin lips,
prominent jaws and nose, receding brow, by no means of
Olympian height ; head, however, is of long form, and super-
lative gray eyes in it. Not what is called a beautiful man ;
nor yet by all appearance what is called a happy. On the
contrary, the face bears evidence of many sorrows, as they
are termed, of much hard labour done in this world, and
seems to anticipate nothing but more still coming. Quiet
stoicism, capable enough of what joys there were, but not
expecting any worth mention ; great unconscious, and some
conscious, pride, well tempered with a cheery mockery of humour—are written on that old face, which carries its chin
well forward, in spite of the slight stoop about the neck ;
snuffy nose rather flung into the air, under its old cocked hat
—like an old snuffy lion on the watch ; and such a pair of
eyes as no man, or lion, or lynx of that century, bore elsewhere, according to all the testimony we have. ' Those eyes,'
says Mirabeau, ' which at the bidding of his great soul, fascinated you with seduction or with terror' ('*portaient, au gré de
son âme héroïque, la séduction ou la terreur* '). Most excellent,
potent, brilliant eyes, swift-darting as the stars, steadfast as
the sun ; gray, we said, of the azure gray colour ; large enough,
not of glaring size, the habitual expression of them vigilance
and penetrating sense, rapidity resting on depth ; which is an
excellent combination, and gives us the notion of a lambent

outer radiance springing from some great inner sea of light and fire in the man. The voice, if he speak to you, is of similar physiognomy : clear, melodious, and sonorous ; all tones are in it, from that of ingenuous inquiry, graceful sociality, light-flowing banter (rather prickly for most part), up to definite word of command, up to desolating word of rebuke and reprobation : a voice 'the clearest and most agreeable in conversation I ever heard,' says witty Dr. Moore. 'He speaks a great deal,' continues the doctor, 'yet those who hear him regret that he does not speak a good deal more. His observations are always lively, very often just ; and few men possess the talent of REPARTEE in greater perfection.' "

JOHN HOOKHAM FRERE.

These additions, selected and abridged from the *Quarterly Review*, January, 1872, will be read with interest, as supplementary to the sketch of Mr. Canning in vol. i. p. 63 of the present work.

Mr. John Hookham Frere may be regarded as a type of a remarkable class of men, of whom we have hardly any representatives in the present day. Of ancient lineage, a fine classical scholar, well read in English literature, with a keen and polished wit, and early brought into parliament and official life, he combined a practical knowledge of the world with that love of letters and refinement which distinguished the statesmen of the last generation. His literary abilities were of the highest order. He was one of the chief writers in the *Anti-Jacobin ;* his poem of *Whistlecraft* was the model upon which Lord Byron framed *Beppo* and *Don Juan ;* and his translation of the plays of Aristophanes is a real work of genius, being, perhaps, the most perfect representation of any ancient poet in a modern language. He was the friend of Pitt and Canning ; and the high estimation in which he was held by Scott, Byron, Coleridge, and his other illustrious contemporaries, appears from the memoirs and literature of the period, in which his name constantly occurs. But to the present generation he is comparatively unknown. Most of his works were privately printed, and were difficult and almost impossible to procure, while others had never been printed at all. Under these circumstances we congratulate his nephews, Mr. W. E. Frere and Sir Bartle Frere, upon the good service they have rendered to literature, by making a complete collection of the works of their uncle. They have prefixed an interesting biography, which will enable us to present to our readers a sketch of Mr. Frere's public and private life, with a brief account of his writings. We do this the more willingly, as Mr. Frere was one of the distinguished men who co-operated with the late Mr. Murray in establishing the *Quarterly Review.*

John Hookham Frere was born in London on the 21st of May, 1769, the year which witnessed the birth of Napoleon and Wellington. He was High Sheriff in Suffolk in 1776, when he composed a High Tory sermon, which his chaplain preached for the edification of a Whig judge. It was pronounced to be "an excellent sermon, much better than judges usually got from High Sheriffs' Chaplains."

To the talents which Mr. Frere inherited from both parents there was added an influence which is always most interesting to trace—the influence of a high-minded and accomplished woman. Such was Lady Fenn, his father's surviving sister, and the widow of Sir John Fenn, editor of the *Paston Letters.* As the authoress of *Cobwebs to catch Flies,* under the name of "Mrs. Lovechild," Lady Fenn shares with Mrs. Barbauld and Mrs. Trimmer the honour of founding that species of fiction for children which was perfected by Miss Edgeworth. In the conversations of his later years, Mr. Frere described this type of a class to be revered the more as it becomes rarer :—

"It is difficult to give any one nowadays an idea of the kind of awe which, in my boyhood, a learned old lady like her inspired. down in the country, not only in us, her nephews and nieces, and in those of her own age and rank who could understand her intellectual superiority, but even in the common people around her. I remember one day, coming from a visit to her, I stopped to learn what some village boys outside her gate were wrangling about—they were disputing whether the nation had any reason to be afraid of an invasion by Buonaparte, and one of the disputants said, with a conscious air of superior knowledge—' I tell ye, ye don't know what a terrible fellow he is : why, he don't care for nobody ! If he was to come here to Dereham, he wouldn't care that,' snapping his fingers ; 'no ! not even for Lady Fenn, there !' "

In his sixteenth year, Frere went from an excellent preparatory school to Eton. His descriptions of the dignified authority of Mr. Davies are valuable as a record of one of the strongest traditions of our public schools. The boys watched with jealous pride the bearing of their head-master on the frequent visits of George III., and the good-natured king used to humour the pedagogue in magnifying his office; like Charles II. and Busby. At Eton, Frere formed a life-long friendship with Canning, "for whom he cherished a love and admiration, which absence never diminished, and neither age nor death itself could dull." He joined Canning and a few other Etonians of their own standing in starting the *Microcosm.*

Frere's contributions to the *Microcosm* already indicated his great critical power; and about the same time he proved the poetic genius, which has placed him at the very head of English translators. Here, too, his knowledge of the brilliant fragments of the Greek lyric poets—of which the elegant imitations by Horace are but the shadow of a shade—prove how far his classical reading went beyond school routine. His exquisite *Lament of Danaë*, from Simonides, is perhaps generally known; but his version of a fragment of Alcæus may be referred to as breathing the patriotism which thus early inspired his poetry.

His account of the relations between Pitt, the king, and the old Tories is very interesting. In answer to a question whether George III. had not a great personal regard for Pitt, he said :—

"Latterly he had, but certainly not at first. It was a choice between him and Fox, and the king inclined to Pitt as the less obnoxious of the two. Pitt's name was best known, in his early days, as an advocate for parliamentary reform. I remember when I was a boy hearing two high Tories of the old school, at my father's house, talking about Pitt when he first became Prime Minister; they said : 'He is a thorn in our side; but one must stick to a bramble to save one from a fall into something worse.' The old Tories at first had very little confidence in him. I recollect they were all in great delight, when the church at Wimbledon, where Pitt lived, was to be repaired, because he sent a hundred pounds, as his subscription, with a request 'that it might be laid out on the steeple, in order that the church might not look like a meeting-house.' The old Tories began then to think that there was really some hope of him after that !"

Mr. Frere repelled with warmth the charge of Pitt's supposed frigidity of disposition.

19—2

"No one who really knew Pitt intimately would have called
him cold. A man who is Prime Minister at twenty-six cannot
carry his heart on his sleeve and be 'Hail, fellow! well met'
with every Jack, Tom, and Harry. Pitt's manner by nature, as
well as by habit and necessity, was in public always dignified,
reserved, and imperious : but he had very warm feelings, and,
had it not been for the obligations of the official position, which
lay on him almost throughout his whole life, I believe he might
have had nearly as many personal friends as Fox."

On Mr. Frere's settling in London his intercourse with
Canning was renewed on the intimate footing of their schoolboy days at Eton. Some severe strictures have been passed
upon Canning for entering public life under Pitt, as if he
had been guilty of an unworthy change of principles.

"Some years after," says Mr. Frere, "when Canning was
going to be married, Pitt felt as keenly about the affair as if Pitt
had nothing else to think of, and Canning had been his only
child. It was a good match for Canning in a worldly point of
view, for his own fortune was not adequate to the political position Pitt would have liked him to hold. Pitt not only took a
personal interest in the match himself, but he made old Dundas
think almost as much about it, as if it had been some important
party combination."

In connection with this marriage Mr. Frere related the following anecdote :—

"'I was to be best man, and Pitt, Canning, and Mr. Leigh,
who was to read the service, dined with me before the marriage,
which was to take place in Brook Street. We had a coach to
drive there, and as we went through that narrow part, near what
was then Swallow Street, a fellow drew up against the wall to
avoid being run over, and peering into the coach, recognized
Pitt, and saw Mr. Leigh, who was in full canonicals, sitting
opposite to him. The fellow exclaimed, "What, Billy Pitt! and
with a parson, too!" I said, "He thinks you are going to
Tyburn, to be hanged privately," which was rather impudent of
me ; but Pitt was too much absorbed, I believe, in thinking of
the marriage, to be angry. After the ceremony, he was so
nervous that he could not sign as witness, and Canning whispered
to me to sign without waiting for him.'"

In 1797, Mr. Frere joined Mr. Canning, George Ellis, and
others of the younger members of their party in bringing out
the *Anti-Jacobin, or Weekly Examiner.*
The *Anti-Jacobin* has suffered the fate of many a famous
work, which is talked about without being known, and

criticised apart from the circumstances which gave it birth and character. People are content to laugh over some of its most hackneyed pieces with ever fresh amusement, or to shake their heads with the grave superiority of professional critics, and pronounce the catch-words—"mere parody"—"no original thoughts"—"*Punch* as good every week." But the *Anti-Jacobin* is neither to be judged by scraps, nor from the point of view of 1872 instead of 1798. The whole (for we may leave the lesser contributors out of sight) is the harmonious work of three ardent minds, working with a definite purpose, and on a joint plan, which made it difficult in later years to distinguish their separate shares in several of the pieces. And the purpose and style of the work arose naturally out of the political crisis of that time.

The writers, who were roughly classed as Jacobins—with what justice or discrimination it is now superfluous to discuss. —themselves suggested the direction of the attack by the puerile theories and sickly sentimentalisms which they uttered in such outlandish guise as Southey's *Dactylics* and *Sapphics*, and those uncouth *Hexameters*, which Byron characterised in words applicable to all similar imitations,

> "He stuck fast in the first Hexameter,
> Not one of all whose *gouty feet* would stir."

Here we must observe, in passing, that the ludicrous swing of the so-called *Sapphics* of the famous *Needy Knife-grinder* (the joint production of Canning and Frere) was purposely adopted from "the *absurdity* of the metre" in Southey's original :—

> "Cold was the night wind; drifting fast the snows fell;
> Wide were the downs and shelterless and naked :
> When a poor wanderer struggled on her journey,
> Weary and way-sore."

Were ever lines more provocative of parody?

The poetry of the *Anti-Jacobin* is not truly described as "mere parody." It is far more than an empty echo of the original, more than an amusing travesty, written for sound or for fun : it gives another version of the sense—or of the lurking nonsense—and that with a set and serious purpose. It is ridicule as well as parody, in the true spirit of the Aristophanic comedy. Its classic tone and allusions appeal to the educated classes, in whose hands the government then was; and its very want of adaptation to an age of household suffrage and penny papers is a testimony to its power at its own time.   Sir Bartle Frere observes :—

"The shafts of ridicule told with greater effect on the more impressible classes, and helped to keep in the ministerial fold many a young literary adventurer or sober dissenter, whose poetical or religious feelings might have been touched by such appeals as Southey's visions of a millennial reign of liberty, or by his description of the beauties of nature, from enjoying which the regicide was debarred."

The final test of merit is the fact that many of these imitations have surpassed and survived the originals, as Sir George Cornewall Lewis observed of the admirable satire on Erasmus Darwin's poems in the *Loves of the Triangles* by Canning and Frere.

German mysticism and enthusiasm come in for their share of ridicule in the *Rovers*, an admirable parody on Schiller's *Robbers*, which, we repeat, can only be judged of as a whole. It was the joint production of Canning, Frere, and Ellis. Canning's inimitable dungeon-song of Rogero, ending—

> "Sun, moon, and thou vain world, adieu,
>   That kings and priests are plotting in :
>   Here doomed to starve on water gru-
>   el, never shall I see the U-
>   niversity of Gottingen—"

is probably familiar to our readers; and to Frere belongs the merit of the well-known scene between Matilda and Cecilia :—

"*Mat.* Madam, you seem to have had an unpleasant journey, if I may judge from the dust on your riding-habit.

Cec. The way was dusty, madam, but the weather was delightful.   It recalled to me those blissful moments when the rays of desire first vibrated through my soul.

Mat. (*aside*). Thank Heaven ! I have at last found a heart which is in unison with my own—(*To Cecilia*)—Yes, I understand you—the first pulsation of sentiment—the silver tones upon the yet unsounded harp. . . .

Cec. The dawn of life—when this blossom—(*putting her hand upon her heart*)—first expanded its petals to the penetrating dart of love !

Mat. Yes—the time—the golden time, when the first beams of the morning meet and embrace one another !—The blooming blue upon the yet unplucked plum ! . . .

Cec. Your countenance grows animated, my dear madam.

Mat. And yours, too, is glowing with illumination.

Cec. I had long been looking out for a congenial spirit !—my heart was withered—but the beams of yours have re-kindled it.

Mat. A sudden thought strikes me—Let us swear an eternal friendship.

Cec. Let us agree to live together !

Mat. (*with rapidity and earnestness*). Willingly.

Cec. Let us embrace. [*They embrace.*"

Frere also was the sole author of the imaginary reports of the *Meetings of the Friends of Freedom*, in which the speeches of Fox, Erskine, and the other great opposition orators are parodied with inimitable felicity.

In the second period of his political and diplomatic service, like his friend, Canning, in the celebrated poetical despatch about the Dutch Customs, Frere relieved the dryness of official work by at least one poetical epistle. Being ordered by Lord Grenville to direct Lord Minto to refund an unauthorized payment by Mr. Stratton for a snuff-box, which had been presented by the British ambassador to some foreign diplomatist, in violation of the Treasury regulations, he conveyed the reproof in the following lines :—

"DRAFT TO LORD MINTO.

" My Lord, when I open'd your letter,
  I confess I was perfectly stunn'd ;
But I find myself now something better,
  Since I'm ordered to bid you *refund.*

" 'Tis a very bad scrape you've got into,
  Which your friends must all wish you had shunn'd,
Says Lord Grenville, ' Prepare to Lord Minto
  Despatches to bid him *refund.*'

" Mr. Hammond, who smiles at your cunning,
  On the subject amusingly punn'd ;
Says he, ' They're so proud of their funning,
  'Twill be pleasant to see them *refunn'd.*'

" As for Stratton, he ought for his sin to
  Be sent to some wild Sunderbund,
But we'll pardon him still, if Lord Minto
  Will instantly make him *refund.*

" Believe me, I don't mean to hurt you,
　　But if you'd avoid being dunn'd,
Of necessity making a virtue,
　　With the best grace you can, you'll *refund.*

" Let the Snuff-box belong to Lord Minto ;
　　But as for the five hundred *pund,**
I'll be judged by Almeida or Pinto,
　　If his Chancery must not *refund.*"

" POSTSCRIPT.

" There are letters from India which mention
　　Occurrences at Roh-il-cund ;
But I'll not distract your attention,
　　Lest I make you forget to *refund.*

" Lord Carlisle's new play is the Story
　　Of Tancred and fair Sigismund,
Our last news is the taking of Gorée,
　　But our best is, that you must *refund.*"

The third period of Frere's life, from 1809 to his death,
was spent in the enjoyment of his taste for literature, and in
the dignified social pleasures of which he was the life and
centre.　On his return to England, he took up his residence
at his country-house at Roydon, his father having died in
1807.　A letter, written by a lady who was staying at Roydon
in 1813, describes him as "a very odd creature, but very
good, and very entertaining ;" getting up early in the morning to teach two little nephews grammar, taking one still
smaller a walk, during which he completed teaching him his
letters, and "spending an hour after dinner in reading to
them the ballad of ' William of Cloudesley,' which delighted
them very much."　But "his favourite pursuits and early
friendships all conspired to draw him to the capital.　In
London society, his polished wit and playful fancy—his varied
learning and great power of conversation, joined to the easy
courtesy of a travelled English gentleman of the old school,
made him everywhere a welcome guest."　He was, in fact,
one of the most popular men in the brilliant literary society
of that period.　But he, or rather the future generations
whom he might have amused and instructed, paid the penalty
of this elegant social life.

* Scotticè pro "pound."—J. H. F.

It is much to be regretted that Mr. Frere wrote so little. His extreme fastidiousness and, we fear we must add, his constitutional indolence, disinclined him to the labour of the pen, and, as his biographer observes :—

"The most characteristic and valuable results of his reading and thinking were lost in every-day use ; what little remains owes its preservation to contemporary friends, and the care of their biographers, who have noted a few of the sayings and anecdotes which survived in the memory of his companions long after Mr. Frere had ceased to be among them. Such are the anecdotes preserved by Moore.

"At one time he is pleased with Frere's comparison of O'Connell's eloquence to the 'aerial potato,' described by Darwin in his Phytologia, and with his severe criticism on Erskine's verses, 'The Muses and Graces will just make a jury.' Another time he refers to 'Frere's beautiful saying that 'next to an old friend, the best thing is an old enemy ;' and again he relates how Madame de ——— having said in her intense style, 'I should like to be married in English, in a language in which vows are so faithfully kept,' some one asked Frere 'What language, I wonder, was she married in ?' '*Broken* English, I suppose,' answered Frere."

A saying attributed to him, that he loved Spain, "as a country in which God had so much land in His own holding," has the true tone of his humour about it.

Judging by his existing remains, in prose and verse, he would have excelled in almost any species of composition. Scott bore the warmest testimony to Frere's powers. One of Frere's earliest literary efforts was a "Metrical Version of an Ode on Athelstan's Victory," originally published in Ellis's "Specimens of Ancient English Poetry." Scott, writing in 1830, says that this is the only poem he has met with in his researches into these matters "which, if it had been produced as ancient, could not have been detected on internal evidence." It was written by Frere, when an Eton schoolboy, during the controversy occasioned by the poems attributed to Rowley, and was intended as an imitation of the style and language of the fourteenth century. At an earlier period, Scott had expressed the same opinion in a letter to Ellis (1804) :— "Frere is so perfect a master of the ancient style of composition, that I would rather have his suffrage than that of a whole synod of your vulgar antiquaries."

As an original poet, Mr. Frere is best known by his " Monks and Giants," which bore the pseudonym of Whistlecraft as its author. The first part was published by Mr. Murray in 1817, as "The prospectus and specimen of an intended national work by William and Robert Whistlecraft, of Stowmarket, in Suffolk, harness and collar makers, intended to comprise the most interesting particulars relating to King Arthur and his Round Table." A second part appeared along with the first in the following year, with the title of the "Monks and Giants." In the subject of the poem Mr. Frere anticipated Mr. Tennyson's Idylls, but the metre he adopted, and his mode of treatment of the subject, were very different.

"In this *jeu d'esprit*," observes his biographer, "Mr. Frere introduced into English poetry the octave stanza of Pulci, Berni, and Casti, which has since been completely naturalized in our tongue. Men of letters were not slow to recognize the service thus rendered to English literature ; and Italian scholars, especially, were delighted to see one of the most beautiful of their favourite metres successfully adopted in a language so different from the dialect in which it was first used. Its value was immediately recognized by Byron. He wrote to Murray, from Venice, in October, 1817, announcing 'Beppo,' and said, 'I have written a poem of eighty-four octave stanzas, humorous, in or after the excellent manner of Whistlecraft (whom I take to be Frere).' And ten days later, 'Mr. Whistlecraft has no greater admirer than myself. I have written a story in eighty-nine stanzas, in imitation of him, called "Beppo."' A few months later (March 26th, 1819), again writing to Murray, of 'Beppo,' he says, 'The style is not English, it is Italian :—Berni is the original of *all ;* Whistlecraft was my immediate model.'"

Mr. William Stewart Rose, himself one of the most elegant Italian scholars of the past generation, addressed Mr. Frere two years afterwards as—

> "O thou that hast revived in magic rhyme
>   That lubber race, and turn'd them out, to turney
> And love after their way ; in after time
>   To be acknowledged for our British Berni ;
> Oh send thy giants forth to good men's feasts,
>   Keep them not close."

The humour and versification as well as the poetical beauty of many passages were appreciated by men of taste and letters, but the poem never achieved the popularity that might have been expected. As the work is now almost forgotten, we subjoin one extract, which will convey some idea of its style, and

probably induce our readers to turn to the poem itself.   The
cause of the quarrel between the monks and the giants is thus
described :—

"In castles and in courts Ambition dwells,
    But not in castles or in courts alone ;
She breathed a wish, throughout those sacred cells,
    For bells of larger size, and louder tone ;
Giants abominate the sound of bells,
    And soon the fierce antipathy was shown,
The tinkling and the jingling, and the clangour,
Roused their irrational gigantic anger.

"Unhappy mortals ! ever blind to fate !
    Unhappy Monks ! you see no danger nigh ;
Exulting in their sound and size and weight,
    From morn till noon the merry peal you ply :
The belfry rocks, your bosoms are elate,
    Your spirits with the ropes and pulleys fly ;
Tired, but transported, panting, pulling, hauling,
Ramping and stamping, overjoy'd and bawling.

"Meanwhile the solemn mountains that surrounded
    The silent valley where the convent lay,
With tintinnabular uproar were astounded,
    When the first peal burst forth at break of day :
Feeling their granite ears severely wounded,
    They scarce knew what to think, or what to say ;
And (though large mountains commonly conceal
Their sentiments, dissembling what they feel,

"Yet) Cader Gibbrish from his cloudy throne
    To huge Loblommon gave an intimation
Of this strange rumour, with an awful tone,
    Thundering his deep surprise and indignation ;
The lesser hills, in language of their own,
    Discussed the topic by reverberation ;
Discoursing with their echoes all day long,
Their only conversation was ' ding-dong.'

"Those giant-mountains inwardly were moved,
    But never made an outward change of place :
Not so the mountain-giants—(as behoved
    A more alert and locomotive race),
Hearing a clatter which they disapproved,
    They ran straight forward to besiege the place
With a discordant universal yell,
Like house-dogs howling at a dinner-bell."

Mr. Frere's reasons for not continuing the work, which he had promised to do, were given by him at a later period (1844) in conversation with a friend.

"You cannot go on joking with people who won't be joked with. Most people who read it at the time it was published, would not take the work in any merely humorous sense ; they would imagine that it was some political satire, and went on hunting for a political meaning ; so I thought it was no use offering my jokes to people who would not understand them. Even Mackintosh once said to me, ' Mr. Frere, I have had the pleasure of reading your *Monks and Giants* twice over '—and then he paused ; I saw what was in his mind, and could not help replying with a very mysterious look, ' And you could not discover its political meaning ?' Mackintosh said, ' Well, indeed, I could not make out the allegory ;' to which I answered, still looking very mysterious, ' Well, I thought you would not.' "

In connection with this poem, Sir Bartle relates an amusing anecdote illustrative of his uncle's frequent absence of mind, of which his friends told many stories. Mr. Frere was married in September, 1816, to the Dowager Countess of Erroll, and on his marriage day called upon Mr. Murray to propose the publication of his *Monks and Giants*.

" It is related that the late Mr. John Murray having for once relaxed his usual rule never to ask an author to read or recite in the sanctum in Albemarle Street, got so interested in some verses which Mr. Frere was repeating and commenting on, that his dinner hour was at hand. He asked Mr. Frere to dine with him, and continue the discussion ; but the latter, startled to find it was so late, excused himself on the plea that ' he had been married that morning, and had already overstayed the time when he had promised Lady Erroll to be ready for their journey into the country.' "

Another story of his absence of mind rests on the authority of Lady Erroll herself :—

" Mr. Frere had just been introduced to her at an evening party, and offered to hand her downstairs and procure some refreshment ; but getting much interested in conversation by the way, became so engrossed in the train of thought he was pursuing, that he drank himself a glass of negus that he had procured for her, and then offered his arm to help her upstairs without any idea of their not having achieved the errand on which they came ; and was only reminded of his mistake by her laughing remonstrance with him on his forgetfulness of her existence. 'This,' she added, 'convinced me that my new acquaintance was, at any rate, very different from most of the young men around us.'"

Mr. Frere settled at Malta in 1821 in consequence of the failing health of Lady Erroll, and there he passed the remaining twenty-five years of his life.

His chief anxiety was the failing health of his wife, whom he tended with the most affectionate care. In 1825 he paid a short visit to England. On this occasion we are told that, while staying with his brother, he "took his night's rest chiefly by sleeping early in the evening, from seven till eleven, and that then he awoke, and entertained his brother and nieces by repeating verses which he had translated or composed, till two o'clock in the morning, which did not prevent his rising early next day."

In speaking of Mr. Frere's translations, Sir Walter Scott repeated a pretty long passage from his version of one of the "Romances of the Cid," and seemed to enjoy a spirited charge of the knights therein described as much as he could have done in his best days, placing his walking-stick in rest like a lance, to "suit the action to the word."

The following is the passage in the poem of the "Cid" to which Scott alludes :—

"Their shields before their breasts, forth at once they go,
Their lances in the rest levell'd fair and low :
Their banners and their crests waving in a row,
Their heads all stooping down toward the saddle bow.
The Cid was in the midst, his shout was heard afar,
'I am Ruy Diaz, the Champion of Bivar ;
Strike amongst them, gentlemen, for sweet mercy's sake !'
There where Bermuez fought, amidst the foe they brake,
Three hundred banner'd knights, it was a gallant show :
Three hundred Moors they kill'd, a man with every blow ;
When they wheel'd and turn'd, as many more lay slain,
You might see them raise their lances and level them again.
There you might see the breastplates, how they were cleft in
      twain,
And many a Moorish shield lie shatter'd on the plain.
The pennons that were white mark'd with a crimson stain,
The horses running wild whose riders had been slain.
The Christians call upon St. James, the Moors upon Mahound.
There were thirteen hundred of them slain on a little spot of
      ground."

Sir Bartle Frere, who passed some weeks under his uncle's roof in 1834 and 1845, has preserved many of Mr. Frere's remarks upon politics, literature, and the current topics of the day.

With all his reverence for ancient uninterrupted usage, he had little sympathy with the revival of forms long obsolete.

"Commenting on some innovations in music and vestments which had troubled an Anglican congregation in the See of Gibraltar, he said in reply to the argument that the change was justified by the custom in Edward the Sixth's time—'But if I were to appear at church in the costume of Queen Elizabeth's time, would the clergyman consider it a sufficient justification for my disturbing the gravity of the congregation that I could prove the dress to be in strict accordance with the usages and sumptuary laws of three hundred years back?'"

He took a very gloomy view of the political future.

"He viewed with alarm the growing tendency of statesmen of all parties to follow, instead of aspiring to lead and direct, public opinion—a tendency which he foresaw must often transfer the initiation of great measures from the wisest and best informed to those who were simply discontented with the existing order of things. He especially disliked the new name under which the broken ranks of the Tories had been rallied after the Reform Bill. 'Why do you talk of Conservatives?' he asked; 'a Conservative is only a Tory who is ashamed of himself.'"

Mr. Frere's chief literary occupation in Malta was, as we have already said, the translation of Aristophanes. He translated five plays in all:—the *Acharnians*, the *Knights*, the *Birds*, the *Frogs*, and the *Peace*.

We subjoin an extract, in the hope of persuading our readers to make acquaintance with the translations for themselves, assuring those who are not scholars that they will obtain from them as vivid an idea of the Aristophanic wit, humour, and poetry as is possible to any one who does not read the original Greek.

The only extract for which we can afford space, is a portion of the dialogue between Bacchus and the Chorus of Frogs, as he rows in Charon's boat across the lake at the entrance of the infernal regions:—

B. (*rowing in great misery*).
   How I'm maul'd,
   How I'm gall'd ;
  Worn and mangled to a mash—
  There they go ! " *Koash, koash !*"
Frogs.   Brekeke-kesh, koash, koash.
B.   Oh, Beshrew,
   All your crew ;
  You don't consider how I smart.
Frogs.   Now for a sample of the Art !
   Brekeke-kesh, koash, koash.

   *   *   *   *

B.   I forbid you to proceed.
Frogs. That would be severe indeed.
  Arbitrary, bold, and rash—
  Brekeke-kesh, koash, koash.
B.   I command you to desist—
  —Oh, my back, there ! oh, my wrist !
   What a twist !
   What a sprain !
Frogs. Once again—
  We renew the tuneful strain,
  Brekeke-kesh, koash, koash.
B.   I disdain—(Hang the pain !)
  All your nonsense, noise, and trash.
  Oh, my blister ! Oh, my sprain !
Frogs. Brekeke-kesh, koash, koash.
  Friends and Frogs, we must display
  All our powers of voice to-day ;
  Suffer not this stranger here,
  With fastidious foreign ear,
  To confound us and abash.
  Brekeke-kesh, koash, koash.
B.   Well, my spirit is not broke,
  If it's only for the joke,
  I'll outdo you with a croak.
  Here it goes—(*very loud*) " Koash, koash."
Frogs. Now for a glorious croaking crash,
   (*Still louder*).
  Brekeke-kesh, koash, koash.
B.   (*splashing with his oar*).
  I'll disperse you with a splash.
Frogs. Brekeke-kesh, koash, koash.
B.   I'll subdue
  Your rebellious, noisy crew—
  —Have amongst you there, slap-dash.
      [*Strikes at them.*

Frogs.   Brekeke-kesh, koash, koash.
            We defy your oar and you.
Ch.   Hold ! We're ashore just—shift your oar. Get out.
            Now pay for your fare.
B.   There—there it is—the twopence.

Mr. Frere died of a paralytic seizure on the 7th of January, 1846. " He was laid beside his wife in the English burial-ground, in one of the Floriana outworks overlooking the Quarantine Harbour." His death was lamented by all classes in Malta, but especially by the poor ; and, even now, " when the generation of those who were the objects of his active sympathy has passed away, there are Maltese who will point out his tomb as the grave of the noble-hearted Englishman, known in his day as the best friend of their fellow-islanders in want or distress."

R. H. BARHAM (INGOLDSBY).

(Continued from vol. i. p. 210.)

THE SEAFORTH PROPHECY.

Sir Walter Scott declared to Mrs. Hughes that, many years before the event took place, he had heard of a prophecy in the Seaforth family, uttered, or said to have been uttered, by a second-sighted clansman more than a century before, to the effect that " when the Chisholm and the Fraser should be baith deaf, and the M'Pherson (? M'Kenzie) born with a buck tooth, the male line of the Fraser should become extinct, and that a white-hooded lassie should come from ayont the sea and inherit a'." All these contingencies happened in the late Lord Seaforth's time, who, on reverting to the prophecy, showed two fine lads, his sons, to Sir Walter, and observed, " After all's said and done, I think these boys will ding the prophet after all." He was wrong, however. The two boys died immediately before their father, and the present Lady Hood, a widow, came from India after his decease and inherited the property.

The prophecy is said to have included yet another family misfortune, and to have foretold that the white-hooded lassie (the widow's cap is clearly alluded to in the epithet) should cause the death of her own sister. This also came to pass. By the upset of a pony-carriage, which Mrs. Stuart M'Kenzie (as Lady Hood had become by marriage) was driving, her sister was instantaneously killed on the spot, and she herself so fearfully injured about the face as to be compelled to wear, for the remainder of her life, a head-dress of a fashion which enabled her to conceal the greater part of her countenance under bands of black velvet.

"Sir Walter Scott," Mr. Barham goes on to say, "gave Mrs. Hughes an account of his visit to Warrender House, the seat of Sir George Warrender, at Bruntsfield, near Edinburgh. He stated that, on an architect being called in to make some repairs there on a large scale, he could not make the ground plan agree with the interior measurement of the edifice. After much discussion he found an old doorway, which the servants assured him was a false one, and 'led nowhere.' Recurring to his plan, however, he suspected that the deficient quantity must be in its vicinity, and accordingly determined to have it opened. It was strongly fastened, but was at length removed, when behind it he found three small rooms, the farthest one fitted up as a bed-room, with two silver candlesticks on the toilet-table, the candles burnt down in their sockets. Half-burnt embers were on the hearth; and an old-fashioned but very handsome dressing-gown was hanging over the back of a chair, at the foot of which was a pair of slippers. The bed appeared to have been left disarranged as when quitted by its last occupant. Not any of the family then living were aware of the existence of these rooms, nor was there any tradition as to the name or character of their inmates. It was also said by Sir George, at the same time, that he had been assured by members of the family that at Glamis Castle there was a secret room, the mode of approaching which was never known to more than the possessor and the heir-apparent of the property."

A True and Particular Report of the Case, Harris *v.* Kemble, as *not* heard in the House of Lords, September 5, 1831.*

"Lord Mulgrave sat there,
With his fine head of hair,
While the Chancellor's look was so glum,
That on t'other side Plunket
Appeared much to funk it,
And Lyndhurst kept biting his thumb.

* The subject of this action was the validity of a lease granted by the proprietors of Covent Garden Theatre to Mr. Charles Kemble.

"In front Sir Edward,
     His brief who had read hard,
Began to address these great men ;
     While behind Mr. Pepys
     Sat drawing little ships
On the back of his brief with his pen.

"Messrs. Pulman and Currie
     Came up in a hurry,
In bag-wigs, knee-breeches, and swords,
     As two gentlemen more
     Set open a door,
And let in three queer-looking lords.

"King Norroy, so great
     In his tabard of state,
To the Chancellor then made a bow ;
     In a kind of a growl, he
     Says, 'Here's my Lord Cowley,
Who is come here to *promise and vow !*'

"Lord Brougham, for the Crown,
     Says, 'My lord, pray sit down,
You're quite welcome—I never dissemble.'
     So Lord C., after that,
     Puts on his cocked hat,
And goes and sits down near Miss Kemble,

"Then was heard a sad rout
     In the lobby without,
As if twenty or more were a-talking ;
     And in came a summons,
     'A message from the Commons !'
Says the Chancellor, 'Pray let 'em walk in.'

"Then Sir John Milley Doyle,
     With a score more who toil
In committee, to wait longer scorning,
     Came and said, 'We agree
     Mrs. Turton to free
From her husband.   We wish you good morning.'

"'Then,' says my Lord Brougham,
     It's high time to go home ;
Sir Edward, pray stop your red rag !'
     Then Councillor Pepys
     Never opened his lips,
But popped his brief into his bag.

"Then Sugden, so sly,
     Gave a wink with his eye,

> And shut up his grief without sorrow,
>   Saying, 'Earned with ease,
>   This morning, my fees,
> And hey for ten guineas to-morrow !'"

Mr. Barham was essentially a peacemaker, and one of the earliest incidents remembered is his being called out one winter's night to interpose his good offices in a slight domestic difference between man and wife, in the course of which the former was enforcing his arguments, by the aid of a broomstick, with rather more action than the neighbours thought necessary or safe. Then there were the ordinary amusements of a country life, for which he had a natural relish, although the crippled condition of his right arm precluded his pursuing them with very great success. It was indeed scarcely to be expected that the cultivation of literature should flourish in so uncongenial an atmosphere, however favourable it might prove for the development of that "holy vegetation of which Mr. Peter Plymley so pleasantly discourses ; still my father, even at this time, was by no means idle with his pen. Of the many amusing trifles which he was in the habit of addressing to his friends, one of the best, perhaps, is an invitation to Dr. Wilmot, of Ashford, conveyed under the form of a parody on 'O Nanny, wilt thou gang with me?'

> "O Doctor ! wilt thou dine with me,
>   And drive on Tuesday morning down ?
> Can ribs of beef have charms for thee—
>   The fat, the lean, the luscious brown ?
> No longer dress'd in silken sheen,
>   Nor deck'd with rings and brooches rare,
> Say, wilt thou come in velveteen,
>   Or corduroys that never tear ?
>
> "O Doctor ! when thou com'st away,
>   Wilt thou not bid John ride behind,
> On pony, clad in livery gay,
>   To mark the birds our pointers find ?
> Let him a flask of darkest green
>   Replete with cherry brandy bear,
> That we may still, our toils between,
>   That fascinating fluid share !
>
> "O Doctor ! can'st thou aim so true,
>   As we through briars and brambles go,
> To reach the partridge brown of hue,
>   And lay the mounting pheasant low ?

20—2

Or should, by chance, it so befall
    Thy path be cross'd by timid hare,
Say, wilt thou for the game-bag call
    And place the fur-clad victim there?

" And when at last the dark'ning sky
    Proclaims the hour of dinner near,
Wilt thou repress each struggling sigh,
    And quit thy sport for homely cheer?
The cloth withdrawn, removed the tray—
    Say, wilt thou, snug in elbow-chair,
The bottle's progress scorn to stay,
    But fill, the fairest of the fair?"

AFTER-DINNER ANECDOTES.

In 1829, Mr. Barham appears to have met for the first time, at the table of their common friend Theodore Hook, Charles Mathews the elder. Their acquaintance was of some years' duration, but never reached intimacy; it was accompanied, nevertheless, certainly on the part of Mr. Barham, by feelings of no ordinary regard. It may, indeed, be questioned whether the golden opinions won by this accomplished actor in his professional career upon the stage were more than commensurate with the esteem which he inspired in private life.

Mathews told an excellent story of an Irish surgeon named Maseres, who kept a running horse, and who applied to him on one occasion for his opinion respecting a disputed race.

" Now, sur," commenced the gentleman, " Mr. Mathews, as you say you understand horse-racing, and so you do, I'll just thank ye to give me a little bit of an opinion, the least taste in life of one. Now, you'll mind me sur, my horse had won the first *hate*, well, sur, and then, he'd won the second *hate*, well—"

" Why, sir," said Mathews, " if he won both the heats, he won the race."

" Not at all, my dear fellow, not at all. You see he won the first *hate*, and then, somehow, my horse fell down, and then the horse (that's not himself, but the other) came up—"

" And passed him, I suppose," said Mathews.

" Not at all, sur, not at all; you quite mistake the gist of the matter. Now, you see, my horse had lost the first *hate*—"

" Won it, you mean—at least, won it, you said."

"Won it! of course, I said won it; that is, the other horse won it, and the other horse, that is *my* horse, won the second *hate*, when another, not himself, comes up and tumbles down —but stop! I'll demonstrate the circumstances ocularly. There—you'll keep your eye on that decanter; now, mighty well; now, you'll remember that's *my* horse, that is, I mane it's not my horse, it's the other, and this cork—you observe this cork—this cork's my horse, and my horse, that is this cork, had won the first *hate*—"

"Lost it, you said, sir, just now," groaned Mathews, rapidly approaching a state of complete bewilderment.

"Lost it, sur, by no manes; won it, sur, I maintain—'pon my soul, your friend there that's grinning so is a mighty bad specimen of an American—no, sur, *won* it, I said; and now I want your opinion about the *hate*, that is, not the *hate*, but the race, you know, not, that is, the first *hate*, but the second *hate*, that would be the race when it was won."

"Why, really, my dear sir," replied the referee, "I don't precisely see the point upon which—"

"God bless me, sur! do ye pretind to understand horseracing, and can't give a plain opinion on a simple matter of *hates*? Now, sur, I'll explain it once more. The stopper, you are aware, is my horse, but the other horse—that is, the other *man's* horse," etc., etc.

And so poor Maseres went on for more than an hour, and no one could tell at last which horse it was that fell; whether he had won the first *hate*, or lost it; whether his horse was the decanter or the cork; or what the point was, upon which Mr. Maseres wanted an opinion.

"Mathews afterwards sang a very amusing song in his best manner, descriptive of a Lord Mayor's day. Yates was no less entertaining, and on his health being drunk, returned thanks in an imitation of Young, which was perfect. Hook had hung a piece of black crape over Peel's picture, which was on one side of his room, and H. Twiss, being Under Secretary of State, thought it incumbent on him to endeavour to remove it. The piece of mourning, however, was more strongly fastened than he had imagined, which induced Lennox to say, on seeing him bungling in his attempt: 'It's of no use, Horace; you'll never be able to get him out of his scrape.'"

"Mrs. Hughes told me that the person whose character was drawn by Sir Walter Scott as 'Jonathan Oldbuck' was a

Mr. Russell, and that the laird whom he mentions as playing cards with Andrew Gimmell (the prototype of 'Edie Ochiltree') through the window, was Mr. Scott, of Yarrow.

"Snivelling Stone, about two miles and a half from the cromlech known as Wayland Smith's Cave, in Berkshire, is a large stone, which it is said that Wayland, having ordered his attendant dwarf to go on an errand, and observing the boy to go reluctantly, kicked after him. It just caught his heel, and from the tears which ensued, it derived its traditionary appellation. It is singular that when Mrs. Hughes, who had this story from a servant, a native of that part of the country, first told it to Sir Walter Scott, he declared that he had never heard of Wayland's having had any attendant, but had got all the materials for his story, so far as that worthy is concerned, from Camden. His creation of 'Dicky Sludge,' a character so near the traditionary one of which he had never heard, is a curious coincidence.

"So also is his description of Sir Henry Lee and the dog, in *Woodstock*. There is a painting in the possession of Mr. Townsend, of Trevallyn, in Wales, representing, according to a tradition long preserved in his family, Sir Henry Lee of Ditchley, with a large dog, the perfect resemblance of Bevis. Mr. Townsend, however, thinks he flourished about a century earlier than the Woodstock hero, and was the same with the Sir H. Lee whose verses to Queen Elizabeth, on his retiring from the tilt-yard in consequence of old age, are preserved in Walpole's *Antiquities*. The strange thing is that Sir Walter knew nothing of this picture till after *Woodstock* was published.

"Told her the story of old Steady Baker, the mayor of Folkestone, whom I well remember. A boy was brought before him for stealing gooseberries. Baker turned over *Burn's Justice*, but not being able to find the article he wanted in the book, which is alphabetically arranged, he lifted up his spectacles, and addressed the culprit thus : 'My lad, it's very lucky for you that, instead of stealing gooseberries, you were not brought here for stealing a goose; there is a statute against stealing geese, but I can't find anything about gooseberries in all *Burn:* so let the prisoner be discharged, for I suppose it is no offence.'

"*October*, 1843.—Dined with T. Haffenden at Lawn House, Hanwell ; Dr. and Mrs. Paris, &c. Dr. Paris told us a ghost story. He said that a Mrs. P——, living and keeping a depôt (in which word she used to pronounce the last syllable as an Englishwoman would) for lace in Leicester Fields, had been a patient of his ; that she had once dreamed that on going upstairs to bed she had seen a black bull come out of a clock-case which stood on the landing-place, and this dream was followed by the immediate death of her sister. It was late one night, several years after this event, that he (Dr. Paris) was summoned, just as he was going to bed, to attend his patient, who was, he was told, in a very alarming state. On reaching Leicester Fields, he found her in a high state of excitement, and insisting on being allowed to go immediately to her brother, as she was sure he was dead, she having just had a recurrence of her former dream. The doctor, who had long known her family, used every argument and persuasion to induce her to forego her resolution ; but finding that opposition only irritated her to a degree bordering on frenzy, he good-naturedly consented to take her with him in his own carriage, then at the door, and convince her of the absurdity of her suspicion. On arriving in the neighbourhood of Bethnal Green, where the brother resided, the doctor, finding her much calmer, renewed his entreaties to her to defer her visit till the morning ; but finding all of no avail, and that her excitement returned at the bare mention of going back, he drove up to her brother's door, determined that, as the house, like every other one in the street, was shut up—for it was now two o'clock in the morning—unless he found somebody stirring, he would not alarm the inmates by a continued knocking, but take his patient back, in spite of her teeth. To his surprise, however, a female servant opened the door at his first summons, and informed him that her master, who had been to his club, had returned about half an hour before, had been suddenly seized, while in the act of putting on his slippers, with gout in the stomach, or some affection of the heart, and that he had expired about a quarter of an hour before, the medical man who had been hastily summoned to his assistance having only that moment left the house."

" At a late fête at Hatfield House, *tableaux vivants* were among the chief amusements, and scenes from *Ivanhoe* were among the selections. All the parts were filled up but that of *Isaac of York*. Lady Salisbury begged Lord Alvanley ' to make the set complete by doing the Jew.' ' Anything in my power your ladyship may command,' replied Alvanley,

' but, though no man in England has tried oftener, I never could *do a Jew* in my life.' "

"He half affronted Mr. Greville, with whom he was dining. The dining-room had been newly and splendidly furnished, whereas the dinner was but a very meagre and indifferent one. While some of the guests were flattering their host on his taste, magnificence, &c., ' For my part,' said his lordship, ' I had rather have seen less gilding and more carving.' "

Of Mr. Samuel Arnold, Mr. Barham relates : " I first met him at Hawes's, several years before the institution of the ' Garrick,' where he was a member of the committee at the same time with myself. I encountered him the morning after his theatre (the English Opera-house, afterwards the Lyceum) was burnt down, by which he lost £60,000, and never saw a man meet misfortune with so much equanimity. His new theatre, which was raised by subscription, completely failed, and when Osbaldiston took Covent Garden in 1835, and reduced the admission to the boxes to four shillings, Arnold reduced his price to two; but this did not succeed, while the property was materially depreciated by the measure. Arnold was one of the leading members of the Beef Steak Club, where he was called ' the Bishop.' "

To authors' oaths, as well as to those of lovers, Jove, it is to be hoped, is particularly indulgent; for, assuredly, whatever amount of affirmative perjury may be incurred by the latter, it is to the full paralleled by the ample negations put forth by the former. Southey distinctly denied the authorship of *The Doctor*. But, perhaps, a greater degree of "nerve" was exhibited by Mr. Sidney Smith, who, positively disowning all connection with the *Plymley Letters* in one edition, actually published them in a collection of his acknowledged works some few months after. The mystery that hung so long around the Wizard of the North is yet more notorious; the anecdote which follows may serve to show the anxiety of the " Great Unknown " to preserve his incognito :—

" Murray told me that Sir Walter Scott, on being taxed by him as the author of *Old Mortality*, not only denied having written it, but added, ' In order to convince you that I am not the author, I will review the book for you in the *Quarterly*" —which he actually did, and Murray still has the MS. in his handwriting."

" Sir George Warrender said that, returning once from Windsor with the Duke of Wellington in his cab, the Duke drove so furiously and so badly, narrowly escaping collision with several drags, &c., that he, Sir George, was much alarmed, and begged him not to drive so fast. ' Pooh, pooh!' said his Grace, ' where there is no fear there is no danger!' ' My dear Duke,' returned Sir George, ' if fear is the criterion of danger, for Heaven's sake stop and let me out, for I was never in such a funk in my life!' "

" From letters of Sir Walter Scott, it appears that Lord Webb Somerset, brother to the Duke of Beaufort, was the author of the note to *Rokeby* containing the legend of Littlecote Hall, and that Miss Hayman furnished him with the ballad, ' The spirit of the blasted tree,' in *Marmion.*

" *Dandie Dinmont* was one Jamie Davison, who lived in Liddesdale, and died in September, 1823. When the minister, who had paid him several visits during his illness, called for the last time on the morning of his death, the good man inquired as to the state of his mind :—

" ' Eh, minister, ye're vara gude, and I'se muckle obleeged to ye ; eh, sir, it's a great mercy that I sulde be able to look out of window the morn, and get a sight o' the hounds ; it's just a mercy they sulde rin this way. 'Twad ha' bin too much for a puir sinner like me to ha' expeckit a sight o' the tod ! sae thank the Lord for a' things !'

" The circumstances attending *Tony Foster's* death, as described in *Kenilworth*, are taken from a real incident recorded in the third volume of the Duc de St. Simon's memoirs. There an account is given of the death of an avaricious Master of Requests at Lyons, named Pecoil, who had contrived a recess within his cellar, closed by a heavy iron door, within which he was in the habit of depositing his hoards. By some means the lock at last got hampered, and on one of his visits he was unable to let himself out again. He was eventually discovered lying on his treasures dead, and having previously begun to gnaw one of his arms.

" Mrs. Hughes repeated several anecdotes which she had heard from the mouth of Sir Walter himself; among them one of Lady Johnson, sister to the late Earl of Buchan and Lord Erskine, and widow of Sir J. Johnson. When on her death-bed, a few hours prior to her dissolution, she had her notice attracted by the violence of a storm which was raging with great fury out of doors. Motioning with her hand to have the curtains thrown open, she looked earnestly at the window, through which the lightning was flashing very vividly, and exclaimed to her attendants : ' Gude faith, but it's an unco awfu' night for me to gang bleezing through the lift !'

" Another story told by Sir Walter was of a drunken old laird, who fell off his pony into the water while crossing a ford in Ettrick.

" ' Eh, Jock,' he cried to his man, ' there's some puir body fa'en into the water; I heard a splash ; wha is it, man ?'

" ' Troth, laird, I canna tell ; forbye it's no yersell,' said John, dragging him to the bank. The laird's wig meanwhile had fallen off into the stream, and John, in putting it on again, placed it inside out. This, and its being thoroughly soaked, annoyed the old gentleman, who refused to wear it :—

" ' Deil ha' my saul, it's no my ain wig; what for do ye no get me my ain wig, ye ne'er-do-weel ?'

" ' Eh, then, laird, ye'll no get ony ither wig the night, sae e'en pit it on again. There's nae sic a wale o' wigs in the burnie I jalouse.'

" Another of his stories was of a party of Highland gentlemen, who continued drinking three whole days and nights successively, without intermission :—

" ' Hech, sirs,' cried one at last, ' but McKinnon looks gash !'

" ' What for should he no,' returned his neighbour; ' has na the chiel been dead these twa hoors ?'

" ' Dead !' repeated his friend, ' an' ye did na tell us before !'

" ' Hoot, man,' was the answer, ' what for should I ha' spoiled gude company for sic a puir bit bodie as yon ?' "

" Dr. Blomberg is fully installed at Cripplegate, where his parishioners have given him a public dinner on his remitting three hundred a year from their tithes. Of course, he is at present very popular there, and goes to reside immediately. A long, flourishing account of the banquet appeared next day in the *Times*, furnished, no doubt, by Mr. W——, who was present on the occasion, and pronounced a panegyrical oration with sufficient emphasis, I say nothing of discretion. Altogether, it appears to have been a mighty silly affair, and I much fear the worthy Doctor may hereafter find himself inconvenienced, when called upon, as he assuredly will be—

for radicals give no quarter—to redeem some of the pledges of hospitality and good-fellowship which escaped from him in the overflowing of his heart. To wind up the whole, his coffee-coloured friend has at last carried his favourite point, and is to be 'his worship's representative, factotum, locum tenens' at the cathedral, *residing in the Residentiary House,* and *presiding* at the weekly dinners! Adkins has, I believe, given up all thoughts of further proceedings at law or otherwise; so you will not have to fear another *subpœna.* Not that I should feel so much for you on a third as I did on the first and second times of your appearance *coram nobis.* The account you gave me of your sensations on the latter occasion put me very much in mind of Beaumont and Fletcher's little French lawyer, excessively alarmed in the first instance, and dragged with difficulty into fighting, but afterwards quite eager for a rencontre with every one he met; nor have I the least doubt that a summons or two more would make you not only dumbfound the counsel, but bully the judge himself in all the majesty of *Domini Regis.*"

"Dined at the 'Garrick;' Mr. Williams, the banker, in the chair; Fladgate, croupier; Charles Mathews (the father), E. Parrott, Westmacott (the sculptor), Mortimer Drummond, T. Clarke, Tom Hill, J. R. Durrant, W. Beloe, myself, and John Murray. We twelve were seated when Hook arrived. He looked at first very blank on finding himself the *thirteenth,* but being told that Charles Young the actor was expected immediately took his seat, and we had a very pleasant evening. C. Mathews gave a very amusing account of poor Dicky Suett's funeral which he had attended as a mourner. Suett lies buried in St. Paul's Churchyard, in the burial-ground belonging to St. Faith, nearly opposite the shop of Dollond the optician, and just within the rails. Suett had been brought up originally as a boy in the choir. Mathews and Captain Caulfield (whom I have often seen perform, and whose personation of Suett, Mathews said, was much more perfect than his own) were in the same coach with Jack Banister and Palmer. The latter sat wrapped up in angry and indignant silence at the tricks which the two younger *mourners* (who, by the way, had known but little of Suett, and were invited out of compliment) were playing off; but Banister, who was much affected by the loss of his old friend, nevertheless could not refrain from laughing occasionally in the midst of his grief and while the tears were actually running from his eyes. Mr. Whittle, commonly called 'Jemmy Whittle,' of the firm of Laurie and Whittle, stationers, in Fleet Street, was an old and intimate friend of Suett's. As the procession approached, he came and stood at his own door to look at it, when Caulfield called out to him from the mourning-coach in Suett's voice,

"'Aha! Jemmy—O la! I'm going to be buried! O la! O lawk! O dear!'

"Whittle ran back into the house absolutely frightened. Similar scenes took place the whole of the way. The burial service was read, when, just as the clergyman had concluded it, an urchin seated on a tombstone close by the rails began clapping his hands. The whole company were struck by this singular conclusion to a theatrical funeral; but the boy when questioned and taken to task for the indecency said,

"'La! there was only them two dogs outside as wanted to fight, and was afraid to begin, so I did it to set 'em on.'

"The following story was told me as a fact by George Raymond. Yates (the well-known actor and manager of the Adelphi Theatre) met a friend from Bristol, in the street, whom he well recollected as having been particularly civil to his wife and himself when at that town, in which the gentleman was a merchant. Yates, who at that time lived at the Adelphi Theatre, invited his friend to dinner, and made a party, among whom were Hook and Mathews, to meet him. On reaching home he told his wife what he had done, describing the gentleman, and calling to her mind how often they had been at his house near the cathedral.

"'I remember him very well,' said Mrs. Yates, 'but I don't just now recollect his name—what is it?'

"'Why, that is the very question I was going to ask you,' returned Yates. 'I know the man as well as I know my own father, but for the life of me I can't remember his name, and I made no attempt to ascertain it, as I made sure you would recollect it.'

"What was to be done? all that night and the next morning they tried in vain to recover it, but the name had completely escaped them. In this dilemma Yates bethought him of giving instructions to their servant which he considered would solve the difficulty, and calling him in told him to be very careful in asking every gentleman, as he arrived, his name, and to be sure to announce it very distinctly. Six o'clock came, and with it the company in succession, Hook,

Mathews, and the rest—all but the anonymous guest, whom Yates began to think, and almost to hope, would not come at all. Just, however, before the dinner was put on the table, a knock was heard, and the lad being at that moment in the kitchen, in the act of carrying up a haunch of mutton which the cook had put into his hands, a maid-servant went to the door, admitted the stranger, showed him upstairs, and opening the drawing-room door allowed him to walk in without any announcement at all. At dinner-time everybody took wine with the unknown, addressing him as 'Sir,'—'A glass of wine, sir?' 'Shall I have the honour, sir,' &c., but nothing transpired to let out the name, though several roundabout attempts were made to get at it. The evening passed away, and the gentleman was highly delighted with the company, but about half-past ten o'clock he looked at his watch and rose abruptly, saying,—

"'Faith, I must be off or I shall get shut out, for I am going to sleep at a friend's, in the Tower, who starts for Bristol with me in the morning. They close the gates at eleven precisely, and I sha'n't get in if I am a minute after, so good-bye at once. Be sure you come and see me whenever you visit Bristol.'

"'Depend on me, my dear friend; God bless you if you must go!'

"'Adieu,' said the other, and Yates was congratulating himself on having got out of so awkward a scrape, when his friend popped his head back into the room, and cried hastily,—

"'Oh, by-the-by, my dear Yates, I forgot to tell you that I bought a pretty French clock as I came here to-day at Hawley's, but as it needs a week's regulating, I took the liberty of giving your name, and ordering them to send it here, and said that you would forward it. It is paid for.'

"The door closed, and before Yates could get it open again, the gentleman was in the hall.

"'Stop!' screamed Yates over the balusters, 'you had better write the address yourself, for fear of a mistake.'

"'No, no, I can't stop, I shall be too late;—the old house, near the cathedral; good-bye!'

"The street door slammed behind him, and Yates went back to the company in an agony.

"Douglas repeated a story very similar of King the actor, who, meeting an old friend, whose name he could not recollect, took him home to dinner. By way of making the discovery, he addressed him in the evening, having previously made several ineffectual efforts :—

" ' My dear sir, my friend here and myself have had a dispute as to how you spell your name ; indeed, we have laid a bottle of wine about it.'

" ' Oh, with two P's,' was the answer, which left them just as wise as before."

" Story of Edward Walpole, who, being told one day at the ' Garrick,' that the confectioners had a way of discharging the ink from old parchment by a chemical process, and then making the parchment into isinglass for their jellies, said, ' Then I find a man may now eat his deeds as well as his words.' This has been very unfairly, like a great many other *bon mots*, attributed to James Smith."

" Moore gave an account of the King's (George IV.) visit to Ireland. One man, whom the King took notice of and shook hands with, cried, ' There, then, the divil a drop of wather ye shall ever have to wash that shake o' the hand off of me !' and by the colour of the said hand a year after it would seem that he had religiously kept his word. Moore told this story to Scott, together with another referring to the same occasion. He spoke of Jeffrey as an excellent judge, and remarked on the difference between his conversation and that of Scott. Scott all anecdote, without any intermediate matter—all fact ; Jeffrey with a profusion of ideas all worked up into the highest flight of fancy, but no fact. Moore preferred Scott's conversation to Jeffrey's : the latter he got tired of."

" ' Anecdote of the little Eton boy invited to dinner at Windsor Castle, and being asked by Queen Adelaide what he would like, replied, ' One of those twopenny tarts, if you please, ma'am.' Lord Lansdowne's description of Sydney Smith as a ' mixture of Punch and Cato.' Moore lamented that though his son had just distinguished himself by gaining an exhibition at the Charterhouse, when his historical essays had been particularly applauded, the prize would be of no use to him, barring the honour, as he is determined to enter the army. His father consoled himself by reflecting that he had given up his original wish, which was for the navy.

" J. Longman's story of the rival convents, each possessing the same (alleged) relics of St. Francis, the one having furnished its reliquary with the beard of an old goat belonging to the establishment, the other asserting its superiority *non pour la grandeur, mais pour la fraîcheur.*

" Moore talked of O'Connell, and said that he had recently met him in a bookseller's shop ordering materials, in the shape of books, for his new *Quarterly Review,* and that he had inadvertently offered to lend him a small volume respecting Ireland, but added that he must manage to slip out of his promise somehow.

" Dan, he said, manœuvred evidently that they might walk away together, but he (Moore) fought shy of the companionship and outstayed him. He spoke of O'Brien, the author of the *Round Towers,* and said that that person's hostility to him was occasioned by his declining a proposal for a sort of partnership in publication. O'Brien wrote to him when he undertook the *History of Ireland,* saying that he had a complete key to the origin and meaning of the Round Towers, and proposed to communicate his secret. If Moore used O'Brien's MS., the compensation was to be a hundred pounds ; if he took the materials and worked them up in his own way, a hundred and fifty was to be the sum. This was refused, and O'Brien was deeply offended. He died of an epileptic fit at Hanwell in 1835, and lies buried in the extreme north-west corner of the churchyard, close to the rector's garden. I happened accidentally to be present at his funeral. Mr. Mahony, the *Father Prout* of *Fraser,* was a mourner, and as I have heard, paid the expenses.

" It was, I believe, on this occasion that one of the Messrs. Longman present mentioned to my father the following quaint answer returned by Sydney Smith to an invitation to dinner :—

" Dear Longman,—I can't accept your invitation, for my house is full of country cousins. I wish they were once removed.—Yours, " SYDNEY SMITH."

One trifling *fracas* which occurred may not altogether have passed out of memory. A portrait of Sir John Soane was presented to the Literary Fund Society by that admirable artist, Mr. Maclise ; but the original, not deeming that his fair proportions had been treated with sufficient tenderness, peremptorily demanded its surrender, promising to replace it with a much handsomer, and *ergo* much more correct, representation by Sir Thomas Lawrence. During the somewhat lengthened discussion which ensued, a certain member of the council remarkable not more for his literary talent than for his social kindness and love of peace, put an end to all contention by entering the committee-room, and cutting the caricature of Sir John (as the latter chose to term it) into pieces with his penknife. The following *Lament* appeared a few days afterwards (May 22, 1836) in the *John Bull :*—

(Dr. Taylor *loquitur.*)

" Ochone ! ochone !
For the portrait of Soane,
Jerdan ! you ought to have let it alone ;
Don't you see that instead of removing the bone
Of contention, the apple of discord you've thrown ?
    One general moan,
    Like a tragedy groan,
Burst forth when the picture-cide deed became known.
    When the story got ' blown,'
    From the Thames to the Rhône,
Folks ran, calling for ether and eau de Cologne ;
All shocked at the want of discretion you've shown.
    If your heart's not of stone,
    You will quickly atone.
The best way to do that's to ask M. RONE-
Y to sew up the slits ; the committee, you'll own,
When it's once stitched together, must see that it's Soane."*

" I dined in company with Tom Moore the other day, who talked to me a good deal about Sydney Smith, and said that Lord Lansdowne, in allusion to his severity as a man of business and levity at the dinner-table, described him as being ' an odd mixture of Punch and Cato.' He could hardly have hit him off better. I know you are not over fond of Moore : *I* hate his politics, but he is a very amusing companion.

" I must tell you one of his stories, because, as Sir Walter Scott is the hero of it, I know it will not be unacceptable to you. When George IV. went to Ireland, one of the ' pisintry,' delighted with his affability to the crowd on landing, said to the toll-keeper, as the King passed through,—

" ' Och, now ! and his Majesty, God bless him, never paid the turnpike ! an' how's that ?'

" ' Oh ! kings never does : we lets 'em go free,' was the answer.

" ' Then there's the dirty money for ye,' says Pat. ' It

* Qy. *Sewn.*—Print. Dev.

shall never be said that the king came here, and found nobody to pay the turnpike for him.'

"Moore, on his visit to Abbotsford, told this story to Sir Walter, when they were comparing notes as to the two royal visits.

"'Now, Mr. Moore,' replied Scott, 'there ye have just the advantage of us. There was no want of enthusiasm here: the Scotch folk would have done anything in the world for his Majesty, but—pay the turnpike.'"*

WHATELIANA. (*See Vol. II., page* 31.)

"Those who are continually calling attention to the empty, or half empty, churches in some parishes, while overlooking the three times as many parishes in which there is a distressing want of church accommodation, seem to proceed in the way that Balak did with Balaam: 'Come, now, and I will bring thee to another place, where thou shalt see but the uttermost part of them, and *shall not see them all*, and curse me from thence.'"

Previously to obtaining the see of Meath, Dr. Dickenson had been appointed by Dr. Whately vicar of St. Anne's, Dublin, in succession to Lord Harburton, under whose incumbency an incident had occurred too amusing to omit. Lord M——, as we are informed by Mr. Daunt, had obtained his title during a venal period, in gracious recognition of some dexterous traffic in parliamentary votes; and he was unprincipled in pecuniary, as in political transactions. When Lord Kerry's house, in Stephen's Green, was for sale, a Mrs. Keating ambitioned to become the possessor of a pew attached to it, which she erroneously assumed belonged to Lord M——, and waited upon him to negotiate a purchase.

"I am not aware that I own any pew in St. Anne's," said Lord M——.

"Pardon me," replied Mrs. Keating; "I find your lord-

---

* Sir Walter, in turn, narrated another anecdote in connection with the same event. "The Marquis ——, in passing through one of the streets of Dublin, during the king's visit, happened accidentally to run against and overturn an old applewoman's barrow. The enraged lady called after him, 'Och, now! go your ways, ye big ugly *comb*. Sure, ye're all back and teeth, anyhow!' To those acquainted with the peculiarities of the noble lord's person, the simile will not, perhaps, appear very inappropriate."

ship has one ; and, if you have no objection, I am willing to buy it."

Thus appealed to, Lord M—— threw out no further obstacle. A bargain was struck ; he took the money ; and, on the following Sunday, Mrs. Keating, in an imposing suit of rustling bombazine, sailed up the nave to take possession of her pew ; but the beadle, with much firmness, interposed, and, in reply to her explanatory remonstrances, declared that it was "the Kerry pew," and had never, at any period, belonged to Lord M——.

The lady, smarting under the combined consciousness of the trick and the slight, retired with considerably less inflation than she had advanced, and lost no time in waiting on Lord M——, in the hope of obtaining some redress.

"My lord," she began, "as regards the pew at St. Anne's——"

"Oh," interrupted the peer, laughing, "you may have twenty more pews on the same terms."

"Pray, don't add injury to insult, my lord ; you must be aware of your mistake, and that you really never held any pew in St. Anne's."

"I told you so, in the first instance," replied Lord M——.

"Under all the circumstances," repeated his fair visitor, "I trust your lordship will kindly refund the money."

"Impossible, my dear madam ; it's gone long ago."

"But your lordship's character——"

"That is also gone," exclaimed Lord M——, leaning back in his easy-chair, and laughing immoderately.

The money was never returned, and Lord M—— subsequently obtained an unenviable notoriety for selling the commissions of a regiment of militia in which he was colonel; and when upbraided with the act by the Lord-Lieutenant, coolly replied, "Your excellency always told us to assimilate the militia, as far as possible, to the line. In the line commissions are sold."

But we must again leave the cap and bells for the mitre. Those who admired Bishop Dickenson were very anxious that Dr. Whately should write his life. The following is his grace's reply to Dr. West on the subject :—

"As for me, you cannot doubt that the very idea of writing the memoir myself was very long, and certainly revolved in my own mind, and discussed with several friends; and I have long been fully satisfied that, whatever I may write on that subject, must not appear but as a posthumous work. I am, on the whole, perhaps, the best qualified of all to state the most important points of character, supposing me to be writing what is not to be read in my lifetime; for that which is, I should be one of the worst qualified, from the very same chances, in a great measure, viz., my being *myself so mixed up* with him, that I could not (in an immediate publication) say, consistently with delicacy, even what many others, or almost any one else, could. It is precisely because, as you say, I dug the diamond up, and set it, and wore it myself, that it would be unbearable for me to describe and particularize, even as others could. In a posthumous work great allowances are made. The delicacy of egotism is pardoned in a dead man, and so is a good deal of stricture in others. Death gives a solemnity to what a man writes, knowing it is not to be seen till he is dead; and, moreover, people have nothing *more* to fear from him. In short, though the 'Palace of Truth' (of Madame Genlis) would be an intolerable place to *live* in, most would deem it a very good place to *die* in, *i.e.*, for the dying man to speak his mind quite freely about himself and others, once for all. So do not think of me, unless it be to ascertain any fact or date."

It cannot be said that Dr. Whately failed to practise what he preached. In his principles and movements he was methodical; and he carried them out with an energetic tread which often crushed the toes of those who placed them in his way. He did not like to see a man turning up the whites of his eyes during dinner or other social hours; and when the Bishop of O——, one day, at his own table, was descanting in a tone more suitable to a Prix Dieu than the easy-chair in which he sat, Dr. Whately, dropping his knife and fork, suddenly exclaimed, "Do you know the best way of dressing cabbage?" and, without waiting for a reply, entered into an elaborate and instructive detail regarding its culture, from the sowing of the seed to the culinary preparation of the plant.

We once heard a good story told, descriptive of a parish in a remote part of Ireland, where the parson and priest lived on terms of great intimacy, owing, doubtless, to the fact that there was not a ghost of a congregation, and was, therefore, exempt from that bitterness to which opposition or rivalry often give birth. "My dear fellow," said the latter, "I have a favour to ask. My bishop is coming down here next week, on his first visitation, and it is absolutely necessary that I should make a respectable appearance.   I want you to lend me your congregation for an hour or two, and you have my word of honour that no religious rite shall be performed." The priest, who was a humourist, as well as a good-natured man, is said to have entered into the joke, and consented, provided that no divine service should be gone through in presence of his flock.   The bargain was struck, the bishop came down ; the congregation was marshalled before him, and the parson was unctuously complimented, and as the story goes, rewarded by preferment, for the highly creditable state of religion in his parish.

Moore records several amusing anecdotes of Lord Dudley, based on his odd habit of making comments aloud.   A gentleman who proposed to walk with him from the House of Commons to the Traveller's Club, heard him mutter—" I think I may endure the fellow for ten minutes."   Lord Auckland used to tell a curious fashion Lord Dudley had of rehearsing over to himself in an undertone the good things he was about to retail to the company, so that the person who sat next to him had generally the advantage of his wit before any of the rest of the party.   The other day, having a number of the foreign ministers and their wives to dine with him, he was debating with himself whether he ought not to follow the continental fashion of leaving the room with the ladies after dinner.   Having settled the matter, he muttered forth in his usual soliloquising tone—" I think we must go out altogether."   " Good God ! you don't say so," exclaimed Lady ——, who was sitting next him, and who is well known to be the most anxious and sensitive of the lady Whigs with respect to the continuance of the present ministry in power. " Going out altogether," might well alarm her.   On another occasion, when he gave somebody a seat in his carriage from some country-house, he was overheard by his companion, after a fit of thought and silence, saying to himself—" Now, shall I ask this man to dine with me when we arrive in town ?"   It is said that the fellow-traveller, pretending not to hear him, muttered out in the same sort of tone, " Now, should he ask me to dinner, shall I accept his invitation ?"— *Note to Memoirs of Richard Whately.   By William John Fitzpatrick, J.P.,* 1864.

INDEX TO VOL. II.

APPENDIX.

THE END.

BILLING, PRINTER, GUILDFORD, SURREY.

Im The Story
personalised classic books

"Beautiful gift., lovely finish.
My Niece loves it, so precious!"

Helen R Brumfieldon

⭐⭐⭐⭐⭐

UNIQUE GIFT

FOR KIDS, PARTNERS
AND FRIENDS

Timeless books such as:

Kids

Alice in Wonderland · The Jungle Book · The Wonderful Wizard of Oz
Peter and Wendy · Robin Hood · The Prince and The Pauper
The Railway Children · Treasure Island · A Christmas Carol

Adults

Romeo and Juliet · Dracula

Highly Customizable

Change Books Title

Replace Characters Names with yours

Upload Photo (at intros page)

Add Inscriptions

Visit
Im The Story .com
and order yours today!